I0821789

Die Päpste und Rom
zwischen Spätantike und Mittelalter

Die Päpste

Herausgegeben von
Stefan Weinfurter, Alfried Wieczorek,
Michael Matheus, Bernd Schneidmüller

Bd. 3

Die Päpste und Rom

zwischen Spätantike und Mittelalter

Formen päpstlicher Machtentfaltung

Norbert Zimmermann, Tanja Michalsky,
Stefan Weinfurter, Alfried Wieczorek (Hg.)

Publikation der Reiss-
Engelhorn-Museen Band 76

Abbildung der vorderen Umschlagseite:
Arnolfo di Cambio, Papst Bonifaz VIII., Marmor, um 1296/1300
(Vatikan, Vatikanpalast, Sala San Giovanni).

Wir danken den Unterstützern und Förderern des Gesamtprojektes.

Gefördert durch

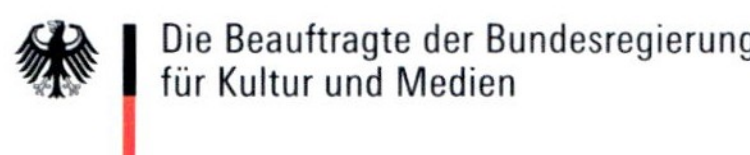

Bibliografische Information der Deutschen Nationalbibliothek:
Die Deutsche Nationalbibliothek verzeichnet diese Publikation in der
Deutschen Nationalbibliografie; detaillierte bibliografische Daten
sind im Internet über http://dnb.dnb.de abrufbar.

1. Auflage 2017

Umschlaggestaltung: Tobias Mittag (Mannheim), Anna Braungart (Tübingen)
Satz: typegerecht, Berlin
Druck: Grafisches Centrum Cuno GmbH & Co. KG, Calbe
ISBN 978-3-7954-3089-4

Weitere Informationen zum Verlagsprogramm erhalten Sie unter:
www.schnell-und-steiner.de

Inhalt

Vorwort

Das Papsttum ist die einzige Institution in Mitteleuropa, die seit der Antike kontinuierlich existiert und bis heute international anerkannt und politisch relevant ist. In Vorbereitung der internationalen Ausstellung *Die Päpste und die Einheit der lateinischen Welt. Antike – Mittelalter – Renaissance* der Reiss-Engelhorn-Museen Mannheim im Luther-Jahr 2017 nahm die Konferenz *Die Päpste zwischen Spätantike und Mittelalter. Formen der päpstlichen Machtentfaltung in Rom* diese Sonderstellung der Päpste und die Dynamik ihrer Selbstdarstellung zwischen Antike und Mittelalter in den Fokus.

Das Deutsche Archäologische Institut, Abteilung Rom, und die Bibliotheca Hertziana, Max-Planck-Institut für Kunstgeschichte, haben damit auch eine lange Tradition gemeinsamer Forschungen und Veranstaltungen wieder aufleben lassen. Die Tagung zum Papsttum bot eine willkommene Gelegenheit, die oft parallel unternommenen Forschungen in Archäologie und Kunstgeschichte auf einer internationalen Forschungsplattform in einen Dialog zu bringen.

Die Konferenz war Teil einer Reihe von wissenschaftlichen Veranstaltungen im Vorfeld der genannten Ausstellung, und wir danken insbesondere den Mitherausgebern dieses Bandes Stefan Weinfurter und Alfried Wieczorek für ihre Initiative zur Konferenz und die Aufnahme der Akten in diese Reihe der Begleitbände.[1] Uns ging es darum, in diachroner Perspektive den Schwerpunkt auf methodische Fragestellungen zu legen und einen großen historischen Rahmen von der Spätantike bis ins späte Mittelalter zu wählen. Die Beteiligung sowohl international renommierter als auch relativ junger Wissenschaftler*innen aus Archäologie, Kunstgeschichte, Geschichte, Kirchengeschichte und Musikgeschichte ergab sowohl in urbanistischer und liturgischer als auch in politischer und diplomatischer Hinsicht ganz neue Facetten im Verständnis der Institution und ihrer Rituale.

Den historischen Rahmen der Tagung bildeten die etwas mehr als 900 Jahre von Damasus I., unter dem sich im späten 4. Jahrhundert das römische Bischofsamt erstmals als Papsttum zu manifestieren begann, bis zu Clemens V., unter dem die Päpste im frühen 14. Jahrhundert für rund hundert Jahre Rom ins Exil nach Avignon verließen.

---

1 S. die übrigen Publikationen dieser Reihe: Bernd Schneidmüller, Stefan Weinfurter, Michael Matheus, Alfried Wieczorek (Hg.), Die Päpste. Amt und Herrschaft in Antike, Mittelalter und Renaissance, Regensburg 2016 (Bd. 1); Michael Matheus, Bernd Schneidmüller, Stefan Weinfurter, Alfried Wieczorek (Hg.), Die Päpste der Renaissance. Politik, Kunst und Musik, Regensburg 2017 (Bd. 2); Stefan Weinfurter, Volker Leppin, Christoph Strohm, Hubert Wolf, Alfried Wiezcorek (Hg.), Die Päpste und ihr Amt zwischen Einheit und Vielheit der Kirche. Theologische Fragen in historischer Perspektive, Regensburg 2017 (Bd. 4).

Dieser Zeitraum umfasst die Entstehung des Papsttums aus dem römischen Bischofsamt in der Spätantike durch die Übernahme von imperialen Ideen und Symbolen des untergehenden römischen Westreiches, die Etablierung und Ausübung seiner kirchlichen und weltlichen Macht im Frühmittelalter sowie ihre Wahrnehmung in den politischen und religiösen Auseinandersetzungen mit den hochmittelalterlichen Herrschern, die mit dem Exil nach Avignon im Verlust der hegemonialen Macht zunächst endeten.

Selbstredend konnte in diesem Rahmen nicht der gesamte Zeitraum umfassend aufgearbeitet werden. Vielmehr sollte die zweitägige Konferenz dazu dienen, in exemplarischer Weise charakteristische Momente oder Formen päpstlicher Machtaneignung und Machtentfaltung darzustellen. Die Beiträge schärfen das Profil des Papsttums als Phänomen in synchroner und diachroner Perspektive seines historischen, kirchenhistorischen, kunst-, musik- und architekturgeschichtlichen Kontextes. So werden Charakteristika, Kontinuitäten, Dynamiken und Differenzen in der Aushandlung, Ausgestaltung und Performanz der päpstlichen Macht beleuchtet.

Zusammengefasst unter den drei Themenbereichen »Repräsentation päpstlicher Ordnung«, »Raum und Performanz« sowie »Politik und Diplomatie« bieten die Fallbeispiele neue Interpretationen der charakteristischen Ausgestaltung sakraler Räume, der Aneignung territorialer Macht in der Stadt und dem Umland sowie des Systems der administrativen Machtausübung, der Interaktion liturgischer Handlungen und ihrer musikalischen Gestaltung, der Funktionen und Agency diplomatischer Geschenke und sakraler Kultgegenstände und nicht zuletzt des Umgangs mit identitätsstiftenden Orten wie dem Grab Petri und der *Confessio* von St. Peter. Die »Formen päpstlicher Machtaneignung und Machtentfaltung« erscheinen so in neuem Licht.

Für die finanzielle Unterstützung danken wir, neben DAI und Max-Planck-Gesellschaft, insbesondere der Deutschen Forschungsgemeinschaft für die großzügige Förderung. Der Botschafterin am Heiligen Stuhl Frau Anette Schavan gilt unser Dank für ihre Gastfreundschaft und den Abendempfang, ebenso den Reiss-Engelhorn-Museen für ihre Unterstützung. Bei der praktischen und logistischen Durchführung in Rom halfen uns besonders I. Balzer, M. Block, A. M. Graatz (DAI Rom) und E. Scirocco (Bibliotheca Hertziana), für die sorgfältige und umsichtige Betreuung der Drucklegung sind wir C. Wawrzinek, S. Herrmann, C. Braun und L. Reiblich besonders verpflichtet. Für die Realisierung dieses Buches im Verlag Schnell & Steiner erhielten wir vom Geschäftsführer Albrecht Weiland und von der Lektorin Elisabet Petersen die gewohnt professionelle Betreuung. Schließlich sei F. Dörr für die Übersetzung der italienischen Beiträge gedankt.

Wir hoffen mit dieser Konferenz und ihren Tagungsakten auch der langen Reihe freundschaftlicher Kooperationen deutscher Institutionen in Rom einen neuen Impuls gegeben zu haben.

Rom, im April 2017 Tanja Michalsky, Norbert Zimmermann

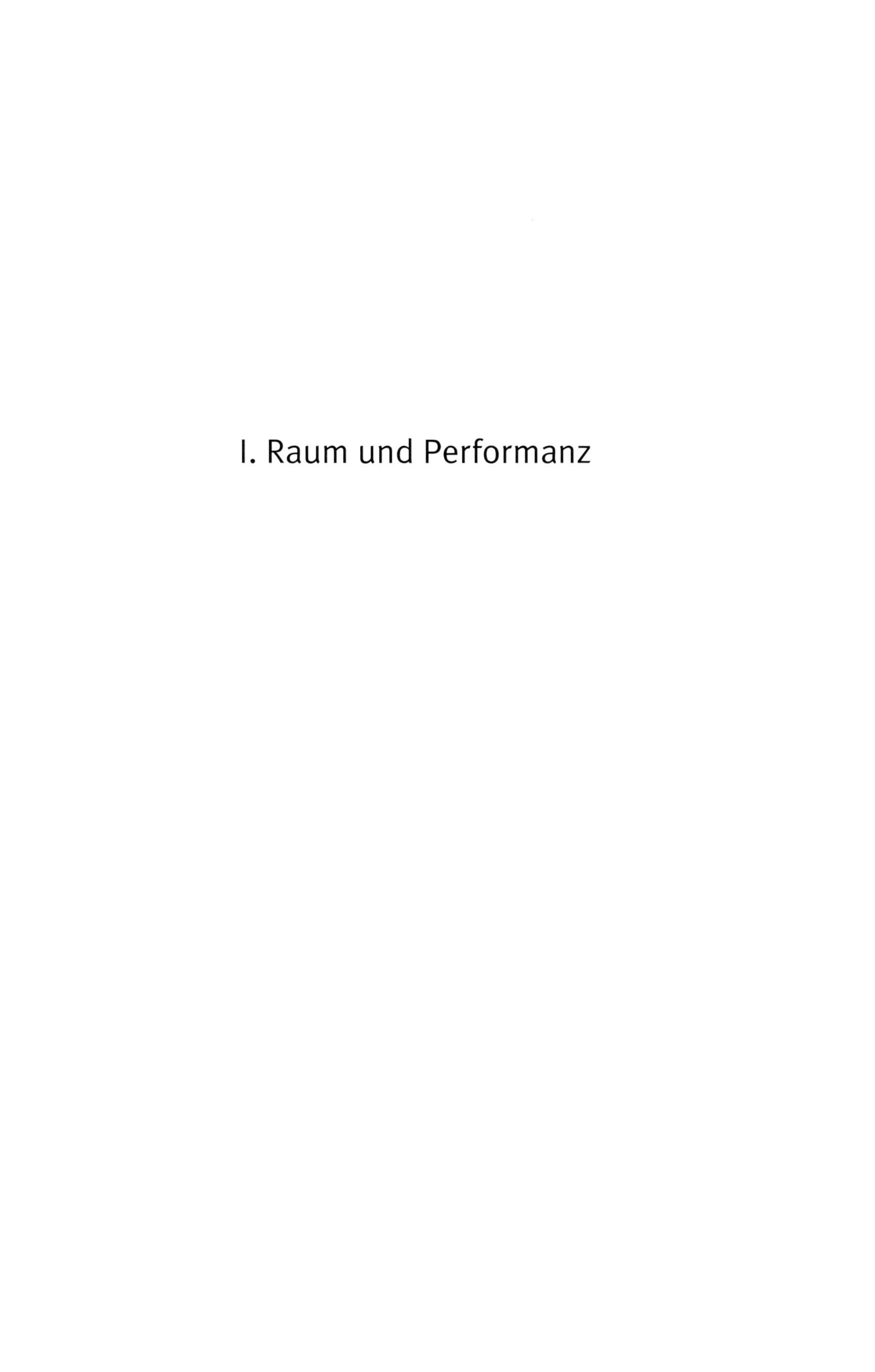

I. Raum und Performanz

Building prestige. Processions, visual codes, and episcopal power in fifth-century Rome

Vladimir Ivanovici

Fifth-century Rome presents us with a particular process, as the period in which the bishop managed to impose himself as one of the leading figures of the city. As recent studies have shown, the void of power supposedly created in the city after the emperors' transfer of the court to Milan and then to Ravenna did not exist.[1] Richard Krautheimer's thesis according to which the leader of the Christian community took advantage of the situation to gain control of the city thus needs to be reevaluated.[2] A complex dynamic emerges from recent analysis, with the senatorial aristocracy taking over and reanimating civic life.[3] It is against this background that the public image the leaders of the Christian community built for themselves on the social stage through gestures, rituals, and buildings needs to be considered.

The present article represents a first personal attempt to ponder how the bishops of Rome appeared to the city. After sketching in thick lines the relation between Church and city in the fifth century, a first part considers the relationship between the stational procession and the bishop's image, while a second focuses on some visual codes bishops included in their design of churches in the period. Both performances, the procession and the liturgy, stressed the relevance of the bishop, who presented himself as a figure of power that combined civic and religious authority. While processing was the city's traditional manner of acquiring and transmitting power, the ritual stage addressed in the second part reflected the Late Antique anthropological ideal represented by the statue-like, iconic religious virtuoso.[4]

1 See Humphries 2003, 2007, 2014 and Machado 2009, as well as Marazzi 2000 and Noble 2001. The bibliography on the topics addressed in the present article is very large. Indicated in the notes are recent studies that serve as starting point on the various topics. In the selection of images, I preferred those less known to those that the reader might be more familiar with, or which are easily found such as, e.g. the apse of Santa Pudenziana.

2 Krautheimer 1983, p. 4–5.

3 Machado 2006, 2009, 2010.

4 Ivanovici 2016.

Church and city in the fifth century

As indicated by the different role played by the leader of the Christian community in two key moments of the city's life, the preparations for Alaric's siege in 408 and the welcoming of Theodoric the Great in 500, the bishop succeeded in becoming a leading figure of the city in the course of the fifth century.[5] Nevertheless, as already stated, the process was not as straightforward as imagined by Richard Krautheimer more than half a century ago. A number of factors contributed to the rise of the bishop on the social scene. Of these, some, like the weakening of the senatorial aristocracy, escaped his authority. It is on the other, on those that the bishop controlled that I wish to focus, with particular accent on the forging of an image of urban potentate. Public gestures, rituals, constructive and decorative programmes influenced his image, which I will consider from the point of view of the non-Christian citizen of Rome.[6] The period is characterized by the adoption of a common visual rhetoric of power by the Church, which, after Constantine's measures, had turned to the world. As pointed out by Dominic Janes, "people's visual symbolic language was rooted largely outside the Church. Therefore, Christian propaganda necessitated secular metaphors, or else such arguments would not have been comprehensible to the masses. [...] The Church adopted many of the images as well as the ways of that world. This enabled the new sect to communicate effectively and so to bring about the maximum number of conversions."[7]

In Rome, perhaps more than elsewhere, the manner in which power was expressed was shaped by the classical norm. As the rest of the western provinces slowly drifted away from the Roman *koiné*, the peninsula, and the city of Rome in particular, regained their importance during the fifth century. The city's symbolic capital represented an important legitimizing instrument, as its history and topography allowed for the creation of powerful symbolic associations.[8] With the city's relevance depending increasingly on its past, the senatorial aristocracy that controlled the city kept traditions alive. Not only the monuments indicative of the city's glory were maintained, but also the cultural fabric particular to the city, in which public visibility, antiquity, and procession – all elements essential to my study – were central.[9] As perceptively noted by Jan Stenger, "Wenn Rom aufgrund seiner singulären Ästhetik so aus der gesamten Erfahrungswelt

5 Latham 2012, p. 301 and p. 318–321.

6 On the relevance of the bishops' public image, see Slootjes 2011, p. 101.

7 Janes 1998, p. 117–118 [...] 45.

8 Prolonged stays by emperors Honorius (393–423) and Anthemius (467–472) attest to the city's growing importance. On the visit and residing of emperors in the city, see Gillet 2001.

9 This is best visible during civic performances related to imperial visits, when the social structure, its relation to the spaces of the city, and with the city's past were synthetically reproduced.

herausfällt, scheint es einen Kosmos für sich zu bilden, dessen Grundprinzip die Transgression oder die Abweichung ist."[10] The "little Renaissance"[11] praised by Krautheimer did in fact take place, but it was not a uniquely Christian phenomenon. Rather, in order to gain recognition on the public scene, bishops adopted the idiom of power of the aristocracy, building and behaving in manners that pertained to Roman elite culture.[12]

The process of constructing for themselves an image of local potentates entwined with a number of other phenomena that marked the evolution of the Roman Church in the fifth century.[13] It is reductive to focus on one element of a complex phenomenon whose very characteristic was its semantic multiplicity but given the ramifications of the process, the extent of the bibliography on the topics it intersects, and the limited space one sole aspect was selected, namely the use of visual codes to create a certain image of the episcopate. The common point in this complex dynamic was the figure of the bishop, who by the end of the century emerged not only as leading figure of the city, but also of the Christian community whom he now controlled in a variety of manners. The success of the endeavor was partly assured by the construction of a public image of the bishop as urban potentate.[14] Given the nature of the audience, which was both Christian and non-Christian, and of the particular accent placed in Rome on aristocratic status, the bishop's image is best understood when considered through a local common sense. As pointed out by Jacob Latham, "... whether 'pagan' or Christian, the result is the same: up through the early-sixth century, aristocratic traditions, their sacred and political rituals, controlled the public sphere, the political core, and monumental center of a still classical city. That is, pagan and Christian aristocrats alike competed for power and prestige in the same classical idiom."[15] It is with this in mind that I ponder the image of the bishop during two fundamental moments for his relationship with the city, the stational procession and the liturgical performance.

10 Stenger 2011, p. 205.

11 Krautheimer 1961.

12 Humphries 2014, 180 stressed that liturgical developments evolved under a lay pressure that influenced their shape. Humphries 2014, p. 172 argued that the same rules of display of status were used inside and outside churches.

13 See Pietri 1976. Internal power struggles, attempts to gain control of the various (ethnic) communities in the city, the extension of the cultic network inside the city walls, or the design and introduction of a coherent 'Taufpolitik' (Bruderer-Eichberg 2002) developed in parallel to their construction of an aristocratic image.

14 Machado 2011, p. 507.

15 Latham 2012, p. 306.

Processing through the city of Rome

Constantine's measures and gifts to the Church of Rome assured a certain recognition of the bishop on the social stage. The consecration of the *episcopalis audientia* supposedly assimilated the bishop to one of the *illustres*, status which translated into a particular costume.[16] The right to the pallium, to a particular headpiece, shoes, and ring indicated one as a *potentissimus.* Constantine's measures thus enmeshed the bishop in what Bernhard Jussen aptly called the Roman "culture of appearance".[17] During the fifth century, as the community, funds, and influence of the bishops of Rome grew, and they came to be elected from the more educated and richer part of the community, the leaders of the Church grew into their costume.[18] The disparaged information we have on the situation in Rome in the fifth century indicates a fast accommodation of the episcopate to the visual rhetoric of power of the elite. This is best indicated by the classical dimension of the spaces and performances staged by the bishops, as well as by symbolic gestures such as the merging of Christ with the sun on the triumphal arch of San Paolo fuori le mura and with Serapis on the apse of Santa Pudenziana, which indicate a surprising confidence for a cult that, in Rome, was not yet dominant.[19]

Of the gestures and motifs one could rely on to gain prestige in Late Antique Rome, none was more symbolically charged than processing.[20] As shown by Diave Favro, the very fabric of the city had been shaped by the triumphal procession, morphed in Late Antiquity into the imperial *adventus*.[21] The assimilation of visibility and authority in Roman urban culture, as well as the particular relation between processing and power in the city of Rome, rendered the stational system a legitimation mechanism.[22] The stational procession – the transfer of the bishop from the Lateran to one of the churches of the city on the Sunday or holiday assigned to it – shaped the way the city perceived

---

16 While they included him into the local magistrature, and allowed him to pertain to the culture of the elite, Constantine's measures seem to not have assured an immediate assimilation of the bishop into the city's elite.

17 Jussen 2001, p. 155.

18 As in other cities, the position became attractive for those already having a high social status, who saw the opportunities for visibility it offered or who were pushed to the top by the brethren who sought influential protectors. Nevertheless, bishops of senatorial status remained few in Italy according to Rapp 2000. On the adoption of Christianity by the aristocracy, see Salzman 2002, esp. p. 77.

19 On Serapis, see Foletti 2015.

20 On Christian processions in Late Antiquity, their various connotations, and impact on Christian architecture and liturgy, see Baldovin 1987; de Blaauw 1994; Bauer 2001; Andrade 2010.

21 Favro 1994. On the triumph and *adventus* see Versnel 1970; MacCormack 1981; McCormick 1990; Dufraigne 1994.

22 Favro 2008, p. 14: "The very act of being seen imparted *dignitas* on the visual target, since visibility implied honesty."

the bishop.[23] As he paraded the various routes of the city together with the community of believers, the rest of the clergy, and the liturgical vessels, the Christian bishop was an ordinary sight for the capital as many other cults had processions. What was extraordinary in the case of the Christian community was the frequency of the procession and the diversity of the paths taken.

While priests of various cults were a constant sight on every street of the city, processions that involved an important number of participants and were led by the leaders of the cult usually had one or a limited number of processional paths. On the contrary, the Christian bishop continuously added new routes through the building of a network of churches that in the fifth century focused on the most inhabited areas of the city.[24] At least once a week, and more often if a holiday fell during the weekdays, he could be seen parading the city, en route to one of the churches. The stational system assured the visibility of the bishop and provided a perfect context to display the growing wealth of the episcopate.[25] As the Church grew, the bishop's entourage did too. In Rome, the size of one's retinue was a clear indication of his power, and probably few, if any individuals could mobilise as often and as many people as the bishop did. The number and richness of the liturgical vessels also likely grew in time; a rather clear indicator of the cult's growing status.

The *vasa sacra* stored in the Lateran and taken to the stational church identified the procession as cultic since the practice of carrying cultic objects in the cortege of statues was famous. The *stauroforus* title carved on the tombstone of a minor clergy member indicates that towards the end of the fifth century or the beginning of the sixth, the Roman Church used the 'pagan' practice of ascribing titles according to the object one carried during the procession.[26] The presence of cross-bearers allows for a further relation with 'pagan' practices, as a fresco from Ostia shows a procession of children, some of whom carry T shaped posts with vines on them. (Fig. 1) Related to this, a ninth-century statement referring to the "mos antiquitus"[27] of having cross-bearers walk in front of the bishop's horse indicates that the procession was a slow pace one. Such a rhythm increased the theatricality of the performance and, of course, the visibility of the bishop.

The stational system does not appear as an official performance sanctioned by the city's authorities as a religious procession. As argued by Jacob Latham, the space of the

---

23 On the stational system, see Baldovin 1987, p. 166.

24 Bruderer-Eichberg 2002.

25 According to Baldovin 1987, p. 151 although the stational practice is discernible as early as the third century CE, the system was established around the middle of the fifth century.

26 Already Ignatius of Antioch († ca. 108) associated the categories existing at that time within his community with the various types of "bearers" in "pagan" processions. On the Roman *stauroforus* and the development of the practice in Rome, see de Blaauw 2001a.

27 *Liber Pontificalis* 125.28, quoted by de Blaauw 2001a, p. 322.

Fig. 1: Children processing with Dionysian symbols, supposedly during the Vendemmia. Early third-century CE fresco from Ostia. Vatican Museums, Inv. 79643.

city remained "pagan" until later, with the first Christian procession organized in the sixth century.[28] The processional dynamic of fifth-century architecture in Rome represents, I believe, a response to this problem and, simultaneously, a confirmation of the role processions had in building prestige. Churches designed under episcopal patronage, to which I will now turn, combined the dynamic of the procession with the staging of the anthropological ideal of period, which promoted the religious virtuoso as an immobile, statue-like embodiment of the divine.

Constructing iconicity in fifth-century Rome

The classical dimension of the churches of Santa Sabina, Santa Maria Maggiore, San Pietro in Vincoli, Santo Stefano Rotondo, and of the restoration and additions to the Lateran Baptistery indicates the bishops' willingness to adopt the common visual rhetoric of power. The latter was, nonetheless, adapted to the ritual needs and, in particular, to the image the bishop constructed for himself. Indeed, it appears that the spaces and rituals

28 Latham 2012 and 2014, p. 129–133.

developed in this period represent more a negotiation between Roman elite culture and the image of the episcopal office rather than the cult's ritual needs.[29] At the centre of a particular architectural and decorative style that combined in a coherent manner classical elements with the Late Antique appreciation of marbles and mosaics considered luminous, stood the figure of the bishop. These spaces, as did other gestures and policies attested in the course of the century, stressed his role inside the community and the city. In so doing, the bishops followed the path set by Constantine's donations, with fifth-century foundations harmonizing the two elements found in the fourth-century Roman basilicas – the processional and the iconic dimensions – with the classicizing gusto of the period.

The two main basilicas in Rome, the Lateran and the Vatican, evince a spatial momentum that is essentially processional. The axiality of the space indicates a liturgical dynamic that placed the accent on the advancement of the bishop as living icon.[30] Whether or not a *solea* was present, the relationship between the spaces inside, and the increase in natural and artificial illumination on the way from the narthex to the apse attest to a growing tension embedded in the space.[31] As Olof Brandt has argued, this momentum is discernible in Christian architecture before Constantine.[32] Nevertheless, Constantine's contribution stimulated it, enmeshing it in an official dimension substantiated by the aesthetic of the spaces. As the presence of the *fastigium* in the Lateran basilica testifies, an important dimension of the programme enacted through the space and decoration regarded the stimulation of the iconic dimension of the bishop.[33] Such object or setting was used in the period to indicate the divinity of emperors, and given the mastery revealed by Constantine in the staging of his own iconicity, most evident in his planning of Constantinople and its ceremonies, it is justified to consider the *fastigium* as an instrument of personal power.[34] Bishops continued on the same path in the following century. What was added was an even stronger accent on the bishop's role, with an emphasis on his appurtenance to Rome's aristocratic elite.

Built with a variety of audiences in mind – 'pagans', Christians, catechumens, Romans, foreigners – cultic spaces of the fifth century afforded a number of simultaneous readings. Of this semantic complexity that added to their effect, I will focus on those elements

---

29 On the relationship between structure, symbolism, and ritual needs in Christian cultic architecture, see Brandenburg 1995 and 2004; de Blaauw 2000 and 2008; Guidobaldi/Guidobaldi 2002; Brandt 2014.

30 Ivanovici 2016.

31 The amount of natural light depended on the size and number of windows, which assured the prominence of the main nave and of the presbytery. The same hierarchy was enacted through the number and richness of the artificial lights, as noticeable from the information preserved in the *L.P.* 34.9–12.

32 Brandt 2014, p. 30.

33 On the *fastigium*, see de Blaauw 1994, p. 117–126 and de Blaauw 2001b; Liverani 1992/93.

34 See the *missorium* of Emperor Theodosius (379–395) and the *prothyron* of Diocletian (284–305) in his palace in Split.

Fig. 2: Relief from the tomb of the Haterii, showing landmarks of second-century CE Rome. Vatican Museum.

that stimulated the perception of the bishop as urban potentate and *summus sacerdos*. As mentioned, the processional dimension of the space, present in fourth-century basilicas and maintained in fifth-century ones, could be read as the bishops' response to the impossibility to have formal processions in the city centre. The carefully choreographed character of the bishop's arrival and entrance, attested by later sources which likely reflect the Late Antique practice, corroborate my reading of the stational procession as focused on the person of the bishop.[35] Contrary to Constantinopolitan practice, and similar to the norm of the Roman *adventus*, the bishop entered last, after the brethren occupied the space and a tension was created through waiting, chanting, and the parading of Christic symbols (cross and gospel book, accompanied both by lights and censers).[36]

The main nave of fifth-century churches cited the spaces one could find in the Forum through the coherent use of ionic (Santa Maria Maggiore) and doric (San Pietro in Vincoli) capitals. The effect is particularly strong in the Marian basilica, where the mosaic scenes beneath the windows furthered the association with urban facades decorated with statues and bas-reliefs.[37] (Fig. 2) Bishop Sixtus III (432–440), to whom the church is attributed, thus built a space for a sort of *adventus* that recommended him simultaneously as both urban potentate and God's representative.[38] Other elements embedded in the design, or present on the Roman scene, strengthened this visual rhetoric.

35 According to the typology proposed by Baldovin 1987, and accepted in the academe, the stational procession was a person-centred performance.

36 Brandenburg 2001 argued for the moulding of the episcopal entrance on the imperial *adventus* ceremony. On the entrance and its role in conferring iconicity to the bishop, see Ivanovici *forthcoming*.

37 The "second population of statues" (Stewart 2003, p. 118) inhabiting the city was a constant and real presence to the Romans, as attested by Cicero who included nearby statues in his speeches.

38 See also the photo in the archive of the Deutsches Archäologisches Institut in Rome (inv. no. 60.1169) of a lost relief showing a procession against a *scaenae frons* or urban background which resembles the main nave of Santa Maria Maggiore.

Fig. 3: Sarcophagus excavated in the Vatican cemetery. Drawing by Antonio Bosio, *Roma Sotterranea*, II.8, p. 85–87.

The display of Christ against an urban background in the art of the period is part, I believe, of the same strategy meant to render the bishop of Rome both a Christ-like and powerful urban figure. On the one hand, scenes such as those depicted on a sarcophagus excavated in the Vatican cemetery (currently in Vatican Museums) and the apse mosaic of Santa Pudenziana established Christianity as an urban cult. (Fig. 3) On the other, by association, the bishop appeared as a Christ-like figure since the buildings against which Christ was shown were the very same associated with the bishop: basilicas and baptisteries/martyria.[39] Similarly, the depiction of Peter wearing the pallium, which the bishops likely wore in the fifth-century,[40] was meant both to establish a direct relation-

39 While the buildings making up the background in the Santa Pudenziana mosaic have been variously interpreted, those on the sarcophagus are obviously Christian, as indicated not only by the typology, but also by the presence of a *chi-rho* on top of one. Furthermore, the main side of the sarcophagus shows a selection of scenes framed by a colonnade covered by an architrave rather than by arches, a classicising detail present also in Santa Maria Maggiore.

40 As shown by Jussen 2001, p. 158, from the fifth to the eighth century, the bishops of Rome argued for the use of a costume suitable to the office's civic status. See Ammianus Marcellinus, *Histories* 27.3.14.

ship between them and the apostle, and indicate the bishops of Rome as urban potentates *ante litteram*.[41] On the doors of Santa Sabina, dedicated during the episcopate of Sixtus III, and on the triumphal arch of Santa Maria Maggiore, attributed to the same bishop, Peter is shown as founding the Church in Rome and representing the city of Rome, respectively. In the Santa Sabina "Acclamation" panel, a man wearing a pallium is shown standing in the door of a basilica. (Fig. 4) The man, who was variously identified in modern scholarship, represents the apostle.[42] His position on the door of the building indicates his assimilation to it, with the stance being used in the period to depict the *committente* with his donation. Showing physiognomic resemblance to Peter as shown in other panels on the same doors, the man is probably the apostle shown against Old St. Peter's. The church is depicted with that element that was its distinctive external mark on the Roman scene, its transept, shown here in a broken perspective. Donning anachronistically the pallium, Peter was founding the Roman church and setting the basis for the local bishop's power.[43]

The same strategy, with Peter dressed as a Roman aristocrat and shown against the city scene, is present on the arch of Santa Maria Maggiore. (Fig. 5) There, the presentation in the temple is shown with the *templum urbis* replacing the Jerusalem one,[44] and with Peter replacing Simeon. Further elements in the mosaic on the arch strengthen the relationship bishop-Peter-Christ-city. The empty throne, a powerful symbol of both divine and civic authority, and element to which the bishop of Rome had a right to through Constantine's measures, created a potent association between the bishop, sitting below the arch on a real throne, Roman aristocrats using similar thrones in virtue of their status, and Christ. Occupied by Christ, reduced to His symbol so that the accent of the *mise-en-scène* fell on the bishop below as His embodiment, the throne was flanked by Peter and Paul, who assured with their presence the link between Christ and the bishop. Sitting below, the latter embodied the Divine Presence, functioning as Christ's *vicarius*.

At the end of an entry procession that established him as visual focus of the community, and placed him in a relationship with the depicted characters that was particularly Roma: above the eyes of the community and below the depictions of the gods, the bishop took his place at the apex of the space. The seated position implied immobility,

---

41 The same technique is found later in Sant'Apollinare in Classe, where the bishops of Ravenna were depicted donning the pallium, by now the symbol of the archbishop, which had only been given to Bishop Maximian (546–556) who supervised the decoration.

42 On the various interpretations of the panel, see Foletti/Gianandrea 2015, p. 190–193.

43 The angel present in the scene is similar to the one shown leading the Jews out of Egypt in another panel. Its presence in the "Acclamation" panel could symbolise the relocation of the Divine Presence from the Tabernacle to the Church and thus be a legitimizing motif.

44 Warland 2003.

Fig. 4: Wooden panel of the "Acclamation" from the doors of the Church of Santa Sabina, Rome, ca. 432 CE.

Fig. 5: Detail from the presentation to the Temple scene. Mosaic on the triumphal arch, Santa Maria Maggiore, Rome, fifth century CE.

which was the new mark of holiness in the period.[45] The *mise-en-scène* in Santa Maria Maggiore represents the merging of two systems of acquisition of symbolic capital, the urban procession and the immobility associated with divine immutability.[46] The latter, an essentially imperial technique in the period, was integrated by Sixtus in the design of the new basilica. Surrounded by an ambulatory, the *cathedra* displayed the bishop as a sort of cultic statue. (Fig. 6) The possibility to circle the throne and observe the bishop from every angle created a contrast between the dynamic mass of believers and the immobile bishop, with the setting simultaneously stressing the statue-like quality of the latter and placing him at the centre. The particular dynamic was famous in Rome, being the mark of the procession of Cybele where the statue of the goddess was surrounded by the circular dance of her priests. Keeping with the general tendency, and similar to the technique already used in the stational procession, the statue had been replaced in the Late Antique church with the living religious virtuoso playing the statue.[47]

45 MacMullen 1964; Ivanovici 2016.

46 Favro 2008.

47 Ivanovici 2016.

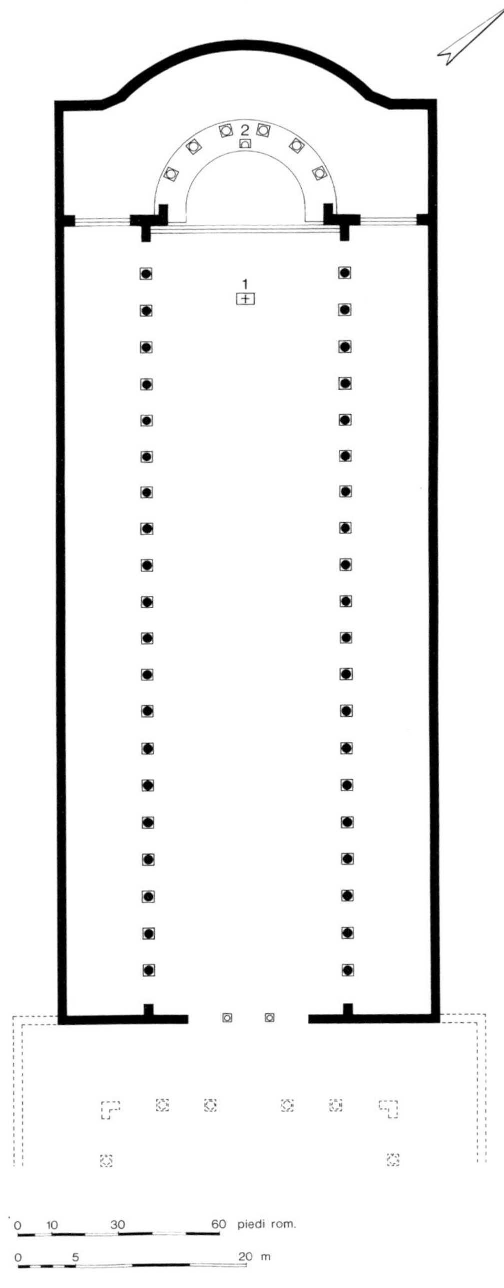

Fig. 6: Reconstructed plan of Santa Maria Maggiore in the fifth century CE, with the position of the altar (1) and episcopal *cathedra* (2). Drawing by Sible de Blaauw 1994.

Conclusion

It appears that during the fifth century the bishops of Rome used every possibility to construct for themselves an image of power. As typical in the period, the ideal leader reunited worldly and divine authority. Both the stational procession and the liturgical *mise-en-scène* conveyed the idea, with the former performance stressing the civic dimension, and the interior of churches striving to confer an iconic aura. While parading the city, the bishop was subjected to a variety of visual codes that escaped his authority. Nevertheless, by moulding the form of the procession on that of other cults and replacing the cult statue with his own person, he managed to create a powerful symbolic association. Inside cultic spaces, a particular visual code was developed, one that followed conventions established outside the Church, as to enable proper communication, but used for a specifically Christian purpose. The complexity of the setting found in Santa Maria Maggiore, with its overlapping rhetorics of power, points to the designer's deep knowledge of Roman visual codes, and indicates his belonging to the elite.[48] It was, I believe, this capacity to merge into one figure of power both civic and divine authority that assured the recognition of the episcopate on the social stage during the fifth century, as bishops successfully adapted to their needs the technique Constantine had used to reform the imperial image.[49]

The strong relationships one is able to establish between Forum and church space, between stational and other processions, or between the decoration of Santa Sabina and Santa Maria Maggiore indicate the dialogic dynamic in which these spaces and performances were designed. Indeed, in this instance, the very scarcity of the information available for the period becomes an argument for the great coherence of the elements we discussed, when the few extant details allow for the reconstruction of such direct concordances. It thus seems that the appearance of the cult – namely built structures, iconographic trends, decorative aesthetic, liturgical shape, and, of course, personal appearance of the clergy – was designed as a combination of Roman elements, Late Antique paradigms, and ritual needs.

48 I hold the coherence of the program to indicate the "meeting and merging" (Salzman 2002, p. 3) of Christian clergy with the aristocracy.

49 Bardill 2012.

Bibliography

Andrade 2010 Nathanael Andrade: The Processions of John Chrysostom and the Contested Spaces of Constantinople, in: Journal of Early Christian Studies 18, 2010, p. 161–189.

Baldovin 1987 John F. Baldovin: The Urban Character of Christian Worship: The Origins, Development, and Meaning of Stational Liturgy (Orientalia Christiana Analecta, 228), Rom 1987.

Bardill 2012 Jonathan Bardill: Constantine: Divine Emperor of the Christian Golden Age, New York 2012.

Bauer 2001 Franz Alto Bauer: Urban Space and Ritual: Constantinople in Late Antiquity, in: Acta ad archaeologiam et artium historiam pertinentia 15, 2001, p. 27–59.

Brandenburg 1995 Hugo Brandenburg: Kirchenbau und Liturgie. Überlegungen zum Verhältnis von architektonischer Gestalt und Zweckbestimmung des frühchristlichen Kultbaues im 4. und 5. Jh., in: Divitiae Aegypti: Koptologische und verwandte Studien zu Ehren von Martin Krause, ed. Cäcilia Fluck et al., Wiesbaden 1995, p. 36–69.

Brandenburg 2000 Hugo Brandenburg: Santo Stefano Rotondo in Roma: funzione urbanistica, tipologia architettonica, liturgia ed allestimento liturgico, in: Arredi di culto e disposizioni liturgiche a Roma da Costantino a Sisto IV, ed. Sible de Blaauw, in: Mededelingen van het Nederlands Instituut te Rome 59, 2000, 27–53, p. 44–45.

Brandenburg 2004 Hugo Brandenburg: Le prime chiese di Roma IV–VII secolo, Mailand 2004.

Brandt 2014 Olof Brandt: The Archaeology of Roman Ecclesial Architecture and the Study of Early Christian Liturgy, in: Studia Patristica LXXI, 2014, p. 21–52.

Bruderer-Eichberg 2002 Barbara Bruderer-Eichberg: Prolegomena zur frühchristlichen und frühmittelalterlichen Tauforganisation Roms: die Baptisterien und die Stifterrolle der Päpste, in: Art, cérémonial et liturgie au Moyen Ages (Études lausannoises d'histoire de l'art 1), ed. Nicolas Bock et al., Rom 2002, p. 321–356.

De Blaauw 1994 Sible de Blaauw: Cultus et decor: Liturgia e architettura nella Roma tardoantica e medievale: Basilica Salvatoris, Sanctae Mariae, Sancti Petri, Vatikanstadt 1994.

De Blaauw 2000 Arredi di culto e disposizioni liturgiche a Roma da Costantino a Sisto IV, ed. Sible de Blaauw, in: Mededelingen van het Nederlands Instituut te Rome 59, 2000.

De Blaauw 2001a Sible de Blaauw: Following the Crosses: The Processional Cross and the Typology of Processions in Medieval Rome, in: Christian Feast and Festival. The Dynamics of Western Liturgy and Culture (Liturgia Condenda, 12), ed. Paulus Post et al., Leuven 2001, p. 319–343.

De Blaauw 2001b Sible de Blaauw: Imperial Connotations in Roman Church Interiors. The Significance and Effect of the Lateran Fastigium, in: Acta ad archaeologiam et artium historiam pertinentia XVI, 2001, p. 137–146.

De Blaauw 2008 Sible de Blaauw: 'v. Kultgebäude', in: Reallexikon für Antike und Christentum XX, 2008, Sp. 227–393.

Dufraigne 1994 Pierre Dufraigne: *Adventus Augusti, adventus Christi.* Recherche sur l'exploitation idéologique et littéraire d'un cérémonial dans l'antiquité tardive, Paris 1994.

Favro 1994 Diane Favro: Rome. The Street Triumphant: The Urban Impact of Roman Triumphal Parades, in: Streets. Critical Perspectives on Public Space, ed. Zeynep Çelik, Diane Favro and Richard Ingersoll, Berkeley 1994, p. 151–164.

Favro 2008 Diane Favro: The Festive Experience: Roman Processions in the Urban Context, in: Festival Architecture, ed. Sarah Bonnemaison and Christine Macy, New York 2008, p. 10–42

Foletti 2015 Ivan Foletti: Dio da dio. La maschera di Cristo, Giove Serapide e il mosaico di Santa Pudenziana a Roma, in: Convivium 2/1, 2015, p. 60–73.

Foletti/Gianandrea 2015 Ivan Foletti und Manuela Gianadrea: Zona Liminare. Il nartece di Santa Sabina a Roma, le sue porte e l'iniziazione cristiana, Rom 2015.

Gillett 2001 Andrew Gillett: Rome, Ravenna, and the Last Western Emperors, in: Papers of the British School at Rome 69, 2001, p. 131–167.

Grig 2006 Lucy Grig: Throwing Parties for the Poor: Poverty and Splendour in the Late Antique Church, in: Poverty in the Roman World, ed. Margaret Aitkens and Robin Osborne, Cambridge 2006, p. 145–161.

Guidobaldi/Guidobaldi 2002 *Ecclesiae Urbis*. Atti del congresso internazionale di studi sulle chiese di Roma (IV–X secolo), ed. Federico Guidobaldi and Alessandra Guiglia Guidobaldi, Vatikanstadt 2002.

Humphries 2000 Mark Humphries: Italy, AD 425–605, in: The Cambridge Ancient History 14. Late Antiquity: Empire and Successors AD 425–600, ed. Averil Cameron, Bryan Ward-Perkins and Michael Whitby, Cambridge 2000, p. 525–551.

Humphries 2003 Mark Humphries: Roman Senators and Absent Emperors in Late Antiquity, in: Acta ad archaeologiam et artium historiam pertinentia 17/3, 2003, p. 27–46.

Humphries 2007 Mark Humphries: From Emperor to Pope? Ceremonial, Space, and Authority at Rome from Constantine to Gregory the Great, in: Religion, Dynasty, and Patronage in a Christian Capital. Rome 300–900, ed. Kate Cooper and Julia Hillner, Cambridge 2007, p. 21–58.

Humphries 2014 Mark Humphries: Liturgy and Laity in Late-Antique Rome: Problems, Sources, and Social Dynamics, in: Studia Patristica LXXI, 2014, p. 171–186

Ivanovici (im Druck) Vladimir Ivanovici: The Ritual Display of Gospels in Late Antiquity, in Clothing Sacred Scripture. Book Art and Book Religions in the Middle Ages, ed. David Ganz and Barbara Schellewald, Berlin 2017.

Ivanovici 2016 Vladimir Ivanovici: Manipulating Theophany. Light and Ritual in North Adriatic Architecture (ca. 400 – ca. 800), Berlin 2016.

Janes 1998 Dominic Janes: God and Gold in Late Antiquity, Cambridge 1998.

Jussen 2011 Bernhard Jussen: Liturgy and Legitimation, or How the Gallo-Romans Ended the Roman Empire, in: Ordering Medieval Society, ed. Bernhard Jussen, Philadelphia 2011, p. 147–199.

Krautheimer 1961 Richard Krautheimer: The Architecture of Sixtus III: A Fifth-Century Renaissance? in: De Artibus Opuscula XL. Essays in Honor of Erwin Panofsky, ed. Millard Meiss, New York 1961, Vol. 1I, p. 291–302.

Krautheimer 1983 Richard Krautheimer: Three Christian Capitals. Topography and Politics, Berkeley 1983.

Latham 2012 Jacob A. Latham: From Literal to Spiritual Soldiers of Christ: Disputed Episcopal Elections and the Advent of Christian Processions in Late Antique Rome, in: Church History 81/2, 2012, p. 298–327.

Latham 2014 Jacob A. Latham: Battling Bishops, the Roman Aristocracy, and the Contestation of Space in Late Antique Rome, in: Religious Competition in the Third Century CE: Jews, Christians, and the Greco-Roman World, ed. Jordan D. Rosenblum, Lily Vuong and Nathaniel DesRosiers, Göttingen 2014, p. 126–137.

Liverani 1992/93 Paolo Liverani, Le colonne e il capitello in bronzo di età romana dell'altare del SS. Sacramento in: Laterano. Analisi archeologica e problematica storica. Atti della Pontificia Accademia Romana di Archeologia, Rendiconti 65, 1992/93, p. 75–80.

MacCormack 1981 Sabine MacCormack: Art and Ceremony in Late Antiquity, Berkeley/Los Angeles/London 1981.

McCormick 1990 Michael McCormick: Eternal Victory. Triumphal Rulership in Late Antiquity, Byzantium and the Early Medieval West, Cambridge 1990.

Machado 2006 Carlos Machado: Building the Past: Monuments and Memory in the Forum Romanum, in: Social and Political Life in Late Antiquity, ed. William Bowden, Adam Gutteridge and Carlos Machado, Leiden 2006, p. 157–192.

Machado 2009 Carlos Machado: Religion as Antiquarianism: Pagan Dedications in Late Antique Rome, in: Dediche sacre nel mondo greco-romano:

diffusione, funzioni, tipologie, ed. John Bodel and Mika Kajava, Rom 2009, p. 331–354.

Machado 2010 Carlos Machado: City as Stage: Aristocratic Commemorations in Late Antique Rome, in: Les frontières du profane dans l'antiquité tardive, ed. Eric Rebillard und Claire Sotinel, Rom 2010, p. 287–317.

Machado 2011 Carlos Machado: Roman Aristocrats and the Christianization of Rome, in: Pagans and Christians in the Roman Empire (IVth–VIth Century A.D.): The Breaking of a Dialogue, ed. Peter Brown and Rita Lizzi Testa, Münster 2011, p. 493–513.

Macmullen 1964 Ramsay MacMullen: Some Pictures in Ammianus Marcellinus, in: Art Bulletin 46, 1964, p. 435–456.

Marazzi 2000 Federico Marazzi: Rome in Transition: Economic and Political Change in the Fourth and Fifth Centuries, in: Early Medieval Rome and the Christian West. Essays in honour of Donald A. Bullough, ed. Julia H. M. Smith, Leiden 2000, p. 21–41.

Noble 2001 Thomas F. X. Noble: Topography, Celebration, and Power, in: Topographies of Power in the Early Middle Ages, ed. Mayke de Jong and Frans Theuws, Leiden 2001, p. 45–92.

Pietri 1976 Charles Pietri: *Roma Christiana*. Recherches sur l'Eglise de Rome, son organisation, sa politique, son idéologie de Miltiade à Sixte III (311–440), Rom 1976.

Rapp 2000 Claudia Rapp: The Elite Status of Bishops in Late Antiquity, Ecclesiastical, Spiritual, and Social Contexts, in: Arethusa 33, 2000, p. 379–399.

Salzman 2002 Michele R. Salzman: The Making of a Christian Aristocracy. Social and Religious Change in the Western Roman Empire, Cambridge 2002.

Slootjes 2011 Daniëlle Slootjes: Bishops and Their Position of Power in the Late Third Century CE: The Cases of Gregory Thaumaturgus and Paul of Samosata, in: Journal of Late Antiquity 4/1, 2011, p. 100–115.

Stenger 2011 Jan Stenger: Ammian und die Ewige Stadt. Das spätantike Rom als Heterotopie, in: Rom und Mailand in der Spätantike. Repräsentationen städtischer Räume in Literatur, Architektur und Kunst, ed. Therese Fuhrer, Berlin/Boston 2011, p. 189–216.

Stewart 2003 Peter Stewart: Statues in Roman Society: Representation and Response, New York/Oxford 2003.

Versnel 1970 H.S. Versnel: Triumphus. An Inquiry into the Origin, Development and Meaning of the Roman Triumph, Leiden 1970.

Warland 2003 Rainer Warland: The Concept of Rome in Late Antiquity Reflected in the Mosaics of the Triumphal Arch of Santa Maria Maggiore, in: Acta ad Archaeologiam et Artium Historiam Pertinentia 17, 2003, p. 127–141.

Von Johannes VII. zu den Renaissancepäpsten

Die Öffnung der Heiligen Pforte in Alt-St. Peter

Antonella Ballardini

Über die Öffnung der ersten Heiligen Pforte in Alt-St. Peter wird bereits seit langer Zeit und kontrovers debattiert. Das Thema könnte in einer Tagung über *Formen der Päpstlichen Machtentfaltung zwischen Spätantike und Mittelalter*[1] marginal erscheinen, aber das vor Kurzem beendete Heilige Jahr der Barmherzigkeit verleiht diesem Aspekt Aktualität und bietet Gelegenheit daran zu erinnern, wie die Öffnungs- und Schließungsriten der Heiligen Pforte in der Vatikansbasilika, die noch heute das Symbol der Kirche von Rom und ihrer Oberhirten ist, ihre Form erhielten.[2]

Der Wunsch, dieser Fragestellung auf den Grund zu gehen, entwickelte sich nach einer Untersuchung der architektonischen Form des Oratoriums, das Papst Johannes VII., *natione grecus*, im Jahr 706 am Nordostende der früheren Basilika weihte.[3] Es war der Muttergottes gewidmet und die erste Grabkapelle, die ein Papst *sibi vivens* in Alt-St. Peter errichten ließ. Dieser abseits gelegene, von sieben Wänden umschlossene Raum soll um das 10. Jahrhundert eine der im Mittelalter meistverehrten Reliquien beherbergt haben, nämlich das legendäre Schweißtuch der Veronika. Es wurde so früh mit dem Heiligen Jahr assoziiert, dass die Heilige Pforte in der Nähe des darüber gebauten Ziboriums angelegt wurde[4] (Abb. 1).

In diesem Zusammenhang ist der Vollständigkeit halber sowohl auf die Erwähnung der heiligen Veronika in Dantes *Göttlicher Komödie* (mit Bezug auf eine ›Reise‹, die der Dichter während des ersten Heiligen Jahres unternahm) (*Paradies*, XXXI, V. 103–108) als auch auf das Pergament von Cortona (1300) hinzuweisen[5] (Abb. 2). In Kanzleimi-

---

1 Im Vergleich zu dem bei der Tagung vorgetragenen Text wurde der vorliegende in manchen Teilen gekürzt, in anderen erweitert, um diverse Details zur Architekturgeschichte der Heiligen Pforte während des 16. Jahrhunderts darzustellen.

2 Ballardini 2016a, S. 19-41. Zur Rolle der Vatikansbasilika bei der Einrichtung des Heiligen Jahres s. Maccarrone 1983, S. 751–753.

3 Ballardini 2011, S. 98–116; Ballardini/Pogliani 2013, S. 190–213.

4 Zu Veronika und ihrer Legende: Dobschütz 1899–1909, S. 197–262, und Wolf 2000, S. 103–114; zum Ziborium des Heiligen Antlitzes: Claussen 2001, S. 229–249.

5 Cortona, Biblioteca dell'Accademia Etrusca, cod. 101, c. 6 (225 × 625 mm), s. Mori/Wolf 2000.

Abb. 1: Abschnitt von Alt-St. Peter, 1606; im ersten Seitenschiff rechts erkennt man das Ziborium für das Schweißtuch der Veronika (Biblioteca Apostolica Vaticana, Arch. Cap. S. Pietro, A 64ter, f. 12).

nuskel geschrieben, enthält das Pergament den Brief des päpstlichen *scriptors* Silvester und die Abschrift der Bulle zur Ausrufung des ersten Jubeljahrs (*Antiquorum habet*, 22. Februar 1300).[6] Am oberen und unteren Rand sind das Heilige Antlitz und die Apostelfürsten gemalt (am unteren Rand auf dem Kopf stehend).[7] Wie schon die Bulle von Bonifaz VIII. liefert auch Silvesters Brief keinerlei Information dazu, ob es bereits im Jahr 1300 eine besondere Eingangstür zum Petersdom gab, bei deren Hindurchschreiten man einen Ablass erlangte. Die Miniaturen des Schweißtuchs zwischen Petrus und Pau-

6 *Magnum Bullarium Romanum*, Bd. 3. 2, 94. Wie wir der *Cronica Urbevetana* (1294–1304) entnehmen, wurde auf päpstliche Anordnung die Bulle auf eine *tabula lapidea affixa parietibus Sancti Petri* gemeißelt, s. Cronica Urbevetana 1902–1929, S. 202. Zur Zeit des Tiberius Alfaranus († 1596) befand sich die Inschrift im Atrium der früheren Basilika rechts von der Porta Argentea, s. Plan der Basilika (1589–1590) in: Alpharanus 1914, Taf. 1, Nr. 129; heute, in der neuen Kirche, ist sie links von der Heiligen Pforte angebracht.

7 Es handelt sich um die älteste bekannte Darstellung des in St. Peter aufbewahrten Schweißtuchs der Veronika; s. Wolf 2000, S. 19–24, sowie Mori/Wolf 2000, S. 176–178.

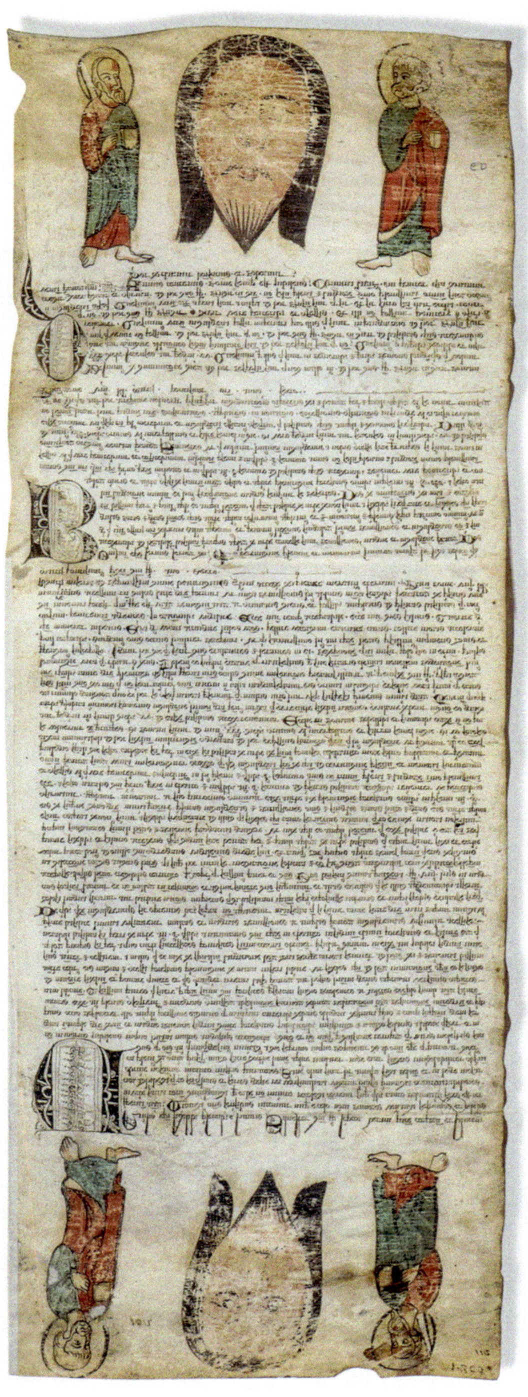

Abb. 2: Brief des päpstlichen *scriptors* Silvester, 1300 (Cortona, Biblioteca dell'Accademia Etrusca).

lus am Anfang und Ende des Textes lassen jedoch die zunehmende Anziehungskraft des Oratoriums Johannes' VII. im Laufe der Zeit erahnen: Die Eröffnungs- und Schlussfeiern der Jubiläumsjahre fanden darin statt.[8] Im Sommer 1610, kurz vor dem Abriss des letzten Fassadentrakts von Alt-St. Peter, befand sich die Heilige Pforte in der Tat an diesem Oratorium (Abb. 3).

Aber seit wann? Wie aus dem Folgenden hervorgeht, ist die Entstehungsgeschichte dieser Ritualtür alles andere als geradlinig, und im Laufe der Zeit wurde sie von der Symbolfunktion, die ihrer Einrichtung zugrunde lag, in den Schatten gestellt. Beim Versuch, die historische Dimension dieses Monuments wiederzugewinnen, werde ich in der Zeit zurückgehen und auf einige unveröffentlichte bzw. wenig bekannte Angaben aufmerksam machen.[9]

Am 7. Juli 1610, dem Oktavtag der Apostel Peter und Paul, wurde in Anwesenheit des Kardinals und Präfekten der Bauhütte von St. Peter Bartolomeo Cesio und des päpstlichen Zeremonienmeisters und Geheimkämmerers Paolo Alaleone die Heilige Pforte des Jubiläumsjahres aus der inzwischen abrissfertigen Fassade von Alt-St. Peter herausgelöst und ins Atrium der neuen Basilika gebracht. Von einem Holzrahmen geschützt und mit Hilfe eines Seilzugs wurde die alte Heilige Pforte mit dem Mauerwerk, das sie verschloss, aufrecht transportiert und – nach einiger Zeit – rechts des nördlichsten Zugangs zur neuen Kirche aufgestellt.[10] Diese Umstellung ist im Plan von Matthäus Greuter (1613, mit dem ›Zusatz‹ von Carlo Maderno) erkennbar, ebenso in der Innenansicht des Atriums von Martino Ferrabosco (um 1620)[11] (Abb. 4).

Aufgrund des bewährten und geschickten Könnens der Belegschaft der Fabbrica waren keine größeren Schwierigkeiten beim Transport zu erwarten. Dennoch verfolgte Giacomo Grimaldi, der diese außergewöhnliche Überführung in einer notariellen Urkunde festhielt, sie mit Sorge, denn seit Januar 1601 war das von diesem Kleriker und Notar verfasste Tagebuch des Heiligen Jahres ins Mauerwerk neben der Türe eingelas-

---

8 Als die Verehrung der heiligen Veronika durch Innozenz III. (1198–1216) einen neuen Impuls bekam, wurde das Oratorium Johannes' VII. mit einem Mosaikzyklus der Apostelfürsten ausgestattet; s. Pogliani 2001, S. 505–523, bes. S. 511–512 (mit Literaturübersicht).

9 Der jüngste bedeutende Beitrag zum Thema stammt von Christoph Luitpold Frommel; s. Frommel 2001, S. 571–592.

10 S. BAV, Barb. lat. 2732, f. 74r; BAV, Barb. lat. 2733, f. 237v–238r; AFSP, Arm. 26, B, 195, c. 90v; schließlich BAV, Urb. lat. 1078, f. 513: »La Porta Santa della chiesa vechia di San Pietro è stata levata intera per conservarla […]«, zit. nach Orbaan 1920, S. 173.

11 BAV, Cart. S. Pietro B, Piante I (Plan von Matthäus Greuter, 1613); Ferrabosco 1684, Taf. 18: Papst Paul V. hatte Martino Ferrabosco († 1623) mit der Erstellung von Bildtafeln zur Beschreibung von Alt- und Neu-St. Peter beauftragt. Das Werk Ferraboscos blieb unvollendet und wurde einige Jahrzehnte später (1684) in Druck gegeben.

Abb. 3: Standort der Heiligen Pforte an der Fassade von Alt-St. Peter, 1606 (Biblioteca Apostolica Vaticana, Arch. Cap. S. Pietro, A 64ter, f. 31).

Abb. 4: Martino Ferrabosco, Innenansicht des Atriums in Neu-St. Peter mit der ersten Neuaufstellung der Heiligen Pforte.

sen, wo es eigentlich bis Weihnachten 1625 verborgen bleiben sollte.[12] Eine der ersten Seiten des Pergamentmanuskripts trägt eine Widmung an den noch unbekannten Papst, der in eben diesem Jahr die Heilige Pforte öffnen würde.[13]

Seinem Titel (*Diarium*, Tagebuch) entsprechend verzeichnet das Buch Tag für Tag die Besuche von berühmten Fürsten wie auch von Pilgerströmen, die in geordneten Prozessionen von den Kirchen der römischen und auswärtigen Bruderschaften bis durch die Pforte zogen.[14] Mit statistischer Genauigkeit registriert Grimaldi die Anzahl der Messen, der ausgeteilten Hostien und der Kollekten sowie der ordentlichen und außerordentlichen Zurschaustellungen des Schweißtuchs *et alia quae ad posterorum memoriam digna visa sunt*. In seinem Bericht finden jedoch auch dramatische und sonst unbekannte Ereignisse Erwähnung, wie die Verbrennung Giordano Brunos auf dem Campo dei Fiori am 17. Februar bzw. die Hochzeit von Margherita Aldobrandini mit Ranuccio Farnese, dem Herzog von Parma, am 7. Juni in der Sixtinischen Kapelle. Schließlich liefert er auch merkwürdige, um nicht zu sagen ›legendäre‹, Informationen wie die über einen Hundertjährigen aus Äthiopien, der zu Fuß von Ferrara nach Rom pilgerte, wo er an einem Augustmorgen ankam.[15]

Unter den zahlreichen Prozessionen verdient die vom 19. September mit den Bruderschaften aus San Ginesio in den Marken besondere Erwähnung:[16] Den Höhepunkt bildete ein selbstfahrender allegorischer Wagen, der die *ecclesia triumphans* darstellte. Diesem voraus und hinterher schritt eine Hundertschaft von Figuranten, die als *tableaux*

12 BAV, Barb. lat. 2210: *Diarium anni iubilei millesimi sexcentesimi. Iacobo Grimaldo Bononiense Basilicae Vaticanae sacrista auctore*; zu Leben und Werk Giacomo Grimaldis (1568–1623) s. Niggl 1971. Über Ablässe und Jubeljahre schrieben um 1600 auch Robert Bellarmin (1600), Caspar Schoppe (1601), Jerónimo Gracián (1599), Rutilio Benzoni (1600) und Agostino Valier (1601). Zu einer kritischen Wertung dieser Schriften, aus denen eine erneuerte Vitalität der Heilig-Jahr-Feiern und ihr zunehmendes internationales Prestige hervorgeht, s. Andretta 1997, S. 355–376 (mit Literatur).

13 BAV, Barb. lat. 2210: Pergamenthandschrift; 122 × 90 mm (f. II, *14, 259); Widmung: f. *13r: *Sanctissimo Patri in sede Petri sedenti Anno Iubilei MDCXXV.* Nach der Auffindung der Trümmer der Heiligen Pforte (1625) wurde das Tagebuch von Giovanni Battista Nardone abgeschrieben (1628); s. BAV, Arch. Cap. di S. Pietro E 36; eine weitere (unvollständige) Abschrift in: BAV, Arch. Cap. di S. Pietro B 111. Ich danke Paolo Liverani für seinen Hinweis auf den späteren *Diarium anni MDCXXVI*, verfasst von Francesco Maria Torrigio. Dem Beispiel Giacomo Grimaldis folgend ließ auch Torrigio sein *Diarium* in die von Urban VIII. geöffnete und geschlossene Heilige Pforte einmauern (BAV, Barb. lat. 2324); s. Liverani 1999, S. 143–144 und 159–160.

14 Zur Rolle der römischen Bruderschaften, besonders der Arciconfraternita della SS. Trinità dei Pellegrini s. Cabibbo 1997, S. 405–430; zu den Prozessions- und Aufnahmeriten s. Visceglia 1999, S. 104–129.

15 Ich habe die gesamte Handschrift mit Blick auf ihre Veröffentlichung in einem anderen Zusammenhang transkribiert; zu den hier zitierten Passagen s. BAV, Barb. lat. 2210, f. 33v: *Iordanus Brunus Nolanus ordinis S. Dominici, propter haeresim, vivus et pertinax c(omb)ustus est, eius libri ante fores nostrae basilicae concremati*; f. 53v–56v: Hochzeit von Margherita Aldobrandini mit dem Herzog von Parma; f. 145r–146r: *Hodie venit ad basilicam senex Aethiops Abissinus, ex civitate Bremaria, nomine Ioannes de Cacuba, centesimum septimum annum agens vitae suae ... Pedes hoc anno Romam venit, pedes Ferrariam rediit* [...].

16 BAV, Barb. lat. 2210, f. 154v–159r.

vivants Propheten, Patriarchen und Heldinnen des Alten Testaments spielten, darunter Abraham mit dem Schwert und sein Sohn Isaak mit den Holzscheiten für seine Opferung, Judith mit dem abgetrennten Haupt des Holofernes, der gehäutete Bartholomäus mit seiner Haut über den Schultern, *summa arte accomodata adeo ut vera, non fictam esse demostraret*, der von Pfeilen durchbohrte Sebastian, der erste christliche Märtyrer Stephanus im Diakonsgewand *cum lapidibus super caput* sowie Petrus und Paulus als Lenker des Wagens mit der Kirche.

Schließlich beschreibt das Manuskript die Öffnungs- und Schließungsriten der Heiligen Pforte, die sich nun seit der Zeit Alexanders VI. (Jubiläumsjahr 1500) regelmäßig alle 25 Jahre wiederholten.[17]

Die Verlegung der alten Jubiläumspforte in die Fassade von Neu-St. Peter ist als Zeichen der Treue zu den althergebrachten Ritualen zu verstehen. Die Heilige Pforte der Peterskirche war gleichsam eine ›Reliquie‹ aus der alten Kirche, und nur der Pontifex war zu ihrer Öffnung und Schließung befugt. Sie blieb intakt, auch als Urban VIII. kurz vor dem Heiligen Jahr 1625 einer weiteren Verlegung zustimmte:[18] Von der Wand, in die sie unter Grimaldis Augen gemauert worden war, gelangte die Pforte in den anliegenden Nordzugang der neuen Basilika, wo sie sich heute noch befindet. Das bezeugt der auf das Heilige Jahr 1575 zurückgehende *titulus* Gregors XIII.[19] (Abb. 5).

Die Gründe für diese neuerliche Verlegung sind in den Dokumenten der für die Bauhütte zuständigen Kongregation dargelegt: Schon im Mai 1623 wurden die »großen Unannehmlichkeiten« betont, die sicherlich aufgetreten wären, hätte man die Pforte an ihrem früheren Standort belassen.[20] Dort nämlich führte die Tür nicht etwa in das Seitenschiff der Basilika, sondern in einen engen Gang, der im Vestibül zur damaligen Kreuzigungskapelle endete.[21] Diese periphere Position der Heiligen Pforte, deutlich von den anderen Zugängen zum Kircheninnern abgesetzt, war quasi eine Wiederherstellung (in Neu-St. Peter) der Position der Tür in der früheren Basilika bis zum Sommer 1610.

Für die weitere Erforschung der Heiligen Pforte muss also von der Veronika-Kapelle, also vom Oratorium Johannes' VII., ausgegangen werden.

---

17 BAV, Barb. lat. 2210, f. 3r–27v (Eröffnung) und f. 223v–240r (Schließung).

18 Zur Zeit Urbans VIII. wurde auch eine Reformierung der Öffnungs- und Schließungsriten vorgeschlagen, die jedoch nicht weiter verfolgt wurde; s. Formica 1997, S. 47–50.

19 Inschrift: Gregorius XIII Pont(ifex) Max(imus).

20 Gregor XV. (Konsistorium, 10. Mai 1623) hatte sich dafür ausgesprochen, aber die Verlegung der Porta Sancta wurde von Urban VIII. ursprünglich blockiert (Congregazione della Fabbrica, 12. Januar 1624), später jedoch durchgeführt; s. AFSP, Arm. 16, A, 159a, f. 58; Arm. 16, A, 159a, f. 64; Arm. 1, B, 13, Nr. 66, f. 193; s. Pollak 1928, Bd. 2, S. 190; vgl. Thelen 1999, S. 18–19.

21 Ein Exemplar von Greuters Plan mit Anmerkungen von Grimaldi befindet sich in: BAV, Barb. lat. 2733, f. 490–491; im neuen Atrium, bei der Türe, die in den Gang führte, verzeichnete der Kleriker *Porta Sancta anni iubilei*.

Abb. 5: Peterskirche, Heilige Pforte.

Zur virtuellen Besichtigung der früheren Kapelle bediene ich mich einer 3D-Rekonstruktion, die das Ergebnis einer Kooperation mit meiner Kollegin Paola Pogliani und mit den Architekten Marco Carpiceci und Giovanni Dibenedetto ist. Für weitere Details verweise ich auf frühere Veröffentlichungen[22] (Abb. 6).

Der Raum entstand in der Nordecke von St. Peter durch das Vermauern der ersten drei Interkolumnien des Kirchenschiffs in südlicher Richtung und war von Westen her zugänglich durch eine Tür, auf deren Architrav der *titulus* des Pontifex zu lesen war: »† Iohannis s[e]rvi s(an)c(t)ae Mariae.«[23]

Die Formel im Genitiv zeigt juristisch ein Besitzverhältnis an und bestätigt den privaten Charakter dieses geweihten Ortes, für den der Papst *auri et argenti quantitatem multam* (LP 88, c. 1) aus seinem persönlichen Besitz investierte.

Die Innenwände waren mit quadratischen Platten aus weißem, geäderten Marmor und grauem Granit verkleidet. Die *crustae* wechselten sich mit Lisenen ab, deren Ranken durch Tiere belebt und die Spolien aus severischer Zeit waren, aber auch mit anderen, die eigens für diesen Ort in den Werkstätten von Johannes VII. gefertigt wurden.

Der Altar war der *Theotokos* geweiht und an die Fassadenrückwand der Basilika angelehnt. Erhalten ist davon noch ein Fragment, das heute in den Vatikanischen Grotten aufbewahrt wird, von Grimaldi jedoch im Innern des Oratorium beschrieben und abgezeichnet wurde.[24] Über dem Altar ruhte eine Archivolte mit der Mosaikinschrift *Domus s(an)c(ta)e Dei Genitricis Mariae* auf zwei mit Rankenwerk verzierten Säulen, die Johannes VII., Sohn des letzten uns bekannten *curator Palatii*, sich beschaffte, um dem Marienaltar dieselbe majestätische Pracht wie dem Petrusaltar zu verleihen.

Oberhalb der Monumentalädikula dehnte sich die Mosaikdekoration auf drei Registern bis zum Dachstuhl aus. Sie zeigte Szenen aus der Heilsgeschichte von der Verkündigung bis zur Passion und Auferstehung Christi. Kernpunkt dieses Bildzyklus war eine von schwarzen Marmorsäulen eingerahmte Nische mit einer Darstellung der *Theotokos* in Begleitung des Stifterpapstes. Zwischen den Säulen mit Rankenwerk und an dem Platz, den früher der Marienaltar eingenommen hatte, wurde nun die Heilige Pforte geöffnet, und von dort wurde sie 1610 in die neue Basilika überführt.

Die genaue Chronologie dieser Heiligen Pforte ist nicht gesichert. Schon Giacomo Grimaldi klagte, er habe keinerlei Dokumente auffinden können, die seine These von einer Initiative seitens der Päpste Nikolaus V. oder Sixtus IV. stützten.[25]

---

22 Zuletzt auch Ballardini 2016b, S. 220–227 und Pogliani 2016, S. 240–259.

23 Ballardini 2016c, S. 231–233.

24 Kommentar und Übersetzung der Inschrift in: Ballardini 2011, S. 104–110 (mit Literaturübersicht).

25 Nach Auswertung der wenigen verfügbaren Quellen (Maffeo Vegio und Johannes Burckard) kommt Grimaldi zu dem Schluss, dass die Öffnung der Heiligen Pforte an der Stelle des Altars Johannes' VII. durch Sixtus IV. erfolgte, … *salva in omnibus veritate*; s. BAV, Arch. Cap di S. Pietro H. 3, f. 27r–v.

Üblicherweise schreibt man die Entstehung dieser Pforte Alexander VI. zu (1499); er soll auch die Eröffnungs- und Schlusszeremonien des Heiligen Jahres festgelegt haben.[26] Zur Lösung dieses Problems muss man auf das Zeugnis des Zeremonienmeisters Johannes Burckard zurückgreifen: Im *Liber notarum* beschrieb er nicht nur die vom Borgia-Papst beauftragte Ausarbeitung der Riten zur Eröffnung des Jubeljahrs, sondern auch die kurz vor Weihnachten 1499 durchgeführten Arbeiten zur monumentalen und funktionellen Umgestaltung des Ortes. Es folgt eine Übersetzung der relevanten Passagen:

> »[...] am Mittwoch, dem 18. Dezember, kam nach der 21. Stunde Seine Heiligkeit Unser Herr zum Petersdom, wo [...] ich Seiner Heiligkeit in der Veronika-Kapelle den Ort zeigte, den die Kanoniker der Basilika für die sogenannte *Porta aurea* erachten, die üblicherweise alle hundert Jahre von den Päpsten geöffnet wird; das habe ich schon öfters gehört und halte es für allgemeine Auffassung (*in vulgo*).
>
> Es gefiel Seiner Heiligkeit, dass die *Porta* in gleicher Weise auch in der Anfangsstunde des Jubeljahrs geöffnet würde, und er ordnete an, Marmorplatten zum Schmuck der Tür bis zu ihrer Innenhöhe zu beschaffen und zu bearbeiten; außerdem befahl er, die Mauern zu entfernen, die die Kapelle von vorne und auf den Seiten umschlossen, damit das Volk sich dort frei bewegen konnte.
>
> [...] [Seine Heiligkeit] beauftragte den römischen Maurer Tommaso Mattarrazzi, die Wand mit der *Porta aurea* bis auf eine Dicke von vier bis fünf Fingerbreit zu verschmälern (»ad grossitudinem quartuor vel quinque digitorum«), ohne sie jedoch zu durchbrechen, damit – wenn Seine Heiligkeit zur Vesperstunde der besagten Vigil Hand anlegte – die Wand ohne Schwierigkeiten nachgibt und der Zugang für alle frei wird.
>
> [...] Nachdem er all dies verfügt hatte, kehrte [Seine Heiligkeit] in den Palast zurück, und der vorgenannte Maurermeister machte sich mit anderen an die Durchführung seines Auftrags: Man fertigte die Marmorarbeiten zur Dekoration der Tür bis zur vorgeschriebenen Höhe, allerdings um etwa zwei Handbreit erweitert (»latiorem ad duos palmos«), und eine Überdachung, da es an diesem Ort noch nie vorher eine Türe gegeben hatte, sondern auf beiden Seiten miteinander verbundene Wände, die gemeinsam die Mauer bildeten. An der genannten Stelle (also der Tür) stand vermutlich ein einfacher Altar; da jedoch das Volk an die Tür glaubte, habe ich dessen Meinung, die eventuell die Verehrung mehren konnte, nicht anzweifeln wollen.«[27]

Aus Burckards Bericht geht zweifelsfrei hervor, dass sich die Ummauerung des alten Oratoriums bis Weihnachten 1499 noch am Platz befand, aber auch, dass der Altar Johannes' VII. schon verschwunden war. Die leer gebliebene Stelle, umrahmt von der

26 Thurston 1900, S. 30; Abbamondi 1997, S. 51–52; Visceglia 1999, S. 86–87.

27 Burckardus 1907–1910, S. 179–180. Der Abschnitt wurde schon mehrfach übersetzt und erläutert; s. bes. Thurston 1900, S. 30–32 und zuletzt Frommel 2001, S. 571–572.

Abb. 6: 3D-Rekonstruktion des Oratoriums von Johannes VII. (digitales Rekonstruktionsmodell: M. Carpiceci, Architekt; grafische Umsetzung: G. Dibenedetto, Architekt).

Archivolte auf den Säulen mit Rankenwerk, war von den Kanonikern schon mit der *Porta aurea* der Basilika identifiziert worden.

Auf päpstliche Anordnung wurde also im Narthex der Basilika an der Stelle der inneren Archivolte (d.h. der über den Säulen mit Rankenwerk) der aus Marmor gefertigte Rahmen eines Portals angebracht; außerdem wurde eine Verschmälerung des Mauerwerks der *Porta aurea* verfügt, damit es bei der Zeremonie an Heiligabend ohne Probleme nachgab.

Der Erklärung des Zeremoniars, der die Arbeit der Werkleute beobachtete, entnehmen wir, dass diese Mauer nicht neu entstand, sondern wohl noch zur Fassade der konstantinischen Basilika gehörte. Sie wies nämlich die althergebrachte dreigeteilte Struktur (Außenwand / Konglomerat / Außenwand) auf, die für eine fortschreitende und sichere Verschmälerung gut geeignet war.[28] Der Umstand, dass Tommaso Mattarazzi bei der Herstellung des äußeren Türrahmens »zwei Handbreit mehr« vorgesehen hatte, ist ebenso bedeutsam als Hinweis darauf, dass der Platz für die Widerlager der Laibung schon einkalkuliert war: Dieser Arbeitsgang konnte erst nach dem Durchbruch der Mauer erfolgen. Auch diese technische Angabe bestätigt, dass sie sehr alt und unangetastet war.

Laut Burckards Aussage war folglich Alexander VI. der erste Papst, der die »neue« Heilige Pforte öffnete. Unbeantwortet bleibt jedoch die Frage, wo in St. Peter die Pforte des Jubiläumsjahres, die mit dem Zusatz *aurea* seit spätestens 1450 bekannt war, vor 1499 geöffnet wurde: Der Schweizer Jurist Felix Hemmerlin († 1458/61) erwähnt sie in seinem *Dialogus de anno Iubileo*, den er kurz nach 1450 verfasste und der innerhalb eines großen Kompendiums seiner Schriften postum in Basel veröffentlicht wurde.[29] Hemmerlin spricht von einer *Porta aurea*, die zu den Feierlichkeiten des Jubeljahrs sowohl in der Lateransbasilika als auch in St. Peter geöffnet wurde.[30]

Der *Dialogus* stellt die *Porta aurea* mit Blick auf ein Zitat aus dem Matthäusevangelium als enges Tor dar: Das weite Tor ist der Weg ins Verderben, und viele beschreiten

28 [...] *quod in eo loco numquam fuit porta prius, sed murus undique altera parte eiusdem muris equalis et colligatur*; s. Burckardus 1907–1910, S. 180. Ich danke Maura Medri für den Ideenaustausch über die Eigenschaften der von Burckard beschriebenen Wand; zu den in der konstantinischen Basilika angewandten Mauertechniken s. Brandenburg 2015, S. 14.

29 Hemmerlin 1500, S. LXIIIr, zit. nach Thurston 1900, S. 36–37. Die Datierung des *Dialogus* wird abgeleitet aus den Hinweisen auf das Unglück auf der Engelsbrücke, das die letzten Tage des Heiligen Jahres überschattete, und auf den amtierenden Papst: *Unde de papa moderno videlicet Nicolao V* [...], s. Hemmerlin 1500, S. LXVIIIv und LXXr.

30 Die Heilige Pforte des Laterans war schon seit 1400 bekannt; s. Pisa, Archivio di Stato, Fondo Datini, filza 545, Nr. 505241: »Èssi aperta una porta, qui, a Santo G(i)ovanni Laterano, che è anni 50 più no' ssi aperesse: che chi passa per essa 3 volte, a lat' a lato, dicie à perdonanza di pena e di cholpa [...]«, s. Esch 1997, S. 288 und 290 Abb. 13; sie wird anlässlich der Heiligen Jahre Martins V. (1423), s. Nicola della Tuccia 1872, S. 213, und Nikolaus' V. (1450) erwähnt. Giovanni Ruccellai, Kaufmann und Humanist aus Florenz, erwähnt ihren feierlichen Durchbruch, nicht jedoch die *Porta aurea* von St. Peter; s. Rucellai 2013, S. 118.

ihn. Aber das enge Tor ist der schmale Weg zum Leben, den nur wenige finden (vgl. Mt 7,13–14).

Für eine *Porta aurea* in St. Peter, genauer am Ort der Veronika-Kapelle, findet sich auch ein Beleg in Nikolaus Muffels *Beschreibung der Stadt Rom*. Er war 1452 in Rom eingetroffen und sah die Tür verschlossen: »die guldenen porte vermaurt ist.« Es handelt sich demnach um die im Januar 1451 nach Abschluss des von Nikolaus V. ausgerufenen Heiligen Jahres geschlossene Heilige Pforte.[31]

Es überrascht hingegen, dass Maffeo Vegio diese *Porta aurea* nicht erwähnt. In seinem nach 1455 entstandenen Werk *De rebus antiquis memorabilibus basilicae S. Petri* schreibt er über das Oratorium von Johannes VII.:

> »[...] Gleich rechts hinter dem Eingang in die Basilika befindet sich das wundervolle, mit Skulpturen und Mosaiken geschmückte Oratorium, das der seligen Jungfrau geweiht ist und in dem immer die erste Weihnachtsmesse gefeiert worden ist. Es wurde von Papst Johannes VII. in Auftrag gegeben, und er selbst wurde unter dem Altar beigesetzt. In der Mitte des Raums steht ein weiterer Altar, darüber ein überaus kunstvolles Ziborium, worin das allerheiligste Schweißtuch Christi [...] mit großer Verehrung aufbewahrt wird.«[32]

Maffeo Vegio, ein hochgebildeter Humanist in den Diensten Eugens IV. (1431–1447) und seines Nachfolgers Nikolaus V. (1447–1455), war auch Kanoniker von St. Peter und hätte das alte Oratorium kennen müssen. Müssen wir daher annehmen, dass Muffels Aussage durch Vegios Schweigen widerlegt wird?

Diesbezüglich hilft uns das Zeugnis des Klerikers von St. Peter Tiberius Alfaranus weiter: In seinem berühmten Plan von 1589–1590 ist im äußersten Norden der Fassade von Alt-St. Peter, fast an der Ecke der Basilika, ein kleiner Durchgang eingezeichnet, der in der Legende als »Porta parvula olim« angegeben ist[33] (Abb. 7). Die handschriftlichen Ausgaben der Zeichenerklärung enthalten detailliertere Angaben: *Porta parvula olim vulg. porta sancta quae centesimo quoque Iubilaei anno a pontifice aperiabatur et claudebatur.*[34]

31 Muffel 1999, S. 48 und 50.

32 Vegio 1953, S. 397; zum Werk von Maffeo Vegio s. zuletzt Della Schiava 2011, S. 139–196.

33 Alpharanus 1914, Taf. 1, Nr. 113; zu den von Alfaranus zwischen 1571 und 1590 gezeichneten Plänen der Peterskirche s. zuletzt Ballardini 2015, S. 38–43 (mit Literatur).

34 S. BAV, Arch. Cap. S. Pietro G. 5, S. 557; aber auch BAV, Barb. lat. 2362 (Nr. 113 und 114), s. Alpharanus 1914, S. 193; s. Cecchelli 1950, S. 229–238, bes. 231. Auch Johannes Severanus (um 1624) erwähnt ein *vetus ostiolum parvulum muro clausum, in angulo Porticus ad Aquilonem, quod vulgo dicebatur Porta Sancta antiqua*, s. Rom, Bibl. Vallicelliana, G 86, c. 85v. Ich denke jedoch, dass dieser Erwähnung auch die Kenntnis des Alfaranus-Plans zugrunde liegen könnte, vgl. Severanus 1630 (mit *Pianta della chiesa antica di San Pietro*: Nr. 77 *Porta Santa* und *Porta Santa antica*).

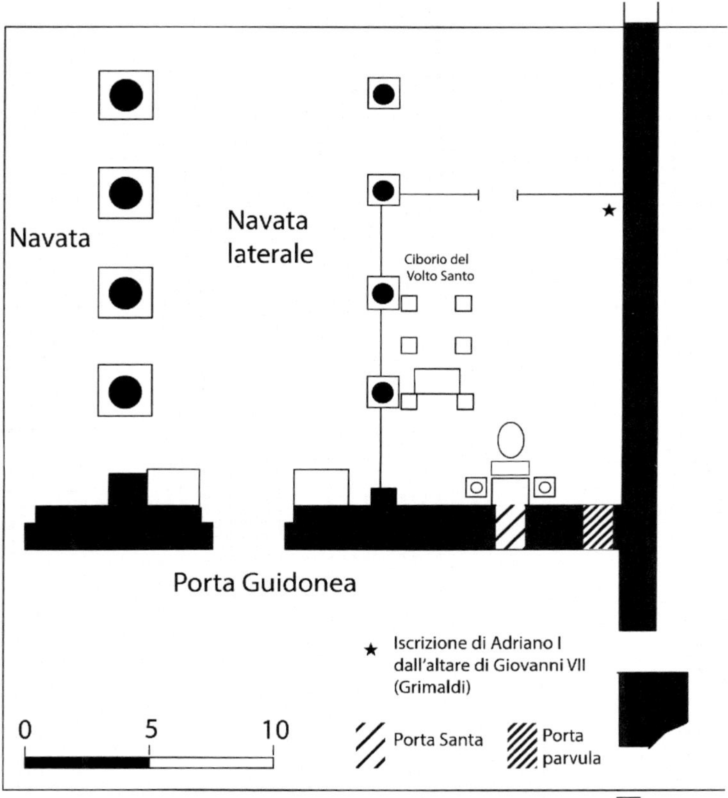

Abb. 7: Grundriss des Oratoriums von Johannes VII. mit der Heiligen Pforte und der »porta parvula«, nach den Angaben von Tiberius Alfaranus, 1589–1590 (Ausführung: E. Viscontini).

Die Assoziation zwischen der »Porta parvula« und dem Jubiläum des ›hundertsten Jahres‹ zeigt eine chronologische Unterscheidung von der jüngeren Heiligen Pforte an, *quae vigesimo quoque quinto Iubilei anno* [...] *aperitur et clauditur.* Es gibt jedoch keine Anhaltspunkte für die Annahme, dass die von Alfaranus genannte Hundertjahrfeier diejenige von Bonifaz VIII. gewesen sei; der Ausdruck könnte einfach nur bedeuten, dass es sich um einen älteren Zugang handelt.[35]

Wir wissen, dass Alfaranus in seinen Plan von Alt-St. Peter auch Bauteile eingezeichnet und beschrieben hat, die zu seiner Zeit schon nicht mehr existierten bzw. umgestal-

35 Zum Turnus der Heiligen Jahre (alle 50, 33, 25 Jahre), wie sie von den Nachfolgern Bonifaz' VIII. abgeändert wurde, s. zusammenfassend die Einführung zum Bollario dell'anno santo 1998, S. XLVII–LI.

tet worden waren. Zum Bespiel war er persönlich Zeuge dafür, dass Gregor XIII. 1574 den Narthex der alten Basilika im Hinblick auf das Heilige Jahr umfassend restaurieren ließ: Die Kassettendecke wurde erneuert, es wurden alle Überreste der Papstgräber überdeckt, die zwischen einer Tür und der nächsten zu sehen waren, die Wände bekamen einen weißen Anstrich und die alten Malereien über den Türen wurden entfernt (»coprire tutti i vestigii dei sepolcri dei pontefici che si vedevano tra una porta e l'altra e facendo imbiancare le pareti e buttare giù le pitture antiche che erano sopra le porte [...]«).[36] Wahrscheinlich verschwand die »Porta parvula«, die zur Zeit Alexanders VI. durch die neue, größere Heilige Pforte ersetzt worden war, während der Restaurierung durch Papst Gregor. Dessen Baumaßnahmen sollten in das tausendjährige Baugefüge der Peterskirche etwas Ordnung bringen. Die ›goldene Pforte‹, von der Felix Hemmerlin und Nikolaus Muffel berichteten, war also keineswegs eine Erfindung, und Muffel, der sie mit Sicherheit gesehen hatte, beschrieb das ihr von Nikolaus V. gegebene Aussehen. Dieser Papst veranstaltete 1450 das erste große Jubiläumsjahr der Moderne.[37]

Fassen wir zusammen: In Alt-St. Peter ist die Existenz einer *Porta aurea* für das Heilige Jahr ab 1450 belegt, also spätestens seit dem Jubeljahr unter Nikolaus V. Die Pforte war als »Porta parvula« gestaltet und befand sich im nördlichsten Teil der Kirchenfassade, beinahe an der Ecke der Basilika, ohne dass ihre Öffnung die liturgische Ordnung des alten Oratoriums von Johannes VII. gestört hätte.

Die »Porta parvula« wurde zum Heiligen Jahr 1450 (Nikolaus V.) und vielleicht auch wieder 1475 (Sixtus IV.) genutzt, somit so lange, bis auf Geheiß von Alexander VI. die »Porta magna« geöffnet wurde (1499).[38] Diese ›große Tür‹ entstand mithilfe eines Durchbruchs in einer alten, nie zuvor geöffneten Mauer, deren Lage im Innern der Basilika der Stelle der Archivolte auf berankten Säulen entsprach. Die Heilige Pforte Alexanders VI. ist auf einem Bild von Hans Burgkmair d. Ä. (Augsburg, Staatsgalerie) zu erkennen, das die Vatikansbasilika und ihren Namensheiligen darstellt[39] (Abb. 8). Auf dem Bild sind die architektonischen Formen verkürzt; die geöffnet dargestellte Pforte

36 BAV, Arch. Cap. S. Pietro G. 5, 153; s. Alpharanus 1914, S. 153.

37 Muffel beschreibt: Die Tür »ist von kostlichen merbelstein und hat Tytus und Vespasianus gen Rom pracht [...]«, s. Muffel 1999, S. 48; zum Heiligen Jahr Nikolaus' V. (1450) s. Miglio 1998, S. 56–73 und Frommel 2001, S. 573.

38 Ohne seine Quelle zu nennen, vertritt Johannes Severanus (um 1624) die Auffassung, zum Heiligen Jahr 1475 habe Sixtus IV. die als gefährlich eingestufte *Porta parvula* entfernt und für die Feierlichkeit die dem Oratorium am nächsten liegende Porta Guidonia genutzt: *Sixtus verus quartus iuxta praedictum ostiolum per quod dificilius admodum et fortasse non absque vitae periculo patebat transitus, anno Domini 1475 eo dismisso, aliam addidit portam supra Guidoneam quae deinceps a summis Pontificibus singulis Iubilei Annis aperiri pariter et claudi consuevit*, s. Rom, Bibl. Vallicelliana, G 86, c. 85v; zu dieser Handschrift s. Formica 1997, S. 48–50.

39 Gärtner 2002, S. 122 und 255.

Abb. 8: Hans Burgkmair d.Ä.: Die Basilica San Pietro mit dem Heiligen Petrus, 1501 (Augsburg, Staatsgalerie).

ist jedoch mit vielen Details wiedergegeben, darunter sogar ein Ausschnitt von einer der Säulen des Oratoriums.[40] Burgkmair malte das Bild anlässlich des Heiligen Jahres 1500, wie die Schriftrolle in Petrus' Hand (1501/ »Auctoritate ap(osto)lica dimitto vob(is)

40 Innerhalb der Reihe der Augsburger Heilig-Jahr-Bilder finden wir einen weiteren Beleg für Burgkmairs dokumentarische Gewissenhaftigkeit in der Darstellung des Laterans: Im Hintergrund sieht man Pilger die Scala Santa auf den Knien hinaufziehen. Die Treppe ist durch ihre Lage im Norden der Basilika und durch ihre auch aus anderen graphischen Quellen bekannte Architektur zu identifizieren; s. Gärtner 2002, S. 145–146 und Taf. IV/2.

om(n)ia p(e)c(ca)ta)« und die Inschrift auf dem Architrav über der Tür (»Alexande(r) Borgia P(a)p(a) VI Pont(ifex) Max(imus)/Anno Iubelei«) bestätigen.

Wie Christoph Luitpold Frommel bemerkte, belegt der Vergleich mit den Scheinädikulen Pinturicchios im Appartamento Borgia (Sala dei Misteri), dass der Augsburger Maler der Heiligen Pforte Alexanders VI. die gleiche Form gegeben hatte, die in jenen Jahren im Apostolischen Palast Anwendung fand.[41]

Wie gelangt man jedoch von der Heiligen Pforte des ausgehenden 15. Jahrhunderts zu derjenigen mit dem *titulus* Gregors XIII., die heute noch verwendet wird?

Wie Eberhard Hempel vorgeschlagen und Frommel nachgewiesen hat, beschränkte sich Gregor XIII. auf die Umgestaltung einer Tür, die schon damals nicht mehr die Alexanders VI. war. 1525 gab Clemens VII. Medici der Heiligen Pforte ein moderneres Aussehen.[42]

Auch Giacomo Grimaldi, der seine Quelle leider ungenannt lässt, schreibt, die (heute noch vorhandenen) Türpfosten aus sorgfältig gearbeitetem Chiosmarmor seien von Clemens VII. in Auftrag gegeben worden. Laut Grimaldi wurde diese Art von geflecktem rotem Marmor danach allgemein als *Portasanta* bezeichnet.[43]

Grimaldis Aussagen werden teilweise durch eine Denkschrift von Paris de Grassis bestätigt, die Marc Dykmans bekannt gemacht hat.[44] Der Zeremoniar Clemens' VII. berichtet, am Vorabend der Beendigung des Heiligen Jahres 1525 habe der Papst sich vergewissert, dass alles *pro clausura* Nötige verfügbar war, *etiam cum stipitibus et cornicibus ac trabibus marmoreis.*

Clemens VII. hatte für den Eröffnungsritus die Besprengung der Türpfosten mit Weihwasser eingeführt und wollte daher, dass sie besonders wertvoll waren; kurz vor der Schließung veranlasste er eine Umgestaltung der Pforte. Damit betraut wurde Baldassare Peruzzi (1481–1537), damals zweiter Architekt von St. Peter.[45] Die Urheberschaft lässt sich einer Anmerkung auf einer anonymen Zeichnung in der Albertina in Wien entnehmen (»Questa è la porta S(anta) di S. Pietro e fu disegno di Baldassarre di Siena«), sie wird aber auch von der überzeugenden Ähnlichkeit mit anderen Türen des Architekten aus Siena bewiesen[46] (Abb. 9).

Die Vorderseite der Zeichnung zeigt das Relief der Pforte mit dem Schnitt des Gesimses, des Frieses und des Architravs, alle mit Maßen versehen; die Rückseite lässt

41 Laut Frommel spiegelt die von Burgkmair dokumentierte Heilige Pforte Alexanders VI. eine Idee Antonio Sangallos d. Ä. wider; s. Frommel 2001, S. 574–575.

42 Hempel 1924, S. 10; Frommel 2010, S. 571–592.

43 BAV, Barb. lat. 2733, f. 175v.

44 BAV, Vat. lat. 56341, f. 239v–249r–v, s. Dykmans 1984, S. 69–70.

45 Frommel 2000, S. 271 und Frommel 2001.

46 Vgl. vor allem das Tor des Palazzo Massimo alle Colonne in Rom (1532).

das Relief und den Schnitt einer Volute, des darüber liegenden Gesimses und anderer Bekrönungselemente erkennen[47] (Abb. 10).

Der Text der Inschrift auf dem Polsterfries (*Gregorio XIII Pont. M.*) beweist, dass der gregorianische *titulus* noch nicht endgültig festgelegt war. So erscheint mir denkbar, dass es sich bei der anonymen Zeichnung in der Albertina um eine Abbildung der Heiligen Pforte von Clemens VII. handelt, die im Hinblick auf die Anpassung des *titulus* an den Namen des amtierenden Papstes (um 1575) angefertigt wurde.

Das Medici-Wappen (noch an seinem Platz über dem Bekrönungsgesims) stützt die Annahme, dass die Zeichnung die ursprüngliche Dekoration der Heiligen Pforte von Baldassare Peruzzi darstellt.

Begibt man sich auf die Suche nach ikonographischen Belegen zur Heiligen Pforte, findet man in den Heilig-Jahr-Medaillen ebenso interessante wie irreführende Informationen. Eine seltene Gedenkmedaille für das Heilige Jahr Gregors XIII., nämlich ein von Federico Cocciola 1575 geprägtes Exemplar, vermittelt jedoch ein unüblich realistisches Bild der Tür. Die *Porta Santa* auf der Rückseite entspricht vollständig Peruzzis Vorgaben: das von Voluten gestützte Gesims, der konvexe Fries, das Medici-Wappen und die *tabula* mit geschweifter Umrandung als oberer Abschluss[48] (Abb. 11). Wie Clemens VII. beseitigte auch Gregor XIII. Wappen und *tabula* erst bei den Schließungsriten; davor trug der *titulus* auf dem Fries wahrscheinlich den Namen seines Vorgängers.[49] Zur Erleichterung der Umarbeitung des Frieses war eine (temporäre) Entfernung des Architravs nötig, der bis heute Zeichen dieses Arbeitsgangs aufweist: Die rechte und die linke Ecke sind rechteckige Ergänzungen, auch das Mittelelement des Architravs zeigt – im Vergleich zu den darunter liegenden Pfosten – eine geringere Herausarbeitung des Reliefs, dessen Wirkung durch die eintönige und glanzlosere Färbung des Marmors weiter eingeschränkt wird.

Wenn man die heutige Ausführung des Gesimses betrachtet und es mit Peruzzis Heiliger Pforte vergleicht, so erfuhren auch die Voluten und die Bekrönung eine Umgestaltung (vielleicht zu unterschiedlichen Zeiten): Das Gesims wurde verkleinert und

47 Wien, Bibl. Albertina, AzRom 750r und v; sowohl Hempel 1924, S. 10, als auch Cola 1999, S. 406 bekannt, wurde die Zeichnung von Frommel veröffentlicht (2001, S. 575–576 und Abb. 12–13). Der Türrahmen war mit dem Medici-Wappen und einer *tabula* auf einem Sockel geschmückt.

48 Auch andere für das Heilige Jahr Gregors XIII. geprägte Exemplare zeigen die Pforte mit dem Medici-Wappen; allerdings geben nur diese kleine, äußerst seltene Medaille (Cabinet des Médailles de la Bibliothèque Nationale de Paris, Dm 25,1 mm) und die Albertina-Zeichnung die Heilige Pforte von St. Peter nach dem Plan Baldassare Peruzzis wieder. Aufgrund der Darstellung eines kreuztragenden Christus auf der Türschwelle hat Adolfo Modesti darin fälschlicherweise die Heilige Pforte des Laterans erkannt; s. Modesti 2004, Bd. 3, S. 414, Nr. 719.

49 Der Polsterfries ist aus grünem Serpentin, die Inschrift darauf in Gelb eingelegt.

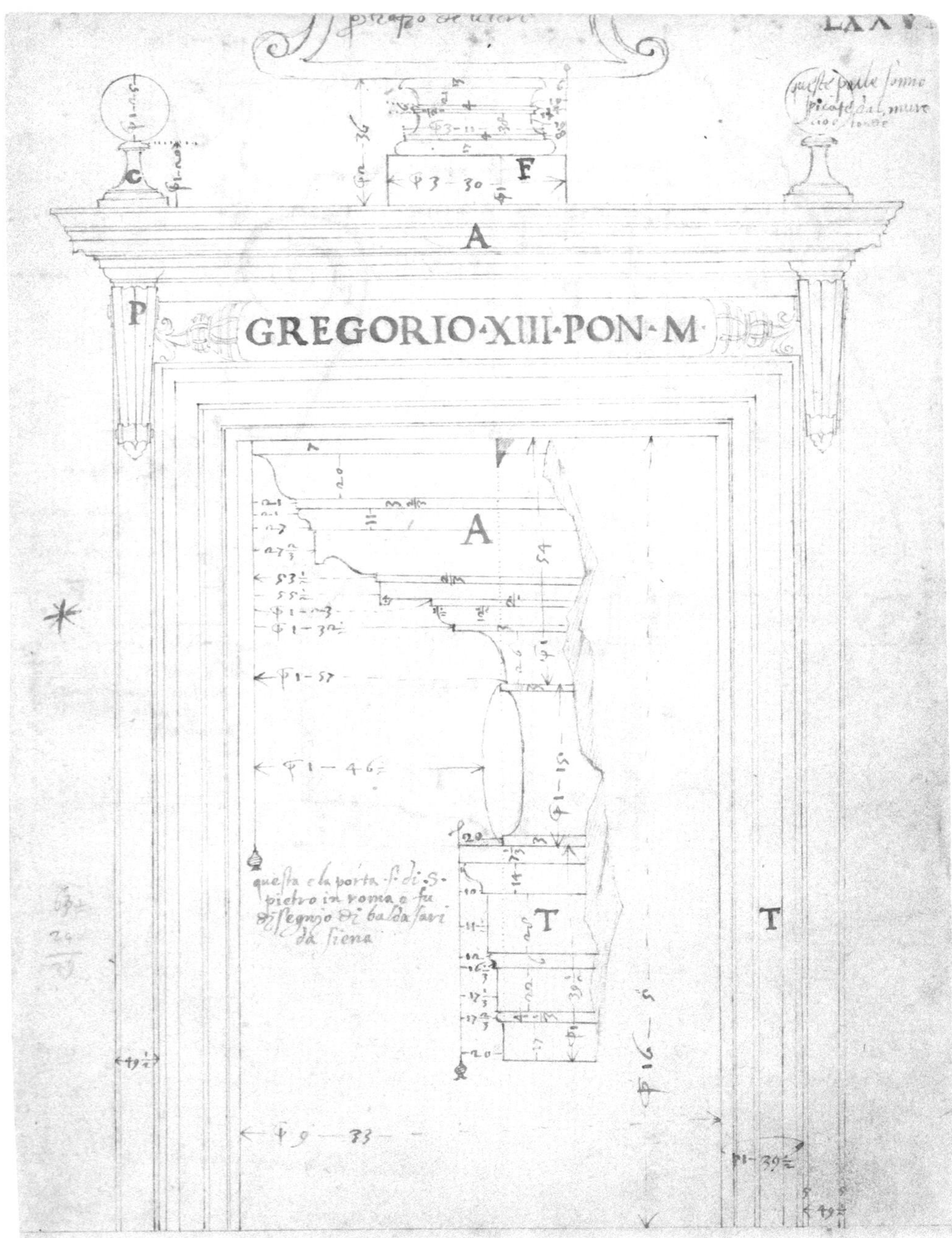

Abb. 9: Aufriss der Heiligen Pforte, um 1575 (Wien, Albertina, AZRom 750r).

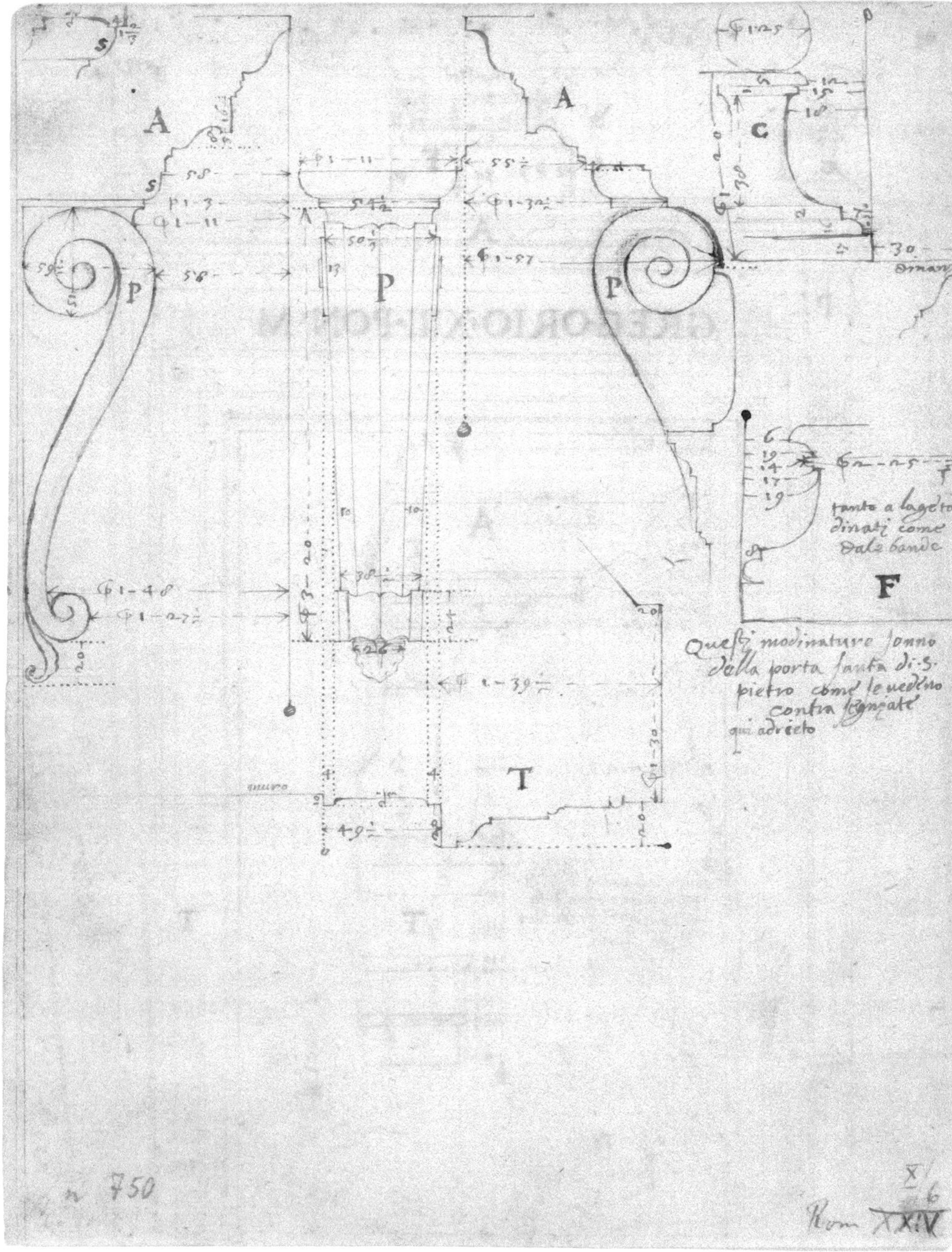

Abb. 10: Aufriss der Heiligen Pforte, um 1575 (Wien, Albertina, AZRom 750v).

Abb. 11: Paris, Cabinet des Médailles de la Bibliothèque Nationale: Originalgedenkmedaille, geprägt vom Medailleur Federico Cocciola, 1575.

an der Sima neu behauen, die Voluten wurden ersetzt.[50] Nach Gregor XIII. wagte kein Papst mehr, die Friesinschrift zu verändern.

Ab 1575 setzte sich der vielleicht schon von Clemens VII. (1525) eingeläutete und bis heute bestehende Brauch durch, eine *memoria* der Päpste, die zuvor das Heilige Jahr gefeiert hatten, in die Wand über der Heiligen Pforte einzumauern.[51]

Zum Abschluss des Heiligen Jahres 1625 beschränkte sich auch der junge Borromini auf eine Ausarbeitung der Gesimse und darauf, in »il piano dele doi inscritioni de marmo« die Namen von Clemens VIII. und Urban VIII. einzumeißeln; er erfand jedoch auch das mit dem Barberini-Wappen geschmückte Kreuz, das die Wand der Heiligen Pforte versiegeln sollte.[52]

50 Ich bin der Ansicht, dass diese Veränderungen (Verkleinerung des Gesimses und Ersetzen der Voluten) nicht zur Zeit Gregors XIII., sondern erst im 17. Jahrhundert erfolgten. Diese Hypothese bedarf noch einer intensiven Archivforschung. Eine nähere ›archäologische‹ Verifizierung wird erst nach Ende des laufenden Heiligen Jahres möglich sein, wenn der Durchgang sein rituelles ›Gewand‹ abgelegt haben wird.

51 Die Zeichnung in der Albertina wurde leider am oberen Rand beschnitten. In der Mitte der Bekrönung ist eine *tabula* mit geschweifter Umrandung auf einem Sockel zu erkennen. Der namenslose Zeichner hat den Text nicht abgeschrieben, sondern merkt nur an: »pitafio de […]«. Tiberius Alfaranus hielt die Gedenkinschriften für die Heiligen Jahre 1550 und 1575 fest (BAV, Arch. Cap. di S. Pietro G. 5, S. 153): »Sopra la Porta Santa vi è l'arme di papa Iulio et è scrito: *Iulius III Pont. Max. portam hanc aperuit et clausit anno iubilaei MDL; aperta prius ab Alexandro VI MD et a Clemente VII anno MDXXV*, ma nell'anno 1576 Gregorio XIII havendo(la) aperta et serrata posse questa altra inscriptione: *Gregorius XIII Pont. Max. hanc Sanctam Portam a Iulio III Anno MDL apertam et clausam aperuit et clausit Anno Iubilei MDLXXV*«.

52 AFSP, ARM. 1, A, 2, Nr. 2 (28. Januar 1626); s. Pollak 1928, Bd. 2, S. 191–192, zuletzt Di Sante 2014, S. 171–185 ; Seifert 2016, S. 457–485; Di Buono 2016, S. 487–497. Mein aufrichtiger Dank gilt Assunta Di Sante vom Archivio Storico della Fabbrica di San Pietro, mit der ich die Neugier und Leidenschaft für die Geschichte der Heiligen Pforte in St. Peter teile.

Bibliographie

Antonella Ballardini *Da Giovanni VII ai papi del Rinascimento. L'apertura della Porta Santa nell'antico San Pietro.*

Abbamondi 1997 Lorenzo Abbamondi: La Porta Santa, in: »Dell'aprire et serrare la Porta Santa«. Storie e immagini della Roma degli Anni Santi (Ausstellung Rom, Biblioteca Vallicelliana 4.12.1997–30.4.1998), hg. von Barbara Tellini Santoni und Alberto Manodori, Rom 1997, S. 51–54.

Alpharanus 1914 Tiberii Alpharani De Basilicae Vaticanae antiquissima et nova structura (Studi e Testi; 26), hg. von Michele Cerrati, Rom 1914.

Andretta 1997 Stefano Andretta: Devozione, controversistica e politica negli anni santi 1550–1600, in: Roma moderna e contemporanea 5, 2–3, 1997, S. 355–376.

Ballardini 2011 Antonella Ballardini: Un oratorio per la Theotokos. Giovanni VII (705–7) committente a San Pietro, in: Medioevo: i committenti, XIII Convegno internazionale di studi, Parma, 21–26 settembre 2010, hg. von Arturo Carlo Quintavalle, Mailand/Parma 2011, S. 98–116.

Ballardini 2015 Antonella Ballardini: Die Petersbasilika im Mittelalter, in: Hugo Brandenburg, Antonella Ballardini und Christof Thönes, Der Petersdom in Rom. Die Baugeschichte von der Antike bis Heute, Petersberg 2015, S. 34–75.

Ballardini 2016a Antonella Ballardini: Piccola ma aurea: la Porta Santa nell'antico San Pietro, in: Quando la Fabbrica costruì San Pietro. Un cantiere di lavoro di pietà cristiana e di umanità (XVI–XIX secolo), hg. von Assunta di Sante und Simona Turriziani, Foligno 2016, S. 19–41.

Ballardini 2016b Antonella Ballardini: Il perduto Oratorio di Giovanni VII nella Basilica di San Pietro in Vaticano. Architettura e scultura, in: Santa Maria Antiqua, tra Roma e Bisanzio (Ausstellung Rom, Santa Maria Antiqua, 17.3.–30.10.2016), hg. von Maria Andaloro, Giulia Bordi und Giuseppe Morganti, Mailand 2016, S. 220–226.

Ballardini 2016c Antonella Ballardini: Il *titulus* dell'oratorio di Giovanni VII, in: Santa Maria Antiqua, tra Roma e Bisanzio (Ausstellung Rom, Santa Maria Antiqua, 17.3.–30.10.2016), hg. von Maria Andaloro, Giulia Bordi und Giuseppe Morganti, Mailand 2016, S. 231–233.

Ballardini/Pogliani 2013 Antonella Ballardini und Paola Pogliani: A reconstruction of the oratory of John VII (705–7), in: Old Saint Peter's, Rome, hg. von Rosamond McKitterick et al., Cambridge 2013, S. 190–213.

Bollario dell'anno Santo 1998 Bollario dell'anno Santo. Documenti di indizione dal Giubileo del 1300, hg. von Erminio Lora, Bologna 1998.

Brandenburg 2015 Hugo Brandenburg: L'antica Basilica Vaticana costantiniana di S. Pietro, in: San Pietro. Storia di un monumento, Mailand 2015, S. 8–33.

Burckardus 1907–1910 Johanni Burckardi *Liber Notarum, ab anno mccccIxxxiii usque ad annum mdvi* (Rerum Italicarum Scriptores; 32,1–2), hg. von Enrico Celani, Città di Castello 1907–1910.

Cabibo 1997 Sara Cabibbo: Civilité e anni santi. La santa opera di »albergar li pellegrini« nelle cronache dei Giubilei (1575–1650), in: Roma moderna e contemporanea 5, 2–3, 1997, S. 405–430.

Cecchelli 1950 Carlo Cecchelli: Origini della Porta Santa, in: Capitolium 25, 1950, S. 229–238.

Claussen 2001 Peter Cornelius Claussen: Il tipo romano di ciborio con reliquie:questioni aperte sulla genesi e la funzione, in: Atti del colloquio internazionale «Arredi di culto e disposizioni liturgiche a Roma da Costantino a Sisto IV» (Istituto Olandese a Roma, 3.–4.12.1999), hg. von Sible De Blaauw, Assen 2001, S. 229–249.

Cola 1999 Maria Celeste Cola: Disegno della Porta Santa (1623–1624), in: Il giovane Borromini. Dagli esordi a San Carlo alle Quattro Fontane (Ausstellung Lugano, Museo Cantonale, 5.9.–14.11.1999), hg. von Manuela Kahn-Rossi und Marco Franciolli, Mailand 199, S. 405–406.

Cronica Urbevetana 1902–1929 Ephemerides Urbevetanae dal Codice Vaticano Urbinate 1745 (Rerum Italicarum Scriptores; 15,5), hg. von Luigi Fumi, Città di Castello/Bologna 1902–1929.

Della Schiava 2011 Fabio Della Schiava: Il »De rebus antiquis memorabilibus« di Maffeo Vegio tra i secoli XV–XVII, la ricezione e i testimoni, in: Italia medioevale e umanistica 52, 2011, S. 139–196.

Di Buono 2016 Paolo Di Buono: La croce per la Porta Santa della Basilica di San Pietro: Calandra e l'uso del mosaico filato, in: Quando la Fabbrica costruì San Pietro. Un cantiere di lavoro di pietà cristiana e di umanità (XVI–XIX secolo), hg. von Assunta di Sante und Simona Turriziani, Foligno 2016, S. 487–497.

Di Sante 2014 Assunta Di Sante: Le croci di Borromini per la dedicazione della Basilica di San Pietro in Vaticano (18 novembre 1626), in: Rivista d'arte 48, 4, 2014, S. 171–185.

Dobschütz 1899–1909 Ernst von Dobschütz: Christusbilder. Untersuchungen zur Christlichen Legende. Einzelausgabe des Darstellenden Teiles, Leipzig 1899–1909.

Dykmans 1984 Marc Dykmans: La Porta d'oro e le sue origini, in: Roma 1300–1875. L'arte degli anni santi (Ausstellung Roma, Palazzo Venezia, 20.12.1984–5.4.1985), hg. von Marcello Fagiolo und Maria Luisa Madonna, Mailand 1982, S. 66–72.

Esch 1997 Arnold Esch: I giubilei del 1390 e del 1400, in: La storia dei Giubilei, hg. von Gloria Fossi, Bd. 1, [o. O.] 1997, S. 278–293.

Ferrabosco 1684 Martino Ferrabosco: Architettura della Basilica di S. Pietro in Vaticano. Opera di Bramante Lazzari, Michel'Angelo Bonarota, Carlo Maderni e altri famosi architetti, Rom 1684.

Formica 1997 Patrizia Formica: Il rito della Porta Santa sotto accusa alle soglie del giubileo di Urbano VIII: l'oratoriano Severano contro Michele Lonigo, in: »Dell'aprire et serrare la Porta Santa«. Storie e immagini della Roma degli Anni Santi (Ausstellung Rom, Biblioteca Vallicelliana, 4.12.1997–30.4.1998), hg. von Barbara Tellini Santoni und Alberto Manodori, Rom 1997, S. 47–50.

Frommel 2000 Christoph Luitpold Frommel: La porta ionica nel Rinascimento, in: Studi in onore di Renato Cevese, hg. von Guido Beltrametti, Adriano Ghisetti Giavarina und James S. Ackerman, Vicenza 2000, S. 251–292 und 575–592.

Frommel 2001 Christoph Luitpold Frommel: La Porta Santa di Alessandro VI e di Clemente VII e un'opera sconosciuta di Baldassarre Peruzzi a S. Pietro, in: Roma di fronte all'Europa al tempo di Alessandro VI, Atti del convegno (Vatikanstadt-Rom, 1.–4.12.1999), hg. von Maria Chiabò, Silvia Maddalo und Massimo Miglio, Bd. 2, Rom 2001, S. 571–592.

Gärtner 2002 Magdalene Gärtner: Römische Basiliken in Augsburg. Nonnenfrömmigkeit und Malerei um 1500, Augsburg 2002.

Hämmerlin 1500 Felix Hämmerlin: De nobilitate et rusticitate dialogus et alia opuscula, Straßburg ca. 1500, S. LIIIIV–LXXIV.

Hempel 1924 Eberhard Hempel: Francesco Borromini, Wien 1924.

Liverani 1999 Paolo Liverani: La Topografia Antica del Vaticano (Monumenta Sanctae Sedis; 2), Vatikanstadt 1999.

Maccarrone 1983 Michele Maccarrone: L'indulgenza del giubileo del 1300 e la Basilica di San Pietro, in: Atti della IV settimana di studi di storia dell'arte medievale dell'Università di Roma ›La Sapienza‹ (Mediaevalia; 1), hg. von Angiola Maria Romanini, Rom 1983, S. 731–752.

Magnum Bullarium Romanum. Bullarum privilegiorum ac diplomatum Romanorum pontificum amplissima collectio, Graz 1964 [Rom 1739–1757], Bd. 3.2, S. 94.

Miglio 1998 Massimo Miglio: Il Giubileo di Niccolò V (1450), in: La storia dei Giubilei, hg. von Marcello Fagiolo und Maria Luisa Madonna, Bd. 2, [o.O.] 1998, S. 56–73.

Modesti 2004 Adolfo Modesti: Corpus Numismatum Omnium Romanorum Pontificum (C.N.O.R.P), Bd. 3, Rom 2004.

Mori/Wolff 2000 Elisabetta Mori und Gerhard Wolf: Lettera dello scrittore pontificio Silvestro, in: Il Volto di Cristo (Ausstellung Rom, Palazzo delle Esposizioni, 9.12.2000–16.4.2001), hg. von Giovanni Morello und Gerhard Wolf, Mailand 2000, S. 176–178.

Muffel 1999 Nikolaus Muffel: Descrizione della città di Roma nel 1452. Delle indulgenze e dei luoghi sacri di Roma (Der ablas und die heiligen stet zu Rom), hg. von Gerhard Wiedmann, Bologna 1999.

Nicola della Tuccia 1872 Nicola della Tuccia: Cronaca di Viterbo, in: Cronache e statuti della città di Viterbo, hg. von Ignazio Ciampi, Florenz 1872.

Orbaan 1920 Johannes Albertus Franciscus Orbaan: Documenti sul Barocco di Roma, Rom 1920.

Pogliani 2001 Paola Pogliani: Le storie di Pietro nell'oratorio di Giovanni VII nella basilica di San Pietro, in: La figura di San Pietro nelle fonti del Medioevo (Textes et études du Moyen âge; 17), Louvain-La-Neuve 2001, S. 505–523.

Pogliani 2016 Paola Pogliani, Il perduto Oratorio di Giovanni VII nella Basilica di San Pietro in Vaticano. I mosaici, in: Santa Maria Antiqua, tra Roma e Bisanzio (Ausstellung Rom, Santa Maria Antiqua, 17.3.–30.10.2016), hg. von Maria Andaloro, Giulia Bordi und Giuseppe Morganti, Mailand 2016, S. 240–259.

Pollak 1928 Oskar Pollak: Die Kunsttätigkeit unter Urban VIII, Bd. 2, Wien 1928.

Rucellai 2013 Giovanni di Pagolo Rucellai: Zibaldone, hg. von Gabriella Battista, Florenz 2013.

Seifert 2016 Veronika Seifert: La recente riscoperta di una croce di Borromini per la Porta Santa di San Pietro, posta al centro di una fioritura di opere di carità, in: Quando la Fabbrica costruì San Pietro. Un cantiere di lavoro di pietà cristiana e di umanità (XVI–XIX secolo), hg. von Assunta di Sante und Simona Turriziani, Foligno 2016, S. 457–485.

Thelen 1999 Heinrich Thelen: Francesco Borromini. Personalità, disegni giovanili, in: Il giovane Borromini. Dagli esordi a San Carlo alle Quattro Fontane (Ausstellung Lugano, Museo Cantonale, 5.9.–14.11.1999), hg. von Manuela Kahn-Rossi und Marco Franciolli, Mailand 1999, S. 13–24.

Thurston 1900 Herbert Thurston S.J.: The Holy Year of Jubilee. An Account of the History and Ceremonial of the Roman Jubilee, London 1900.

Vegio 1953 Maffeo Vegio: De rebus antiquis memorabilibus basilicae S. Petri Romae, in: Codice Topografico della città di Roma, hg. von Roberto Valentini und Giuseppe Zucchetti, Bd. 4, Rom 1953, S. 375–398.

Visceglia 1999 Maria Antonietta Visceglia: *Haec est porta Domini. Justi intrabunt in eam. I rituali del Giubileo*, in: La storia dei Giubilei (1600–1775), hg. von Alessandro Zuccari, Rom 1999, S. 84–129.

Wolf 2000 Gerhard Wolf: »Or fu sì fatta la sembianza vostra«: sguardi alla ›vera icona‹ e alle sue copie artistiche, in: Il Volto di Cristo (Ausstellung Rom, Palazzo delle Esposizioni, 9.12.2000–16.4.2001), hg. von Giovanni Morello und Gerhard Wolf, Mailand 2000, S. 103–114.

Geschichtsschreibung und Erinnerung

Die Rolle von Papst Silvester in der Selbstdarstellung des römischen Papsttums (6.–12. Jahrhundert)

Manuela Gianandrea

Als historische Persönlichkeit ist Papst Silvester (314–335) nicht klar umrissen. Zur Symbolfigur des neuen, christlichen Roms wurde er jedoch als Zeitgenosse von Kaiser Konstantin, was eine offensichtliche Verherrlichung dieses Pontifex in Gang setzte, nämlich als Abglanz eines historischen Bewusstseins, das sich mit der näheren Vergangenheit auseinandersetzt.[1] Da der *Liber pontificalis* die Gründung der wichtigsten frühchristlichen Gebäude Roms Konstantin und nicht etwa Silvester zuschreibt[2], enthüllt das aufmerksame Lesen der *Actus Silvestri* diesbezüglich interessante Anhaltspunkte.[3] Dieser Text entstand nicht zur stärkeren Verehrung Silvesters, sondern zu anderen Zwecken, zu deren Erfüllung der Papst ein höchst geeignetes literarisches Werkzeug war: das Prestige des römischen Bischofssitzes, die anti-jüdische Polemik, vor allem aber die Notwendigkeit einer Korrektur der früheren Geschichte von Konstantins Taufe, die erst auf dem Totenbett und durch einen arianischen Geistlichen gespendet worden war. Zwischen dem 4. und dem 6. Jahrhundert wird Silvester unbewusst zum Protagonisten einer Erzählung, die eigentlich nicht seiner persönlichen Glorifizierung dient, sondern hauptsächlich einer Neufassung des Andenkens an Konstantin,[4] dem eigentlichen Angelpunkt des Geschehens. Die Gleichzeitigkeit mit der sogenannten konstantinischen Wende hat dem Pontifikat Silvesters eine erhebliche symbolische Tragweite verliehen und ihn, als Inhaber des apostolischen Stuhls zur Zeit Konstantins, zum archetypischen Vermittler in der fortdauernden Dialektik zwischen kirchlicher *auctoritas* und weltlicher Macht gemacht. Im römischen Mittelalter, als das Gleichgewicht zwischen diesen beiden Gewalten immer wieder wankte, wird Silvester zum geschichtlichen Präzedenz-

---

1 Scorza Barcellona 2000, S. 321–332.

2 LP I, S. 170–187.

3 Zu den *Actus* s. die Studien von Loenertz (1975) und Pohlkamp (1992) sowie zuletzt Canella 2006.

4 Die Literatur zu diesem grundlegenden und vielschichtigen Aspekt ist sehr umfangreich. Der Kürze halber verweise ich auf Linder 1975, Pohlkamp 1984, Beiträge in: Costantino il Grande 1992–1993, Amerise 2005, Costantino il Grande 2008 sowie Maraval 2013, S. 197–202.

fall ohnegleichen und zum politisch-intellektuellen Werkzeug der Durchsetzung des Papsttums; er verkörpert den Vorrang der Kirche über das Imperium.

Die Bedeutung, die Silvesters Pontifikat im Laufe der Jahrhunderte annahm, war jedenfalls das Ergebnis einer längeren Entwicklung von der Spätantike bis zum 12./13. Jahrhundert, die wir als ›historische Stratifikation‹ bezeichnen könnten, womit eine progressive Entwicklung historiographischer Deutungen gemeint ist, die auf eine politische Nutzbarmachung Papst Silvesters als geschichtlichen Präzedenzfall abzielen. Letztendlich hat das legendenhafte Bild den historischen Silvester vollständig überdeckt; der entstandene Mythos entspricht nur teilweise der Wahrheit, hat aber in Rom im Laufe der Zeit sogar den früher vorherrschenden Mythos Konstantins überholt. Das dokumentierte Bild des Papstes wurde mehrfach im Sinne einer Legende überarbeitet, und die Geschichten, die man sich über ihn erzählt, sind das Ergebnis ausgefeilter literarischer Korrekturen, die zu guter Letzt seine tatsächliche geschichtliche Tragweite nicht mehr widerspiegeln. Vor diesem Hintergrund ist die Knappheit rein historischer Quellen über den Papst nicht erstaunlich; erheblich zahlreicher sind hingegen spätere hagiographische Dokumente, darunter die berühmte Konstantinische Schenkung.[5] Zum korrekten Verständnis der Lebensgeschichte Papst Silvesters und ihrer strategischen Verwendung seitens der römischen Kirche im geschichtlich-künstlerischen Bereich muss man sich daher hauptsächlich auf verschiedene sozio-anthropologische Methoden verlassen, wie z. B. historische Stratifikation und Aufarbeitung des Andenkens.

Die oben genannten Überlegungen scheinen in der Erforschung von Monumenten und Darstellungen, die Papst Silvester betreffen, ihre Bestätigung zu finden. Sie zeigen, dass er vor allem ab der Mitte des 8. Jahrhunderts vermehrt in kunstwissenschaftlichen Chroniken auftritt. Obwohl es schon durch die *Actus Silvestri* zu bedeutenden Veränderungen und Korrekturen in der Darstellung des Pontifex gekommen war, betrafen diese doch hauptsächlich die Vita Konstantins, der in der Spätantike und dem frühen Mittelalter *de facto* der absolute Protagonist der Geschichtsschreibung blieb. Obwohl in den wenigen, ebenfalls nur aus Texten bekannten Zeugnissen für die damalige Zeit fast ausschließlich Bildnisse des Kaisers vermutet werden[6], bildet das angebliche Silvesterbild, das einige Forscher in einem Raum unter der römischen Kirche S. Martino ai Monti zu erkennen glauben, eine Ausnahme.[7] Das Mosaik mit dem Brustbild wird dem Euergetismus von Papst Symmachus (498–514) zugeschrieben und ist nur schwer zu

5 Vian 2004, Fried 2007.

6 Nach Meinung einiger Forscher befanden sich Kaiserbilder am Triumphbogen und an der Fassade der Vatikansbasilika, vgl. Liverani 2006, S. 90–91, mit früherer Literatur, und Liverani 2008, S. 155–172. Für Konstantinopel wird eine Darstellung der Taufe Konstantins in der Portikus der Polyeuktoskirche angenommen, vgl. Fowden 1994. Allgemein s. auch Falla Castelfranchi 2014, S. 375–382.

7 Davis-Weyer/Emerick 1984, S. 3–60; Andaloro 2002, S. 877–884.

identifizieren. Es könnte leicht mit dem *titulus Equitii* in Verbindung gebracht werden, der laut *Liber pontificalis* von Silvester gegründet und von selbigem Symmachus weiter ausgeschmückt wurde.[8] Dessen Pontifikat war von den Konflikten mit dem Gegenpapst Laurentius geprägt, und deshalb wurde zur Unterstützung und Rechtfertigung von Symmachus' Aktionen eine ganze Reihe von Texten verfasst, in denen daher falsche Ereignisse erfunden und früheren Päpsten (Marcellus, Liberius, Sixtus III.) und insbesondere Silvester unwahre Ereignisse zugeschrieben wurden.[9]

Trotz des recht beschränkten Rahmens einer persönlichen Geschichte ist es doch bemerkenswert, dass zu Symmachus' Unterstützung gerade Silvester als Akteur erfundener Ereignisse herhalten musste, denn diese erforderten notwendigerweise eine Persönlichkeit von hohem Ansehen, also einen über jeden Zweifel erhabenen Gewährsmann, um offiziell Anerkennung zu finden. Silvester musste also schon eine gewisse Verehrung durch das Kirchenvolk genießen, auch in der vom Erfolg der *Actus* vorgezeichneten Spur. In der Tat ist ein ihm geweihtes Oratorium schon für das späte 7. Jahrhundert belegt, das sich nicht zufällig im Areal der Papstresidenz am Lateran befand.[10] Dennoch steht fest, dass Silvesters Gestalt erst ab der Mitte des 8. Jahrhunderts in den Fokus gezielten Interesses rückte, was sich auch in bildlichen Darstellungen niederschlug. Damals nämlich standen Rom und sein Bischof auf dem schmalen Grat zwischen dem oströmischen Reich und den Franken; sowohl die Stadt als auch der Papst wussten, dass sie gegenüber diesen beiden politischen Nachbarn ihre Unabhängigkeit behaupten mussten. Im Unterschied zum Jahrhundert davor, als die römische Kirche – trotz ihrer lehramtlichen Auseinandersetzungen mit Byzanz – sich noch tief im Imperium verortet fühlte[11], war das Papsttum nun zu einem wirklich autonomen politischen Programm bereit.[12] Genau darauf zielte die in jenen Jahren formulierte Konstantinische Schenkung ab[13], die sicher nicht einem damals völlig unrealistischen Anspruch auf Kontrolle über das Abendland diente. Sie sollte vielmehr eine solide Grundlage für den weltlichen Herrschaftsanspruch der Päpste bieten. In diesem Zusammenhang war die ›Wiederbelebung‹ der Person Silvesters eine wohldurchdachte Entscheidung, nicht zuletzt als Fortsetzung des Goldenen Zeitalters der Religionsfreiheit, jener ersten bedeutenden Errungenschaft der christlichen Welt; dabei waren seine in den *Actus Silvestri* beschriebenen erstaunli-

8 LP I, S. 170 und 262. Zu Symmachus' Euergetismus: Guiglia 2016, S. 109–116.

9 Wirbelauer 1993; Sardella 1996.

10 Das Gebäude fiel erst dem Abrissprogramm Sixtus' V. zum Opfer und wird schon in der Biographie Sergius' I. genannt: LP I, S. 371. Zu seiner Standortbestimmung im Laterankomplex s. Luchterhandt 1999, S. 109–122, und Ballardini 2015, S. 889–927.

11 Bertolini 1941; Bertolini 1958, S. 733–789; Ekonomou 2007.

12 Azzara 1997; Noble 1998; Delogu 2001.

13 Laut der glaubhaftesten These wurde die gefälschte Schenkung zwischen den Pontifikaten von Stephanus II., Paul I. oder Hadrian II. verfasst. Vgl. Anm. 5.

chen Aktionen von besonderer Bedeutung. Gegen Mitte des 8. Jahrhunderts tritt Silvester zusammen mit Leo dem Großen und Gregor dem Großen[14] in der Reihe westlicher und östlicher Heiliger auf, die im linken Seitenschiff der Kirche S. Maria Antiqua gemalt wurde. Den beiden Päpsten Leo und Gregor hatte das Mittelalter schon eine außerordentliche geschichtliche und geistige Bedeutung zuerkannt.[15] In ihrem Fall beruhte sie jedoch auf konkreten Tatsachen, nicht auf phantasievoll-strategischen Erfindungen wie bei Silvester. Papst Zacharias (741–752) ließ das Silvester-Oratorium am Lateran,[16] der damals gerade wieder zum neuralgischen Zentrum der römischen Päpste wurde, mit Heiligenbildnissen ausstatten. Sein Nachfolger Stephanus II. (752–757) intensivierte hingegen die Verehrung Silvesters im Vatikan und benannte dort eine Diakonie nach ihm.[17] Auf Paul I. (757–767), der sich stark für die päpstliche Unabhängigkeit einsetzte[18], gehen zwei besonders wichtige Maßnahmen zurück: die Umgestaltung persönlicher Besitztümer zur Errichtung eines nach den Heiligen Silvester und Stephanus benannten Klosters (heute S. Silvestro in Capite), vor allem aber die Überführung der Reliquien des Papstes aus der Priscilla-Katakombe in die Neugründung[19], wobei vermutlich ein Oratorium oder Monument zur würdigen Unterbringung gebaut wurde. Ganz allgemein unterstreicht diese Aktion Pauls I. die wesentliche Rolle des Märtyrerkults und der damit zusammenhängenden Handlungen bei der Durchsetzung des Primats und der Unabhängigkeit der Kirche von Rom.[20] Die Überführung der Reliquien Silvesters, also eines Papstes der ›modernen Zeit‹, muss jedoch auch in einem anderen Licht betrachtet werden: Davor nämlich war das Privileg einer Umbettung der sterblichen Überreste von der ursprünglichen Grablege in ein zu diesem Zweck errichtetes Monument innerhalb einer Basilika nur Leo dem Großen (440–461) zuteil geworden; sein Leichnam befand sich zunächst in der Portikus der Peterskirche und wurde auf Veranlassung von Papst Sergius I. (687–701) von dort in ein reich ausgestattetes Grab an der Südwand der Kirche verbracht. Sergius ließ auch eine Lob- und Gedenkinschrift anbringen.[21]

Zwischen dem 8. und 9. Jahrhundert vollzieht sich demnach eine nachhaltige, intensive Aufwertung der Silvesterverehrung durch die Päpste. Auf diese Zeit geht auch die erste gesicherte Darstellung Silvesters im Raum M der sogenannten *sala a sei vani* unter S. Martino ai Monti zurück (Abb. 1). Konstantin kommt darin nicht vor, wohl aber der

14 Romanelli/Nordhagen 1999, 63; Grafova [im Druck].

15 Gianandrea 2017, S. 61–75. Zu den beiden Päpsten s. Cavalcanti 2000, S. 423–442 und Boesch Gajano 2000, S. 546–574.

16 LP I, S. 432.

17 LP I, S. 441.

18 Delogu 2000, S. 665–670.

19 LP I, S. 464. Zum Komplex von S. Silvestro in Capite s. Gaynor/Toesca 1963.

20 Bauer 2004, S. 121–147.

21 Gianandrea 2017, S. 61–75.

Abb. 1: Aquarellierte Fotografie von Wilpert-Tabanelli: Wandmalerei mit Silvester und dem Drachen im Raum M der sog. *sala a sei vani* unter S. Martino ai Monti.

Triumph über den Drachen, der in den *Actus Silvestri* erzählt wird[22] und der den Kampf gegen das teuflische Monstrum der Apokalypse mit der christologischen Episode des Abstiegs in die Unterwelt verbindet. Silvester tritt hier als Nachfolger Christi in direkter Linie auf. In diesem Zusammenhang spielt auch Petrus eine wichtige Rolle: Als Mittler und Garant des Sieges über den Drachen segnet und legitimiert er Silvesters Papstamt, das ja als Leitung und Schutz der (vor allem römischen) Christenheit gedacht ist. Wenn einerseits diese Darstellung in dem laut Überlieferung von Silvester gegründeten *titulus* nicht erstaunt, drängt sich andererseits die Frage auf, warum manche als Auftraggeber Hadrian I. (772–795)[23], andere Leo IV. (847–855)[24] annehmen.

Es besteht kein Zweifel, dass das Interesse für die Geschichte um Konstantin und Silvester (und demzufolge deren Instrumentalisierung) unter Papst Hadrian[25] stark zunimmt. Im Bereich der Kunst erneuert er die *basilica beati Silvestri* [...] *in Orfea*, deren genauer Standort innerhalb des *titulus Equitii* leider noch nicht bestimmt werden konnte; er lässt die Kirche S. Martino *iuxta titulum Sancti Silvestri*[26] renovieren und gründet eine Diakonie *quae appellatur Sancti Silvestrii* im Vatikan.[27] Weiterhin veranlasst Hadrian eine Umgestaltung der berühmten Priscilla-Katakombe, die jedoch von seinem Biographen *cymiterium sancti Silvestri*[28] genannt wird; schließlich gibt er das Bild mit der *Theotokos* und den Heiligen für das Atrium von S. Maria Antiqua in Auftrag, auf dem Silvester an privilegierter Stelle neben der Gottesmutter auftritt (Abb. 2).[29]

Ebenso deutlich sind die Bezugnahmen auf theoretischer und intellektueller Ebene. In einem Brief aus dem Jahr 778 über die Taufe eines Sohnes Karls des Großen ermahnt Hadrian den König, sich wie ein *novus Constantinus* zu verhalten und erinnert ihn daran, dass jener Kaiser der Kirche zu erheblichem Wachstum verholfen und ihr die Oberhoheit über verschiedene Gebiete abgetreten habe.[30] Recht deutlich wird im Brief Hadrians Wunsch, die Güter in Tuszien, in der Sabina, in Spoleto und Benevent zu übernehmen, die Pippin ihm zugesagt hatte, die dann jedoch weder von diesem

22 Pohlkamp 1983, S. 1–100; Santangeli Valenzani 2007, S. 379–395.

23 Andaloro 2005, S. 525–540.

24 Wilpert 1916, I, S. 333–334; Davis-Weyer/Emerick 1984, S. 25–29.

25 Zur historischen Gestalt Hadrians s. Bertolini 2000, S. 681–695; zu seinem Wirken als Kunstmäzen: Bauer 2001–2002, S. 189–203; Barral i Altet 2016, S. 181–212.

26 LP I, S. 505–507.

27 LP I, S. 506.

28 LP I, S. 509. Es sei betont, dass, obwohl Silvesters sterbliche Überreste von Paul I. in das von ihm gegründete Kloster überführt worden waren, das ursprüngliche Grab weiterhin als Gedenkstätte gepflegt und verehrt wurde. Es handelte sich um eine der letzten derartigen Aktionen vor dem von Papst Paschalis I. (817–824) begonnenen weitreichenden Überführungsprogramm.

29 De Grüneisen 1911, S. 93–94, S. 178–179, S. 492–493; Romanelli/Nordhagen 1999, S. 64 mit Literatur.

30 *Codex Carolinus*, Nr. 60, 1892, S. 586. Angenendt 1980, S. 70–80; Becher 2008, S. 35–38.

noch von Karl dem Papsttum zurückgegeben worden waren.[31] Der allgemeine Ton des Schreibens und bestimmte Wendungen erinnern manche Forscher so stark an den Text des *Constitutum Constantini*, dass sie von direkten Ableitungen bzw. von einer Abfassung des Briefs im selben intellektuellen Milieu ausgehen.[32] Der Biographie Papst Hadrians entnehmen wir außerdem, dass Karl der Große bei einem Romaufenthalt in den Lateran eingeladen wurde, um dort während der Osterfeierlichkeiten dem Taufsakrament beizuwohnen, gleichsam als indirekter, aber klarer Hinweis auf die Geschichte von Silvester und Konstantin.[33]

Genauso wurde Hadrians Besuch bei Karl dem Großen, der erneut zur Erfüllung von Pippins Gebietszusagen aus dem Jahr 754 aufgefordert werden sollte, absichtlich auf den Mittwoch vor Ostern gelegt, denn am gleichen Tag hatte Konstantin seine Konzessionen an Silvester besiegelt, wie in den *Actus Silvestri* und mit weiteren Nuancen im *Constitutum* dargelegt.[34] Karl ließ sich davon jedoch nicht beeinflussen und übersah geflissentlich den wiederholten Vergleich mit Konstantin. Dies beweist, dass erhebliche Meinungsunterschiede zwischen den Franken und dem Papsttum über ihre Partnerschaft bestanden. Auf Seite der Franken galt der König als wichtigste politisch-moralische Instanz der christlichen Welt und daher würdig, als Kaiser in Rom anerkannt zu werden. Demgegenüber verstanden die Päpste Rom sowohl als heiligen Ort als auch als Kaiserstadt, in der die Kirche über kaiserliche Rechte, Titel und Würden verfügte, will heißen: Die Kaiserwürde stand seit jeher dem Papst und dem römischen Volk zu, und diese verliehen sie nach Belieben einem befreundeten Souverän. Eine eindeutige visuelle Umsetzung dieser Auffassung findet sich im Mosaik des Trikliniums, das Leo III. (795–816) kurz vor dem Jahr 800 im Lateran anlegen ließ[35], auch wenn speziell in Bezug auf die ursprüngliche Gestaltung des rechten Zwickels der Apsisstirnwand mit Konstantin und Silvester weiterhin Zweifel bestehen. Bereits im 16. Jahrhundert schon vollständig verloren, wurde dieses Mosaikelement von Francesco Barberini *ex novo* rekonstruiert. Wir wissen jedoch nicht, ob er sich dabei auf (nie explizit genannte) Quellen stützte oder ob seine artifizielle wie geniale Neugestaltung den Vorgaben der katholischen Gegenreform gehorchte.[36] Ganz gleich, ob es sich dabei um eine Abbildung des Heiligen Petrus oder Silvesters handelte: Der strategische Zweck der Darstellung änderte sich nicht, ging es doch darum zu zeigen, dass die politische Investitur weltlicher Herr-

31 Classen 1968, S. 27–35; Bertolini 2000, S. 683–693.

32 Ewig 1966, S. 69–75; Becher 2008, S. 37–38.

33 Becher 2008, S. 34–35.

34 Becher 2008, S. 34–35.

35 Nuzzo in diesem Band, Abb. 1; vgl. Belting 1976, S. 167–182; Iacobini 1989, S. 189–196; Luchterhandt 1999, S. 109–122; Ballardini 2015, S. 918–922.

36 Zu diesem grundlegenden Aspekt s. Iacobini 1989 und Herklotz 1995, S. 175–196.

Abb. 2: Rom, Santa Maria Antiqua: Wandmalerei mit der Gottesmutter, Heiligen und Papst Hadrian I. (links mit dem eckigen Nimbus). Papst Silvester erscheint an privilegierter Stelle links neben Maria.

scher von Christus kam und demnach von Petrus und dessen Nachfolgern, also von der römischen Kirche. Die Botschaft des leoninischen Trikliniums von der Unabhängigkeit des Papstes und von seiner sowohl weltlichen wie religiösen Dimension war leicht verständlich und sowohl an Byzanz als auch an die Franken gerichtet. Wie fränkische Quellen belegen, wurde die im *Constitutum* enthaltene politische Vorlage jedoch von Karl und seinen Nachfolgern nicht anerkannt: Sie weigerten sich, als *novi Constantini* zu agieren. Sie lehnten das Kaisertum zwar nicht prinzipiell ab, sehr wohl aber das Modell, das die Päpste ihnen aufzwingen wollten, um sie zu territorialen Zugeständnissen zu bewegen. Das bedeutet nicht, dass die karolingischen Herrscher den Vergleich mit dem berühmten römischen Kaiser verschmähten, was aufgrund von Konstantins Ruhm ja auch unvorstellbar war, aber sie wollten das auf ihre Weise tun, indem er z.B. symbolhaft in die Stammbäume der Monarchen aufgenommen wurde, und in jedem Fall außerhalb der legendären Erzählungen der *Actus* bzw. des *Constitutum.*[37] In der Tat spielt Silvester nördlich der Alpen praktisch keine Rolle und bleibt im Wesentlichen die farblose Figur der Primärquellen. Es ist dagegen das römische bzw. stark romanisierte Papsttum, das, zusammen mit der Lokalaristokratie, die Verherrlichung Silvesters entschlossen vorantreibt: Seit der *Actus Silvestri* und dem *Constitutum Silvestri* aus der Zeit von Papst Symmachus bis zur Konstantinischen Schenkung verändert sich nicht

37 Valenti 2012, S. 115–137.

so sehr die historische Persönlichkeit Silvesters bzw. seine Legende, als vielmehr die Ansprüche der Päpste, die sich durch Silvester weitere Privilegien und weiter reichende Funktionen aneignen wollten. Ab der Mitte des 8. Jahrhunderts entsprechen die intensivere Verwendung von Silvesterdarstellungen, die ihm geweihten Denkmäler wie auch eine gesteigerte Aufmerksamkeit gegenüber den schon bestehenden einem dringenden Bedürfnis der Gegenwart: Nicht mehr Konstantin sollte der absolute Protagonist der Erzählung sein, sondern auch und vor allem Silvester, d.h. die Kirche von Rom. Diese steht nämlich vor diversen Herausforderungen, die deren Symbolfigur bestimmen: Das Streben nach politischer Unabhängigkeit und weltlicher Macht findet in Silvester eine ausgezeichnete Galionsfigur, denn die schon großenteils umgearbeitete Erinnerung schreibt ihm eine ›konkrete‹ Gebietsschenkung und weltliche Souveränität zu. Inwieweit die Silvester-Legende den Mechanismus zu einer auf Selbstdefinition abzielenden Aufarbeitung der Geschichte stützt und inwiefern sie das Ergebnis zeitgenössischer Umgestaltungen ist, geht deutlich aus der Tatsache hervor, dass noch wenige Jahrzehnte zuvor Leo der Große gleichsam der Medienstar der römischen Kirche gewesen war. Damals ging es darum, Roms Autonomie in Religionsfragen und die Würde des apostolischen Stuhls zu betonen, und Leo – der große Theologe, Beschützer der *Urbs* gegen Attila und vor allem Verteidiger des orthodoxen Glaubens beim Konzil von Chalcedon – war der beste Repräsentant des römischen Klerus.[38] Aus diesem Grunde, und angesichts der doktrinären Konflikte mit Byzanz, wird das Andenken an Papst Leo vom kirchlichen Selbstdarstellungssystem neu belebt: Sowohl Sergius I. (687–701) als auch Johannes VII. (705–707) feiern ihn mit Ehrenmälern und Bildwerken.[39] In jenen Jahren ist eine Persönlichkeit wie Silvester den Zielsetzungen des Papsttums noch nicht dienlich; sie wird es jedoch, sobald sich die Bedürfnisse der Päpste verändern und diese eine Gestalt mit starker kommunikativer Wirkung suchen, wozu Silvester ohne größere Schwierigkeiten gemacht werden konnte.

Zu diesem Zweck diente er der römischen Kirche sicher auch während der gregorianischen Reform. Der Streit der römischen Reformer gegen die Frankenherrscher zur Durchsetzung der *libertas ecclesiae* stützte sich im Wesentlichen auf die Rolle und Bedeutung der Märtyrer, und in der zweiten Hälfte des 9. Jahrhunderts förderte das Papsttum die Heiligenverehrung auf der Grundlage des Märtyrertums: Verehrung der Apostel, allen voran Petrus und Paulus, und der Märtyrerbischöfe. Dieses geistige Erbe wurde in karolingischer Epoche gerne wieder aufgenommen. Seit Gregor VII. (1073–1085) jedoch spielte die Heiligkeit der Päpste im ekklesiologischen Profil des römischen Papsttums eine immer größere Rolle; aus dessen *collectio canonum* stammt nämlich das wirk-

38 Gianandrea 2017, S. 61–75.

39 Gianandrea 2017, S. 61–75.

lich epochemachende Konzept, wonach der rechtmäßig gewählte Papst eine funktionsgebundene Heiligkeit genießt, die sich direkt aus den Verdiensten des heiligen Petrus ableitet. Daraus wiederum ergibt sich die Möglichkeit, zugleich geistliche und irdische Macht auszuüben.[40] Diese ›göttliche‹ Verortung der Papstmacht hatte unmittelbare Auswirkungen auf die – weitgehend instrumentale – Funktion der Darstellung und Verehrung der zeitgenössischen bzw. vor kurzem verstorbenen *pontifices*, die inzwischen als *sancti inter sanctissimos* galten. Dazu zählte auch Silvester, das perfekte Abbild des Widerstands gegen jegliche Einmischung durch weltliche Herrscher und des päpstlichen Vorrangs über alle kirchlichen Strukturen. Emblematisch ist in dieser Hinsicht die von Calixtus II. (1119–1124) und Anaklet II. (1130–1138) für die Nikolaus-Kapelle im Lateran gewählte Ikonographie (Abb. 3).[41] Die Gestaltung wird nur im Zusammenhang mit der anschließenden *camera pro secretis consiliis* verständlich, denn letztere, ebenfalls auf Geheiß von Calixtus II. entstanden, um dort den Triumph der rechtmäßigen Päpste über die Gegenpäpste zu zelebrieren, endete mit einer Darstellung des Wormser Konkordats.[42] Diesen ideologischen Extremismus finden wir auch in der Nikolaus-Kapelle: Das Mittelbild der Apsiskalotte war eine Wiederaufnahme der *Madonna della Clemenza* von S. Maria in Trastevere und zeigte Calixtus und Anaklet kniend mit Quadratnimbus; ihnen zur Seite waren bezeichnenderweise zwei berühmte Vorgänger gestellt: Anaklet I., dem die mittelalterliche Überlieferung der *Decretales Pseudo-Isidorianae* verschiedene Briefe über die päpstliche Oberhoheit zuschrieb[43], und Silvester I., der inzwischen in den ›Begründer‹ der politischen Autonomie des Papsttums verwandelt worden war. Calixtus stellt sich also bewusst neben Silvester und nicht neben seinen gleichnamigen Vorgänger. Die Bildbotschaft wurde im darunter liegenden Register weiter betont: Dort war eine Reihe von Päpsten dargestellt, die alle mit Tiara, Pallium, Aureole und dem Zusatz *sanctus* vor ihrem Namen versehen waren. Es handelte sich um ›moderne‹ Päpste der vergangenen fünfzig Jahre (Alexander II., Gregor VII., Viktor III., Urban II., Paschalis II. und Calixtus II.), denen man zum ersten Mal den Status der sofortigen Heiligkeit zusprach als Nachfolger Petri, dessen Erbe sie in Ehren gehalten hatten, indem sie gegen die römisch-deutschen Herrscher für die *libertas ecclesiae* kämpften. In diesem Rahmen, der die Wirklichkeit zur Zeit der gregorianischen Reform perfekt widerspiegelt, ist die zen-

40 Es handelt sich um den Leitsatz 23 der berühmten *Dictatus papae*, vgl. Hofmann 1933; Capitani 2000, S. 188–212.

41 Von Calixtus II. begonnen, wurde sie wahrscheinlich von Anaklet II. fertiggestellt; dieser ging als Gegenpapst in die Geschichte ein, weshalb sein Gedenkbild durch das von Anastasius IV. ersetzt wurde. S. Gandolfo 1981, S. 9–28; Herklotz 2000, S. 151–153; de Blaauw 2014, S. 129–152.

42 Herklotz 2000, S. 95–151.

43 Die Sammlung wurde vermutlich im 9. Jahrhundert zusammengestellt und bestand aus gefälschten Dekreten, die verschiedenen Päpsten (darunter Anaklet I.) zugeschrieben waren und bis ins 18. Jahrhundert für gültig gehalten wurden: vgl. Decretales Pseudo-Isidorianae Ausg. 1863, Nr. 74, 84, 85.

Abb. 3: Stich von Caetani mit dem Apsisdekor der Nikolaus-Kapelle im Lateran (1638).

trale Rolle Leos I. und Gregors I. beachtenswert: Sie führten die Papstreihe als unermüdliche Verteidiger ihres kirchlichen Amts an. Ebenso wichtig ist natürlich Silvester als Verfechter und Emblem desselben Kampfes. Das wird nicht zuletzt in der Verbreitung – zwischen der zweiten Hälfte des 11. und dem 12. Jahrhundert – der Darstellungen Silvesters mit dem Drachen deutlich (Unterkirche von S. Crisogono in Rom, Heiligengrotte von Calvi, Immacolata-Kirche in Ceri und S. Silvestro in Alatri).[44] Diese Wahl, die zweifellos als ein Element der Förderung päpstlicher Heiligkeit durch die römische Kirche zu verstehen ist, gilt als bester Beweis für Silvesters Funktion nicht nur in Bezug auf die Verehrung früherer Päpste, sondern auch hinsichtlich der gewollten Kontinuität Christus-Petrus-Silvester und daher aller Päpste. Auf diese grundlegende Entwicklung spielt die Anwesenheit der Heiligen Petrus und Paulus in der Wandmalerei in Ceri an (Abb. 4), die Silvester zum Sieg über den Drachen führen. Letzterer verkörpert nunmehr alles Schlechte: rebellische Herrscher, Ketzer und alle Feinde der Kirche, über die Silvester im Namen eben dieser Kirche triumphiert. Die Ikonographie der Drachentötung, in der sich bis zum Ende des 12. Jahrhunderts der Ruhm dieses Papstes verdichtete, macht in der Folgezeit einer außergewöhnlichen Erweiterung in der Erzählung Platz. Den *Actus Silvestri* und dem *Constitutum Constantini* wird eine ganze Reihe von Vorkommnissen mit wirkungsvoller ideologisch-politischer Wertigkeit entnommen: Silvester verkörpert die triumphierende römische Kirche, während Konstantin mit der Rolle des ruhmreichen Nebendarstellers vorlieb nehmen muss. Die erhebliche Zunahme von Silvesterbildern bescheinigt einen bemerkenswerten ›Klimawandel‹, der sich inzwischen auch in der Darstellung des Papsttums in der ekklesiologischen Glaubenslehre ereignet hatte. Äußere Umstände zwangen die Kirche dazu, die Fundamente ihrer Stärke durch eine wirksame, deutliche visuelle Kommunikation zu betonen. Dazu gehörte zweifellos auch die Mosaikdekoration am Architrav der Portikus der Lateranbasilika, die nur noch aus Kopien und Beschreibungen bekannt ist (Abb. 5).[45] Unterbrochen von ›kosmatenartig gestalteten‹ Marmor-Clipei waren einige Episoden aus den Viten der zwei namensgebenden Heiligen (Enthauptung des Täufers und Martyrium des Evangelisten) zu sehen, aus der Verehrung der alttestamentlichen, in der Kirche verwahrten Reliquien (Feldzug des Titus und Belagerung Jerusalems), von den Ursprüngen der Basilika und des ›modernen‹ Papsttums (Silvester fängt den Drachen, Taufe Konstantins und seine Schenkung) zusammen mit Bildern rein eschatologischer Bedeutung (Jesu Abstieg in die Unterwelt)[46].

44 Zu S. Crisogono: Brenk 1984, S. 57–65, und Mazzocchi 2007, S. 247–274; zur Grotte von Calvi: Piazza 2002, S. 169–208. Zu den Fresken in Ceri: Zchomelidse 1996, S. 53–168, und Maddalo 2012, S. 678–685; zu Alatri: Maddalo 2011, S. 115–121.

45 De Blaauw 1990, S. 299–316; Herklotz 2000, S. 159–209; Maddalo 2007, S. 424–434; Claussen/Senekovic 2008, S. 60–89. Zuletzt De Strobel /Bernacchio [im Druck].

46 Ebd.

Abb. 4: Ceri (RM), Chiesa dell'Immacolata: Der Heilige Silvester und der Drachen.

Panvinius dokumentiert außerdem die Darstellung der Apostel Petrus und Paulus (von Mellini bestätigt) und von Papst Calixtus II.; auf letzteren bezog sich vielleicht die von Ciampini in sehr schlechtem Zustand gesehene Szene mit einem Papst, der zwei Männer empfängt (ein Hinweis auf das Wormser Konkordat?).[47] Wie Herklotz annahm und Claussen jüngst bekräftigte, geht die Portikus höchstwahrscheinlich auf Nicola d'Angelo[48] zurück, was eine Datierung um das Jahr 1200 ermöglicht. Vermutlich aufgrund des Todes dieses anerkannten Marmorkünstlers vergab Innozenz III. alle späteren Aufträge an die Werkstatt Lorenzos und insbesondere an dessen Sohn Jacopo.[49] Im Übrigen scheint gerade die Verarbeitung ausschließlich von Marmorsteinchen (diejenigen aus Glas gehören zu einer späteren Einfügung) eine Datierung spätestens kurz vor dem 13. Jahrhundert zu bestätigen. Damals traute man sich offenbar noch nicht, für Kunstwerke und liturgischen Dekor senkrechte Oberflächen aus Glaspaste zu gestalten, was

47 Panvinio 1570, S. 139; Mellini metà XVII secolo, f. 11v–12r; Ciampini 1693, S. 13.
48 Zu dieser facettenreichen Gestalt s. Bassan 1997, S. 684–685.
49 Zu diesem Aspekt: Gianandrea 2014, S. 29–43; Pistilli 2015, S. 517–531.

Abb. 5: Stich von Ciampini mit einigen Szenen des Frieses an der Ostportikus der Lateransbasilika (1693).

sich vermutlich erst mit dem Aufstieg von Jacopo di Lorenzo durchsetzte. Diese Datierung passt außerdem gut zur bildlichen Botschaft der uns bekannten Mosaikszenen: Fokussierung auf die römische *Ecclesia* als Erbin der Kirche von Jerusalem, auf den Vorrang des Bischofs von Rom über die anderen Patriarchate, auf die weltliche Souveränität des Papsttums und auf die geschichtliche Bedeutung der Lateranbasilika. Dies waren im 12. Jahrhundert heiße politische Themen, denn damals kommt es zu einem allgemeinen Wachstum der päpstlichen Institutionen und ihrer Macht in allen Bereichen, auch in säkularer und finanzieller Hinsicht. Die Anbringung des Mosaikzyklus über dem von den Gläubigen meistgenutzten Haupteingang der Basilika, der für den Ablauf des päpstlichen Zeremoniells und für die *liturgia stazionale* ebenfalls von besonderer Bedeutung war,[50] lässt ein intellektuell-universalistisches Bildprogramm annehmen, das in keiner Weise auf lokale Themen beschränkt war. Spezifisch beziehe ich mich auf die Polemik zwischen Lateran und Vatikan, die oft herangezogen wird, wenn es um eine Klärung der Entstehung und Begründung des Mosaiks in der Lateranportikus geht. Diese Erklärung ist genauso breitgetreten wie unbegründet und basiert auf einer historiographischen Meinung des späten 19. Jahrhunderts, die aus einer (diesmal reellen) Polemik zwischen den beiden religiösen Polen Roms zur Zeit der Gegenreformation entstanden war.[51] Im Gegensatz dazu – und es konnte gar nicht anders sein – war die Botschaft des Zyklus im Lateran viel weiter gefasst; bei genauem Hinsehen bemerkt man, dass sie in Wirklichkeit an alle Elemente gerichtet war, die sich im Laufe der Zeit dem Wachstum der Kirchenmacht entgegengestellt hatten: die deutschen Kaiser, die römische Stadtverwaltung, den byzantinischen Kaiser und den Patriarchen von Konstantinopel. Dieser Notwendigkeit entsprach also vollkommen dieser ganze Silvester-Zyklus, der nach unserem Wissensstand zum ersten Mal die Konstantinische Schenkung darstellt.

Zu den Konflikten mit den Kaisern, die das gesamte 12. Jahrhundert geprägt hatten, gesellten sich nun auch Auseinandersetzungen mit der neu eingesetzten *Comune romano*, die in der Anfangsphase einen ausgesprochen städtischen Charakter betonte.[52] Als anti-päpstliche Institution entstanden, verbrachte sie schon Jahrzehnte vor den berühmten Ereignissen im Jahr 1143 die meiste Zeit damit, den Papst zu bekämpfen bzw. einen heiklen *modus vivendi* mit ihm zu finden. Die Darstellung der Konstantinischen Schenkung und der Lebensgeschichte von Papst Silvester an der Fassade der Kathedrale von Rom sollte natürlich die Legitimität der päpstlichen Regierung und die Autonomie des Papsttums gegen die Einmischung der Stadt und der römisch-deutschen Herrscher hervorheben. Nicht zufällig hatten die Kaisertreuen in dieser Zeit angefangen, die Legenden um Silvester und insbesondere das *Constitutum Constantini* immer mehr zu

50 Andrieu 1938; ebenfalls: de Blaauw 1994, I, *passim*.

51 Lucherini 2009, S. 297–318.

52 Carocci/Vendittelli 2001, S. 80–88; Vigueur 2001, S. 118–132; Wickham 2013, S. 468–520.

diskreditieren, um ihre eigene Position zu stärken. Von ersten Zweifeln unter Otto III. über den berühmten Wezel-Brief von 1152 bis zu den Worten der *Graphia*, die den Lateran als *palatium Neronis* bezeichnen und im Reiter des Laterans nicht Konstantin erkennen[53], war die römische Kirche nun in der Pflicht, den Wert der Schenkung und ihres Inhalts zu bekräftigen. Dies war im Übrigen auch ein wesentlicher Aspekt in der konfliktreichen Diskussion mit der byzantinischen Welt, die nun nicht mehr gewillt war, wie es hingegen im frühen Mittelalter der Fall gewesen war, den Primat des Bischofs von Rom anzuerkennen. In den höfischen und kirchlichen Kreisen von Byzanz war es jedoch allgemeine Auffassung, wenn auch mit unterschiedlichen Nuancierungen zwischen polemisch und konziliant, dass die Primatansprüche Roms, so wie sie sich im 11. und 12. Jahrhundert herauskristallisiert hatten, abzulehnen seien; allenfalls sei ein Ehrenprimat unter Schwesterkirchen denkbar.[54] Zu den Elementen, an denen Byzanz am meisten auszusetzen hatte, gehörten: die enge Verbindung zwischen Christus und dem Papst, die ›exklusive‹ Beziehung zwischen dem heiligen Petrus und Rom, die Überzeugung, dass die römische Kirche *mater omnium ecclesiarum* sei, und vor allem der Grundsatz der *monarchia Petri* im Gegensatz zur *monarchia Imperii.*[55]

Roms Antworten auf diese Kritikpunkte scheinen in der Dekoration der Lateranportikus perfekt dargestellt, insbesondere in der strategischen Verwendung der Gestalt Silvesters. Die Vorstellung vom Pontifex als *vicarius Christi*, die auf theologischer Ebene von Innozenz III. (1198–1216) endgültig festgeschrieben wurde[56], ist in der Szene mit Silvester und dem Drachen ganz offensichtlich. Sie stellt eine Verbindung her zwischen dem Papst (der den Drachen besiegt), Petrus (Mentor und Leiter des Unternehmens) und Christus (impulsgebend durch die *Anastasis*) und besiegelt das direkte Verhältnis zwischen diesen drei (wie von Rom gewollt). Die von Panvinius und Mellini beschriebenen Geschichten von Petrus und Paulus beantworten die Frage nach dem privilegierten Verhältnis zwischen den Aposteln, insbesondere Petrus[57], und der *Urbs*, und die Inschrift der Portikus wird zum Banner des Prinzips der römischen *Ecclesia* als Mutter und Haupt aller Kirchen[58] und deshalb auch als Erbin der Kirche von Jerusalem, wie in den Geschichten über Titus und Vespasian angedeutet.[59] Auf die Besessenheit der byzantinischen Polemiker, die davon ausgingen, dass Rom zusammen mit der Kaiserwürde auch den kirchlichen Primat verlieren würde, und das natürlich zugunsten

53 Herklotz 2000, S. 68–75.

54 Spiteris 1979.

55 Spiteris 1979, S. 300–322.

56 Maccarone 1952.

57 Meyendorff 1965, S. 101–113; Paravicini Bagliani 1996.

58 Herklotz 2000, S. 193–204.

59 De Blaauw 1990, S. 299–316.

Abb. 6: Tivoli (RM), San Silvestro: Fresken in der Apsis mit Szenen aus dem Leben von Silvester.

Konstantinopels[60], bestand Roms angemessene Antwort in der Geschichte Silvesters, des wahren Retters von Kaiser Konstantin, vor allem aber in dessen Schenkung mit der Abtretung der Herrschaft über das Abendland an den Papst.

Das ›neue‹ Papsttum, wie es sich seit dem 11. Jahrhundert herauskristallisierte, hatte in Silvester ein höchst eindrucks- und wirkungsvolles mediales Abbild gefunden – allerdings nicht im historischen, dokumentierten Silvester, sondern in dessen mittelalterlicher Aufbereitung, wobei einzelne Details den jeweiligen Umständen angepasst wur-

60 Lemerle 1965, S. 228–246.

den. Das legendäre, als einzige Erfolgsgeschichte dargestellte Leben des Papstes hatte in etwas weniger als zehn Jahrhunderten dazu geführt, dass er Kaiser Konstantin in den Schatten stellte; dies nur deshalb, weil es den Bedürfnissen des damaligen Papsttums sehr entgegenkam und es sich besser mit Silvester als mit dem Kaiser identifizieren ließ. Die narrative Überhöhung ab dem 12. Jahrhundert zeigt ihn uns als unangefochtenen Protagonisten der ersten Hälfte des 4. Jahrhunderts: Die Fresken von Tivoli (Abb. 6) wie auch der berühmte Zyklus im Komplex in SS. Quattro Coronati[61] konzentrieren sich auf ihn; Konstantin wird zur Nebenfigur. Dessen Rolle hätte die Kirche von Rom in Silvesters Namen gern auch den römisch-deutschen Herrschern, der römischen Kommune und dem byzantinischen Kaiser zugeteilt.

---

61 Zu Tivoli: Lanz 1983; zu den Malereien im Oratorio dei Santi Quattro Coronati s. zusammenfassend Draghi 2012, S. 191–208 (mit früherer Literatur).

Bibliographie

Abkürzungen

LP = Le Liber Pontificalis. Texte, introduction et commentaire par Louis Duchesne, 2 Bde., Paris 1886–1892.

Amerise 2005 Marilena Amerise: Il battesimo di Costantino il Grande. Storia di una scomoda verità, Stuttgart 2005.

Andaloro 2002 Maria Andaloro: Il mosaico del *Titulus* di Equizio di San Martino ai Monti a Roma, in: I mosaici. Cultura, Tecnologia, Conservazione, Atti del convegno di studi (Brixen, 2.–5.7.2002), hg. von Guido Biscontin und Guido Driussi, Venedig, S. 877–884.

Andaloro 2005 Maria Andaloro: I papi e l'immagine prima e dopo Nicea, in: Medioevo: immagini e ideologia, Atti del Convegno internazionale di studi (Parma 2002), hg. von Arturo Carlo Quintavalle, Mailand 2005, S. 525–540.

Andrieu 1938 Michel Andrieu: Le pontifical romain du XIIe siècle, Vatikanstadt 1938.

Angenendt 1980 Arnold Angenendt: Das geistliche Bündnis der Päpste mit den Karolingern (754–796), in: Historisches Jahrbuch 100, 1980, S. 1–94.

Azzara 1997 Claudio Azzara: L'ideologia del potere regio nel papato altomedievale, Spoleto 1997.

Ballardini 2015 Antonella Ballardini: »In antiquissimo ac venerabili Lateranensi palatio«: la residenza dei pontefici secondo il *Liber Pontificalis*, in: Le corti nell'Alto Medioevo, Atti della LXII Settimana di Studio del CISAM (Spoleto 2014), Spoleto 2015, S. 889–927.

Barral i Altet 2016 Xavier Barral i Altet: L'VIII secolo: da Giovanni VI (701–705) ad Adriano I (772–795), in: La committenza artistica dei papi a Roma nel Medioevo, hg. von Mario D'Onofrio, Rom 2016, S. 181–212.

Bassan 1997 Enrico Bassan: Nicola d'Angelo, in: Enciclopedia dell'Arte Medievale, Bd. VIII, Rom 1997, S. 684–685.

Bauer 2001–2002 Franz Alto Bauer: Il rinnovamento di Roma sotto Adriano I alla luce del *Liber Pontificalis*: immagine e realtà, in: Mededelingen van het Nederlands Instituut te Rome 60/61, 2001–2002, S. 189–203.

Bauer 2004 Franz Alto Bauer: Das Bild der Stadt Rom im Frühmittelalter. Papststiftungen im Spiegel des *Liber Pontificalis* von Gregor dem Dritten bis zu Leo dem Dritten, Wiesbaden 2004.

Becher 2008 Matthias Becher: Costantino il Grande, l'incoronazione imperiale nell'816 e le relazioni tra papato e Franchi dopo la prima metà del secolo VIII, in: Costantino il Grande fra medioevo ed età moderna, hg. von Giorgio Bonamente, Giorgio Cracco und Klaus Rosen, Bologna 2008, S. 15–50.

Belting 1976 Hans Belting: I mosaici dell'aula leonina come testimonianza della prima »renovatio« nell'arte medioevale di Roma, in: Roma e l'età carolingia, Atti delle giornate di studio (Rom 1976), hg. von Istituto di Storia dell'arte dell'Università La Sapienza di Roma, Rom 1976, S. 167–182.

Bertolini 1941 Ottorino Bertolini: Roma di fronte a Bisanzio e ai Longobardi, Bologna 1941.

Bertolini 1958 Ottorino Bertolini: Riflessi politici delle controversie religiose con Bisanzio nelle vicende del secolo VII in Italia, in: Caratteri del secolo VII in Occidente, Atti della V Settimana di Studio del CISAM (Spoleto 1957), Bd. II, Spoleto 1958, S. 733–789.

Bertolini 2000 Ottorino Bertolini: Adriano I, in: Enciclopedia dei Papi, Bd. I, Rom 2000, S. 681–695.

Boesch Gajano 2000 Sofia Boesch Gajano: Gregorio I, santo, in: Enciclopedia dei Papi, Bd. I, Rom 2000, S. 546–574.

Brenk 1984 Beat Brenk: Die Benediktszenen in S. Crisogono und Montecassino, in: Arte Medievale 2, 1984, S. 57–65.

Capitani 2000 Ovidio Capitani: Gregorio VII, santo, in: Enciclopedia dei Papi, Bd. I, Rom 2000, S. 188–212.

Canella 2006 Tessa Canella: Gli *Actus Silvestri*. Genesi di una leggenda su Costantino imperatore, Spoleto 2006.

Carocci/Vendittelli 2001 Sandro Carocci und Marco Vendittelli: Società ed economia (1050–1420), in: Roma medievale, hg. von André Vauchez, Rom/Bari 2001, S. 71–116.

Cavalcanti 2000 Elena Cavalcanti, Leone I, santo, in: Enciclopedia dei Papi, Bd. I, Rom 2000, S. 423–442.

Ciampini 1693 Giovanni Giustino Ciampini: De sacris aedificiis a Constantino Magno constructis: synopsis historica, Romae 1693.

Classen 1968 Peter Classen: Karl der Grosse, das Papsttum und Byzanz. Die Begründung des karolingischen Kaisertums, Düsseldorf 1968.

Claussen/Senekovic 2008 Peter Cornelius Claussen und Darko Senekovic: San Giovanni in Laterano (Corpus Cosmatorum 2,2), Stuttgart 2008.

Codex Carolinus 1892 Codex Carolinus, hg. von Wilhelm Gundlach, in: Epistolae Merowingici et Karolini aevi, I (MGH, Epistulae, III), Berlin 1892.

La committenza artistica 2016 La committenza artistica dei papi a Roma nel Medioevo, hg. von Mario D'Onofrio, Rom 2016.

Costantino il Grande 1992–1993 Costantino il Grande dall'antichità all'umanesimo, Atti del colloquio sul Cristianesimo nel mondo antico (Macerata 1990), hg. von Giorgio Bonamente und Franca Fusco, Macerata 1992–1993.

Costantino il Grande 2008 Costantino il Grande tra medioevo ed età moderna, hg. von Giorgio Bonamente, Giorgio Cracco und Klaus Rosen, Bologna 2008.

Davis-Weyer/Emerick 1984 Cecilia Davis-Weyer und Judson J. Emerick: The Early Sixth-Century Frescoes at S. Martino ai Monti in Rome, in: Römisches Jahrbuch für Kunstgeschichte 21, 1984, S. 3–60.

De Blaauw 1990 Sible de Blaauw: A mediaeval portico at San Giovanni in Laterano: the Basilica and its ancient conventual building, in: Papers of the British School at Rome 58, 1990, S. 299–316.

De Blaauw 1994 Sible de Blaauw: Cultus et decor. Liturgia e architettura nella Roma tardoantica e medievale. Basilica Salvatoris, Sanctae Mariae, Sancti Petri, 2 Bde., Vatikanstadt 1994.

De Blauuw 2014 Sible de Blaauw: Kirchenbau und Erinnerung in Rom unter Anaklet II. und Innozenz II., in: *Damnatio in memoria*. Deformation und Gegenkonstruktionen in der Geschichte, hg. von Sebastian Scholz, Gerald Schwedler und Kai-Michael Sprenger, Köln/Weimar/Wien 2014, S. 129–152.

Decretales Pseudo-Isidorianae ed. 1863 Decretales PseudoIsidorianae et Capitula Angilramni, hg. von Paulus Hinschius, Leipzig 1863.

De Grüneisen 1911 Wladimir De Grüneisen: Sainte Marie Antique, Rom 1911.

Delogu 2000 Paolo Delogu: Paolo I, santo, in: Enciclopedia dei Papi, Bd. I, Rom 2000, S. 665–670.

Delogu 2001 Paolo Delogu: Il passaggio dall'Antichità al Medioevo, in: Roma medievale, hg. von André Vauchez, Rom/Bari 2001, S. 3–40.

De Strobel/Bernacchio [im Druck] Anna Maria De Strobel und Nicoletta Bernacchio: Il Portico medievale di S. Giovanni in Laterano, in: The Lateran Basilica. A conference held at the British School at Rome (19.–21.9.2016) [im Druck].

Draghi 2012 Andreina Draghi: La decorazione della Cappella di San Silvestro, in: Serena Romano: Il Duecento e la cultura gotica (La pittura medievale a Roma 312–1431. Corpus, V), Mailand 2012, S. 191–208.

Ekonomou 2007 Andrew J. Ekonomou: Byzantine Rome and the Greek Popes, Lanham 2007.

Ewig 1966 Eugen Ewig: Das Zeitalter Karls des Großen (768–814), in: Handbuch der Kirchengeschichte, hg. von Hubert Jedin, Bd. III/1, Freiburg i. Br. 1966, S. 62–118.

Falla Castelfranchi 2014 Marina Falla Castelfranchi: Sull'origine e la funzione »politica« dell'immagine del battesimo di Costantino nel portico della basilica lateranense, in: L'officina dello sguardo. Scritti in onore di Maria Andaloro, I. I luoghi dell'arte, hg. von Giulia Bordi et al., Rom 2014, S. 375–382.

Fowden 1994 Garth Fowden: Constantine, Silvester and the Church of S. Polieuctus in Constantinople, in: Journal of Roman Archaeology 7, 1994, S. 274–284.

Fried 2007 Johannes Fried: Donation of Constantine and *Constitutum Constantini*: the Misinterpretation of a Fiction and its Original Meaning, Berlin/New York 2007.

Gandolfo 1981 Francesco Gandolfo: Simbolismo antiquario e potere papale, in: Studi Romani 29, 1981, S. 9–28.

Gaynor/Toesca 1963 Juan Santos Gaynor und Ilaria Toesca: S. Silvestro in Capite (Le chiese di Roma illustrate 73), Rom 1963.

Gianandrea 2014 Manuela Gianandrea: L'arredo liturgico medievale del San Francesco di Vetralla tra perduto e restauri, in: La chiesa di San Francesco a Vetralla. Le origini, hg. von Elisabetta De Minicis und Carlo Tedeschi, Vetralla 2014, S. 29–43.

Gianandrea 2017 Manuela Gianandrea: Leone Magno e i pontefici del Medioevo romano: l'esegesi di un mito e la strumentalizzazione della sua immagine, in: Survivals, Revivals, Rinascenze. Studi in onore di Serena Romano, hg. von Nicolas Bock, Ivan Foletti und Michele Tomasi, Rom 2017, S. 61–75.

Grafova [im Druck] Maria Grafova: The Decorations in the Left Aisle of Santa Maria Antiqua Within the Context of the Political History of the Iconoclastic Era, in: Santa Maria Antiqua: »The Sistine Chapel of the 8th Century« in Context. A Consideration of the site from the 4th–9th Century, Proceedings of International Congress (Rom, 2013) [im Druck].

Guiglia 2016 Alessandra Guiglia: Il VI secolo: da Simmaco (498–514) a Gregorio Magno (590–604), in: La committenza artistica dei papi a Roma nel Medioevo, hg. von Mario D'Onofrio, Rom 2016, S. 109–144.

Herklotz 1995 Ingo Herklotz: Francesco Barberini, Nicolò Alemanni, and the Lateran triclinium of Leo III. An episode in restoration and Seicento medieval studies, in: Memoirs of the American Academy in Rome 40, 1995, S. 175–196.

Herklotz 2000 Ingo Herklotz: Gli eredi di Costantino. Il papato, il Laterano e la propaganda visiva nel XII secolo, Rom 2000.

Hofmann 1933 Karl Hofmann: Der »Dictatus Papae« Gregors VII. Eine rechtsgeschichtliche Erklärung, Paderborn 1933.

Iacobini 1989 Antonio Iacobini: Il mosaico del Triclinio Lateranense, in Fragmenta picta. Affreschi e mosaici staccati del Medioevo romano (Ausstellung Rom, Museo Nazionale di Castel Sant'Angelo, 15.12.1989–18.2.1990), hg. von Maria Andaloro et al., Rom 1989, S. 189–196.

Lanz 1983 Hanspeter Lanz: Die romanischen Wandmalereien von San Silvestro in Tivoli. Ein römisches Apsisprogramm der Zeit Innozenz III., Bern [u.a.] 1983.

Lemerle 1965 Paul Lemerle: L'Orthodoxie byzantine et l'oecuménisme médiéval: les origines du »schisme« des Eglises, in: Bulletin de l'Association Guillaume Budé 2, 1965, S. 228–246.

Linder 1975 Amnon Linder: The Myth of Constantine the Great in the West. Sources and Hagiographic Commemoration, in: Studi Medievali XVI, 1975, S. 43–95.

Liverani 2006 Paolo Liverani: Costantino offre il modello della basilica sull'arco trionfale, in: Maria Andaloro: L'orizzonte tardoantico e le nuove immagini 312–468 (La pittura medievale a Roma. Corpus, 1), Rom 2006, S. 90–91.

Liverani 2008 Paolo Liverani: Saint Peter's, Leo the Great and the leprosy of Constantine, in: Papers of the British School at Rome 76, 2008, S. 155–172.

Loenertz 1975 Raymond Joseph Loenertz: *Actus Silvestri*. Genèse d'une légende, in: Revue d'Histoire Ecclésiastique LXX, 1975, S. 426–439.

Lucherini 2009 Vinni Lucherini: Memorie della Roma monumentale, riflessi della politica papale nelle *descriptiones* di Giovanni Diacono e Pietro Mallio dedicate ad Alessandro III, in: Medioevo: immagine e memoria, Atti del Convegno internazionale di studi (Parma 2008), hg. von Arturo Carlo Quintavalle, Mailand 2009, S. 297–318.

Luchterhandt 1999 Manfred Luchterhandt: Päpstlicher Palastbau und höfisches Zeremoniell unter Leo III., in 799. Kunst und Kultur der Karolingerzeit, Karl der Große und Papst Leo III., in: Paderborn, Beiträge zum Katalog der Ausstellung Paderborn 1999, hg. von Christoph Stiegemann und Matthias Wemhoff, Mainz 1999, S. 109–122.

Maccarone 1952 Michele Maccarone: *Vicarius Christi*. Storia del titolo papale, Rom 1952.

Maddalo 2007 Silvia Maddalo: «Caput et vertex omnium ecclesiarum«. La cattedrale di Roma tra XII e XIII secolo, in: Medioevo: l'Europa delle cattedrali, Atti del convegno internazionale di studi (Parma 2006), hg. von Arturo Carlo Quintavalle, Mailand 2007, S. 424–434.

Maddalo 2011 Silvia Maddalo: Una leggenda in immagine. Un episodio delle storie di Silvestro negli affreschi della chiesa di San Silvestro ad Alatri, in: Tempi e forme dell'arte. Miscellanea di studi offerti a Pina Belli D'Elia, hg. von Luisa Derosa und Clara Gelao, Foggia 2011, S. 115–121.

Maddalo 2012 Silvia Maddalo: I santi Giorgio e Silvestro e l'ideologia politica della Riforma nel ciclo pittorico dell'Immacolata di Ceri, in: Le plaisir de l'art du Moyen Âge. Commande, production et réception de l'œuvre d'art. Mélanges en hommage à Xavier Barral i Altet, Paris 2012, S. 678–685.

Maraval 2013 Pierre Maraval: Il Battesimo di Costantino, in: Costantino I. Enciclopedia Costantiniana sulla figura e l'immagine dell'imperatore del cosidetto Editto di Milano 313, Rom 2013, S. 197–202.

Mazzocchi 2007 Eleonora Mazzocchi: Il cuore antico della Riforma: le pitture della basilica di S. Crisogono a Roma, in: Roma e la Riforma gregoriana, Actes du colloque (Lausanne 2004), hg. von Serena Romano und Julie Enckell Julliard, Rom 2007, S. 247–273.

Mellini metà XVII secolo Benedetto Mellini: Dell'antichità di Roma, metà XVII secolo, Biblioteca Apostolica Vaticana, Vat. Lat. 11905.

Meyendorff 1965 Jean Meyendorff: Saint Pierre, sa primauté et sa succession dans la théologie byzantine, in: La Primauté de Pierre dans l'Église orthodoxe, hg. von Nicolas Afanassieff et al., in: Revue des études byzantines 23, 1965, 1, S. 101–113.

Noble 1998 Thomas F. X. Noble: La Repubblica di S. Pietro. Nascita dello Stato pontificio (680–825), Genova 1998.

Panvinio 1570 Onofrio Panvinio: De Praecipuis urbis Romae sanctioribusque basilicis, quas septem ecclesias vulgo vocant, Romae 1570.

Paravicini Bagliani 1996 Agostino Paravicini Bagliani: Il trono di Pietro. L'universalità del papato da Alessandro III a Bonifacio VIII, Rom 1996.

Piazza 2002 Simone Piazza: La Grotta dei Santi a Calvi e le sue pitture, in: Rivista dell'Istituto Nazionale d'Archeologia e Storia dell'Arte, 3. Ser., 25, 2002, 57, S. 169–208.

Pistilli 2015 Pio Francesco Pistilli: Il »magister Iacobus«, Innocenzo III e il chiostro di Subiaco, in: Medioevo: natura e figura, Atti del Convegno internazionale di studi (Parma 2011), hg. von Arturo Carlo Quintavalle, Mailand 2015, S. 517–531.

Pohlkamp 1983 Wilhelm Pohlkamp: Tradition und Topographie. Papst Silvester I. (314–335) und der Drache vom Forum Romanum, in: Römische Quartalschrift für christliche Altertumskunde und Kirchengeschichte 78, 1983, S. 1–100.

Pohlkamp 1984 Wilhelm Pohlkamp: Kaiser Konstantin, der heidnische und die christliche Kult in den Actus Sylvestri, in: Frühmittelalterliche Studien. Jahrbuch des Instituts für Frühmittelalterforschung der Universität Münster XVIII, 1984, S. 357–400.

Pohlkamp 1992 Wilhelm Pohlkamp: Textfassungen, literarische Formen und geschichtliche Funktionen der römischen Silvester-Akten, in: Francia. Forschungen zur Westeuropäischen Geschichte XIX/I (Mittelalter – Moyen Âge) 1992, S. 117–196.

Roma medievale 2001 Roma medievale, hg. von André Vauchez, Rom/Bari 2001.

Romanelli/Nordhagen 1999 Pietro Romanelli und Per Jonas Nordhagen: Santa Maria Antiqua, Rom 1999.

Santangeli Valenzani 2007 Riccardo Santangeli Valenzani: Il vescovo, il drago e le vergini. Paesaggio urbano e paesaggio del mito nella leggenda di S. Silvestro e il drago, in: Res bene gestae. Ricerche di storia urbana su Roma antica in onore di Eva Margareta Steinby, hg. von Anna Leone, Domenico Palombi und Susan Walker, Rom 2007, S. 379–395.

Sardella 1996 Teresa Sardella: Società, Chiesa e Stato nell'età di Teodorico. Papa Simmaco e lo scisma laurenziano, Messina 1996.

Scorza Barcellona 2000 Francesco Scorza Barcellona: Silvestro I, in: Enciclopedia dei Papi, Bd. I, Rom 2000, S. 321–332.

Spiteris 1979 Yannis Spiteris: La critica Bizantina del Primato Romano nel secolo XII, Rom 1979.

Valenti 2012 Devis Valenti: L'iconografia del potere imperiale. Carlo Magno come »Novus Constantinus«, in: Ikon 5, 2012, S. 115–138.

Vian 2004 Giovanni Maria Vian: La donazione di Costantino, Bologna 2004.

Vigueur 2001 Jean-Claude Marie Vigueur: Il Comune romano, in Roma medievale, hg. von André Vaucher, Rom/Bari 2001, S. 117–157.

Wickham 2013 Chris Wickham: Roma medievale. Crisi e stabilità di una città (900–1150), Rom 2013.

Wilpert 1916 Josef Wilpert: Die römischen Mosaiken und Malereien der kirchlichen Bauten vom IV. bis XIII. Jahrhundert, Bd. I, Freiburg i. Br. 1916.

Wirbelauer 1993 Eckhard Wirbelauer: Zwei Päpste in Rom. Der Konflikt zwischen Laurentius und Symmachus (498–514). Studien und Texte, München 1993.

Zchomelidse 1996 Nino Zchomelidse: Santa Maria Immacolata in Ceri. Pittura sacra al tempo della Riforma Gregoriana, Rom 1996.

Musik und Liturgie bei päpstlichen Zeremonien im Mittelalter: Gesten, Symbole, Strukturen

Galliano Ciliberti

Die problematische, vielfältige und faszinierende Entstehung der Struktur und der fortschreitenden Schichtenbildung des päpstlichen Zeremoniells zwischen dem 10. und dem 13. Jahrhundert stellte sich als äußerst facettenreicher Prozess zum Verständnis von Musik und Liturgie innerhalb der zahlreichen rituellen Bräuche heraus. Da in diesem Rahmen nicht jeder Aspekt der wechselhaften Entwicklung des päpstlichen Protokolls erörtert werden kann, soll es hier insbesondere um die Zeremonie beim Amtsantritt des Papstes gehen. Bei diesem zentralen Hoheitsritus war die Musik Teil einer ausgetüftelten szenischen Organisation, in der die Gesten zu einer sich ständig weiter entwickelnden Identifikation bzw. Unterscheidung in einer ineinander verflochtenen Schichtung wurden. Musik fand an einem ganz bestimmten Ort statt, an Kultstätten von hoher Symbolkraft, innerhalb einer dynamischen Liturgie, in der nur die handelnden Akteure des Zeremoniells interagieren konnten: im Südosten der Lateranskomplex (die Erlöserbasilika und der Palast), »abgelegen am Stadtrand«,[1] Residenz der Päpste als Bischöfe von Rom, Symbol des universalen Patriarchats und Mittelpunkt der Verwaltung des Patrimonium Petri, und der Vatikan im Nordwesten »außerhalb der Stadtmauern« mit der Peterskirche, »Symbol des päpstlichen Primats und der Vorherrschaft Roms über Konstantinopel, […] Apostolischer Stuhl, Standort der Cathedra Petri«.[2] Die beiden konstantinischen Basiliken, »die von der Stadtmitte getrennt in Randbezirken und in entgegengesetzter Richtung lagen«,[3] waren demnach die feierlichen und maßgebenden Orte, an denen gesungen und Kirchenmusik gespielt und komponiert wurde. Auch sie war – wie das Zeremoniell – das Ergebnis verschiedener Einflüsse und Ablagerungen, die zweckmäßige Darstellung einer normierten, in keiner Weise improvisierten liturgischen Theatralisierung, die sich schrittweise entwickelte und den symbolischen Inhalten der päpstlichen Rituale entsprach.

---

1 Visceglia 2002, S. 55.

2 Visceglia 2002, S. 55–56.

3 Visceglia 2002, S. 55.

Am 27. Dezember 795 wurde Papst Leo III. in St. Peter in sein Amt eingesetzt. Es war ein Sonntag, entsprechend der althergebrachten Sitte der frühesten Bischofsweihen.[4] Leo III. stieß aufgrund seiner theokratischen und karolingerfreundlichen Vorstellungen bei einem erheblichen Teil der städtischen Aristokratie auf Widerstand, fand aber beim Klerus und beim Volk starken Rückhalt für seinen Plan zur Stärkung der päpstlichen Autorität.

Der Gewählte erscheint in seiner ganzen Pracht kostbarer Pontifikalgewänder und betritt die Petersbasilika – so erzählt es der *ordo* XXXVI am Schluss des Berichts – in Begleitung jenes *universo clero vel populus*, die ihn so sehr unterstützt hatten.[5] Der Pontifex begibt sich sofort zur *confessio Sancti Petri*,[6] um sich dort niederzuwerfen und im hieratischen Gebet zu verharren. In diesem feierlichen Augenblick geben die Kantoren den Einsatz zur majestätischen Liturgie der Weihemesse: Die Schola singt das »*introitum Elegit te Dominus*« (Abb. 1).[7] Die Sängergruppe ist der zweite wichtige Akteur, der in dem knappen Bericht über die Zeremonie genannt wird. Beim Einzug stehen die Kantoren hinter dem Papst, dem Klerus und dem Volk; es beweist, wie sehr dem Erzähler die »Verhaltenskodizes der Kurienelite in ihrer hierarchischen Struktur«[8] bewusst waren. Der Vortrag des Introitus, wie im *ordo* XXXVI dargestellt, besaß eine bedeutende Funktion in der Sinneswahrnehmung und nicht nur in liturgischer und politischer Hinsicht, denn er verdeutlicht den Teilnehmern die Wichtigkeit des Zeremoniells, seiner Handlungen und vor allem seiner Gesänge. Da das Musikstück einem Ritualprotokoll angehört, steht es für einen Brauch, eine Erinnerung. Es ist Teil eines vermutlich schon bewährten Verfahrens, aber auch wenn es sich um eine neue Praxis handelte, wäre es sicherlich keine oberflächliche und simple Verschönerung einer Funktion. Nicht zufällig gehört der Introitus *Elegit te Dominus* zum gallikanischen Ritual und wird im Frankenreich während der Messe für die Bischofsweihe gesungen.[9] Auch dies macht deutlich, wie eng die Beziehungen zum karolingischen Hof waren und vor allem in Zukunft noch sein werden. Es gibt zwar viele liturgische Bücher, die den Text überliefern, aber nur eines gilt als maßgebliche Quelle, auch im Hinblick auf die Musik: MS latin 903 der Bibliothèque Nationale de France, ein Graduale des 11. Jahrhunderts aus dem cassinensisch-benediktinischen Kloster von Saint-Yrieix.[10] Die Quelle, in aquitanischen Neumen geschrieben, fügt den Introitus (f. 116v) genau in die Messe *In natali*

4 Andrieu 1974, S. 582–583 (Fascicule, 24).

5 Andrieu 1965, S. 203 (Fascicule, 28).

6 Andrieu 1965, S. 203.

7 Andrieu 1965, S. 203.

8 Visceglia 2002, S. 124.

9 Andrieu 1965, S. 187.

10 Mocquereau 1925.

Elegit te Dominus

Introitus

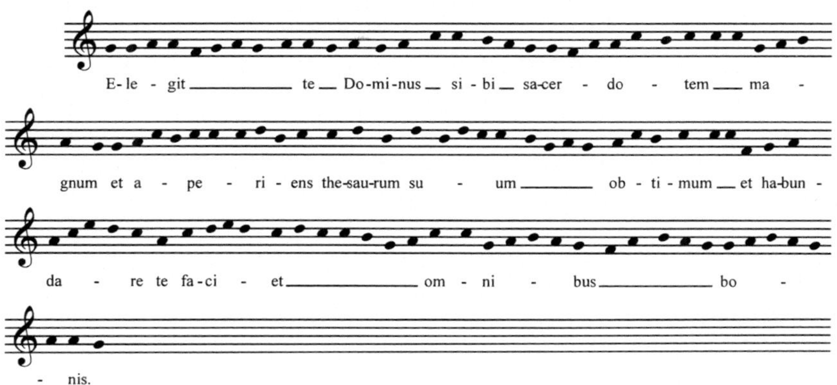

Abb. 1: *Elegit te Dominus*, Introitus, Paris, Bibliothèque Nationale de France (MS Latin 903, f. 116v), Transkription.

pontificis ein, die ihrerseits teilweise ein Unikum darstellt (Abb. 2). Geburt ist ein Synonym für Erschaffung bzw. für Wahl und Weihe, d. h. zwei für einen Papst grundlegende Ereignisse. Das Graduale von Saint-Yrieix könnte daher das *proprium* des Ritus bei der Amtsübernahme Leos III. in liturgisch-musikalischer Hinsicht abbilden:

Proprium missæ
zur Wahl Leos III.

Introitus
*Elegit te Dominus**

Psalmus
Exaudiat te … Seculorum Amen

Graduale
R. *Memor sit Dominus omni sacrificii tui** V. *Mittat tibi auxilium**

Alleluja
R. *Alleluia** V. *Mittat tibi Dominus auxilium**

Tractus
Desiderium anime

Offertorium
R. *Memor sit Dominus** V. *Mittat tibi auxilium**

Communio
*Unguentum in capite quod descendit in barbam**

Im aquitanischen Graduale folgt auf den Introitus *Elegit te Dominus* der Psalm 20 (19) *Exaudiat te Dominus* mit abschließendem *Gloria Patri, et Filio et Spiritui Sancto*, um die Feierlichkeit des Geschehens hervorzuheben (Abb. 2). Die Verwendung dieses Psalms (*Oratio pro regis victoria*) ist von besonderer Bedeutung und belegt ebenfalls den Einfluss liturgischer Elemente von jenseits der Alpen. In der Tat wurde dieser Text im Laufe der Jahrhunderte zu *dem* Symbol für die Liturgie der Königskrönung: Wir finden ihn im *Ordo* für die Krönung Ludwigs VIII. (1223),[11] vor allem aber in den entsprechenden Zeremonien, die in der Nikolauskapelle der Kathedrale von Reims stattfanden. Der Schlussvers des Psalms (*Domine, salvum fac regem*) setzte sich als die für die gallikanische Liturgie spezifische *Prière pour le Roy* durch, das nach der Kommunion gesprochene Schlussgebet, das bis ins späte 18. Jahrhundert immer wieder vertont wurde. Erstaunt stellt man fest, dass das Graduale, das Alleluja und das Gabengebet zusammen mit den entsprechenden Folgeversen demselben Text entnommen sind, obwohl sie in musikalischer Hinsicht Unikate darstellen: das Alleluja *Mittat tibi Dominus* stammt aus Vers 3, aus Vers 4 das Graduale (Abb. 3) und das Gabengebet *Memor sit*, beide mit den Versen *Mittat tibi auxilium* (Abb. 4). Diese textliche und liturgische Einheit verstärkt die Bedeutung von Psalm 20 als »Erwählung« im Graduale von Saint-Yrieix und erklärt seine Aufnahme in die Krönungsformeln für Könige wie auch in die Liturgie von Bischofs- und Papstweihen. Die *longue durée* besteht ebenso im Tractus *Desiderium animæ* [*ejus*]; dieser ist zwar in der Messe des MS 903 in Paris auf f. 117r nur in verkürzter Form wiedergegeben (ausführlich auf f. 26v im *proprium* für den Märtyrerheiligen Valentin) (Abb. 5), er wird jedoch später eine spezifische Einordnung im *Graduale romanum* finden (*Missa de uno martyre pontifice*).[12] Dieser Tractus paraphrasiert Vers 3 des Psalms 21 (20), der als *Gratiarum actio pro regis victoria* gesungen wurde, also ebenfalls einen Bezug zum königlichen Zeremoniell besaß. Der Kommunionvers *Unguentum in capite* (Abb. 6) bleibt hinsichtlich der Musiktra-

11 Godefroy 1649, Bd. 1, S. 13.
12 Liber usualis 1961, S. 1131.

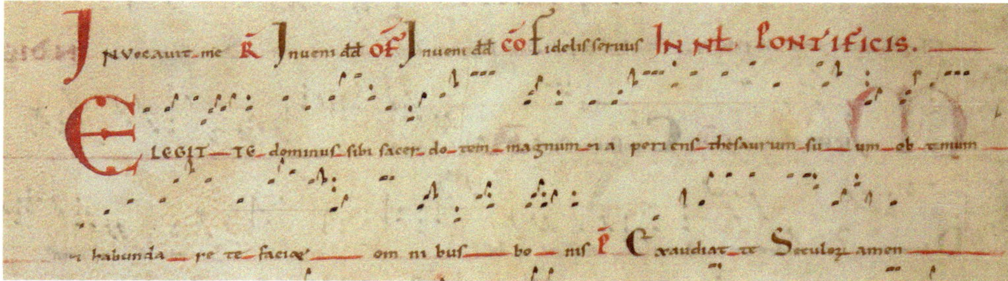

Abb. 2: Paris, Bibliothèque Nationale de France (MS Latin 903, f. 116v).

Abb. 3: Paris, Bibliothèque Nationale de France (MS Latin 903, f. 116v).

Abb. 4: Paris, Bibliothèque Nationale de France (MS Latin 903, f. 117r).

Abb. 5: Paris, Bibliothèque Nationale de France (MS Latin 903, f. 26v).

Abb. 6: Paris, Bibliothèque Nationale de France (MS Latin 903, f. 117r).

dition hingegen ein Unikum. Der Text stammt aus Psalm 133 (132), der später in der Liturgie der Templer eine bevorzugte Rolle spielen sollte, vor allem in den Gebeten der Ritter. Nach dem Graduale, bei dem der thronende Papst laut das *Gloria in excelsis Deo* anstimmt, ist die Schola an der Reihe und *canit ei laudem*: *Dominus Leo papa, quem sanctus Petrus elegit in sua sede multis annis sedere.*[13] Diese Lobgesänge werden auch am Ende der Zeremonie wiederholt, wenn der Papst aufs Pferd steigt, um sich zum Lateran zu begeben.[14] Die Krönung bildet den Abschluss und den Höhepunkt des Weiheritus.

13 Andrieu 1965, S. 204.
14 Andrieu 1965, S. 205.

Bei Papst Benedikt III. fand die Musik ihren Platz bei Feierlichkeiten, deren Zeremoniell außer der zentralen mystischen Gestalt des Pontifex auch verschiedene Stätten Roms als Bühnenbild und Thema der Handlung hervorhebt. Der Klerus, die weltliche Aristokratie, die Plebs und das Volk akklamierten dem neugewählten Papst und eilten dann zur Kirche San Callisto, wo dieser tief im Gebet versunken war.[15] Nachdem sein Widerstreben mit Mühe überwunden werden konnte und man ihn aus diesem besonderen Meditationsort herausgezerrt hatte, wurde er in einer Prozession von seiner großen Anhängerschar bis zur Lateranbasilika begleitet, *cum ymnis et canticis*, wie es seit jeher Brauch war. Die ganze Stadt, ja die ganze Kirche freute sich.[16] Der *Liber pontificalis* sagt leider nicht, um welche Gesänge und Hymnen es sich bei der Prozession handelte. An diesem Bericht beeindruckt besonders, wie die notwendigen Abschnitte der Zeremonie Räume und Menschen zusammenführten, sodass »Stimmen und Musik der feierlichen Riten« erklingen konnten und man »eine Vorstellung von der Kollektivbewegung der Prozessionen«[17] bekam. Innerhalb des jubelnden *mixtus populus* ist die weibliche Präsenz nicht zu unterschätzen: *ovantes divinas modulant virgines laudes*,[18] also junge, unberührte Frauen, die Lobgesänge vortrugen – eine wichtige Vorwegnahme des künftigen liturgischen Gesangs in Frauenklöstern. Benedikt III. wurde aber erst Ende September 855 offiziell gewählt, aufgrund eines genauso grausamen wie linkischen Absetzungsversuchs durch den Gegenpapst Anastasius III., der den rechtmäßigen Pontifex im Lateran einkerkern ließ. Nach seiner Befreiung dank der Unterstützung durch die Bischöfe, den Klerus und die römische Bevölkerung musste er sich einer neuerlichen Amtsantrittszeremonie unterziehen: Er wurde im *patriarchium Lateranensem* eingeführt und erneut *cum ymnis et canticis spiritalibus*[19] gefeiert. Am darauffolgenden Sonntag, dem 29. September 855, wurde Benedikt III. schließlich in St. Peter in sein Amt eingesetzt.

Die allgemeine Formel von Hymnen und geistigen Gesängen kommt im *Liber pontificalis* noch einmal vor, nämlich nach der Krönung von Nikolaus I. im Petersdom am 24. April 858. Die Prozessionsliturgie wird erneut zur Protagonistin des Ritus; die wichtigste Etappe ist der Festzug, der den neuen Pontifex von St. Peter zum Lateran mit solchen Gesängen und Hymnen feierlich begleitet.[20]

Die Schola sang diese geistlichen Gesänge und Hymnen in den Basiliken, im Freien und bei den Prozessionen unmittelbar hinter dem Designierten, dem Gewählten bzw.

15 Bertolini 1966.

16 Duchesne 1892, S. 140.

17 Schmitt 1991, S. 107.

18 Duchesne 1892, S. 140.

19 Duchesne 1892, S. 144.

20 Duchesne 1892, S. 152.

dem Gekrönten. Trotz aller Wiederholungen und vager Erzählungen schaffen die Musikstücke beeindruckende Rituale mit stark kennzeichnenden Gesten: die der Sänger auf der einen Seite und die des Volkes (Klerus, Adel und Laien verschiedener Stände) auf der anderen. Jeder gehört einer Ordnung an, besser: einem *Ordo* (der Begriff stammt ja aus der Liturgie) mit eigenen Zeichen, Verhaltensweisen, gemeinsamen und erkennbaren Handlungen.

Bezüglich der Amtsübernahme von Innozenz II., der am 23. Februar 1130 geweiht wurde, müssen wir auf den *ordo* XI des Benedikt, eines Kanonikers von St. Peter, zurückgreifen, der ihn während Innozenz' Pontifikat zusammenstellte. In seiner Beschreibung der Amtseinführungen schreibt Cancellieri: »Aus dieser Quelle geht hervor, dass am zweiten Sonntag nach Ostern die Päpste üblicherweise jedes Jahr den Festzug wiederholten, in dem sie sich nach ihrer Krönung vom Vatikan zum Lateran begeben hatten.«[21] Der *ordo* XI liefert zwar keine konkreten Hinweise zum Inhalt des *proprium missæ*, aber er ist dennoch ein wichtiges Dokument, weil er den Ablauf der Vesperliturgie am Ostermontag beschreibt. Die eigentliche Weihezeremonie des Papstes konnte nämlich schon am Vorabend mit einer feierlichen Vesper beginnen. Der Gottesdienst fand in St. Peter *ad Matutinum statt*, gesungen wurden das Alleluja (*Surrexit Dominus vere*), drei Psalmen (*Cum invocarem*, *Verba mea*, *Domine ne in ira* mit dem Vers *Hæc diem quam fecit Dominus*), drei Lesungen mit Predigt, zwei Tagesresponsorien und das *Te Deum laudamus*.[22]

Auch wenn diese Riten und Abfolgen in den Gottesdiensten eigentlich nur Pflichterfüllung gegenüber Gott waren, so sind sie doch oft von jenem besonderen Zusammenspiel von Ritualität und Politik beeinflusst, das sogar bis in die Funktion der liturgischen Musik reicht. In diesem Zusammenhang ist z. B. die plötzliche Unterbrechung des *Te Deum* durch die Familie Frangipani während der Weihezeremonie des Gegenpapstes Cölestin II. (Tebaldus Buccapecus romanus) am 15. Dezember 1124 zu verstehen. Die schreckliche Schändung des feierlichen, heiligen und unantastbaren Investiturritus durch Todesdrohungen und Schläge gegen Tebaldus, der offenbar daraufhin sofort auf die Weihe verzichtete, ereignete sich zu Beginn des Loblieds (*inceptus est Te Deum laudamus gaudendo*).[23] Der alsdann Bejubelte hieß Lambert von Ostia; als ihm die Unrechtmäßigkeit seiner Wahl bewusst wurde, legte er die päpstlichen Insignien (Mantel und Mitra) wenige Tage später freiwillig ab (21. Dezember 1124). Die Kardinäle würdigten seine Demut und bestätigten ihn »laut singend« im Amt mit dem Namen Honorius II.[24]

---

21 Cancellieri 1802, S. 10.

22 Migne 1862, Sp. 1025–1058.

23 Duchesne 1892, S. 327, und Cerrini 2000.

24 Duchesne 1892, S. 327.

Die schockierende Unterbrechung des festlichen *Te Deum* für den Gegenpapst einerseits und der folgende Gesang der Kardinäle zur Bestätigung des rechtmäßigen Papstes andererseits zeichnen ein System offensichtlich gegensätzlicher Handlungen, deren Symbolwirkung jedoch unverändert bestehen bleibt, sei es beim Bruch des Protokolls oder bei seiner Bestätigung. Der Abbruch des Singens durch Waffengewalt und auch seine Verstärkung durch die prominenten Stimmen der Kardinäle (quasi als solle der Vorrang ihres kirchlichen Amtes betont werden) entwerten keineswegs die nach dem Normenspektrum der *ordines* vorgetragenen Gesänge, sondern bestätigen, was Boethius als *musica humana* bezeichnet, d.h. die Sphäre der liturgischen Musik, die eine Beziehung zwischen Menschseele und Gott herstellt. Dem entgegengesetzt ist die niedrigste Stufe des künstlerischen Ausdrucks: die *musica instrumentalis* der praktischen Musiker. Laut Pandolfus, Autor des *Liber pontificalis* und Anhänger der Pierleoni-Familie sowie des Gegenpapsts Cölestin II., wären die Unruhen im Zusammenhang mit der Wahl Honorius' II. interessanterweise auf die Frangipani zurückgefallen. Ihren berühmtesten Vertreter verbindet Pandolfus verächtlich mit einer Anspielung auf Boethius' *musica instrumentalis* (*Robertus impius Fraipane verti fecit in luctum cytharam*[25]). Der Hinweis auf die Zither, für Pandolfus nur zur Begleitung der traurigen Klage des gottlosen Schuldigen geeignet, ist insofern sehr speziell, als die Zither damals von Spielmännern verwendet wurde, die Honorius Augustodunensis (1080–1154) zur gleichen Zeit als »Diener Satans«[26] bezeichnete.

In seinem Traktat *Gemma animæ* (1130) betonte Honorius, Chöre seien Ausdruck von Eintracht, Gemeinschaft und Einheit der Sänger (*concordia canentium*).[27] Diese allegorische Auffassung vertrat auch der heilige Augustinus in der *Enarratio in Psalmum CXLIX*: *Chorus est consensum cantantium. Si in choro cantamus, concorditer cantemus.*[28] Die gleiche Situation trat nach der Inthronisation Eugens III. (18. Februar 1145) ein, als während seines Ritts von St. Peter zum Lateran *clerus et populus romanus cum magna letitia occurrit, cantans Benedictus qui venit in nomine Domini.*[29] Die Worte sind Teil der Antiphon zum Psalmsonntag oder für eine feierliche Prozession und passen gut zum festlichen Anlass der Papstkrönung: *Turba multa quæ convenerat ad diem festum clamabat Domino: benedictus qui venit in nomine Domini, hosanna in excelsis.*[30]

25 Duchesne 1892, S. 327.

26 Schmitt 1991, S. 241.

27 Schmitt, S. 73 und 348, aber auch Migne 1854b, Sp. 588.

28 Migne 1854a, Sp. 1953.

29 Duchesne 1892, S. 449.

30 Liber usualis 1961, S. 588.

Während im ältesten Protokoll »die Krönung den Weiheritus abschloss und in gewisser Weise dessen Höhepunkt darstellte«,[31] kam es ab dem 12. Jahrhundert zu tiefgreifenden Veränderungen im Aufbau des Zeremoniells. Der »Inthronisationsritus beginnt und endet im Lateran«; die gleichsam kreisförmige Ritenstruktur – mit ihren Veranstaltungen, Handlungen und Bedeutungsebenen – verwandelt letztlich sogar das Bild des Papstes: 1) Amtsübernahme im Lateran; 2) Weihe in St. Peter am folgenden Sonntag; 3) Krönung vor der Basilika nach der feierlichen Messe; 4) Rückkehr in den Lateran. Diese angeordnete Route durchdringt den hieratischen, von königlicher Unbeweglichkeit ummantelten Pontifex; er ist eine Art göttliche Majestät auf Erden, und daher ist sein Schreiten betont langsam und feierlich, quasi als »Attribut der Macht« und »Sakralität« bzw. als »Zeichen der Vollkommenheit und Souveränität«.[32] In dieser Hinsicht wird der liturgische Gesang seinerseits zum »Zeichen der Sammlung und des Hörens auf das Göttliche«.[33]

Albinus, Kardinal und Bischof von Albano (1189–1196), berichtet, der gewählte und mit einem roten Mantel eingekleidete Papst habe sich vor dem Lateran auf die *sedes stercoraria* genannte Marmorkathedra gesetzt; von dort sei er vom Prior der Kanoniker, vom Subdiakon und vom Primicerius in die Kirche geführt worden. Der Papst warf sich nieder und betete, während die *schola cantorum* das *Te Deum Laudamus* sang.[34] Das strenge, würdevolle Bild des knienden und ins Gebet versunkenen Pontifex, umgeben von den Tönen des Weihehymnus schlechthin, »verherrlicht die Feierlichkeit der Handlung und die Würde des Handelnden«.[35]

Im *ordo* XII, verfasst vom Kämmerer Cencio (1192–1198*c*)[36] über die Weihe Cölestins II. am 26. September 1143, wird das *Te Deum* von verschiedenen Personen (Primicerius, Schola cantorum und Kardinäle) sofort nach der Amtsübernahme im Lateran gesungen. Die Lobgesänge sind erst am darauffolgenden Sonntag während der Krönungsmesse zu hören.[37] Die Schilderung im *ordo* XII liefert nur sehr spärliche Informationen zur Rolle des liturgischen Gesangs, stellt jedoch die Amtsübernahme im Lateran als zentrales Ritual der Papstwahl dar, da auch die *schola cantorum* daran beteiligt war. Das *Pontificale Romanum* des 12. Jahrhunderts bringt zusätzliche Informationen zur Papstweihe: Nach dem Beginn der Messe in St. Peter *Primicerius cum schola inchoat antiphonam ad introitum*,[38] und erst danach begibt sich der Gewählte aus der Sakristei

31 Visceglia 2002, S. 56.
32 Schmitt 1991, S. 18.
33 Schmitt 1991, S. 18.
34 Fabre 1905, S. 123–125; Andrieu 1945, S. 267.
35 Schmitt 1991, S. 18.
36 Fabre 1889, S. 311.
37 Fabre 1889, S. 312.
38 Andrieu 1938, S. 249.

zur *confessio*, wo Litaneien gesungen werden. Im Anschluss an das Anlegen des Palliums stimmt der Papst das *Gloria in excelsis* an.[39] Die kommunikative Funktion dieser Geschehnisse ist beachtlich, denn sie prägt die Ritenstruktur für die päpstliche Majestät und begrenzt ihre Bewegungen. Das Erkennungsmerkmal der Souveränität ist feierliche Starrheit. Die Menge hingegen befindet sich in großer Bewegung. Zwischen Beweglichkeit und Starrheit besteht nicht nur »ein Gegensatz«, sondern auch »eine Hierarchie«.[40] Vom Lateran nach St. Peter (für die Weihe am 22. Februar 1198) wird Innozenz III. von einer Prozession in folgender Aufstellung begleitet: vier Erzbischöfe, 28 Bischöfe, sechs Presbyter, neun Kardinalsdiakone, zehn Äbte, der Prior mit den Subdiakonen, der Primicerius mit den Kantoren und schließlich Richter, Anwälte und Schreiber. Nach dem Hochamt ist es Aufgabe des Volkes, den Pontifex in gestenreicher Bewegung *cum psalmis* bzw. *cum hymnis, et canticis* zum Lateran zurückzuführen[41] und seine Magnifizenz öffentlich zu verkünden. Die Funktion des Volkes am Ende der Pontifikalmesse und beim Heraustreten des Papstes aus der Peterskirche wurde schon im Zusammenhang mit anderen Weihen angemerkt. Bei Innozenz III. scheinen die Quellen zu trennen zwischen der Musik im Innern (die des Zeremoniells, wozu die Dokumente nur spärliche Anhaltspunkte bieten) und der Musik im Freien in Verbindung mit der erhabenen, ja fast göttlichen Erscheinung des Papstes vor der Welt. Diese Unterscheidung wird für den Abschluss der Krönung Gregors IX. am 21. März 1227 noch weiter beschrieben und betont. Nicht nur *concrepant cantica*: In jeder Straße *resonant Kyrie eleison* und *tubarum clangore turba concutitur.*[42] Der Gestus der Musik als Lobpreis und Akklamation der *Populi jubilantis*, die *exurgunt*, steht ganz im Dienste einer religiösen Macht, die durch solche Ovationen »das eigentliche Fundament des sozialen Zusammenhalts« zu vermitteln scheint.[43] Der Krönungszug wird auf diese Weise »zu einer zweiten Inbesitznahme des Laterans, wohingegen die ursprüngliche Zeremonie inzwischen bedeutungslos erscheint«.[44] Kurz: Gesänge, Psalmen und Lieder im Freien, zu denen sich der Silberklang der Trompeten gesellt, untermauern das Geschehen der Papstkrönung, erkennen deren Autorität und Willensäußerung an und prägen ihr lebendiges und weltliches Bild. Aufgrund ihrer Eindrücklichkeit werden diese klanglichen Gesten selbst zum wichtigen Bestandteil des Zeremoniells, wie zwei bedeutende Quellen aus dem 13. Jahrhundert belegen: das *Pontificale Romanum* und das Zeremoniell Gregors X.

39 Andrieu 1945, S. 263.

40 Schmitt 1991, S. 18.

41 Cancellieri 1801, S. 17–18.

42 Fabre 1905, S. 19.

43 Schmitt 1991, S. 6.

44 Boureau 1991, S. 108; Visceglia 2002, S. 56.

Das *Pontificale Romanum* aus der ersten Hälfte des 13. Jahrhunderts beschreibt vor allem die Weiheprozedur, die in St. Peter zu erfolgen hat. Wie es die Tradition befiehlt, *Primicerius cum scola sua inchoat antiphonam ad introitum.*[45] Die Beschreibung geht sofort *in medias res*, denn es werden weder die Wahl noch andere Formalitäten (Anlegung des Mantels, Ausrufung, usw.) behandelt.[46] Der Gewählte wird an der Schwelle zur Basilika von Kardinälen und Prälaten empfangen. Während er seinen Segen gibt, singt er *Sit nomen Domini benedictum.*[47] Auf dem Weg zur Gregorskapelle intoniert er den Psalm 84 (83) *Quam amabilia* (eine frühere Version des *Quam dilecta tabernacula*).[48] Nach der *confessio* setzt er sich auf den Faltstuhl im Hauptschiff zwischen dem Altar und den Stufen zum Papstthron. *Et scola cantet introitum et Kyrie eleison.*[49] Der Neugewählte schaut zum Altar; rechts und links von ihm werfen sich die Bischöfe nieder. Der Prior der Basilika *incipiat et prosequatur letaniam cum cantu, respondentibus aliis cappellanis.*[50] Nach dem Ende der Weihe nimmt der Papst auf seinem Thron in der Apsis Platz, und alle Kardinäle und Prälaten erweisen ihm danach ihre Ehrerbietung. Sodann stimmt der Pontifex das *Gloria in excelsis Deo* an, *et sic peragitur missa ordine suo.*[51] Der Bericht im Pontifikale geht glücklicherweise auf die Besonderheiten dieser Messe ein, insbesondere auf die Ausführung der Lobgesänge unter der Leitung des Priors der Diakone; dieser befand sich *ad pectorale dextrum, ante crucifixum argenteum*, Auge in Auge mit den anderen Musikern, die sich in zwei Reihen vor dem Altar aufgestellt hatten.[52] Der Vortrag erfolgt *alta voce in cantu, quasi legendo*; es handelt sich demnach um einen syllabischen Gesang, sehr ähnlich dem der Hymnen und Psalmen.[53]

Nach Beendigung der Lobgesänge begibt sich die ganze Prozession zur Schwelle der Basilika: Der Papst nimmt auf einem Stuhl vor dem Eingang Platz, der Prior der Diakone nimmt ihm die Mitra ab und setzt ihm die Tiara auf. Das Kirchenvolk steht gedrängt im Atrium *clamante: Kyrie eleison.*[54] Danach beginnt der Papst seinen Ritt zum Lateran, von einer Prozession begleitet, in der die Kantoren an achter Stelle gehen.[55] In der Laterankirche nimmt er die Huldigung des Priors und der Kanoniker entgegen

45 Andrieu 1945, S. 369.
46 Andrieu 1945, S. 271.
47 Andrieu 1945, S. 370.
48 Andrieu 1945, S. 371.
49 Andrieu 1945, S. 371.
50 Andrieu 1945, S. 372.
51 Andrieu 1945, S. 374 (kritischer Apparat).
52 Andrieu 1945, S. 375.
53 Andrieu 1945, S. 375.
54 Andrieu 1945, S. 376.
55 Andrieu 1945, S. 377.

und wird dann »mit Gesang« von der Portikus der Basilika zum Palast begleitet.[56] Dort setzt er sich auf den Faltstuhl und hört abermals die Lobgesänge unter der Leitung des ersten Kardinalpriesters.

Die Beschreibung im Zeremoniell Gregors X. ist viel kürzer gefasst als im *Pontificale Romanum*. Es fehlt gänzlich an Ortsangaben. Während das Pontifikale sogar die einzelnen Örtlichkeiten in St. Peter (Gregorskapelle, Papstkathedra in der Apsis, usw.) und die Offizianten (die Bischöfe von Ostia, Albano und Porto) nennt, spielt sich im *ordo* Gregors X. die gesamte Zeremonie in einer nicht näher genannten Kirche ab. Für die Beichte begibt sich der Gewählte zum Altar *interim choro vel scola cantorum cantante introitum et Kyrieleison*.[57] Danach setzt sich der Papst auf den Faltstuhl; ihm assistieren zwei Kardinaldiakone zu seiner Rechten *et cappellanus subdiaconus dicit letaniam cantando, aliis cappellanis respondentibus*,[58] nicht etwa der Prior der Diakone, die Richter und Schreiber wie im Pontifikale. Nach den von zwei Kardinalbischöfen vorgetragenen Gebeten hält ein dritter, *ordinator sive consecratur* genannt, ein geöffnetes Evangeliar über den Kopf des neuen Papstes, und alle hohen Kleriker stellen sich im Kreis auf.[59] Der *ordinator* stimmt den Vers *Deus honor in cantu* an, während die Ordensleute ihn sprechen.[60] Während der Messe wird auch der Lobpreis gesungen, die Texte sind im Pontifikale und im *ordo* identisch wiedergegeben.[61] Nach Abschluss der Krönung, nach der Huldigung und dem Aufsetzen der Tiara ist das Volk an der Reihe *clamante Kyrieleison*.[62] Die Prozession setzt sich hinter dem Papst zu Pferde in Richtung Lateran in Bewegung; auch hier gehen die Kantoren an achter Stelle.[63] Bei seiner Ankunft begleiten Prior und Kanoniker den Papst zur Kirchentür *cantando Sit nomen Domini*.[64]

Das Zeremoniell Gregors X. erwähnt die Bedeutung der Orte nur in dem Kapitel über die Ankunft eines bereits geweihten oder *extra urbem* gewählten Pontifex in Rom: Nach Entgegennahme des Pluviales und der Mitra von den Kardinälen in der Kapelle S. Maria Maddalena am Fuß des Monte Mario begibt sich der Papst zur Peterskirche. Dort wird er vom Erzpriester und von den Kanonikern empfangen, die ihn mit Gesang in die Kirche führen. In der Mitte der Basilika ist der Introitus *Protector noster aspice Deus et respice in faciem Christi tui* vorgesehen, gefolgt vom Psalm 84 (83) *Quam*

56 Andrieu 1945, S. 378.
57 Dykmans 1977, S. 166.
58 Dykmans 1977, S. 166.
59 Dykmans 1977, S. 167.
60 Dykmans 1977, S. 167–168.
61 Dykmans 1977, S. 169–171.
62 Dykmans 1977, S. 172.
63 Dykmans 1977, S. 173.
64 Dykmans 1977, S. 177.

dilecta tabernacula. Am Altar angelangt, verharrt der Papst im gesammelten Gebet, während die »canonici cantant *Te Deum laudamus*«.

Die Gesangseinlagen von Papst, Chor, Klerus und Volk werden sowohl im Pontifikale als auch im Zeremoniell als streng geordnet dargestellt: Psalmen, Lobgesänge und Hymnen in strengem Rhythmus sind zum wesentlichen Bestandteil einer einzigen Symbolebene geworden. Die römischen Basiliken sind das Haus Gottes, in dem eine Liturgie, die ganze Kirchengemeinschaft umfassend, in einer allegorischen Abbildung der Eintracht verschmilzt – eine Art Verherrlichung, wobei die Chorgesänge eine mystische Verbindung schaffen zwischen den Spiegelungen der Fenster und der Portiken, zwischen den Kirchenschiffen und Kapellen: Körper und Seelen, Materielles und Immaterielles, Menschliches und Engelsgleiches, Sichtbares und Unsichtbares streben zu einer himmlischen Lichtfülle voller Schwingungen, Farben und Klänge.[65]

65 Schmitt 1991, S. 108–109.

Bibliographie

Andrieu 1938 Michel Andrieu: Le Pontifical Romaine au Moyen-Age, Bd. I: Le Pontifical Romaine du XIIe siècle (Studi e testi, 86), Vatikanstadt 1938.

Andrieu 1945 Michel Andrieu: Le Pontifical Romaine au Moyen-Age, Bd. II: Le Pontifical de la Curie Romaine au XIIIe siècle (Studi e testi, 87), Vatikanstadt 1945.

Andrieu 1965 Michel Andrieu: Les *Ordines romani* du haut Moyen Age, Bd. IV: Les textes (suite) (*Ordines XXXV–XLIX*), Louvain 1965.

Andrieu 1974 Michel Andrieu: Les *Ordines romani* du haut Moyen Age, Bd. III: Les textes (suite) (*Ordines XIV–XXXIV*), Louvain 1974.

Bertolini 1966 Ottorino Bertolini: Benedetto III papa, in: Dizionario Biografico degli Italiani, Bd. 8 [online], Rom 1966.

Boureau 1991 Alain Boureau: La papessa Giovanna, Turin 1991.

Cancellieri 1802 Francesco Cancellieri: Storia de' solenni possessi de' sommi pontefici, Rom 1802.

Cerrini 2000 Simonetta Cerrini: Onorio II, in: Enciclopedia dei Papi, Rom 2000 [online].

Duchesne 1892 Le *Liber pontificalis*, Bd. II, hg. von Louis Duchesne, Paris 1892.

Dykmans 1977 Le Cérémonial papal de la fin du Moyen Âge à la Renaissance, Bd. I: Le cérémonial papal du XIIIe siècle, hg. von Marc Dykmans, Brüssel/Rom 1977.

Fabre 1889 Le *Liber Censuum* de l'Église Romaine, Bd. I, hg. von Paul Fabre, Paris 1889.

Fabre 1905 Le *Liber Censuum* de l'Église Romaine, Bd. II, hg. von Paul Fabre, Paris 1905.

Godefroy 1649 Theodore Godefroy: Le ceremonial françois, Bd. I, Paris 1649.

Liber usualis 1961 Liber usualis missæ & officii pro dominicis et festis cum cantu Gregoriano, Tournai 1961.

Migne 1854a Aurelius Augustinus, *Opera omnia*, tomus IV/pars altera (Patrologia Latina, XXXVII), hg. von Jacques-Paul Migne, Paris 1854.

Migne 1854b Honorius Augustodunensis, *Opera omnia* (Patrologia Latina, CLXXII), hg. von Jacques-Paul Migne, Paris 1854.

Migne 1862 Gregorius Papa I, *Opera omnia*, Bd. IV (Patrologia Latina, LXXVIII), hg. von Jacques-Paul Migne, Sp. 1025–1058, Paris 1862.

Mocquereau 1925 Le Codex 903 de la Bibliothèque Nationale de Paris (XIe siècle). Graduel de Saint-Yrieix (Paléographie Musicale, XIII), hg. von Dom André Mocquereau, Tournai 1925.

Schmitt 1991 Jean-Claude Schmitt: Il gesto nel medioevo, Rom/Bari 1991.

Visceglia 2002 Maria Antonietta Visceglia: La città rituale. Roma e le sue cerimonie in età moderna, Rom 2002.

II. Repräsentation päpstlicher Ordnung

The Power and Display of Writing: From Damasus to the Early Medieval Popes

Erik Thunø

In what follows I examine how the early medieval popes used the medium of monumental writing as a strategy to articulate and consolidate their power. I consider not only the content of such inscriptions, but also look at how they were displayed and interacted with their associated imagery (in this case apse mosaics) and with another channel of papal power, namely the relics of early martyrs. A case can thereby be made that monumental inscriptions, besides simply being verbal messengers, also served as visual agents capable of creating networks across time and place and attracting more than just a literate or even semi-literate audience.[1]

Golden texts, saints and popes in mosaic

Between the sixth and ninth centuries, the popes commissioned a series of splendid apse mosaics that hold a unique place in the medieval visual culture of the *Urbs*. A well-known example is the mosaic decoration in the church of S. Prassede on the Esquiline, built and decorated between 817 and 824 (Fig. 1). The mosaic in the apse vault is the most eye-catching and interactive part of the whole impressive early ninth-century visual ensemble. Terminating the nave and suspended above the main altar, a shimmering hierarchy of frontally gazing saints, gathered against a deep-blue background around a hovering golden robed Christ, attracts and then fixes the eye of the beholder as he or she enters the early medieval basilica. From here, the viewer's gaze is drawn upward to the other parts of the mosaic decoration that are configured to interact with the celestial realm in the apse: the Book of Revelation's Adoration of the Lamb by the Four Living Creatures and the Twenty-Four Elders on the apsidal arch surrounding the vault, and the unique depiction of the Heavenly Jerusalem, as defined by a gem and pearl encrusted golden wall, on the monumental triumphal arch in front. In this way, the mosaic

1 The arguments presented in this paper have been more extensively discussed in my book Thunø 2015.

Fig. 1: S. Prassede, Rome, general view of mosaic decoration, 817–824.

in the apse conch serves as the fulcrum around which the entire pictorial decoration pivots and the locus that both begins and concludes the viewer's visual journey (Fig. 2).

Augmenting the interest of the apse vault as a point of attraction for the beholder is the monumental inscription that runs across its lower rim. Its Latin hexameter verse, executed in golden capital letters that flicker against a deep-blue background, honors the saint to whom the church is dedicated and credits the pope with its patronage. Moreover, it consciously and purposefully emphasizes the power of its apse mosaic to pervade the entire space of the church with dazzling light: "[This is the] hall of the devout Praxedis ... It shimmers in light, adorned with diverse metals through the zeal of Paschal the supreme pontiff, foster-son of the Apostolic See."[2]

2 The entire inscription reads: EMICAT AVLA PIAE VARIIS DECORATA METALLIS/PRAXEDIS D[OMI]NO SVPER AETHRA PLACENTIS HONORE/PONTIFICIS SVMMI STVDIO PASCHALIS ALVMNI/SEDIS APOSTOLICAE PASSIM QVI CORPORA CONDENS/PLVRIMA S[AN]C[T]ORVM

Fig. 2: S. Prassede, Rome, apse vault, 817–824.

Within the visual ensemble, it is the non-narrative imagery in the apse vault, the focal point within the basilica, which undergoes the most significant transformations during the Roman Middle Ages. The triumphal arch mosaic of S. Prassede showing the Heavenly Jerusalem, to be sure, is an unusual *ad hoc* expansion of a decorative program that typically consists only of the apse vault and its surmounting arch. The representation of the Adoration of the Lamb, by contrast, is standard on apsidal arches from the early Christian to the late medieval period. Thus, whereas this narrative theme from the Apocalypse remains largely unchanged in that it continues to include all or some of the same protagonists (Lamb/Living Creatures/Elders), the apse vault in S. Prassede displays a number of specific features that are as distinctive among early medieval apse

SVBTER HAEC MOENIA PONIT/FRETVS VT HIS LIMEN MEREATVR ADIRE POLORVM; Thunø 2015, p. 211.

Fig. 3: Ss. Cosmas and Damian, Rome, general view, 526–530.

mosaics in Rome as they are unprecedented in the mosaics of the fourth and fifth centuries and discontinued in those of the twelfth and thirteenth centuries.[3]

Certainly the idea of making a timeless hierarchy of heavenly figures organized around Christ directly face the viewer goes back to the earliest known apse decorations, but it is the choice of some of those figures within that celestial order that should draw our attention. Similarly, while inscriptions are known to have accompanied apse mosaics from the earliest times, their contents and appearance become particularly uniform among the early medieval apse mosaics I shall deal with here. These, as we have seen with S. Prassede, largely focus on the presence of post-apostolic saints – that is, saints who lived and were martyred in eras post-dating the apostles, chiefly during the Christian persecutions of the second and third centuries. In this way, the mosaics always

3 Examples from those centuries are the apse mosaic of S. Pudenziana and S. Clemente. For more on this issue, see Thunø 2015, p. 29–38.

Fig. 4: S. Agnese fuori le Mura, Rome, apse vault, 625–638.

represent the basilica's dedicatee(s), but often introduce other related saints. In the apse of S. Prassede, for instance, S. Prassede is accompanied by her sister, S. Pudenziana. The Roman sisters, recorded to have lived in the second century, are shown presenting their crowns of martyrdom as they are introduced to Christ by Ss. Peter and Paul. In the far right margin of the group stands an additional saint who is represented as a deacon holding a book (S. Zeno?). Along with the introduction of post-apostolic saints, another and somewhat unexpected type of figure was chosen for inclusion in the heavenly hierarchy of saints – that is, the living pope as patron. Thus, in S. Prassede from the left margin of the apse conch, Pope Paschal presents a model of his newly built church to Christ.[4]

In addition to the inclusion of such figures – post-apostolic saints (titular saint included) and donor pope – the inscriptions glossing the early medieval apse mosaics also

4 See also Wisskirchen 1990, p. 29.

stand out among their earlier and later counterparts in Rome, both, it would appear, for formal qualities (golden capital letters on deep blue) and for their combined concern with the titular saint(s) and papal patron on the one hand and the light emitting qualities of the artistic medium on the other. In this way, the shimmering mosaics and their golden inscriptions jointly underline the new figures, while making light and material splendor key topoi. As we shall see, the saints, the popes, and the topos of radiating light are thereby intertwined in ways that originate in the cult of relics and are in turn significant for the embodiment of the divine as well as for the agenda of the papal self-promotion.

This particular combination of iconographic and epigraphic features, as witnessed by the apse vault in S. Prassede, constitutes what I define a 'formula' that is constituent to the early medieval apse mosaic in Rome. Hence, the presence of the titular saint(s) and the patron pope in conjunction with an inscription similar in appearance and contents to that discussed earlier is far from new to S. Prassede but is shared by a larger number of apse mosaics created in Rome between the sixth and ninth centuries and still *in situ* in their churches, as for example: Ss. Cosmas and Damian (526–530; Fig. 3); S. Agnese fuori le Mura (625–638; Fig. 4); the San Venanzio Chapel in the Lateran Baptistery (640–642); S. Cecilia in Trastevere (817–824); and San Marco (827–844). Except for S. Agnese and S. Cecilia, the mosaic decoration in these settings to this day comprises the apse vault, or apse conch, and the arch above it, the apsidal arch.[5]

Formula and chronology

The apse vaults discussed here, to be sure, reveal obvious compositional and iconographic differences in the choice, number, and arrangement of figures. The background color and paradisiacal landscape elements also differ from one another. The mosaics in question, then, may at first sight appear unrelated, indeed heterogeneous, especially in view of the fact that they were made in widely separate historical eras and in disparate styles. However, their fundamental contiguities become evident if a closer look is given to the types of figures that occupy their compositions. Whether or not Christ continues to dominate the center, it is clear that all of the apse mosaics are strongly focused on celebrating their titular (and sometimes additional) saints as well as the popes who built and adorned the churches. In fact, the latter continue to be present even when such typical components as Christ and the apostle princes are left out. Whereas the saints are post-apostolic martyrs who typically hold books, scrolls, or the victorious crowns of

5 Also the apse mosaic in S. Maria in Domnica could be added to this series, but for reasons of brevity I have excluded this mosaic from the present discussion. See Thunø 2015, p. 60.

their martyrdom, the bishop – still alive at the completion of the church and its mosaic – usually wears a square halo and presents a model of the church to the protagonist at the center: Christ or the titular saint.

The stylistic and compositional differences among the apse mosaics recede further into the background when one also takes into account their golden inscriptions. Thus, the mosaics in question not only share an established cast of characters, but they also feature lengthy and eye-catching inscriptions that stretch across the entire lower rims of their apse conches. With the exception of the inscription in the San Venanzio Chapel, consisting of white capital lettering against a deep-blue background, these monumental poetic texts are all set in large capital letters in gold that shimmer against a deep-blue background. Although largely ignored both in content and visual appearance, the golden hexameters deserve much closer scrutiny than they have until now been given. As is true of the figural compositions, they are far from identical. They differ in length as well as in content. Yet, although each inscription therefore deserves to be individually studied, each (San Venanzio included) consistently acknowledges the titular saint(s) and the papal patron shown in the mosaics as well as it evokes the splendor of the church it decorates by self-referentially emphasizing its own and the entire apse mosaic's power to dazzle and glitter with light. As such, the apse inscriptions demonstrate a marked uniformity in which appearance and content mutually reinforce each other.

Seen in this perspective, the early medieval apse mosaics share what I consider a formula of visual and textual features in which titular saint(s), the papal patron, and the focus on material splendor are the constituent elements. The formula transcends changes in style and composition over time and links the mosaics as parts in a series. In their search for cultural specificity in the mosaics, the attempt to make them into manifestations of certain historical moments in time, art historians have, however, turned a blind eye to those features that link rather than separate the mosaics from each other.[6] Indeed, the proposed formula makes it possible to use a new and more wide-ranging lens to view a ninth-century apse mosaic like the one in S. Prassede, for example, not just in relation to a more or less direct prototype of the sixth century or earlier, but also as connected to examples from the period in between. Conversely, the apse mosaics from San Venanzio and S. Agnese may not merely appear as isolated instances from a period when Rome was under 'eastern' influence that was later eclipsed by the Carolingian 'Renaissance', but take their place in a continuum that stretches from the apse mosaic of Ss. Cosmas and Damian to those of the ninth century, carrying on a formula that thereby creates an interconnected series of early medieval apse mosaics. The proposed formula, in other words, rearranges the apse mosaics from the sixth to the ninth

6 See for example Krautheimer 1980, p. 126–134; Andaloro/Romano 2002, p. 83; Poeschke 2010, p. 17.

centuries in ways that are at odds with the traditional narrative that tends to compartmentalize the material into separate groups each belonging to a particular historical period. In this paper, I therefore prefer to ignore the renowned aura of the apse mosaic in Ss. Cosmas and Damian as mediating between early Christian prototypes and their later Carolingian followers on both a specific and more general level. I disregard the 'foreign' and hence isolated characteristics of San Venanzio and S. Agnese and, finally, I choose to overlook the much celebrated Roman revival as embodied by S. Prassede, S. Cecilia, and San Marco. The formula that I have just proposed thus works as a tool that flattens this traditional trajectory in favor of a new alignment that is not submerged by what are perceived as the historical ups and downs of Rome, but which is underpinned by their own visual and textual features.

Mosaics and radiating relics

The early medieval apse mosaics we have looked at thus far are found in churches with different origins and functions in the sacred topography of Rome, a fact that may seem surprising in light of their shared visual and textual formula that identifies them as a distinct group. Just as this formula persisted over three successive centuries, so it appears to rise above the specificity of each church. What instead motivated the formula were the relics of saints. The reburial and orchestration of saints' relics – whether they were imported from abroad, left in their original burial places, or transferred into the city from their suburban cemeteries – in new architectural settings sponsored by the papacy coincide with the continuous manifestation of the formula in the early medieval apse mosaics. In fact, by visualizing some of the newly installed saints in conjunction with the pope as patron and by often recording in words the circumstances that prompted the new church and its mosaic, the formula engages directly with its own origins.[7]

The formula linking the early medieval apse mosaics to one another as a series and the newly orchestrated relics of martyrs should therefore be considered as two sides of the same coin. Indeed, the golden inscriptions in particular played a key role in linking the early medieval apse mosaics and their churches to the presence of the relics. As most recently explained by Cynthia Hahn, essential to the empowerment of relics was an understanding of them as generators of light, a "light not stable but one that flickers, flashes, and coruscates; in short it is incandescent."[8] In suggesting the healing power of the relics of S. Stephen, Augustine writes how "it [his body] shed its light on

7 Such circumstances are for example recorded in the apse inscriptions of S. Prassede (see n. 2) and S. Cecilia.

8 Hahn 2012, p. 26–27.

many lands," and Gregory of Tours describes how the relics of S. Martin and other saints were brought into the oratory of S. Illidius whereby "a frightening flash filled the room . . . and flared about through the entire oratory" that he identified as the power (*virtus*) of the saint.[9] Patricia Cox Miller has argued that the association of relics with such physical qualities as light and brilliance was essential to an apprehension of the relics as not opaque and dead bones, but as spiritual and living objects.[10] Seen against this background, the focus on glitter and brilliance in the golden apse inscriptions is as much about the relics installed in their churches as it is about the materiality of the apse mosaics. Executed in flickering, flashing letters of gold within *tesserae* of glass, the inscriptions – along with the multicolored apse mosaics above them – operate to enhance the experience of their relics as embedded with sacred power. By amplifying the luminous power of the mosaics, the inscriptions imbue them with that sanctifying potential. Rather than objectively 'describing' the power of the medium of mosaic, however, these texts represent an emotional and living response to the mosaics aiming at making their subject – the relics – alive to the congregation in the church.[11] Just like a shimmering reliquary of precious metals, so does the church, decorated with mosaic and sheltering relics, become both a generator and receptacle of light – the spiritual light of the saints.[12] In this way, the inscriptions clearly demonstrate the inter-dependence between the early medieval apse mosaics on the one hand and the bodily remains of the saints present in the altar or crypt within their churches on the other.

Saints and writing under Pope Damasus (366–384)

The early medieval apse mosaics were generated by papal patrons whose goal was to create ornate and accessible liturgical settings for the bodily remains of early martyrs, thereby subjecting them to stronger institutional control than had hitherto been the case. Crucial to this undertaking were the monumental apse inscriptions that drew attention to the presence of the saints in the church, pointed out their intercessory powers, emphasized the material splendor of their new abode, and highlighted the pope as their benefactor. Although unprecedented in apse mosaics, the central role that these eye-catching texts play in promoting the martyrs and their papal sponsors can be demonstrated to have had a venerable tradition in Rome. Thus, we may parallel the undertakings of the early medieval popes to Pope Damasus's (366–384) promotion of

9 Hahn 2012, p. 26; de Nie 1987, p. 183–193; Angenendt 2002, p. 387–399.

10 Cox Miller 2000, p. 213–236.

11 Cox Miller 2000, p. 219–220.

12 Hahn 2012, p. 26.

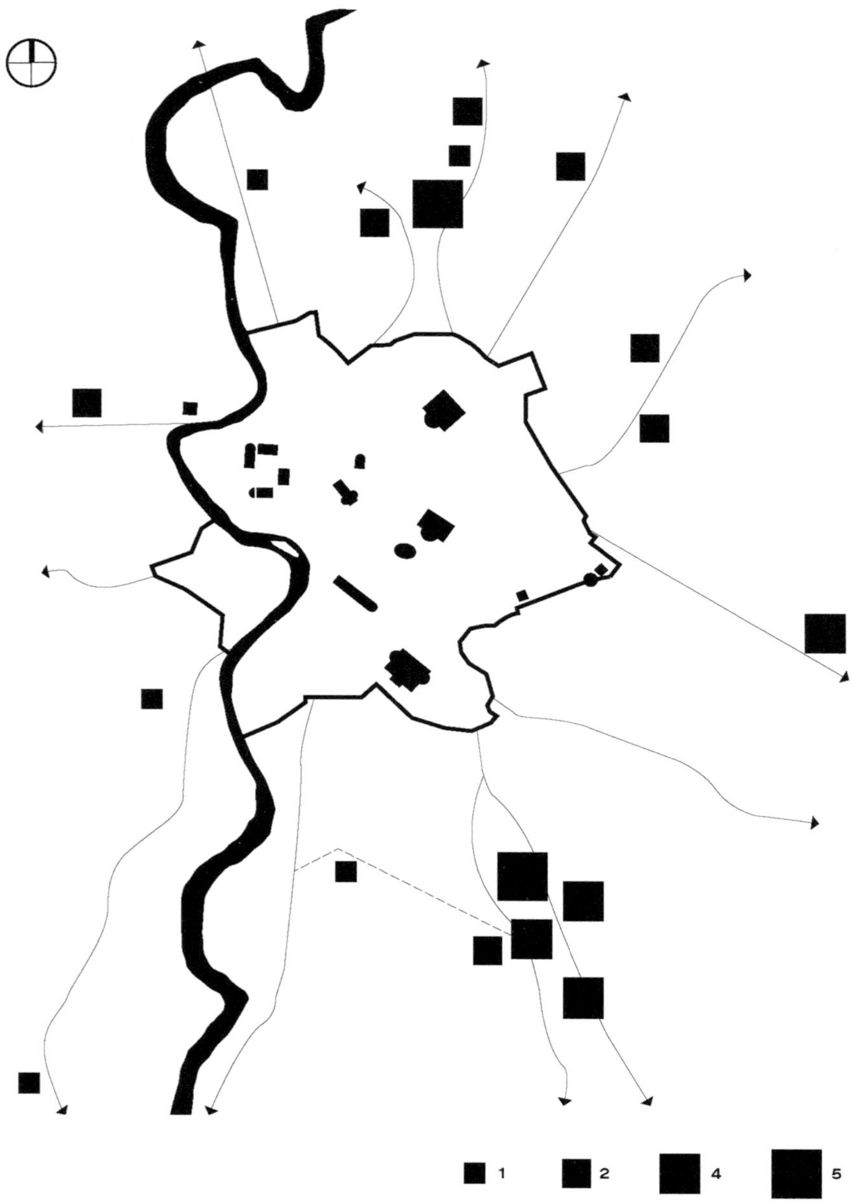

Fig. 5: Map of Rome with extra-urban sites marked by Damasian epigrams (drawing: James Huemoeller after Guyon, Damase e l'illustration des martyrs).

the early martyrs in the city's suburban cemeteries. Essential to the latter's campaign was the creation of monumental inscriptions, also known as the 'Damasian epigrams', engraved on blocks of marble, which were installed near the tombs at eighteen separate sites encircling the city (Fig. 5).[13] These exceptional texts, widely recorded by pilgrims of the early Middle Ages, were executed in the most elegant script of the time. Composed in hexameter verse and incorporating citations from the writings of both Virgil and Ovid, the Damasian epigrams frequently offered a short eulogy of the deceased martyr revolving around his or her triumph over a tortuous death, followed by an invocation of the martyr's intercessory power in heaven. It is fortunate for our purposes that one of the few still intact Damasian epigrams was placed on S. Agnes's tomb in the catacomb on the Via Nomentana (Fig. 6). The large epigram was subsequently removed by Pope Honorius to serve as a paving stone in his new basilica *ad corpus*. In his epigram, which represents the earliest known hagiographical recollection in Rome, Pope Damasus offered the following panegyric of the much venerated Roman martyr:

> According to tradition, some time ago her devout parents reported that when the trumpet summoned her with its mournful melody, their daughter Agnes suddenly left her nurse's bosom; voluntarily she scorned the cruel tyrant's threats and rage when he decided to burn her noble body in the flames: Despite her weakness he failed to inspire in her a powerful fear. She let her hair flow down over her naked body so that no mortal man should gaze upon the temple of the Lord. You whom I revere, gentle and holy ornament to virginity, look kindly, O glorious martyr, on the prayers of Damasus, I pray.[14]

---

13 The epigrams, many of which exist only in very fragmentary condition, have been critically edited by Ferrua 1942, who counted almost sixty authentic examples in stone composed by Damasus himself or by clerics commissioned by this pope. Recent literature includes Diefenbach 2007; Reutter 2009; Löx 2013 and Trout 2015.

14 [FAM]A REFERT SANCTOS DUDUM RETULISSE PARENTES/
[AG]NEN CUM LUGUBRES CANTUS TUBA CONCREPUISSET/
[N] UTRICIS GREMIUM SUBITO LIQUISSE PUELLAM/SPONTE
TRUCIS CALCASSE MINAS RABIEMQ(UE) TYRANNI URERE CUM
FLAMMIS VOLUISSET NOBILE CORPUS/VIRIB(US) INMENSUM
PARVIS SUPERASSE TIMOREM/NUDAQUE PROFUSUM CRINEM
PER MEMBRA DEDISSE/ NE DOMINI TEMPLUM FACIES
PERITURA VIDERET/O VENERANDA MIHI SANCTUM DECUS
ALMA PUDORIS/UT DAMASI PRECIB(US) FAVEAS PRECOR
INCLYTA MARTYR; trans. White 2000, p. 43–44. Ferrua 1942, no. 37, p. 175–178.
The epigram, now attached to the wall of the staircase that leads down to the narthex of the church, measures 3 m by 0.85 m.

Fig. 6: Damasian epigram, S. Agnese fuori le Mura, Rome, 366–384.

A comparison between this text and the later Honorian apse inscription at the same site reveals no contingent relationship. The latter says:

> A golden picture arises from specks of metal
> and daylight itself, shut out [from here], embracing it is in it enclosed.
> Dawn, you could believe, mounts over the gathered clouds
> as though from snowy fountainheads
> wetting the fields with dew.
> Or [you could believe] the sort of light that rainbow will produce
> among the stars and a purple peacock himself gleaming with color.
> He who was able to set the boundary of night or light
> has here beaten chaos back from the tombs of martyrs.
> Any who once casts an eye overhead sees
> these votive offerings the bishop Honorius has given.
> By his garments and offering, his works are signified, as also
> bearing light [inwardly] in his heart of hearts
> he shines [outwardly] to the beholder's eye.[15]

---

15 AVREA CONCISIS SVRGIT PICTVRA METALLIS
ET COMPLEXA SIMVL CLAVDITVR IPSA DIES.
FONTIBVS E NIBEIS [NIVEIS] CREDAS AVRORA SVBIRE
CORREPTAS NVBES RVRIBVS [RORIBUS] ARVA RIGANS.
VEL QVALEM INTER SIDERA LVCEM PROFERET IRIM
PVRPVREVSQVE PAVO IPSE COLORE NITENS.
QVI POTVIT NOCTIS VEL LVCIS REDDERE FINEM
MARTYRVM E BVSTIS HINC REPPVLIT ILLE CHAOS.

While the Damasian epigram narrates from the life of the martyr, whose intercession is being invoked by Damasus personally toward the end of the poem, the seventh-century mosaic inscription is mainly focused on the material splendor of Honorius's new church. This type of subject is generally absent from the Damasian epigraphical poetry. This is not to say that all Damasian epigrams are completely distinct in substance from the golden apse inscriptions; indeed, frequently, both types of inscription evoke the heavenly abode in which the saints are present, and the saints through whose intercessions the pope and the faithful can hope to enter that abode. The Damasian epigrams, too, like the apse inscriptions, sometimes place emphasis on the pope as patron. But with their primary focus on the individual martyr, the epigrams qualify as a separate genre, distinct from the apse inscriptions, which, as I have argued elsewhere, tap into a long tradition of ancient building *ekphrasis*.[16]

Notwithstanding differences in content and medium, the two inscriptions are comparable in other meaningful ways. First, both give an elaborate and visually conspicuous text a central place in a new setting created to promote and venerate a saint. The Damasian epigrams, like the golden apse inscriptions, exemplify a papal strategy of seizing control of the tombs and relics of saints while facilitating public access to them. To that end, Pope Damasus carried out various works in the catacombs such as enlarging their *cubicula*, expanding the galleries leading down to the tombs, and installing new stairways and light wells.[17] In an epigram for Ss. Protus and Hyacinthus, which conjures up the apse inscriptions in S. Agnese, Damasus promotes himself as restorer of the catacombs describing how he brought the tomb to light again after it had been buried deep beneath the mountain.[18] Typically, the renovated tomb was equipped with a *mensa* and flanked by a pair of pillars or columns topped by an architrave, as well as being further monumentalized by the addition of a ciborium-like arch. Finally, the epigram would be situated either between the columns or above the arch. Either way, just as is true of the apse inscriptions, the monumental text was centrally and directly exposed to the visitor.[19]

EVRSVM [SVRSUM] VERSA NVTV QVOD CVNCTIS
CERNITVR VNO PRAESVL HONORIVS HAEC
VOTA DICATA DEDIT. VESTIBVS ET FACTIS
SIGNANTVR ILLIVS O[PE]RA LVCET ET ASPECTV
LVCIDA CORDA GERENS; Thunø 2015, p. 210.

16 Thunø 2015, p. 50–52.

17 Reutter 2009, p. 103–110; Löx 2013, p. 83–88, p. 193–214, who points out the archeological difficulties in determining if certain of these alterations were made during or shortly after Damasus's pontificate, and thus tends to limit the extent of Damasus's architectural interventions.

18 Ferrua 1942, p. 142, no. 47,1. See also Reutter 2009, p. 104–105.

19 Löx 2013, p. 76–77. For the pictorial embellishment of Damasus's tombs, see Reekmans 1986; Paleani 1986.

What really makes the apse inscriptions more akin to the Damasian epigrams than to earlier examples of texts embedded in mosaics, however, is their standardized format. As I mentioned earlier, the format of the apse inscriptions, manifest in both style and content, is unique. While no earlier or later group of apse inscriptions in Rome submits to a similar formulaic consistency like that of these golden texts, the Damasian epigrams of several centuries earlier illustrate the same tendency toward visual and verbal standardization. Jean Guyon has called attention to the strong visual resemblance among the epigrams through their Philocalian lettering on large rectangular marble blocks. To the French scholar, this visual uniformity among the epigrams was deliberate: it served to relate the incised texts to one another and to further an experience of the disparately placed martyrs they commemorated as a unified and collective body, a *communio sanctorum* which, in turn, would identify with the *Ecclesia Romana*. This idea has also recently been endorsed by Steffen Diefenbach.[20]

Building a *communio sanctorum*

The notion that the Damasian epigrams create a network of martyrs yields a fresh perspective on the famous enterprise of the fourth-century pope, which, in turn, seems to have wide-ranging implications for how we understand the early medieval apse mosaics and their shared formulaic nature. Rather than merely considering the repetitions in the apse inscriptions for what they are, *topoi* taken from ancient *ekphrasis* on pagan buildings, they may, just as their counterparts on the Damasian epigrams, have served as the reference points within a network of churches. If so, this dynamic is amplified by the joint visual representation of the patron pope and titular martyrs that always accompanies the apse inscriptions. Moreover, the idea that this repetitive formula serves to establish a communal body of saints is suggested by the tendency in almost every church with an early medieval apse mosaic to assemble larger numbers, even masses of martyrs, whether through visual representation alone or through relics.[21] Similar to the Damasian epigrams, the individuality of the martyrs is obscured by their stereotypical inscriptions. The early heroes of the Church appear more as types in a universe in which numbers and general intercessory qualities enjoyed priority over individual powers and histories. The efforts to create a certain type of apse mosaic whose constituent features are repeated again and again thus coincide with effacing the celebrated saints as singular characters while multiplying their numbers.[22]

20 Guyon 1995, p. 162–163; Diefenbach 2007, p. 303.
21 Thunø 2015, p. 40–47; p. 179–180.
22 Thunø 2015, p. 180.

Pope Damasus' use of monumental inscriptions infused with patterns of visual and textual repetition was thus fundamental in linking the saints and their sacred sites with one another. It is safe to say that as far as their role as impresarios of the saints is concerned, the papal patrons of the early medieval apse mosaics followed in the footsteps of their distinguished fourth-century predecessor. Crucial to implementing those strategies was both parties' use of the medium of script. Although the location and nature of their artistic enterprises differ considerably, what made us associate the early medieval apse mosaics with the Damasian epigrams in the first place was – whether incised in stone or composed of golden *tesserae* – the central and consistent display of monumental writing in sacred spaces.

Writing as image

Pope Damasus has been credited with being the first pope to realize the potential of script in exposing the masses to the teachings of the Church.[23] Yet, despite his keen interest in this exclusive medium, the power of writing as a vehicle to reach the broader populace does not seem immediately obvious. In his famous letters to the Bishop of Marseille, Pope Gregory the Great recommended that not texts, but images – that is, narrative scenes (*historia*) – serve the illiterate to access Scripture. With this authoritative suggestion in mind, the monumental Old and New Testament narrative cycles that typically adorned the nave of early Christian basilicas, have often been seen as serving precisely this didactic or missionary purpose.[24] Pope Gregory was no pioneer in articulating this idea, which in his case was generated by a dispute over the legitimacy of images. Two hundred years earlier, Paulinus of Nola had his basilica at Nola decorated with story-telling images to convert "countryfolk not without belief but unskilled in reading."[25] While these writings indicate the difficulties a majority of the faithful faced in reading a text, inscriptions continued to be an important part of medieval imagery. Paulinus added descriptive and explanatory verses, the so-called *tituli*, to his pictures so that "the written word reveals the theme outlined by the painter's hand." The fifth-century bishop explained that everyone in the church would then "point out and read over to each other the subjects painted," suggesting that those more proficient in reading

23 Cardin 2008, p. 17.

24 Gregory the Great, *Epistola*, 9, 209, and 11, 10, ed. D. Norberg, CCSL 140A, p. 768 and 873–876; Kessler 1985. For a different view, see Brenk 2005.

25 Paulinus of Nola, *Carmen 27*, 11, p. 548–549, CSEL 30, p. 286; trans. Walsh 1975, p. 290. See also Trout 1999, p. 182–183.

Fig. 7: Trajan's Column, Rome, base with inscription, 113.

helped others decipher the written texts.[26] Reading inscriptions was not just an individual matter but a group exercise for those with different levels of literacy. Words in pictures described not merely what was visualized, but typically revealed the larger theological and spiritual implications of the pictured events through classical and theological references. Herbert Kessler has argued that whereas the narrative pictures delivered Scripture to the masses in a most basic and literal way, the embedded texts contained the mystery and knowledge accessible only to the educated few.[27] By addressing both parties, but through different means, the captioned picture would at once stratify and unite the medieval audience. However, this dynamic, I will argue in the following, did not necessarily have to unfold between text and image, but could also evolve in the text itself.

There can be little doubt that both the Damasian epigrams and the apse inscriptions were only fully comprehensible to the privileged few. The many borrowings from Virgil and Ovid and the literary metaphors pervading these texts would have 'veiled' them even further and required an educated audience to transmit their contents to the less literate. The inaccessibility of the inscriptions, however, stands in sharp contrast to their central exposure in the sacred space where they were clearly meant to be seen and admired by the entire congregation. Aside from creating a network of martyrs across time and place, both epigrams and mosaic inscriptions generate a series of associations important

26 Paulinus of Nola, *Carmen 27*, 11, p. 584–587, CSEL 30, p. 288; trans. Walsh, *Poems*, p. 291; Arnulf 1997, p. 47–50.

27 Kessler 1985; Kessler 1989.

Fig. 8: S. Maria Maggiore, Rome, triumphal arch (apex), 432–440.

to both literates and illiterates. The distinct visual format of the epigrams, for example, was a hallmark of Damasus's patronage; even without comprehending the text, viewers would have been reminded by its expressive Philocalian script of the fourth-century pope's personal investment in Rome's early martyrs. Yet, the script undoubtedly also prompted powerful allusions to Rome as *caput mundi*; the Roman capitals on which the Philocalian script was based were also used on public monuments by the Roman emperors and epitomized grandeur, authority, and universal supremacy. Particularly fine examples are present on the triumphal arch of Titus (AD 81) and the base of Trajan's column (AD 113; Fig. 7).[28] The popes were quick to realize the visual potential of this ideologically charged and prestigious script. By adapting it to their own sacred monuments, they conveyed an aura of classical tradition that could bolster the Roman Church in its claim for universality. Preserved examples include Pope Sixtus III's (432–440) inscription above the columns of the Lateran Baptistery, the lettering of which emulates the Damasian epigrams. Early examples in mosaic appear on the entrance wall of S. Sabina (422–432) and the triumphal arch of S. Maria Maggiore (432–440; Fig. 8).[29] At once employing and personalizing the celebrated classical writing, Pope Damasus aimed to integrate his own patronage of Rome's early martyrs with allusions to imperial Rome and its triumphs. Hence, it may also not be fortuitous that the square marble tablets of the epigrams are closely reminiscent of the format used for the inscriptions on the triumphal arches of Rome. The inscriptions in the apse mosaics were rendered *all'antica* not only through their lettering but also by virtue of their golden shimmer reminiscent

28 Thunø 2015, p. 186.
29 Thunø 2015, p. 186.

of the same type of imperial inscriptions, whereby they too could elicit connotations of papal patronage, imperial heritage, and Church primacy. In addition to the associations generated by specific visual features, the presence of writing itself was meaningful. As a tool to gain insight and knowledge, writing was held in higher esteem than pictures. Augustine, for instance, distinguished pictures from writing in the following way:

> "For a picture is seen in one way, letters are seen in another way. When you have seen a picture, to have seen it, to have praised it, is all that is. When you have seen letters, this is not all that is because you are put in mind also to read them ... therefore, because we have seen, because we have praised, let us read and understand."[30]

It seems appropriate that Pope Damasus chose to commemorate the early martyrs not in pictures but in writing – the less easily intellectually more profound and therefore more authoritative medium. With such connotations, both the epigrams and the golden apse inscriptions did not actually need to be read: the mere physical presence of these texts sufficed to validate the saints, their shrines, and, ultimately, their patrons. To that end, the inscribed verses are made manifest on a monumental scale at the center of the sanctuary, and their finely executed script reminds us that their presence mattered as much as their content. In a number of different ways, then, writing was made meaningful to peasants and elites alike. If those proficient in reading read the inscriptions to the less educated, the broad social appeal of monumental script would have been even stronger. Serving as both text and image, the inscriptions alone were capable of stratifying as well as uniting their audience. Were pictures, then, really intended for the illiterate and texts for the literate? The elaborate Damasian epigrams and golden, glinting inscriptions in the Roman apse vaults demonstrate that in reality it was not that simple. Just as the imagery in the church could function as text, and sometimes at such complex theological levels that an educated audience was required to release the content, so could texts in the same space serve as pictures that at their most basic level required no literacy.

30 Augustine, *Tractates on the Gospel of John 11–27*, trans. Rettig 1988, p. 232–233 (*Tractate* 24, 2, 2). See also Kessler 1989, p. 129.

Bibliography

Sources

Augustine, Tractates on the Gospel of John II-27, trans. John W. Rettig (The Fathers of the Church 79), Washington D.C. 1988.

Gregory the Great, Epistola, 9, 209, and 11, 10, ed. Dag Norberg, CCSL [Corpus Christianorum Series Latina] 140A, Turnhout 1982, p. 768 and p. 873–876.

Paulinus of Nola, Poems, trans. P. G. Walsh, Ancient Christian Writers 40, New York 1975.

Literature

Andaloro/Romano 2002 Maria Andaloro und Serena Romano: L'immagine nell'abside, in: Arte e iconografia a Roma. Dal Tardoantico alla fine del Medioevo, ed. Maria Andaloro and Serena Romano, Mailand 2002, p. 73–102.

Angenendt 2002 Arnold Angenendt: Der Leib is klar, klar wie Kristal, in: Frömmigkeit im Mittelalter. Politisch-soziale Kontexte, visuelle Praxis, körperliche Ausdrucksformen, ed. Klaus Schreiner, München 2002, p. 287–399.

Arnulf 1997 Arwed Arnulf: Versus ad Picturas. Studien zur Titulusdichtung als Quellengattung der Kunstgeschichte von der Antike bis zum Hochmittelalter, München 1997.

Augustine 1988 Augustine, Tractates on the Gospel of John 11–27, trans. John W. Rettig (Fathers of the Church, 79), Washington D.C. 1988.

Brenk 2005 Beat Brenk: Visibility and (Partial) Invisibility of Early Christian Images, in: Seeing the Invisible in Late Antiquity and the Early Middle Ages, ed. Giselle de Nie, Karl F. Morrison and Marco Mostert, Turnhout 2005, p. 139–183.

Cardin 2008 Luca Cardin: Epigrafia a Roma nel Medioevo (secoli IV–X). Modelli grafici e tipologie d'uso, Rom 2008.

Cox Miller 2000 Patricia Cox Miller: 'The Little Blue Flower is Red': Relics and the Poetizing of the Body, in: Journal of Early Christian Studies 8, 2000, p. 213–236.

De Nie 1987 Giselle De Nie: Views from a Many-windowed Tower. Studies of imagination in the works of Gregory of Tours, Amsterdam 1987.

Diefenbach 2007 Steffen Diefenbach: Römische Erinnerungsräume. Heiligenmemoria und kollektive Identitäten im Rom des 3. bis 5. Jahrhunderts n. Chr., Berlin 2007.

Ferrua 1942 Epigrammata Damasiana. Recensuit et adnotavit Antonius Ferrua, Rom 1942.

Guyon 1995 Jean Guyon: Damase et l'illustration des martyrs. Les accents de la dévotion et l'enjeu d'une pastorale, in: Martyrium in Multidisciplinary Perspective, ed. Mathijs Lamberigts, Leuven 1995, p. 157–177.

Hahn 2012 Cynthia Hahn: Strange Beauty. Issues in the Making and Meaning of Reliquaries, 400–circa 1204, University Park, P.A. 2012.

Kessler 1985 Herbert L. Kessler: Pictorial Narrative and Church Mission in Sixth-Century Gaul, in: Pictorial Narrative in Antiquity and the Middle Ages, ed. Herbert L. Kessler and Marianna Shreve Simpson, Washington D.C. 1985, p. 75–91.

Kessler 1989 Herbert L. Kessler: L'antica basilica di San Pietro come fonte e ispirazione per la decorazione delle chiese medievali, in: Fragmenta Picta. Affreschi e mosaici staccati del Medioevo romano (Exhibition Rom, Museo Nazionale di Castel Sant'Angelo 15.12.1989–18.2.1990), ed. Maria Andaloro et al., Rom 1989, p. 45–111.

Krautheimer 1980 Richard Krautheimer: Rome: Profile of a City, 312–1308, Princeton 1980.

Löx 2013 Markus Löx: Monumenta sanctorum. Rom und Mailand als Zentren des frühen Christentums. Märtyrerkult und Kirchenbau unter den Bischöfen Damasus und Ambrosius, Wiesbaden 2013.

Paleani 1986 Maria Teresa Paleani: Probabili influssi dei carmi damasiani su alcune pitture cimiteriali a Roma, in: Saecularia Damasiana. Atti del Convegno internazionale per il XVI centenario della morte di papa Damaso I (11.12.384–10/12.12.1984), Vatikanstadt 1986, p. 259–281.

Poeschke 2010 Joachim Poeschke: Italian Mosaics 300–1300, trans. Russell Stockman, New York 2010.

Reekmans 1986 Louis Reekmans: L'œuvre du Pape Damase dans le complexe de Gaius a la Catacombe de S. Callixte, in: Saecularia Damasiana. Atti del Convegno internazionale per il XVI centenario della morte di papa Damaso I (11.12.384–10/12.12.1984), Vatikanstadt 1986, p. 259–281.

Reutter 2009 Ursula Reutter: Damasus, Bischof von Rom (366–384). Leben und Werk, Tübingen 2009.

Thunø 2015 Erik Thunø: The Early Medieval Apse Mosaic in Rome. Time, Network, and Repetition, New York 2015.

Trout 1999 Dennis Trout: Paulinus of Nola. Life, Letters, and Poems, Berkeley/Los Angeles 1999.

Trout 2015 Dennis Trout, ed.: Damasus, The Epigraphic Poetry. Introduction, Text, Translations, and Commentary, Oxford 2015.

White 2000 Carolinne White: Early Christian Latin Poets, London 2000.

Wisskirchen 1990 Rotraut Wisskirchen: Das Mosaikprogramm von S. Prassede in Rom. Ikonographie und Ikonologie, Münster 1990.

Inhalte und Intentionen bildlicher Kunst in Sakralräumen zwischen Damasus und Sixtus III. in Rom

Norbert Zimmermann

Einleitung

Im Folgenden sollen Inhalte und Aussageabsichten von Bildern in römischen Sakralräumen der Zeit von Damasus I. (366–384) bis Sixtus III. (432–440) betrachtet werden: ab Damasus, weil er der erste römische Bischof ist, von dem sich überhaupt Kulträume mit malerischer Ausstattung erhalten haben, nämlich in einigen seiner Anlagen zur Verehrung von Märtyrern in den Katakomben, und bis Sixtus III., da die Mosaikausstattung der unter ihm geweihten Kirche S. Maria Maggiore die ersten in Rom erhaltenen, großen Teile eines Bildprogramms sind, und zwar in Form von komplexen theologischen Bilderzyklen. In der Entwicklung der Bildkunst im genannten Zeitraum spiegelt sich viel von der gleichzeitigen Entwicklung der Kirche allgemein wie auch speziell vom Anspruch des römischen Bischofs und seines Primats vor allen übrigen Bischöfen des Reiches. Die Betrachtungen seien eingebettet in einen kurzen Rückblick auf die Entstehung der christlichen Kultarchitektur und Bildkunst, und es scheint mir besonders wichtig, auch deren Wurzeln in der Kunst der römischen Kaiserzeit noch einmal offenzulegen. Denn da fast ausschließlich spätere christliche Kultbauten die Zeit überdauert haben und zum Vergleich herangezogen werden können, ist es hilfreich, sich die Herkunft *von* und Konkurrenz *zu* solchen älteren Gebäuden abzuleiten, mit denen die christlichen damals in direkten visuellen Kontext traten.

1. Das Umfeld

An sich ist es ohnehin erstaunlich, dass ein orientalischer Erlösungskult, der eigentlich dem alttestamentlichen Bilderverbot verpflichtet ist, derart bildermächtige Kultlokale betreibt.[1] Aber durch die Missionstätigkeit und das Fußfassen in der gesamten griechisch-römischen Welt übernahmen Christen mit der Zeit auch die römische Bilderkultur. Man könnte es so formulieren: Noch bevor die große Masse der Römer im

1 Vgl. etwa Deckers 2007, S. 15–52.

4. und 5. Jahrhundert christianisiert wurde, hatten die Christen, speziell in Bezug auf ihr Verhältnis zu Bildern, im Verlauf des 3. Jahrhunderts längst begonnen, sich zu romanisieren. In allen Bereichen des öffentlichen und privaten Lebens spielten Bilder in der römischen Kultur eine tragende Rolle in der Kommunikation, und so erlagen die Christen in Rom gewissermaßen der Macht der Bilder und fingen trotz des expliziten Bilderverbotes an, sich durch Bilder auszudrücken.

Im 3. Jahrhundert waren es zunächst Privatleute, die ihre Gräber in den Katakomben mit einfachen Szenen des Alten und Neuen Testaments schmückten und so die Jenseitshoffnung ihrer Verstorbenen ausdrückten.[2] Bis ins frühe 4. Jahrhundert überwogen dabei relativ moderate Grabformen, und Gruppen ausgewählter Wunder- und Heilsszenen wurden additiv um die Gräber gelegt. Strukturierte Bildprogramme[3] bleiben in dieser privaten Sepulkralkunst die Ausnahme, aber es tauchen häufiger Anordnungen von Szenen nach alt- und neutestamentlichen Entsprechungen auf, bisweilen in chiastischer Stellung. Für eine kirchliche Kunst, also von Klerikern beauftragte Architektur oder Malerei, gibt es so früh keine archäologischen Spuren in Rom, abgesehen vielleicht von der ursprünglichen Kammer für Klerikerbestattungen in der Katakombe S. Callisto.[4]

Welche Formen liturgisch genutzte Räume vor Konstantins Sieg an der Milvischen Brücke hatten und wie ihre Bildausstattungen aussahen, wissen wir nicht, auch wenn das Bilderverbot der Synode von Elvira in Spanien im frühen 4. Jahrhundert zumindest deren Existenz möglich erscheinen lässt.[5]

2. Konstantins Stiftung der *Basilica Salvatoris* (heute S. Giovanni in Laterano)

Die Lage änderte sich schlagartig und grundsätzlich mit Konstantins Sieg im Zeichen Christi an der Milvischen Brücke von 312, der Erlaubnis zur Kultausübung für Chris-

2 Der mit figürlichen Bildern ausgemalte Kultraum in Dura-Europos ist in der lokalen Tradition, in der auch eine figürlich ausgemalte Synagoge Platz hat, verständlich, darf aber als Ausnahme gelten, zumindest solange sich keine weiteren Spuren bebilderter christlicher Kulträume finden. Eine Einführung in die Mechanismen der Bildentstehung zuletzt bei Bisconti 2009, als Überblick zur Entstehung und Entwicklung der Katakombenmalerei im 3. und 4. Jahrhundert auch Zimmermann 2015, mit weiterer Literatur.

3 Bildprogramm meint hier nicht nur eine allgemein inhaltlich abgestimmte Szenenauswahl, sondern eine so genau geordnete Szenenfolge, dass ein Vertauschen einzelner Bilder den Sinn des Ensembles verändert. Solche echten Bildprogramme sind aber sehr selten in den Katakomben.

4 Zuletzt konnte für die unter Damasus umgebaute sog. Papstgruft in S. Callisto eine Rekonstruktion des ursprünglichen Doppelcubiculums vorgestellt werden, das eine den sog. Sakramentskapellen ähnliche Ausstattung mit Malereien gehabt haben wird, vgl. Fiocchi Nicolai/Guyon 2006, S. 133–145 mit Abb. 14 und 15. Man darf annehmen, dass die Malereien dieser Kammer mit den Bestattungen der Bischöfe auch von diesen bzw. offiziellen Kirchenvertretern beauftragt waren.

5 De Blaauw 2010, S. 22–25.

ten mit der Mailänder Vereinbarung von 313 und der von Konstantin dem römischen Bischof geschenkten und spätestens 324 unter Silvester (314–335) geweihten Salvator-Kirche, heute S. Giovanni in Laterano.[6]

Von der Rolle des verfolgten Staatsfeindes stieg der römische Bischof in nicht einmal zehn Jahren auf zum Priester des neuen Schutzgottes des Kaisers. Es ist nicht bekannt, in welchem Ausmaß der Bischof auf die bauliche Ausführung der Salvator-Basilika Einfluss nahm und eventuell bereits für die christliche Liturgie erprobte Raumlösungen wiederholte, da wir wie gesagt keine vorkonstantinischen Kulträume kennen. Aber es liegt angesichts der Pracht und Ausmaße des fünfschiffigen Baus von 100 m Länge und 55 m Breite nahe, hier weniger ein Anliegen des beschenkten Bischofs verwirklicht zu sehen als vielmehr eines des schenkenden Kaisers. Formal bot die Basilika dem christlichen Kult eine zuvor nie dagewesene Bühne, die sich als so kultgerecht erwies, dass sie für Jahrhunderte zur Leitform christlicher Kirchen wurde. Vor allem entsprach sie aber auch der imperialen Selbstdarstellung Konstantins.[7] Am Ende sei auf diese oft bedachte Bauform der Basilika und ihre Abhängigkeit von römischen Marktbasiliken noch einmal zurückgekommen. Tatsache ist jedenfalls, dass die baulichen Motive der öffentlichen Basiliken wie die Mehrschiffigkeit bei erhöhtem Mittelschiff und die Säulengliederung nun durch ihre Längsausrichtung auf die Apsis in eine klare Kultrichtung gebracht und so zu einem Sakralraum mit eigener Identität gefügt werden. Über einen Widerstand Silvesters gegen die einvernehmende Schenkung des Kaisers, die noch kurz vorher undenkbar gewesen wäre, ist nichts bekannt.[8] Sicherlich ist aber die früher als ›nur‹ peripher bezeichnete Lage der Salvator-Kirche[9] am südwestlichen Stadtrand im Gegenteil eher als absolutes Privileg zu deuten. Denn die Basilika vollzog dort ja nicht nur topographisch-materiell die *damnatio memoriae* der *equites singulares,* deren Kasernen abgerissen und von der Kirche überbaut wurden, sondern sie nahm auch ideell ihren Platz ein: Sie belegte nicht einfach den Bauplatz, sondern ersetzte die persönliche Schutzgarde des Kaisers durch den Kultbau für den Christengott.[10] Und so darf man

6 Brandenburg 2013, S. 20–37; Guidobaldi 2016.

7 Zur Dynamik der Verwirklichung von Kirchenbauten zwischen kaiserlicher Administration und Bischöfen s. Liverani 2003, Guidobaldi 2016, S. 461–463.

8 Josef Engemann hat vor Kurzem noch einmal darauf hingewiesen, dass durch die Anerkennung des Christentums auch das Problem christlicher Soldaten gelöst war, die ja bislang durch den Konflikt mit dem Kaiseropfer zu Staatsfeinden wurden – Konstantin war Realpolitiker und wurde keineswegs Monotheist; vgl. Engemann 2011, S. 61.

9 Etwa Krautheimer 1987, S. 41–42; zur Diskussion zuletzt Guidobaldi 2013, bes. S. 459–460.

10 Ganz ähnlich ist das Vorgehen Konstantins beim Bau seines Mausoleums, in dem später seine Mutter Helena bestattet wurde: Die große Umgangsbasilika an der via Labicana zerstört den Soldatenfriedhof im Bereich der Kaiservilla und vollzieht mit den in ihren Fundamenten verbauten Grabstelen der *equites singulares* diese *damnatio memoriae*, während das angebaute kaiserliche Mausoleum zugleich den Schutz der hier

die Geste hoch symbolisch verstehen. Vielleicht geht die Symbolik sogar noch einen Schritt weiter, da der Bauplatz inmitten des Wohnareals und des Palastes von Konstantins eigener Familie lag – er band also den Kult seines neuen Schutzgottes, der ihm den Sieg geschenkt hat, sozusagen direkt an ›sein‹ Haus an.[11] Dies erinnert unmittelbar an die seinerzeit von Augustus inszenierte Verbindung seines Hauses auf dem Palatin mit dem Tempel Apolls.[12] Aus diesem Blickwinkel scheint es angebracht, die baupolitischen Entscheidungen sowie die Bau- und Schmuckformen, um die es im Folgenden gehen soll, insgesamt viel mehr aus der römisch-imperialen Tradition und den gleichzeitig noch stehenden Bauten, mit denen sie konkurrierten, zu betrachten denn aus der Sicht der Kirche, wie wir sie heute kennen.

Über die ursprüngliche Ausstattung der Salvator-Basilika mit Bildern wissen wir so gut wie nichts.[13] Es ist aber kaum wahrscheinlich, dass die erst für das 5. Jahrhundert sicher bezeugten Bilderzyklen, genauso wie jene von S. Pietro, bereits dem ursprünglichen Bau angehörten. Sie bezeugen einen Grad an Entwicklung, der sinnvoller in den Kontext des 5. Jahrhunderts einzubetten ist.[14]

Mit der Salvator-Basilika werden also die ›offizielle‹ Kirche und der Bischof von Rom archäologisch greifbar – zunächst als vom Kaiser Beschenkte, erst in der Folge auch selbst als Bauherr bzw. Auftraggeber. Der Beginn bischöflicher Patronanz über sakrale Bauprojekte und ihre Ausstattung ist daher untrennbar mit Konstantin verbunden, der Initiator und Stifter der Bauten ist: So ist es außer für den Lateran, S. Pietro und

---

unterirdisch bestatteten christlichen Märtyrer Marcellinus und Petrus sucht, vgl. zur Anlage Guyon 1987, S. 367–399.

11 Zum Problem der genauen Besitzverhältnisse von Grundstücken in dem Bereich, dessen Bezeichnung auf die Familie der Laterani zurückgeführt wurde, s. Liverani 2004. Für die hier vorgeschlagene symbolische Dimension des Baus sind die exakten Besitzverhältnisse im Bereich der Kirche und ihre Chronologie allerdings insofern irrelevant, als fast das gesamte Stadtviertel bis zum Sessorium in kaiserlicher Hand war, weswegen dort ja auch der Palast der Kaisermutter Helena entstand. Schon für die Wahl des Bauplatzes der *castra nova equitum singularium*, die unter Septimius Severus zwischen 193 und 196 errichtet wurden, war die Nähe zum severischen Palatium Sessorium zentral, vgl. Busch 2011, S. 75–80, bes. S. 79. Konstantin selbst hat nie länger in Rom gewohnt, er besuchte die Stadt nach dem Sieg 312 nur noch zur Decennalienfeier 315 und zur Vicennalienfeier 326.

12 Augustus hatte dem Apoll nach der Schlacht bei Actium aus Dankbarkeit für den Sieg einen Tempel gestiftet, und zwar neben seinem Wohnhaus auf dem Palatin, wie es der Gott durch Blitzschlag selbst angezeigt hatte, vgl. Sueton, Augustus 29, 2. Die Symbolik des Zusammenhanges von Kirche (Tempel) und Wohn/Palastbereich (Residenz) machten sich hier im Lateran die römischen Bischöfe zumindest seit dem Ende des 4. Jahrhunderts und bis ins Mittelalter hinein zunutze, vgl. Luchterhandt 2015.

13 Wenn das *fastigium* mit seinen silbernen Figuren von Christus zwischen Engeln bzw. den zwölf Aposteln tatsächlich zum ersten Bestand zählt, hat es jedenfalls, anders als die Basilika selbst, keine vergleichbare Nachfolge gehabt.

14 Für die Zusammenfassung der Diskussionen über die Bildausstattung vgl. mit weiterer Literatur Andaloro 2006, S. 306–346 (S. Maria Maggiore), S. 366–410 (S. Paolo), S. 411–418 (S. Pietro).

S. Paolo auch für vier der sechs suburbanen Umgangsbasiliken bezeugt.[15] Für alle diese frühen Bauten gilt ebenfalls, dass wir keine gesicherten Quellen zu einer ursprünglichen bildlichen Ausstattung haben, zum Teil wegen der schlechten Überlieferungslage, mehr noch aber wohl, weil es komplexe Bildprogramme in der Art, wie man sie etwas später antrifft, kaum schon gegeben haben kann, da auch die theologischen Diskurse, die sie reflektieren, erst im Verlauf des 4. bzw. 5. Jahrhunderts stattfanden.

3. Reflexe der Monumentalkunst in den Katakomben

Der Prozess der Entwicklung der christlichen Ikonographie in Kulträumen lässt sich in Rom wie gesagt für das 4. Jahrhundert aufgrund der nur wenigen erhaltenen Monumente nicht direkt nachvollziehen. Als erste Ausstattung einer monumentalen Anlage haben sich in S. Costanza, dem Mausoleum für Konstantins Tochter Konstantina (nach der Mitte des 4. Jahrhunderts), die Mosaiken der Ringtonne mit den beiden Konchen erhalten. Hier nehmen Petrus im Bild der *traditio clavis* sowie Petrus und Paulus zu Seiten Christi im Bild der *traditio legis* bereits eine Sonderstellung ein. Der Prozess, ihre Bedeutung als Apostelfürsten in eigenen Bildformeln herauszustellen, war also schon im Gange. Das ist bemerkenswert, da beide Aspekte, die Rolle Petri als Empfänger des Gesetzes / der Schlüssel wie auch die Rolle von Petrus und Paulus als der wichtigsten Apostel gleich im ersten erhaltenen Monument die Richtung vorgeben für ihre spätere, besondere römische Ausdeutung. Zugleich zeigte das verlorene Kuppelmosaik wohl kleine biblische Szenen, eingebettet in traditionelle Genreszenen.[16] Die erste figürliche Ausstattung einer Kirche in Rom ist im Apsisbild aus S. Pudenziana erst aus dem frühen 5. Jahrhundert erhalten, wenig später datiert das Mosaik der Eingangswand von S. Sabina, und das erste (fast) vollständige Programm bewahrte S. Maria Maggiore (dazu s. u.).

Es klafft also zwischen der Salvator-Kirche und S. Pudenziana eine große, fast hundertjährige Lücke im Bildbestand der Kirchen Roms, die man jedoch zum Teil füllen kann, indem man die Veränderungen der privaten Grabmalerei in den Katakomben in die Betrachtung einschließt. Im 3. Jahrhundert hatte sich dort wie angedeutet ein Repertoire alt- und neutestamentlicher Rettungsszenen etabliert, welches der Jenseitshoffnung der Verstorbenen Ausdruck gab. Zunächst charakterisieren diese Malerei innovative Ikonographien und ein Stadium des Experimentierens, da viele biblische Szenen erstmals

15 Vgl. Brandenburg 2013, S. 54–95; De Blaaw 2010. Nur jene zwischen via Appia und via Ardeatina hat Bischof Markus selbst gestiftet, vgl. Fiocchi Nicolai et al. 1995–1996, Brandenburg 2013, S. 93. Allgemein zu den Bautätigkeiten der Bischöfe im Westen zwischen dem 3. und 6. Jahrhundert Fiocchi Nicolai 2013.

16 Ausführlich zum Bau und allen Fragen seiner Ausstattung s. Rasch/Arbeiter 2007.

eine Bildform finden mussten.[17] Doch ab konstantinischer Zeit veränderten sich Räume und Bilder deutlich: Es ist ein klarer Trend zu monumentaleren Raumformen mit Arkosolen und größeren Bildfeldern auszumachen, in denen auch die Bildszenen wachsen. Zudem erfuhr die Ikonographie Christi in der zweiten Hälfte des 4. Jahrhunderts eine deutliche Imperialisierung, da er nun kaiserliche Attribute wie Nimbus, Gold- oder Purpurgewand, Thron und Suppedaneum erhielt. Auch häuften sich Bilder, die nicht biblischen Ursprungs sind, sondern auf theologischer Reflexion beruhen, etwa Christus zwischen Petrus und Paulus oder die Apostelversammlung. Offensichtlich reflektieren die Grabtypen und Malereien die ›oberirdische‹ Entwicklung, und die Vorlagen dürfen insbesondere in verlorenen Ausstattungen auch kirchlich beauftragter Monumental- bzw. Sakralkunst vermutet werden. Aus Platzmangel sei hier eine solche Entwicklung nur an einer einzigen Szene beispielhaft nachvollzogen:

Die Apostelversammlung zeigt ein Lehrgespräch Christi mit seinen Jüngern, das keine konkrete biblische Vorlage hat, sondern aus theologischer Reflexion der überzeitlichen Erwartung entstand. Im frühen 4. Jahrhundert, im Moment der Bildschöpfung, erkannte man noch den Ursprung aus dem Schema der halbkreisförmig sitzenden Sieben Weisen, und zwar im Mittelmedaillon der Decke des Cubiculum 58 der Katakombe SS. Marcellino e Pietro.[18] Etwas später erscheinen im Lunettenfeld eines niedrigen Arkosols der Domitilla-Katakombe bereits alle zwölf Apostel, die allerdings zunächst ohne physiognomische Differenzierung um Christus herum sitzen. Er sitzt im Typ des jugendlichen Philosophen auf einer Art Thron oder Kathedra und hält einen Rotulus oder einen geöffneten Codex.[19] Ab der Mitte des 4. Jahrhunderts wurde die Physiognomie von Petrus und Paulus ausgearbeitet, ab der zweiten Hälfte des 4. Jahrhunderts konnte die Stelle des jugendlich-langhaarigen Christus auch ein bärtiger im Typ eines Vatergottes, etwa Serapis, Aesculap oder Jupiter, einnehmen.[20] Nun traten zudem immer öfter imperiale Symbole wie ein (licht-)blauer oder (gold-)gelber Nimbus, das Suppedaneum oder ein Purpurgewand als Attribute Christi hinzu. Am Ende des 4. und im frühen 5. Jahrhundert gab es dann eine ganze Gruppe von Darstellungen Christi mit Aposteln, die ihren Ursprung in Apsidenbildern durch die selbst in unterirdischen Kammern spürbare Monumentalität nicht leugnen können (s. u. Abb. 5).[21] Zugleich änderte sich auch das Verhältnis von Bild und Grabraum, da die Malereien nun tendenziell nicht mehr um die Gräber gelegt wurden, sondern die Kammern nun mitunter Kult-

---

17 Zuletzt Bisconti 2009; Zimmermann 2015.

18 Deckers/Seeliger/Mietke 1987, S. 297–300.

19 Fasola 1989, S. 61 Abb. 21; Wilpert 1903, Taf. 148,2.

20 Das Paradebeispiel für den Pantokratortyp ist das Christusporträt in der Decke des sog. Cubiculum Leonis in Commodilla, vgl. Anm. 41.

21 Etwa das Cubiculum der *mensores* (Domitilla 74), vgl. Anm. 52.

räume mit Apsiden und Bilderfriesen an den Längswänden nachahmten, in die zudem Gräber eingefügt sind. Dafür sind die kapellenartigen Räume wie Kammer 33 in Domitilla mit ›Apsisbild‹ und Bilderfriesen an den Seitenwänden[22] oder das ›Apsisgemälde‹ im Gewölbe der Kammer 3 in SS. Marcellino e Pietro mit dem thronenden Christus zwischen Petrus und Paulus und den Märtyrern der Katakombe beste Beispiele.[23]

Alle die gerade genannten Malereien sind jedoch Teil von privaten Grabausstattungen, die, selbst wenn ihre Datierung nicht ganz exakt festzulegen ist, zumindest als Reflexe einige wichtige Entwicklungsschritte der verlorenen Monumentalkunst nachvollziehen lassen.[24]

4. Damasus und die Ausgestaltung der Märtyrergräber

Eine weitere neue Phase begann, für die Kirchengeschichte wie auch für die archäologischen Evidenzen, mit Damasus, von 366–384 Bischof von Rom.[25] Seine Amtszeit war einerseits von der heftigen Auseinandersetzung mit dem Gegenbischof Ursinus überschattet, die z. T. sogar blutig geführt wurde mit über 130 Toten in der Basilica Liberiana.[26] Andererseits verfolgte Damasus, vielleicht auch um dieser sehr unerfreulichen Situation entgegenzuwirken, eine bis dahin nicht gekannte Agenda eines religiöspastoralen Bauprogrammes für Rom und die römische Kirche, indem er die Märtyrer der Verfolgung und weitere vorbildliche Christen in den Mittelpunkt der kultischen Verehrung rückte.[27] Dies geschah in einem bewussten Rückgriff auf die Heroenverehrung mythischer oder in der Schlacht gefallener Kriegshelden, und auch in der Sprache seiner Lobgedichte für die Märtyrer lehnte sich Damasus immer wieder an Vergil und damit an Roms große Tradition an.[28]

Höchstes Interesse verdienen die Ausbaumaßnahmen und Ausstattungen der Märtyrergräber in den Katakomben für Kulthandlungen und Pilgerbesuch. Ein gut erforschtes, zentrales Element der Verehrung sind Damasus' Epigramme, die er selbst zu Ehren der Märtyrer dichtete und von Filocalus in einem eigens geschaffenen Schrifttyp auf große Marmorplatten schreiben und an den Kultstätten anbringen ließ. Von rund

22 Zimmermann 2002, S. 242–246.

23 Deckers/Seeliger/Mietke 1987, S. 199–201.

24 Vergleichbare Entwicklungsstufen kann man auch anhand der Sarkophagkunst nachvollziehen, in den ihr eigenen Gesetzmäßigkeiten; mehr dazu demnächst in einer Studie, die gemeinsam mit M. Studer-Karlen in Vorbereitung ist.

25 Reutter 2009; Carletti 2000.

26 Reutter 2009, S. 31–56.

27 Zusammenfassend zu Damasus' Bautätigkeit zuletzt Löx 2013, S. 43–88.

28 Vgl. etwa Reutter 2009, S. 137–153.

Abb. 1: Damasianische Ausstattungen römischer Märtyrergräber: 1) Sixtus II (Callisto); 2) Felix und Adauctus (Commodilla); 3) Nereus und Achilleus (Domitilla); 4) Januarius (Pretestato); 5) Urbanus?; 6) Marcellinus und Petrus (nach Spera 2012).

59 überlieferten Epigrammen sind 20 der Erinnerung und Verehrung römischer Märtyrer gewidmet, und zwar zumeist einzelnen oder Paaren von Männern, nur einmal auch einer Märtyrerin, nämlich S. Agnese.[29] Die Märtyrerepigramme waren in der Regel direkt an den Gräbern in den Katakomben angebracht, wie man aus etwa zehn archäologisch zumindest in Ansätzen bekannten Anlagen erschlossen hat.[30]

Schon lange ist ein regelmäßiges Schema von Damasus' Ausbauten erkannt, das der jeweils konkreten Situation des Märtyrergrabes in den Katakomben angepasst wurde (Abb. 1).[31] Die damasianischen Anlagen boten einen ausreichend breiten Zugang, der

29 Ferrua 1942; Reutter 2009, S. 57–98, 111–130.

30 Vgl. die kritische Gesamtschau bei Löx 2013, S. 72–88.

31 Fiocchi Nicolai 2001, S. 79–92; Fiocchi Nicolai 2008; Spera 1998, S. 44; Spera 2012, S. 38.

Pilger über ggf. neue Treppenanlagen möglichst nah zum verehrten Grab herabführte. Die Grabstätte selbst bewahrte man wohl *in situ*, doch der Raum um sie herum wurde moderat erweitert, die Grabstelle durch Einfassungen mit Marmor monumentalisiert, durch *opus sectile*-Verkleidung und Transennen dekoriert sowie durch Mensen für kultische Belange hergerichtet.[32] Unmittelbar beim Grab wurde die Marmorplatte mit dem Epigramm angebracht. Durch neue Lucernare waren Pilgerweg und Sanktuar direkt beleuchtet.[33] Ein eigener Ausgang ließ einen geregelten Pilgerstrom zu, als Vorform der späteren Ringkrypten.

Nach diesem Muster schuf Damasus vor den Mauern Roms ein Netz von kleinen Sanktuaren, die Pilgern in einer Art Ringverkehr in kleinen Gruppen von kaum mehr als etwa zehn Personen die Märtyrergräber als Kultplätze erschlossen. Der Erfolg war offensichtlich so groß, dass die Sanktuare schon bald zu klein für den Pilgerstrom wurden.[34] Zudem führte der Wunsch nach Eucharistiefeiern direkt auf dem Grab bald zu oft massiven Erweiterungen, die in der Regel die Sanktuare nach Damasus stark überformten, bisweilen zu regelrechten Basiliken *ad corpus*.[35] Dennoch ließ sich eine Reihe von damasianischen Anlagen rekonstruieren, und in zumindest zwei Fällen haben sich auch Reste der Malerei dieser Sanktuare erhalten. Um diese soll es im Folgenden gehen:

4a. S. Felix und Adauctus in der Commodilla-Katakombe

Bereits länger bekannt ist das damasianische Sanktuar für Felix und Adauctus in der Commodilla-Katakombe, das A. Weiland rekonstruiert hat.[36] In der später stark veränderten sogenannten Basilichetta ließen sich Architektur und Ausstattung der Märtyrergräber für diese Phase wie folgt ermitteln:[37] Die Märtyrer waren wohl in zwei übereinanderliegenden Loculi in einer Nische an der Rückwand eines breiten Ganges bestattet.[38] Putzabdrücke und Marmorelemente zeigen, dass Damasus den länglichen Zugangsraum zu den Gräbern durch eine halbrund geöffnete Transenne auf Pilastern inszenierte, die den Blick freigab auf die Gräber unten und eine Malerei im Bogenfeld darüber (Abb. 2). Hier erschien ein rot gerahmtes Bild mit den zwei Märtyrern auf

32 Ein Altar gehörte hingegen noch nicht regelmäßig zu den damasianischen Anlagen.

33 Fiocchi Nicolai 1995.

34 Berühmt ist etwa die Schilderung des spanischen Dichters Prudentius von seiner Teilnahme an einer Prozession und einem Besuch am Grab des Märtyrers Hippolytus im frühen 5. Jahrhundert zusammen mit einer großen Anzahl von Pilgern, Prud. Perst. 11 (= CSEL 61, 417–418), vgl. Bauer 2004, S. 149–154.

35 Daher sind auch nur selten die damasianischen Anlagen erhalten, abgesehen von den Zerstörungen im Mittelalter nach der Translation der Reliquien in die Stadtkirchen.

36 Weiland 1994; vgl. die ausführliche Beschreibung mit Literatur bei Deckers/Mietke/Weiland 1994, S. 75–80.

37 Zuletzt zur topographisch-chronologischen Entwicklung Carletti 1994.

38 Vgl. Carletti 1994, S. 6–7: der breite Gang (»galleria B«) war ursprünglich ein Arenar.

blauem Malgrund zu Seiten einer großen *capsa* mit *rotuli*. Beide erheben ihre rechte Hand, um einem Christogramm zwischen sich zu huldigen. Wohl über der Malerei war die Filocalus-Inschrift angebracht, und Gräber, Malerei und Inschrift waren durch den Lichtschacht darüber direkt beleuchtet. Ferner war die Öffnung zu einem Gang auf der linken Seite bemalt, u.a. mit einer auffälligen Lisene mit einem Lorbeerblattstab, ein Motiv, auf das gleich zurückzukommen sein wird.[39]

Während wie gesagt die Bedeutung der damasianischen Epigramme oft gewürdigt wurde,[40] ist die Wirkung der Malerei bislang kaum bedacht worden. Dabei dürften etliche Pilger des Lesens nicht mächtig gewesen sein, und die sechs bis zehn Zeilen langen Gedichte werden ohne eine Abschrift auch kaum in Erinnerung geblieben sein. Die Bildbotschaft aber war sofort verständlich und sehr einprägsam. Bild und Text sollen zwar hier nicht gegeneinander ausgespielt werden, sie ergänzen sich ja sinnvoll. Jedoch kann die Breitenwirkung, die das Bildmotiv der Verehrung des Christogramms durch Märtyrer und ähnliche Bilder, die andere damasianische Sanktuare gehabt haben dürften (s. u.), kaum überschätzt werden. In der Tat wurde das Bild schon kurze Zeit später im berühmten *Cubiculum Leonis*, dem Grab eines Offizialen der Annona namens Leo unweit der Heiligenbestattung ebenfalls in der Commodilla-Katakombe, um 374 gleich zweimal wiederholt: einmal im Hauptbild, das Felix und Adauctus in gleicher Pose zu Seiten Christi *in persona* zeigt, und dann über einer Kultnische der linken Wand der Kammer, wo eine exakte Kopie der Verehrung des Christogramms durch beide als kleine Bildvignette eingefügt ist.[41]

4b. S. Nereus und Achilleus in der Domitilla-Katakombe

Nicht weniger interessant ist das Sanktuar, das Damasus mit aller Wahrscheinlichkeit in der Domitilla-Katakombe zur Verehrung von Nereus und Achilleus, zwei Märtyrern der diokletianischen Verfolgung, ausbauen ließ.[42] Zwar hat die spätere Basilika *ad corpus* den eigentlichen Kultraum weitgehend zerstört, doch können eine monumentale neue Treppe, die Erweiterung des älteren Zugangs, die Vergrößerung der Grabkammer

39 Deckers/Mietke/Weiland 1994, S. 69. Der Zugang zu diesem Sanktuar ist nicht sicher zu klären, der Rest eines Treppenabgangs im Bereich des Lichtschachtes könnte aber auf Damasus zurückgehen. Der heute durch die Anlage der Basilichetta zerstörte Treppenabgang führte von Norden wohl zu einer Galerie herab, die dann von Süden zum Sanktuar führte, an dessen Rückwand die Gräber von Felix und Adauctus lagen. Die breite Treppenanlage E gehört erst zur Anlage der Basilichetta, die das damasianische Sanktuar weitgehend überformt, vgl. Carletti 1994, S. 21.

40 Beginnend mit Ferrua 1942; zusammenfassend Carletti 2000; Reutter 2009, S. 57–98.

41 Deckers/Mietke/Weiland 1994, S. 89–104.

42 Seine Reste konnten im Rahmen der Vorbereitung des Repertoriums der Malereien der Domitilla-Katakomben analysiert werden, vgl. für die detaillierte Analyse Zimmermann 2012.

Abb. 2: Rekonstruktion des damasianischen Sanktuars für Felix und Adauctus in der Commodilla-Katakombe (nach A. Weiland 1994).

auf doppelte Länge, ihre Öffnung durch einen Lichtschacht und schließlich ein neuer Ausgang für den Pilgerstrom, der eine Art Ringverkehr ermöglichte, nachgewiesen werden. Trotz der späteren Zerstörungen an der Apsis der Basilika sind ausreichend Malereireste erhalten, die erstmals auch ein Leitsystem in Malerei nachvollziehen lassen. Das gesamte Tonnengewölbe des neuen Treppenabgangs war mit einem paradiesischen Streublütendekor mit Pfauen und Früchten bemalt, an den Wänden begleiteten Tierfriese den Treppenlauf. Die Treppe führte direkt auf ein Lunettenfeld zu, unter dem man den Durchgang zum Sanktuar betrat. Diese Lunette war durch eine heute schlecht erhaltene Malerei ausgezeichnet, die aber rekonstruiert werden kann. Hier standen, flankiert von Grableuchtern, zwei Personen in Orantengestus, zwischen denen wohl ein Kreuz oder ein Christogramm in einem Kranz erschien (Abb. 3).[43] Der Kontext macht es sehr wahrscheinlich, dass es sich um ein Bild der Titelheiligen Nereus und Achilleus handelt, das wie ein Titulus über dem Eingang angebracht war. Zudem ist im Scheitel des Durchgangs zum Sanktuar ein Staurogramm mit Alpha und Omega erhalten, wodurch die Bewegungsrichtung der Pilger deutlich ist. Diese traten demnach seitlich in den länglichen Kultraum, um ihn anschließend durch die Öffnung in der Rückwand wieder zu verlassen. Schließlich sei der Rest eines Lorbeerblattstabs in der Wandung des Durchgangs erwähnt, weil er seine Entsprechung am Grab der Heiligen Felix und Adauctus hat (s.o.) und so, trotz nur weniger Malreste, eine Verwandtschaft auch im gemalten Dekor besteht. Vom eigentlichen Sanktuar mit den Gräbern der Heiligen, einem wohl längsrechteckigen, tonnenüberwölbten Raum, hat sich leider nur ein Raumeck in der späteren Apsiswand mit Spuren weißer Malerei und einem roten Rahmen erhalten. Die Raumbreite entsprach genau der Breite der Damasus-Inschrift, weshalb diese gut an der Rückwand angebracht gewesen sein könnte, also hinter den Bodengräbern, in denen vermutlich die Märtyrer bestattet waren.[44]

In den Dimensionen, mit dem Lichtschacht und der Position der Inschrift gleicht der Raum auffallend der Anlage der Papstgruft in S. Callisto[45], in deren Eingangsbogen ebenfalls ein – oft übersehenes – Christogramm gemalt ist.[46] Generell fällt auf, dass auch die Disposition der Papstgruft mit zwei Säulen an den Längswänden und die etwas spätere Erweiterung zu einem größeren Raum (heute S. Cecilia genannt), vielleicht als

43 Während die beiden Oranten und zumindest einer der Leuchter in Resten recht gut erkennbar sind, können die Farbspuren in der Mitte nur hypothetisch als Kranz mit Kreuz oder Christogramm ergänzt werden. Eine Restaurierung dieser wichtigen Malereien wäre wünschenswert. Für die Ausführung der Rekonstruktionszeichnung danke ich M. Limoncelli.

44 Vgl. im Detail Zimmermann 2012, S. 192–204.

45 Vgl. Fiocchi Nicolai/Guyon 2006, S. 133–145.

46 Vgl. Styger 1935, Farbtaf. I.

Abb. 3: Rekonstruktion des Zugangs zum Sanktuar der Hl. Nereus und Achilleus in der Domitilla-Katakombe (Zimmermann, Limoncelli, DAI Rom).

Feierraum für die Eucharistie, die Sanktuare in Domitilla und Callisto eng miteinander verbinden.[47]

Alle übrigen damasianischen Anlagen zur Märtyrerverehrung sind heute zu stark zerstört, in der Regel bereits durch Umbauten für größere Kultplätze oder sonst später durch die Translation der Reliquien oder den daraus resultierenden Verfall, sodass keine Reste von Malerei erhalten sind.[48] Umso wichtiger ist daher der Befund in den Katakomben Commodilla und Domitilla (und rudimentär in Callisto): Neben den Inschriften gehörten auch Malereien zur Ausstattung eines solchen Kultraumes, die einerseits die Besucher bildlich leiteten, andererseits durch die Darstellung der Märtyrer in der Verehrung Christi bzw. seines Zeichens einen starken visuellen Impuls für die

47 Vgl. den trapezförmigen Raum, der später in die Basilika der Heiligen Nereus und Achilleus integriert wurde, Krautheimer 1971, S. 131–133, und Reste von heute noch zwei Säulen, bei denen sich auf einer die Darstellung des Martyriums des Achilleus erhalten hat. R. Kanzler hatte einen Altar mit Ziborium rekonstruiert, für den im damasianischen Sanktuar aber nie Platz gewesen sein kann.

48 Es mag hier genügen, an die Märtyrergräber in S. Agnese, S. Lorenzo und SS. Marcellino e Pietri zu erinnern, deren damasianische Phase durch die Anlage von Basiliken oder Kapellen *ad corpus* vollständig ausradiert wurde.

Verbreitung der damasianischen Märtyrertheologie bildeten.[49] Erstmals können wir einen römischen Bischof als Schöpfer und Verbreiter kultischer Bilder fassen, und die folgende Allpräsenz der propagierten Märtyrer-Ikonographie belegt den Erfolg der damasianischen Maßnahme.

Damasus veränderte mit seinen Märtyreranlagen aktiv ihre Wahrnehmung und Kultpräsenz, durch die Architektur und die Inschriften, aber auch visuell durch Bilder, was bislang kaum wahrgenommen wurde. Er schuf eine neue Kultrealität: Generell wurde der Märtyrerkult mit den Märtyrern als Patronen propagiert, besonders für die Apostelfürsten Petrus und Paulus, zudem in der Papstgruft aber auch für die römischen Bischöfe als Nachfolger Petri. Diese Inszenierung von Petrus und Paulus als Apostelfürsten und Patrone Roms und der römischen Kirche hatte auch im wörtlichen Sinne unmittelbar sichtbare Folgen.

Die Märtyrerverehrung und die Verehrung von Petrus und Paulus auf die Initiative von Damasus hin bilden das Rückgrat für alle kommenden Entwicklungen: Die Sonderstellung Roms als Stadt der Märtyrer und Apostelfürsten ist klar akzentuiert, die Stadt ist eingekreist von einem Ring geschickt beworbener Sanktuare und Pilgerstätten, in denen nicht zuletzt der Bischof selbst prominent präsent ist.

5. Die Ausbildung von Bildern in römischen Apsiden (bzw. ihre Spuren)[50]

Da, wie bereits mehrfach festgestellt, aus dem 4. Jahrhundert keine oberirdischen Monumente erhalten sind, sollen nochmals die Katakomben helfen, die Entwicklung nachzuvollziehen, die für Apsidenbilder von Kulträumen erfasst werden kann. Den Einfluss damasianischer Märtyrerverehrung spiegelt etwa die Hauptwand eines Cubiculums in der Katakombe SS. Gordiano ed Epimaco: Hier thront Christus zwischen Petrus und Paulus im mittleren Bildfeld, während in zwei flankierenden Bildfeldern Gordianus und Epimacus den drei mittleren Figuren mit Kränzen huldigen.[51] Auf das monumentale, kultraumartige Cubiculum 33 in der Domitilla-Katakombe mit einer Apostelversammlung im apsidenartigen Hauptbild und dem pantokratorartigen Christus im Deckengewölbe ist bereits hingewiesen worden.[52] Auch ein Cubiculum der Thekla-Katakombe mit einer großen Apostelversammlung im Bildfeld über dem Eingang zählt zu dieser Gruppe.[53]

49 Dies ist ausdrücklich gegen Filacchione 2007 festzuhalten.

50 Allg. immer noch Ihm 1960, zuletzt Brenk 2010.

51 Zimmermann 2002, S. 246–249, mit weiter Literatur.

52 Zimmermann 2002, S. 129–134.

53 Zuletzt Mazzei 2010; vgl. Zimmermann 2002, S. 251.

Abb. 4: Domitilla-Katakombe, Kammer der *mensores* (Nr. 74): rechte Konche mit Apostelversammlung, Lithographie für G. B. De Rossi.

Ein weiteres Beispiel aus den Katakomben mag die Dynamik belegen: In der spektakulären Kammer 74, der sogenannten Kammer der *mensores*, erscheinen in der rechten von zwei regelrechten Apsiden Petrus und Paulus in der Apostelversammlung (Abb. 4) als einzige sitzend, und zwar auf einer *sella curulis.*[54] Um dieses Bild zu verstehen, muss man sich vor Augen halten, dass es genau dem Anblick entsprach, der sich bei Senatssitzungen in der Curia auf dem Forum bot, wo der Kaiser erhöht zwischen den beiden Konsuln auf ihrer jeweiligen *sella curulis* thronte – Petrus und Paulus sind hier klar als die Konsuln Christi inszeniert.[55] Deutlicher kann man die Ideen römisch-imperialer Machtstrukturen kaum auf Christus und Petrus und Paulus übertragen, ein solches Bild musste man in Rom auch nicht erklären. Es scheint wenig wahrscheinlich, dass eine solch komplexe Bildidee hier unterirdisch im Kontext einer Katakombe entstand. Eher ist zu vermuten, dass sie vom Apsisbild einer vielleicht nahe gelegenen Basilika angeregt wurde, es böte sich etwa des Themas wegen die Basilica Apostolorum von S. Sebastiano an, wo Petrus und Paulus ja besondere Verehrung genossen.[56]

54 Zimmermann 2002, S. 133.

55 Freyberger 2016. Ich danke Stefan Freyberger für die Diskussion.

56 Nieddu 2009, S. 7–13.

Auch ohne den oberirdischen Erhalt auch nur einer einzigen Ausstattung eines Kultraumes ist es möglich, eine Vorstellung von der Entwicklung zu bekommen.

Die früheste Apsis einer Kirche hat sich in Rom in S. Pudentiana erhalten, wobei die Kirche selbst bereits unter Damasus in ein älteres Gebäude eingebaut und mit Stiftungen von Privatleuten und Klerikern verschönert worden war, bis unter Innozenz (401–417) das Apsismosaik gestiftet wurde.[57] Deutlich mischen sich imperiale Motive und theologische Aussagen, Christus erscheint in Gold und Purpur, lehrend auf dem Thron, unterhalb des Gemmenkreuzes, das zugleich Triumph über den Tod und Zeichen der Wiederkehr ist, und umgeben von den vier apokalyptischen Wesen. Die Apostelversammlung um ihn herum, vor der Stadtkulisse des himmlischen Jerusalem, führt die Sonderstellung von Petrus rechts und Paulus links nochmals weiter, da sie hier bekränzt werden von den Personifikationen der beiden Kirchen *ex circumcisione* und *ex gentibus*. Die Versöhnung zwischen den Christen aus dem Judentum und denen aus den übrigen Völkern in der Paarung der römischen Apostelfürsten Petrus und Paulus, beide zugleich römische Märtyrer, unterstreicht noch einmal mehr die Sonderstellung Roms. Diese Versöhnung beider Teile der Kirche ist auch im Mosaik der Eingangswand von S. Sabina in Wort (der monumentalen Inschrift) und Bild (in Gestalt der Personifikationen der beiden Kirchen *ex circumcisione* und *ex gentibus*) aufgegriffen: Das Anliegen ist damit als weitere wichtige Botschaft der römischen Bischöfe im frühen 5. Jahrhundert bestätigt.[58]

6. S. Maria Maggiore als Höhepunkt eines programmatischen Bildgefüges

S. Maria Maggiore auf dem Esquilin ist die erste von einem Bischof gestiftete Kirche Roms, deren Bildausstattung umfassend erhalten ist. Ihre Mosaiken markieren zugleich einen Höhepunkt und einen Paradefall der theologischen Verdichtung von Bilderfolgen zu einem echten Bildprogramm.

Die dreischiffige Basilika von 79 m Länge, 35 m Breite und im Hauptschiff 18 m Höhe wurde unter Sixtus III. wohl 434 geweiht, der Bau geht also großenteils bereits auf Coelestin I. (422–432) zurück.[59] Der in weiten Teilen erhaltene Mosaikschmuck

57 Andaloro 2006, S. 292–297, mit ausführlicher Literatur; vgl. Brandenburg 2013, S. 145–151. Das Thema der ersten Apsidenbilder in Rom kann hier aus Raumgründen nicht weiterverfolgt werden, aus den archäologischen Quellen scheint aber evident, dass Apsidenbilder, zunächst insbesondere mit Christus zwischen Petrus und Paulus bzw. in der Apostelversammlung, ab der zweiten Hälfte des 4. Jahrhunderts auftauchen. Vgl. zum Thema allg. Ihm 1960, Brenk 2010.

58 Zusammenfassend Andaloro 2006, S. 114–124; Brandenburg 2013, S. 145–151, mit ausführlicher Literatur.

59 Brandenburg 2013, S. 195–208.

spiegelt erstmals direkt Anspruch und Selbstverständnis des römischen Bischofs, wie es die Stifterinschrift »XYSTUS EPISCOPUS PLEBI DEI« über der Apsisstirn verkündet (vgl. Thunø Abb. 8). Während die nicht erhaltene Apsis und die Inschrift der Eingangswand Maria als *Theotokos,* Gottesgebärerin, feierten und damit wohl das marianische Konzil in Ephesos 431 reflektieren, überlagern sich vielfältige Bedeutungsschichten in dem Mosaikschmuck, der sich im Hauptschiff in Bilderfriesen unterhalb der Fenster bis zur Apsis und auf ihrer ursprünglichen Stirnwand erstreckt. Aus den zahlreichen Forschungen zu Inhalt, Form und Verteilung[60] können hier aus Platzgründen nur die wichtigsten Ergebnisse angeführt werden: An Süd- und Nordwand des Hauptschiffes sowie der Apsisstirnwand sind Felder mit den Szenen der biblischen Heilsgeschichte verteilt, wobei 27 der ursprünglich 42 Felder erhalten sind. Im Langhaus ist das Alte Testament angebracht, wobei die linke (Nord-)Seite die Ereignisse um Abraham, Isaak und Jakob behandelt, die heilsgeschichtlich die Zeit *ante legem* bilden, die rechte Seite mit den Geschichten von Mose und Josua den Zeitraum *sub lege* und die Apsisstirnwand in vier Registern die Kindheitsgeschichte Jesu und damit die Zeit *sub gratia* des Neuen Testaments zum Thema haben. Im Zenit des Bogens, über der Stifterinschrift, erscheint das Bild der Hetoimasie, des für den *secundus adventus Christi* bereiteten Throns. Die in der Kirche versammelte Gemeinde – die in der Stifterinschrift genannte *plebs dei* – wird im Raum umfangen von Bildern, die in den wichtigsten Stationen die biblische Heilsgeschichte vom Alten (Langhaus) über das Neue Testament (Apsiswand) bis zur überzeitlichen bzw. zukünftigen Erwartung der Wiederkehr Christi in der Hetoimasie (Bogenscheitel) vorführen, als großartige bildsymbolische und zugleich performative Verortung der Gemeinde im Kultraum wie im christlichen Kosmos.

Generell ist die Szenenverteilung damit an sich bereits theologisch klar durchdacht, sie wird aber zusätzlich durch eine große Fülle von weiteren künstlerischen Maßnahmen wie die Anordnungen der Szenen und Figuren in den Feldern, den Stil ihrer Darstellung und durch zahllose ikonographische Details weiter aufgeladen und um programmatische Aussagen erweitert. Für diese intensive inhaltliche Gestaltung seien hier nur zwei berühmte Beispiele referiert: So sind etwa zwei Bilder im Langhauszyklus aus ihrer chronologischen Ordnung herausgelöst, nämlich die Begegnung Abrahams mit Melchisedek, der Brot und Wein bringt, und Abraham in Mamre. In beiden Fällen wird durch ihre räumliche Nähe zum Altar und die Anreicherung mit weiteren Bilddetails eine typologische Verbindung zum Vollzug des eucharistischen Mahls erzeugt.[61] Die

60 S. zu den Mosaikzyklen insbesondere Brenk 1975 und Deckers 1976, sowie, die Forschung zusammenfassend, Andaloro 2006, S. 306–346.

61 Schrenk 1995, S. 53–58.

Realität des aktuellen eucharistischen Geschehens wird durch die typologische Verankerung in der biblischen Geschichte heilsgeschichtlich weiter verdichtet.

Eine solche Verknüpfung mit der Jetztzeit kann auch im Bild selbst geschehen, wie das zweite Beispiel vorführen mag: Im rechten oberen Bildfeld der Apsisstirn spielt sich die Szene von Jesus im Tempel vor einem Tempelbau ab, dessen Giebelschmuck ihn deutlich als Roma-Tempel ausweist. Unabhängig davon, wie man die Personengruppe vor dem Tempel deutet, ist ganz klar, dass Rom und seine alten Götter sich im Bild des Roma-Tempels hier der Verehrung des neuen Messias anschließen.[62]

Ohne diese intensive Gestaltung von Aussagen durch Bilddetails weiter vertiefen zu können, ist offensichtlich, dass der Bildausstattung in S. Maria Maggiore inhaltlich tiefe theologische Reflexion und Konzeption zur Schaffung eines originär-christlichen, hoch komplexen Bildprogramms zu Grunde liegen.[63]

Für die Beurteilung der formalen Aspekte scheint oft jedoch in gewisser Weise viel zu kompliziert und vor allem zu exklusiv (im Sinne einer christlichen Interpretation) gedacht worden zu sein. Schon oft hat man auf einen Wechsel in der Darstellungsweise der Mosaikfriese von Langhaus und Apsisstirnwand hingewiesen, denn während im Langhaus die Bilder figurenreich und oft in zwei Registern die Geschichten bildlich erzählen, sind die Mosaike der Apsisstirn durch statischere Einzelbilder gekennzeichnet.[64] Man muss nicht lange nach Vergleichsbeispielen suchen – ein solcher Wechsel der Darstellungsweisen ist etwa auch in den umlaufenden Friesen am Konstantinsbogen bewusst eingesetzt, bei denen bewegte und statische Szenen je nach Inhalt und Binnentopographie angeordnet sind.[65] Die Triumphmonumente sind für noch weitere formale Vergleiche sehr ergiebig, zu Recht ist etwa der Septimius-Severus-Bogen im horizontalen Aufbau seiner vier Bildregister mit dem viergliedrigen Apsisbogen in S. Maria Maggiore verglichen worden.[66]

Die Grundlage der Darstellung ist also zweifelsohne die Verarbeitung historischer Themen in der römischen Kunst, und speziell in der Triumphalkunst, wie am besten

---

62 Andaloro 2006, S. 335 ff., mit ausführlicher Literatur zur Deutung der Szene.

63 Vgl. zuletzt etwa Steigerwald 2016.

64 Zuletzt hat G. Steigerwald dem Phänomen, bei dem er einen ›monumentalen‹ und ›erzählenden Stil‹ unterscheidet, ein ausführliches Kapitel gewidmet, vgl. zusammenfassend Steigerwald 2016, S. 206–215; Andaloro 2006, S. 306–309, mit der älteren Literatur.

65 Vgl. Engemann 1997, S. 45–49. Während die von der Stadt weg weisenden Seiten des Bogens einmalige historische Ereignisse wie die Belagerung von Verona oder die Schlacht an der Milvischen Brücke in Bewegung von links nach rechts im Friesband zeigen, erscheinen dem Forum zugewandt die wohl öfters in der Realität auf dem Forum stattfindenden Ereignisse der *adlocutio* des Kaisers und der *largitio* in statischen, frontalen Bildfeldern.

66 Grabar 1968, S. 48–53.

Abb. 5: Angriff der Amoriter auf Gibeon (Jos 10,10) und deren Vernichtung (Jos 10,11).

die Trajanssäule zeigen mag.[67] Auf ihr wird nämlich durch die Darstellung des Kriegs- und Siegesberichts von Trajans Dakerkriegen (101–102 und 105–106) in einem einzigen durchgehenden Friesband im sogenannten kontinuierenden Stil[68] die Kriegsgeschichte zur sichtbaren Geschichte und damit zur historischen Wahrheit erhoben, ein Verfah-

67 Vgl. Hölscher (im Druck) und die übrigen Beiträge dieses Tagungsbandes.

68 Zum Begriff des kontinuierenden Stils, bei dem die Einheit von Raum und Zeit in einheitlicher Fläche durch das mehrfache Auftreten gleicher Protagonisten aufgehoben wird, um comicartig mehrere Stationen einer Geschichte zu erzählen, s. Wickhoff 1895, S. 7; Zimmermann 2004, S. 208.

ren, das man am besten vielleicht mit dem Begriff des ›Chronikstils‹ benennen kann.[69] Das meint einen Stil, der durch seine erzählende Darstellungsweise eine erzählte Geschichte zur Historie – im Sinne einer Chronik – überhöht. Im Falle der Trajanssäule wird etwa die Geschichte von Trajans Kriegen und Siegen zur Geschichte Roms und seiner Sieghaftigkeit generell, Trajans Triumph ist Roms Triumph. Ganz analog dazu ist die biblische Geschichte bis zur erhofften Wiederkehr Christi in S. Maria Maggiore behandelt.[70] Dieses Verfahren hat sehr alte Wurzeln, in Rom erscheint es ähnlich bereits z. B. im Statilier-Grab aus augusteischer Zeit, wo die mythologische Geschichte von Romulus und Remus als Chronik der Stadt und als persönliche Chronik im Grab erzählt wurde.[71] Ein identisches Verfahren der Erhöhung der Darstellung durch den kontinuierenden Stil ist hier in S. Maria Maggiore nun angewendet, um die biblische Geschichte zunächst als Heilsgeschichte des Volkes Gottes, zugleich damit aber auch als neue Weltgeschichte und als neuen Mythos Roms zu definieren.[72] Ohne Zweifel war auch ›traditionelles‹ römisches Denken bei der Szenenauswahl für die Langhausmosaike mit beteiligt, denn nur so erklärt sich die Häufung regelrechter Schlacht- und Kriegsszenen, besonders in der Josua-Geschichte mit den Bildern der Schlacht von Raphidim (Ex 17,10–13), der Belagerung und Eroberung Jerichos (Jos 6, 4–25), des Angriffs der Amoriter auf Gibeon (Jos 10,10) und deren Vernichtung (Jos 10,11). Vor dem Hintergrund der Friedens- und Liebesbotschaft des Christentums wundert diese Auswahl, aber aus dem Blickwinkel römischer Staatskunst ist das Herausstellen der Sieghaftigkeit Teil des Selbstverständnisses.

Wenn man sich zudem vergegenwärtigt, zu welchen Gebäuden S. Maria Maggiore visuell in Kontext und in gewisser Weise in Konkurrenz trat, so sind es nicht in erster Linie die römischen Tempel, sondern die eingangs bereits erwähnten großen Basiliken auf dem Forum, die z. T. in ähnlicher Weise wie die Kirche mit Bildern geschmückt waren. Im Falle der Basilica Aemilia wissen wir aus den Quellen nicht nur, dass sie zusammen mit dem Augustus-Forum und dem Templum Pacis zu den schönsten Bauwerken überhaupt gezählt wurde,[73] sondern es haben sich auch Teile ihrer Marmorfriese

69 Die im kontinuierenden Stil erzählten Geschichten sollen oft die erzählte Geschichte eben durch die Bildform zur faktischen Geschichte erheben, gewissermaßen als Chronik ausweisen, weswegen der Terminus Chronikstil angemessen erscheint, vgl. Zimmermann/Salvadori (im Druck).

70 Vgl. etwa Deckers 1976, S. 304, der davon spricht, dass die Säule sozusagen in die Basilika gebracht wird.

71 Vgl. Baldassare et al. 2002, S. 173–177.

72 Es ist dies übrigens nicht das erste Mal, dass die christlich-biblische Heilsgeschichte als kontinuierender Fries erzählt wird: Bereits in der Kammer C der via Latina Katakombe waren Auszug aus Ägypten, Durchzug durch das Rote Meer und Einzug ins Gelobte Land über zwei Kammerseiten als Heilsgeschichte erzählt und so in einer Drehung im Raum erfahrbar geworden, vgl. Tronzo 1986, S. 51–65; Zimmermann 2002, S. 73–79 mit Fig. 5.

73 Plin. Nat. 36, 102.

erhalten, in denen die Stadt- und Staatsgeschichte Roms als Gründungsmythos in gleicher Weise gefeiert wurde, etwa im Bild der Stadtgründung und dem des Raubes der Sabinerinnen.[74] Von hier aus betrachtet erscheinen Darstellungsweise und Bildauswahl typisch römisch – die zahlreichen Kriegsszenen des Alten Testaments übertragen nun die Sieghaftigkeit, die vorher dem Kaiser eignete, auf Gott und die Heilsgeschichte seines Volkes (und auf seinen Bischof).[75] Dies ist alles ganz römisch gedacht und ins Bild gesetzt.

Aus diesem formalen Blickwinkel betrachtet überraschen die Mosaiken von S. Maria Maggiore nicht, sie schmücken ein prächtiges Monument, das alle üblichen Register römisch-imperialer Triumphalkunst abruft. Aus der Sicht des ursprünglich bilderlosen Christentums wird hier zumindest in gleichen Maße das Christentum selbst vom Bischof neu definiert wie für die Stadt Rom und die Römer ihre eigene Heilsgeschichte neu erzählt wird, nun in christlichem Gewand. An die Stelle des *SPQR* der Triumphmonumente ist das *Xystus episcupos plebi dei* getreten, an die Stelle römischer Siege und Stadt- und Staatsmythen die biblisch-theologische Heilsgeschichte.

Von der Intensität und Vielfalt der Botschaften und Aussagen her sind die Mosaike für eine visuelle Rezeption eine ähnliche Überforderung, wie dies ganz ähnlich bereits bei der Trajanssäule der Fall war (und immer noch ist). Im Sinne der Möglichkeiten inhaltlicher Ausdrucksweisen zeigt sich die christliche Kunst damit vollends römisch.

7. Ausblick und Rückblick

Schließlich sei noch ein kurzer Ausblick auf die Bildprogramme Leos des Großen gegeben, speziell auf die Langhauszyklen von S. Paolo fuori le mura: In ihnen wird, ebenso wie zur selben Zeit auch in S. Pietro, eine ähnliche Geschichtlichkeit wie zuvor in S. Maria Maggiore durch die Verschränkung von Zyklen des Alten und des Neuen Testamentes bewirkt.[76] Interessant ist, dass im Vergleich zu den Bildern in S. Maria Maggiore wieder mehr Wert auf Rezipierbarkeit gelegt wurde: Die Anzahl der Personen in den Bildern ist stark reduziert, zugleich ihre Größe aber gesteigert, sodass durchaus mit ihrer Lesbarkeit mit bloßem Auge zu rechnen ist. Dieses Phänomen ist gut bekannt von den spätantiken Bildsäulen in Konstantinopel, die im Vergleich zur Trajanssäule in Rom deutlich die Szenenzahl reduziert, zugleich aber die Frieshöhe und damit die

74 Zu den figürlichen Friesen der Basilica Aemilia, die die mythische Stadtgeschichte als Bilderfries wohl erhöht im Innenraum vorführten, s. Carettoni 1961; Hölscher 1993, S. 79; zuletzt Freyberger/Ertel 2016, S. 111–115, bes. S. 114.

75 Vgl. etwa für die Bezüge der Sieghaftigkeit zur Epik Vergils: Geyer 2006.

76 Zusammenfassend Andaloro 2006, S. 366–410.

Rezipierbarkeit gesteigert haben.[77] Vor allem tritt ein weiteres, wiederum traditionell römisches Element an den Hauptschiffwänden von S. Paul hinzu, nämlich die Tondi mit Papstbildnissen.[78] Sie nehmen die gleiche Stelle im Wandaufriss des Innenraumes ein, an der auch in der Basilica Aemilia die *Clipei* mit Porträts erscheinen (Abb. 6), nur dass sie jetzt die Bilder von Petrus und seiner Nachfolger beinhalten.[79] Damit ist ein weiterer Entwicklungsschritt auf dem Weg zum Papsttum markiert, da nämlich die Folge der römischen Bischöfe zum bildlichen Maß der Ordnung und Messung von Zeit wird, denn ursprünglich erfolgte die Zeitrechnung ja nach Konsulaten. Auf diese Weise sind nicht nur die mythische Vergangenheit biblisch und die eschatologische Erwartung christlich geworden, sondern auch die historische Gegenwart Roms ist endgültig in eine christliche Zeit verwandelt. Nicht zufällig okkupiert Leo zugleich auch den seit der Kaiserzeit den römischen Kaisern zukommenden Titel des Pontifex Maximus.

Auch in dieser symbolischen Definition der Zeit durch die Bildnisse der Bischöfe wird keine neue Form erfunden, sondern ›nur‹ ein christlicher Inhalt in den traditionellen Rahmen gefügt. Auf dem Weg zum Papsttum eignet sich die Kirche in umfassendem Maße die römische Tradition zu ihren eigenen Zwecken an.

In der Auseinandersetzung mit den paganen Göttern schlägt das Christentum jene sozusagen mit ihren eigenen Waffen, nicht im Verzicht auf die traditionellen Ausdrucksformen, sondern in deren Aneignung und Übertrumpfung im christlichen Kultbau. Diese Strategie bedient sich der Bilder, die sich den gesamten Raum erobern und ihn zur Projektionsfläche der Heilsgeschichte einschließlich der Endzeit machen, indem die Geschichte des Volkes Gottes als Geschichte der Römer erzählt wird. Neu sind die christlichen, theologischen Inhalte, deren Darstellungsweisen an die lange Tradition römisch-imperialer Kunst anschließen und dabei die Sehgewohnheiten des Publikums bedienen.

Im Rückblick werden Etappen eines Prozesses erkennbar, der die Entwicklung des römischen Papsttums für die kommenden Jahrhunderte entscheidend mitprägt: Mit Konstantin beginnt die Nähe zur römisch-imperialen Tradition. Erste Ausstattungen von Sakralräumen sind in den damasianischen Sanktuaren der Märtyrer erhalten, und Spuren der Bildentwicklung sind immer wieder in Reflexen der privaten Grabkunst zu fassen. In Bau und Mosaikausstattung von S. Maria Maggiore erscheint der Prozess besiegelt. In ihren Inhalten ist diese Kunst christlich und hoch theologisch, zugleich zeigt sie sich in ihren Ausdrucksformen als Teil der römischen Antike, die nicht imitiert erscheint, sondern vielmehr nahtlos fortlebt. Die römischen antiken Formen werden nicht

---

77 Ebenso ist die Figurenzahl reduziert, vgl. Engemann 1988, S. 985–988.

78 Brandenburg 2013, S. 128–130; Andaloro 2006, S. 400–410.

79 Freyberger/Ertel 2016, Farbtafel 8; Freyberger 2016, mit ausführlicher Literatur zu den *imagines clipeatae* und dem Vergleich zu den Papstbildnissen in S. Paolo; ich danke Stefan Freyberger für die Disskussion.

Abb. 6: 3-D-Rekonstruktion der Innenansicht der Basilika Aemilia (nach Freyberger/Ertel 2016).

unterbrochen oder unterdrückt, sondern umfassend angeeignet. Die Abwesenheit der Kaiser von Rom mag diesen Prozess gefördert haben,[80] in dem die Bischöfe allmählich auch die Rolle der Kaiser als Bauherren und Stifter sakraler Großbauten übernahmen. Der Prozess prägte und veränderte jedenfalls letztlich das Christentum selbst auf dem Weg zur römischen Papstkirche.

80 Vgl. zum Phänomen und den Auswirkungen, wenngleich für das frühe 4. Jahrhundert, Bauer 2012.

Bibliographie

Andaloro 2006 Maria Andaloro: La pittura medievale a Roma, L'orizzonte tardoantico e le nuove immagini 312–468, Corpus vol. I, Rom 2006.

Baldassare et al. 2002 Ida Baldassare, Angela Pontrandolfo, Agnès Rouveret und Monica Salvadori: Pittura romana, Mailand 2002.

Bauer 2004 Franz Alto Bauer: Das Bild der Stadt Rom im Frühmittelalter (Palilia, 14), Wiesbaden 2004.

Bauer 2012 Franz Alto Bauer: Stadt ohne Kaiser: Rom im Zeitalter der Dyarchie und Tetrarchie (285–306 n. Chr.), in: Rom und Mailand in der Spätantike: Repräsentationen städtischer Räume in Literatur, Architektur und Kunst, hg. von Therese Fuhrer, Berlin/Boston 2012, S. 5–85.

Bisconti 2009 Fabrizio Bisconti: L1–L2, A1–A6, X–Y, C–E. Relitti iconografici e nuovi tracciati figurativi alle origini della pittura catacombale romana, in: Rivista di Archeologia Cristiana 85, 2009, S. 7–53.

Brandenburg 2013 Hugo Brandenburg: Die frühchristlichen Kirchen in Rom vom 4. bis zum 7. Jahrhundert. Der Beginn der abendländischen Kirchenbaukunst, Regensburg [3]2013.

Brenk 1975 Beat Brenk: Die frühchristlichen Mosaiken in S. Maria Maggiore zu Rom, Wiesbaden 1975.

Brenk 2010 Beat Brenk: The apse, the image and the icon, Wiesbaden 2010.

Busch 2011 Alexandra W. Busch, Militär in Rom. Militärische und paramilitärische Einheiten im kaiserzeitlichen Stadtbild (Palilia, 20), Wiesbaden 2011.

De Blaauw 2010 Sible De Blaauw: Le origini e gli inizi dell'architettura cristiana, in: Storia dell'architettura italiana, hg. von Sible De Blaauw, Mailand 2010, Bd. I, S. 22–53.

Carettoni 1961 Gianfilippo Carettoni: Il fregio figurato della Basilica Emilia, in: Rivista dell'Istituto nazionale d'archeologia e storia dell'arte 10, 1961, S. 5–78.

Carletti 1994 Carlo Carletti: Il santuario dei Santi Felice e Adaucto e la catacomba di Commodilla, in: Deckers/Mietke/Weiland 1994, S. 3–27.

Carletti 2000 Carlo Carletti: s.v. Damaso I, in: Enciclopedia dei papi. Bd. I, Rom 2000, S. 349–372.

Deckers 1976 Johannes G. Deckers: Der alttestamentliche Zyklus von S. Maria Maggiore in Rom, Bonn 1976.

Deckers 2007 Johannes G. Deckers: Die frühchristliche und byzantinische Kunst, München 2007.

Deckers/Seeliger/Mietke 1987 Johannes G. Deckers, Hans Reinhard Seeliger und Gabriele Mietke: Die Katakombe »Santi Marcellino e Pietro«. Repertorium der Malereien, Vatikanstadt/Münster 1987.

Deckers/Mietke/Weiland 1994 Johannes G. Deckers, Gabriele Mietke und Albrecht Weiland: Die Katakombe »Commodilla«. Repertorium der Malereien, Vatikanstadt 1994.

Engemann 1988 Josef Engemann: Art. Herrscherbild, in: Reallexikon für Antike und Christentum 14, 1988, S. 966–1047.

Engemann 1997 Josef Engemann: Deutung und Bedeutung frühchristlicher Bildwerke, Darmstadt 1997.

Engemann 2011 Josef Engemann: Konstantin und das Jahr 312 im Blickpunkt der Forschung, in: Das antike Rom und sein Bild, hg. von Hans-Ulrich Cain, Annette Haugg und Yadegar Asisi, Berlin/Boston 2011, S. 49–65.

Fasola 1989 Umberto M. Fasola: Die Domitilla-Katakombe, Vatikanstadt 1989.

Ferrua 1942 Antonio Ferrua: Epigrammata Damasiana, Vatikanstadt 1942.

Fiocchi Nicolai 1995 Vincenzo Fiocchi Nicolai: »Itinera ad sanctos«: Testimonianze monumentali del passaggio del pellegrini nei santuari del suburbio romano, in: Akten des XII. Internationalen Kongresses für christliche Archäologie, Bonn, 22.–28. September 1991, Jahrbuch für Antike und Christentum, Erg. Bd. 20, Münster 1995, S. 763–775.

Fiocchi Nicolai 2001 Vincenzo Fiocchi Nicolai: Strutture funerarie ed edifici di culto paleocristiani di Roma dal IV al VI secolo, Vatikanstadt 2001.

Fiocchi Nicolai 2008 Vincenzo Fiocchi Nicolai: Sacra martyrum loca circuire. Percorsi di visita dei pelligrini nei santuari martiriali del suburbio romano, in: Christiana Loca. Lo spazio cristiano nella Roma del primo millennio, hg. von Letizia Pani Ermini, Rom 2008, S. 221–230.

Fiocchi Nicolai 2013 Vincenzo Fiocchi Nicolai: Interventi monumentali dei vescovi nelle aree suburbane delle città dell'Occidente (III–VI secolo), in: Akten CIAC [Internationaler Kongress für christliche Archäologie] XV, Toledo 2008, Vatikanstadt 2013, Bd. I, S. 213–234.

Fiocchi Nicolai/Guyon 2006 Vincenzo Fiocchi Nicolai und Jean Guyon: Relire Styger: Les origines de l'*area* I di cimetière de Calliste et la crypte des Papes, in: Origine delle catacombe romane. Atti della giornata tematica dei Seminari di Archeologia Cristiana (Rom, 21.3.2005), hg. von Vincenzo Fiocchi Nicolai und Jean Gyuon, Vatikanstadt 2006, S. 121–161.

Fiocchi Nicolai et al. 1995–1996 Vincenzo Fiocchi Nicolai, Maria Paola Del Moro, Donatella Nuzzo und Lucrezia Spera: La nuova Basilica circiforme della via Ardeatina, in: Atti della Pontificia accademia romana di archeologia, Rendiconti 68, 1995–1996, S. 69–233.

Filacchione 2007 Penelope Filacchione: »Presenze invisibili«. Considerazioni sulle assenze iconiche nelle cripte martiriali damasine, in: Studi sull'Oriente cristiano 11, 2007, S. 67–77.

Freyberger 2016 Klaus Stefan Freyberger: Die Rezeption stadtrömischer Repräsentationsbauten und deren Ausstattung in den römischen Munizipien und Kolonien, in: Dialog Schule – Wissenschaft, Band 50. Formen der Antikenrezeption in Literatur und Kunst, hg. von Rolf Kussl, Speyer 2016, S. 209–266.

Freyberger/Ertel 2016 Klaus Stefan Freyberger und Christine Ertel (†): Die Basilica Aemilia auf dem Forum Romanum in Rom, Wiesbaden 2016.

Geyer 2006 Angelika Geyer: Bibelepik und frühchristliche Bildzyklen. Die Mosaiken von Santa Maria Maggiore in Rom, in: Mitteilungen des Deutschen Archäologischen Instituts, Römische Abteilung 112, 2005–06, S. 293–321.

Grabar 1968 André Grabar: Christian iconography. A study of its origins, Princeton 1968.

Guidobaldi 2013 Federico Guidobaldi: Roma costantiniana, in: Costantino. Enciclopedia costantiniana sulla figura e l'immagine dell'imperatore del cosidetto Editto di Milano 313–2013, Bd. I, Rom 2013, S. 453–469.

Guidobaldi 2016 Federico Guidobaldi: La formulazione progettuale della basilica cristiana come ulteriore espressione dell'innovazione costantiniana nel campo dell'architettura, in: Acta XVI Congressus Internationalis Archaeologiae Christianae, Romae 22–28.9.2013, Vatikanstadt 2016, Bd. I, S. 461–492.

Guyon 1987 Jean Guyon: Le cimetière aux deux lauriers: recherches sur les catacombes romaines, Rom/Vatikanstadt 1987.

Hölscher 1993 Tonio Hölscher: Mythen als Exempel der Geschichte, in: Mythos in mythenloser Gesellschaft. Das Paradigma Roms, hg. von Fritz Graf, Stuttgart 1993, S. 67–87.

Hölscher (im Druck) Tonio Hölscher: Ideologie der Realität – Realität der Ideologie: Narrative Struktur, Sachkultur und (Un-)Sichtbarkeit eines bildlichen Kriegsberichts, in: Columna Traiani. Siegesmonument und Kriegsbericht in Bildern, hg. von Fritz Mitthoff und Günther Schörner, Wien 2017, S. 15-39.

Ihm 1960 Christa Ihm: Die Programme der christlichen Apsismalerei vom vierten Jahrhundert bis zur Mitte des achten Jahrhunderts, Wiesbaden 1960.

Krautheimer 1971 Richard Krautheimer, Spencer Corbett und Wolfgang Frankl: SS. Nereo ed Achilleo on the via Ardeatina, in: Richard Krautheimer, Corpus Basilicarum Christianarum Urbis Romae (saecc. IV–IX), Bd. III, Vatikanstadt 1971, S. 129–135.

Krautheimer 1987 Richard Krautheimer: Tre capitali cristiane, Turin 1987.

Liverani 2003 Paolo Liverani: Progetto architettonico e percezione comune in età tardonatica, in: Bulletin Antieke Beschaving 78, 2003, S. 205–219.

Liverani 2004 Paolo Liverani: L'area lateranense in età tardoantica e le origini del patriachio, in: Mélanges de l'École française de Rom, Antiquité, 116, 2004, S. 17–49.

Löx 2013 Markus Löx: Monumenta sanctorum: Rom und Mailand als Zentren des frühen Christentums. Märtyrerkult und Kirchenbau unter den Bischöfen Damasus und Ambrosius, Wiesbaden 2013.

Luchterhandt 2015 Manfred Luchterhandt: Vom Haus des Bischofs zum Locus Sanctus: Der Lateranpalast im kulturellen Gedächtnis des römischen Mittelalters, in: The Emperor's house. Palaces from Augustus to the Age of Absolutism (Urban Spaces, 4), hg. von M. Featherstone et al., Berlin 2015, S. 73–92.

Mazzei 2010 Barbara Mazzei: Il cubicolo degli apostoli nelle catacombe romane di Santa Tecla: cronaca di una scoperta, Vatikanstadt 2010.

Nestori/Bisconti 2000 I mosaici paleocristiani di Santa Maria Maggiore negli Acquarelli della collezione Wilpert, hg. von Aldo Nestori und Fabrizio Bisconti, Vatikanstadt 2000.

Nieddu 2009 Anna Maria Nieddu: La Basilica Apostolorum sulla Via Appia e l'area cimiteriale circostante, Vatikanstadt 2009.

Rasch/Arbeiter 2007 Jürgen J. Rasch und Achim Arbeiter: Das Mausoleum der Constantina in Rom (Spätantike Zentralbauten in Rom und Latium, 4), Mainz 2007.

Reutter 2009 Ursula Reutter: Damasus, Bischof von Rom (366–384), Tübingen 2009.

Saecularia Damasiana 1986 Saecularia Damasiana. Atti del convegno internazionale per il XVI centenario della morte do Papa Damaso I, Vatikanstadt 1986.

Schrenk 1995 Sabine Schrenk: Typos und Antitypos in der frühchristlichen Kunst, Jahrbuch für Antike und Christentum, Erg.-Bd. 21, Münster 1995.

Spera 1998 Lucrezia Spera: Ad limina apostolorum. Santuari e pellegrini a Roma tra la tarda antichità e l'alto medioevo, in: La geografia della città di Roma e lo spazio del sacro, hg. von Claudio Cerretti, Rom 1998, S. 1–104.

Spera 2012 Lucrezia Spera: I santuari di Roma dall'antichità all'altomedioevo: morfologie, caratteri dislocativi, riflessi della devozione, in: Santuari d'Italia, hg. von Roberto Rusconi, Rom 2012, S. 33–58.

Steigerwald 2016 Gerhard Steigerwald: Die frühchristlichen Mosaiken des Triumphbogens von S. Maria Maggiore in Rom, Regensburg 2016.

Styger 1935 Paul Styger: Römische Märtyrergrüfte, Berlin 1935.

Tronzo 1986 William Tronzo: The Via Latina catacomb. Imitation and discontinuity in fourth-century Roman painting, Philadelphia 1986.

Weiland 1994 Albrecht Weiland: »*Conposuit tumulum sanctorum limina adorans*«. Die Ausgestaltung des Grabes der hl. Felix und Adauctus durch Papst Damasus in der Commodillakatakombe in Rom«, in: Historia pictura refert. Miscellanea in onore di Padre A. Recio Veganzones O.F.M, Vatikanstadt 1994, S. 625–645.

Wickhoff 1895 Franz Wickhoff: Der Stil der Genesisbilder und die Geschichte seiner Entwicklung, in: Die Wiener Genesis, hg. von Wilhelm von Hartel und Franz Wickhoff, Wien 1895, S. 1–98.

Wilpert 1903 Joseph Wilpert: Die Malereien der Katakomben Roms, Freiburg i. Br. 1903.

Wilpert/Schumacher 1976 Joseph Wilpert und Walter N. Schumacher: Die römischen Mosaiken der kirchlichen Bauten vom IV.–XIII. Jahrhundert, Freiburg 1976.

Zimmermann 2004 Barbara Zimmermann: Erzählte Geschichte im Bild. Die narrative Darstellungsweise der Trajanssäule als Vermittlung historischer Ereignisse, in: Kleine Erzählungen und ihre Medien, hg. von Herbert Hrachovec, Wolfgang Müller-Funk und Birgit Wagner, Wien 2004, S. 201–226.

Zimmermann 2002 Norbert Zimmermann: Werkstattgruppen römischer Katakombenmalerei, JbAC Erg.-Bd. 35, Münster 2002.

Zimmermann 2012 Norbert Zimmermann: Rilettura di pitture a Domitilla: tracce del santuario damasiano dei SS. Nereo e Achilleo?, in: Scavi e scoperte recenti nelle chiese di Roma. Atti della giornata tematica dei Seminari di Archeologia Cristiana (Rom, 13.3.2008), hg. von Hugo Brandenburg und Federico Guidobaldi, Vatikanstadt 2012, S. 189–212.

Zimmermann 2015 Norbert Zimmermann: Catacombs and the beginnings of Christian tomb decoration, in: Blackwell Companions to the Ancient World: A Companion to Roman Art, hg. von Barbara Borg, Oxford 2015, S. 452–470.

Zimmermann/Salvadori (im Druck) Norbert Zimmermann und Monica Salvadori: Vom Geschichtenerzählen zum Erzählen von Geschichte. Historische Friese und ihre Verwendung in der römischen Sepulkralkunst vor und nach der Trajanssäule, in: Columna Traiani. Siegesmonument und Kriegsbericht in Bildern, hg. von Fritz Mitthoff und Günther Schörner, Wien 2017, S. 181–192.

Papst Theodor (642–649) und die Künste: ein ›pragmatisches‹ Verhältnis

Alessandro Taddei

Eine Diskussion zu Papst Theodor als Auftraggeber von Kunst ist zweifellos eine spannende Herausforderung. Im Unterschied zu anderen römischen Bischöfen des 7. Jahrhunderts, die eine ideologische Förderung der Kirche durch mehr oder weniger ehrgeizige Bauvorhaben bzw. Ausschmückung und Ausstattung schon existierender Gebäude vorantrieben, zeigte Theodor anscheinend ein deutlich schwächeres Profil, obwohl er sich dieser Verpflichtung nicht entzog. Dieser Eindruck könnte jedoch teilweise trügen.[1] So ist dieser Beitrag als Prämisse gedacht für eine künftige, detaillierte Studie zu diesem hochinteressanten Pontifex.

Man darf nicht vergessen, dass wir außer dem *Liber pontificalis* keine weiteren ausführlichen Quellen über seine Aktivitäten besitzen. Aufgrund der bekannt freien Gliederung der Lebensbeschreibungen im *Liber* werden die diversen Tätigkeitsbereiche des Papstes (innere Kirchenverwaltung, Diplomatie und Politik, Lehre, Kunstaufträge) je nach Bedarf mehr oder weniger umfangreich ausgestaltet. Auch der *Vita Theodori* gab der namenlose Autor eine besondere, nämlich ›politische‹ Prägung.

Wer sich heute mit den politischen und religionsgeschichtlichen Aspekten von Theodors Pontifikat auseinandersetzen möchte, steht vor der schwierigen Aufgabe, eine Epoche großer Veränderungen im mediterranen Raum zu untersuchen, insbesondere im Hinblick auf die komplexen Beziehungen zwischen dem römischen Westen und der Reichshauptstadt Konstantinopel. Dies ist nicht der richtige Rahmen zur Erläuterung der Initiativen Theodors innerhalb der lehramtlichen Kontroversen, vor allem in Bezug auf die zwei großen Debatten über den einen Willen (Monotheletismus) bzw. das eine Handeln (Monoenergismus), die von Konstantinopel ab den 630er Jahren vorangetrieben wurden. Die Erforschung des umfangreichen Corpus an exegetischen Schriften und Briefen wirft auf die Gestalt Theodors und auf seine Beziehungen zu Kaiser Konstans II. (641–668) und dem Patriarchen von Konstantinopel Paul II. (641–653) ein viel stärkeres Licht als die knappen Quellen in den Annalen.[2] Religionsdiplomatische Be-

1 Manche Ergebnisse dieser Studie sind in Taddei 2016, S. 160–163 vorweggenommen.

2 Susi 2000; Ekonomou 2007, S. 96–100; Booth 2014, S. 262, 280, 282–284, 286–287.

mühungen gab es – trotz vielerlei Spannungen – immer wieder auf beiden Seiten bis ca. 645/646, als Rom und das byzantinische Italien sich ihres erhöhten Prestiges und ihrer zentralen Stellung schnell bewusst wurden (im Vergleich zu einem sich verändernden Reich, das im Nahen Osten und Nordafrika schon viele Gebiete verloren hatte).

Laut *Liber pontificalis* entstammt Theodor einer syrisch-hellenophonen Familie in Jerusalem (*Natione grecus, ex patre Theodoro episcopo de civitate Hierusolima*). Er ist also Sohn eines gleichnamigen Bischofs in Palästina.[3] Vermutlich verließ der künftige Papst seine Heimat schon zwischen 614 und 628, als die Heilige Stadt von den Persern besetzt wurde. Der Rückeroberung durch Heraklius im Jahr 634 wurde durch das Heer ʻUmar ibn al-Khaṭṭābs 637/638 für immer ein Ende gesetzt. Aus diesem Grunde konnte Theodor in Rom auf eine wachsende Gruppe befreundeter Kleriker zählen, die aus Syrien, Palästina und Ostanatolien geflohen waren. Aufgrund der ›unkonventionellen‹ Predigten charismatischer Persönlichkeiten wie Johannes Moschus, Sophronius von Jerusalem und Maximus Confessor war bei diesen Kirchenleuten die Aversion gegen die lehramtlichen Neuerungen Konstantinopels besonders stark.[4] Maximus selbst residierte ab 645 in Rom. Gemeinsam mit ihm leiteten Theodor und der zukünftige Papst Martin die Vorbereitungen für die Lateransynode von 649, bei der es zum ersten tiefen Bruch zwischen Rom und Konstantinopel im 7. Jahrhundert kam.[5]

Wie Ovidio Capitani bemerkt, entstand die *Vita Theodori* nach der Synode und unter dem Eindruck der ideologischen Stellungnahmen, die auf dieses Ereignis folgten.[6] Ähnliches gilt für die Biographie seines Nachfolgers Martin, eine hagiographische Überhöhung des Papstes und ein Manifest gegen die lehramtliche Position Konstantinopels. Theodors *Vita* berichtet ausgesprochen detailreich über die innenpolitischen Ereignisse im byzantinischen Exarchat von Italien, liefert hingegen nur ein sehr knappes und konventionelles Bild des Papstes: *Hic fuit amator pauperum, largus, benignus super omnes et multum misericors*. Es fehlt jedoch nicht an Hinweisen auf seinen starken, entschlossenen Charakter.[7] Die Tatsache, dass den politischen Ereignissen in Italien so viel Raum gegeben wird, spiegelt vermutlich die kritische Phase in der byzantinischen Verwaltung der Halbinsel. Der *Liber* berichtet, der *chartularius* Mauritius habe in seiner Funktion als *dux* im Jahr 639 unter Papst Severinus einen Teil des Schatzes des *Episcopium lateranense* unterschlagen, wahrscheinlich um den *exercitus romanus* zu besolden. Mithilfe des Heeres lehnte sich Mauritius 641 oder 642 gegen die kaiserliche

3 LP, I, 331.
4 Booth 2014, S. 290–300.
5 Zur Synode allgemein s. die Einführung zur kritischen Ausgabe der Akten in Price 2014, S. 5–58.
6 Capitani 1992.
7 Anathema und förmliche Absetzung des ehemaligen Patriarchen von Konstantinopel Pyrrhos in St. Peter 645 in LP, I, 332. Derselbe Vorfall ist auch der mittelbyzantinischen Geschichtsschreibung noch zu Beginn des 9. Jahrhunderts bekannt: Theoph., *Chron.*, I, 331.

Autorität von Konstans II. auf, um die Kontrolle über das Herzogtum von Rom zu gewinnen. Das Heer des Exarchats von Ravenna bereitete dem Aufstand ein Ende, und der *chartularius* wurde auf Befehl des Exarchen Isaakios (625–643) hingerichtet.[8]

Nichts deutet im *Liber pontificalis* darauf hin, dass Theodor die interne Verwaltung der römischen Kirche oder sein Zuständigkeitsgebiet vernachlässigt hätte: Er weiht Priester, Diakone und 46 Bischöfe *per diversa loca*[9]. Die wenigen Kunstaufträge, die im *Liber* nur sehr knapp behandelt werden, sind in der Tat eng mit der Verwaltung und Instandhaltung seines Territoriums verbunden. Diese Feststellung wirft eine Frage auf: Gab es wirklich nur so wenige bzw. so unbedeutende Bauten und Ausstattungsaufträge von Theodor? Die Antwort fällt nicht leicht. Seine Biographie ist nicht so ausführlich wie die anderer Päpste (Martin I., Vitalianus), bei denen das Fehlen von Kunstaufträgen ins Auge sticht. Vielmehr ist – wie bei Sergius I. (687–701) – anzunehmen, dass der Autor sich nur oberflächlich mit dem Mäzenatentum von Papst Theodor beschäftigte.

Was den rein künstlerischen Aspekt betrifft, musste sich Theodor mit verschiedenen illustren Vorgängern messen. Ein – auch literarisch – heikles Problem war in diesem Zusammenhang die noch sehr lebendige Erinnerung an seinen Vorgänger Honorius I. (625–638): In dessen Passion für den Erhalt des städtischen *decus* und der Schätze des christlichen Roms lag der Grund für eines der vielschichtigsten, umfangreichsten und breitgefächertsten Bauvorhaben des Frühmittelalters. Es ist jedoch keineswegs erkennbar, ob der ›Grieche‹ Theodor die gleichen Möglichkeiten, Ambitionen und Kenntnisse besaß wie Honorius, der auf seine engen Beziehungen zu den römischen Senatoren und den mittel- und süditalienischen Großgrundbesitzern stolz war. Falls die Anekdote der Veruntreuung des Lateranschatzes im Jahr 639 keine absichtlich eingefügten Elemente geschichtlicher Mystifizierung enthält, könnte man an eine zeitweilige Verarmung der Kirchenkassen denken. Dies hatte Johannes IV. (640–642) aus Dalmatien jedoch nicht daran gehindert, erhebliche Ausgaben im *Episcopium lateranense* zu tätigen (vielleicht aus eigenen Mitteln). Dieses Oratorium war den Märtyrern von Salona und dem heiligen Venantius, dem Namensheiligen von Johannes' Vater, geweiht und ein Vorbild für S. Stefano Rotondo, wie wir noch sehen werden. Das Apsismosaik der Venantius-Kapelle ist übrigens einer der Problemfälle eines doppelten Papstporträts ohne identifizierende Beischriften, weshalb stets für eine Fertigstellung durch Theodor aufgrund des vorzeitigen Ablebens seines Vorgängers plädiert wurde.[10] Ich neige jedoch dazu, diese frühe Initiative aus dem ›Katalog‹ der Aufträge Theodors auszuschließen, denn die Annahme ist in keiner Quelle belegt und steht sogar im Widerspruch zur Aussage

8 LP, I, 328–329, 331–332.

9 LP, I, 333.

10 Gandolfo 2004, S. 16–17; Marin 2009, S. 212–213.

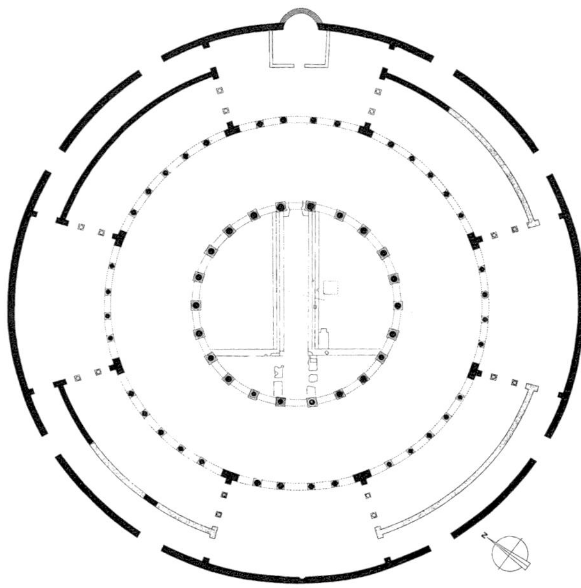

Abb. 1: Rom. S. Stefano Rotondo, Grundriss der Kirche im Frühmittelalter.

im *Liber pontificalis*, wonach Johannes IV. sein Oratorium gebührend vollendet und geweiht habe.[11]

Es gilt also, den Blick auf die Gesamtheit der Baukomplexe zu richten, die, wenn auch nur zaghaft, in Theodors Biographie und in den wenigen zeitgenössischen Quellen auftauchen. Zunächst muss jedoch gesagt werden, dass bei seiner Wahl (642) mit Sicherheit noch bedeutende, von Honorius I. initiierte Bauvorhaben im Gange waren, vor allem im *suburbium*, und es liegt nahe, dass Theodors Vorgänger Severinus und Johannes IV. aufgrund ihrer kurzen Pontifikate so gut wie nichts vollendet hatten. Eine der schwierigsten Entscheidungen, die Theodor bei Amtsantritt treffen musste, betraf zweifellos die Fortsetzung von Honorius' Politik zur Instandhaltung und nachträglichen Ausstattung der *memoriae martyrum* im *suburbium*. Diese Politik drückte sich in flächendeckenden und sicherlich kostspieligen Baumaßnahmen aus: Wiederherstellung

11 LP, I, 330. Zu einer völlig neuen Sicht auf Doppelporträts von Päpsten im römischen Frühmittelalter s. Gianandrea 2012, S. 665–666.

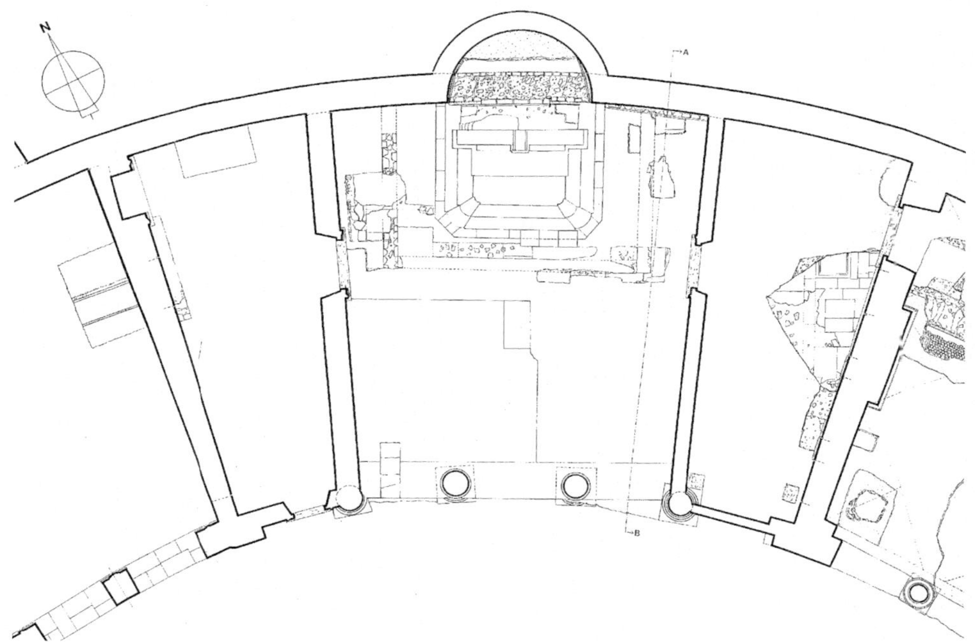

Abb. 2: Rom. S. Stefano Rotondo, Kapelle der Heiligen Primus und Felicianus, Grundriss.

von Friedhöfen und Katakomben, Bau von Ädikulen, Basiliken *ad corpus* und Gedächtniskapellen. Als Beispiel sei S. Agnese an der Via Nomentana genannt.[12]

Auch bei flüchtigem Lesen des *Liber* bleibt kein Zweifel, dass Theodors Episkopat diesbezüglich eine Wende darstellt. Die Liste seiner Maßnahmen beginnt mit einer Reliquienüberführung *intra moenia*; er wird somit zum Vorreiter einer Praxis, die innerhalb kurzer Zeit weit um sich greifen wird. In diesem Fall ging es um die Verlegung der sterblichen Überreste der Märtyrer Primus und Felicianus aus einem Coemeterium an der 14. Meile der Via Nomentana in die neue Kapelle, die der Papst in der Kirche S. Stefano Rotondo auf dem Caelius anlegen ließ. Die Kapelle wird mit wertvollem Gerät ausgestattet: *gabatas aureas III, tabula ex argento ante confessionem, arcos argenteos II* (Abb. 1).[13]

Der Ausbau einer Kirche, die dem ersten Märtyrer und Diakon aus Jerusalem geweiht war, in *Caelio monte* ergab sich zweifelsohne aus den noch engen Beziehungen

12 Zur Umgestaltung von S. Agnese durch Honorius s. den Beitrag von Gambuti 2014–2015, auf den für frühere Literatur verwiesen wird.

13 LP, I, 332.

Abb. 3: Rom. S. Stefano Rotondo, Kapelle der Heiligen Primus und Felicianus, Apsiskalotte.

Abb. 4: Rom. S. Stefano Rotondo, Kapelle der Heiligen Primus und Felicianus, Apsis. Darstellungen der Heiligen Primus (oben) und Felicianus (unten).

des Pontifex zu seiner Heimat.[14] Diese Hypothese wird von dem Umstand gestützt, dass der Papst auch seinen Vater dort bestatten ließ, wie aus einer verlorenen, aber durch de Rossi noch bekannten Inschrift hervorgeht: *Exquirens pietas tectum decorare sacratum / pastoris summi Theodori cordem erexit / qui studio magno sanctorum corpora cultu / hoc dedicavit non patris neglecta reliquit*.[15] In S. Stefano veränderte Theodor den nordöstlichen Kreuzarm, den einzigen heute noch erhaltenen von den vieren des ursprünglichen Baus aus dem 5. Jahrhundert, durch die Einfügung einer Apsis in die Außenwand und sieben Mauereinheiten (nach der Wiederherstellung des ursprünglichen Fußbodenniveaus heute nicht mehr vorhanden), die eine Kapelle von 6,70 auf 4,40 m bildeten (Abb. 2). Die Apsis besteht aus Mauerwerk mit unregelmäßigen Backsteinschichten und wurde im Innern mit einer Marmorverkleidung versehen.[16] Durch die Wahl des Nordostarms wurde eine ideale Linie zum Hauptaltar hergestellt, der sich früher im südwestlichen Bereich des Mittelschiffs befand.[17]

Die Apsiskalotte des kleinen Oratoriums wurde mit einem Mosaik aus *tesserae* in Stein und Glaspaste geschmückt; es ist heute mit zahlreichen Ergänzungen aus dem 18./19. Jahrhundert und nach Restaurierungen des 20. Jahrhunderts zu sehen.[18] Seine Ikonographie ist in hohem Maße symbolisch: ein monumentales goldenes Gemmenkreuz, dessen senkrechter Arm einen Clipeus mit Christusbüste berührt; über dem Clipeus liegt ein Sternenhimmel mit der *manus Domini* (Abb. 3). Zu beiden Seiten des Kreuzes sind der ältere Heilige Primus und der jüngere Felicianus die Hauptdarsteller; durch *tituli* identifiziert, treten sie in Militäruniform auf (Tunika und Chlamys mit *tablion*) (Abb. 3 und 4). Das Kreuz und die zwei Märtyrer heben sich von einem goldenen Hintergrund ab; den Boden bildet eine schlichte Wiese mit weißen und roten Blumen. Am Ansatz der Kalotte besagt eine aus zwei Hexametern gebildete Inschrift in vergoldeten Lettern auf blauem Grund: »Aspicis auratum caelesti culmine tectum / astriferumque micans praeclaro lumine fultum.«[19] Der Auftraggeber ließ sich also weder selbst ins Bild setzen noch in der Hauptinschrift nennen.[20] Nicht vergessen sollte man allerdings die verlorene Widmungsschrift, die Theodors *pietas* erwähnte und sich in früheren Zeiten im selben architektonischen Kontext befand; sie war vermutlich als Beiwerk zur Darstellung eines Stifterpapstes besser geeignet.

Zahlreiche technische und formale Aspekte in der eleganten Ausführung der Ausstattung sowie die kombinierte Verwendung von Stein und Glas wurden angeführt, um

14 Davis-Weyer 1989, S. 71–72.

15 LP, I, 332. De Rossi 1888, S. 152.

16 Ceschi 1982, S. 90–97.

17 Davis-Weyer 1988, S. 388–389; Davis-Weyer 1989, S. 79.

18 Davis-Weyer 1988, S. 392–395; Basile 2000.

19 De Rossi 1888, S. 152.

20 Thunø 2015, S. 56–57.

die These von Handwerkern aus dem östlichen Mittelmeerraum bzw. aus Konstantinopel zu untermauern. Bei genauerer Überlegung war jedoch die Berufung fremder Mosaikkünstler gar nicht nötig, denn Theodor war ja mit den orientalischen, in Rom lebenden Kreisen vertraut, und diesen gehörten aller Wahrscheinlichkeit nach auch Künstler an, weshalb er sicher auch vor Ort jemanden finden konnte, der ihm die gewünschten, bis heute geschätzten Werke liefern konnte.[21] Es war schon die Rede davon, dass das Kreuz unmittelbar auf die heiligen Stätten verwies, an einem Ort, der in Rom durch den Stefanskult sogleich zum Zentrum der aus Jerusalem stammenden Verehrer wurde. Die Einfachheit des ikonographischen Aufbaus, die schon durch die kleine Dimensionierung der Kapelle bedingt ist, entspricht den Malereien in den *memoriae martyrum*, auf deren Einfügung Theodor zwar verzichtet, die er jedoch keineswegs ideologisch ablehnt. In dieser Hinsicht ist eine Überlegung reizvoll, die auch aus den Studien von Simone Piazza und Mara Minasi hervorgeht: Demnach wäre Theodors Mosaik Inspirationsquelle bzw. maßgebliches Vorbild für das Fresko mit den Heiligen Miles/Milix, dem Perser, und Pymenius zu Seiten eines Gemmenkreuzes in der Pontianus-Katakombe an der Via Portuense.[22] Die Malerei sollte ja in erster Linie eine der zahlreichen von ›Fremden‹ genutzten Verehrungsstätten in den römischen Coemeterien schmücken.[23]

Um zu Primus und Felicianus zurückzukommen, drängt sich die Frage auf, warum Theodor ausgerechnet diese beiden Märtyrer wählte. In Ermangelung konkreter Hinweise darf man annehmen, Honorius I. habe die Umgestaltung der beliebten *memoria* von Nomentum unvollendet gelassen und der Plan sei dann aufgrund des *modus operandi* des neuen Pontifex endgültig gestrichen worden. Dafür gibt es wohlgemerkt keine Beweise, aber die Überführung von Primus und Felicianus führte zur zunehmenden Preisgabe einer bedeutenden Basilika *ad corpus* in der Nähe des *castrum* von Mentana, deren Überreste noch in der ersten Hälfte des 17. Jahrhunderts sichtbar waren.[24] Nach Ansicht Theodors bzw. seiner Mitarbeiter war es bequemer, besonders verehrte, aber weitab vom Stadtzentrum aufbewahrte Reliquien in eine Kirche innerhalb der Aurelianischen Mauer zu überführen.

Zum ›Erbe‹ von Honorius gehörte auch eine der wichtigsten unvollendeten Baustellen im Rom des frühen 7. Jahrhunderts, nämlich die Erweiterung der Basilika zu Ehren des Märtyrers Valentin, dessen römische *memoria* an der zweiten Meile der Via Flaminia lag. Eine erste, oberirdische Basilika ließ Papst Julius I. (337–352) am Fuß des nördlichen Steilhangs der Monti Parioli anlegen, wobei wahrscheinlich mindestens zwei frühere Mausoleen eingegliedert wurden, die dann die Ostabschlüsse der Seitenschiffe

21 Matthiae 1965, S. 110–111; Andaloro 1987, S. 247.

22 Piazza 2006, S. 104; Minasi 2012, S. 568.

23 Spera 2012, S. 41.

24 Passigli 1985, S. 315–323.

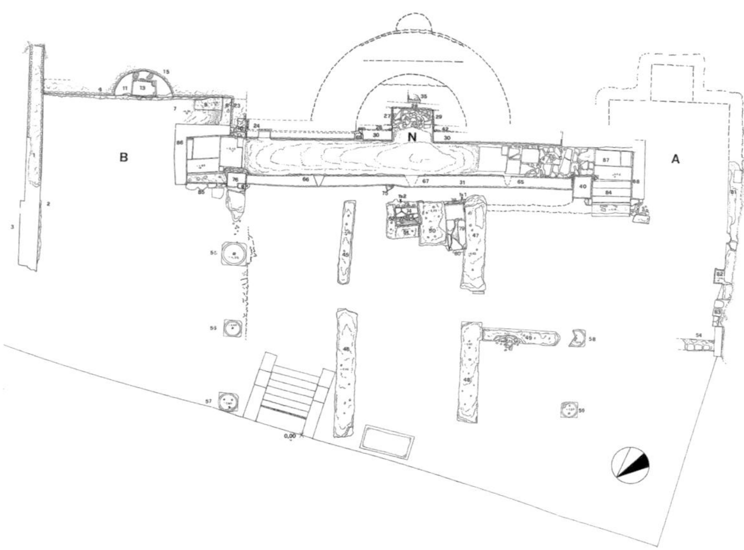

Abb. 5: Rom. Basilika des heiligen Valentin, Plan der Grabungsstätte.

bildeten. Zahlreiche epigraphische Zeugnisse aus dem 4. und 5. Jahrhundert überliefern die rege Verehrung dieses Märtyrers, dessen Ansehen noch im 7. Jahrhundert sehr hoch war, weshalb Honorius sich für ein neues, ehrgeiziges Projekt eines extraurbanen Heiligtums entschied. *Basilica magna quam Honorius reparavit*, steht in der *Notitia ecclesiarum*; *Mirifice ornata*, wird in *De locis sanctis martyrum* bezüglich der glanzvollen Dekoration des Neubaus betont.[25] Die beiden Quellen aus dem 7. Jahrhundert bezeugen ein beachtliches Bauvorhaben (Abb. 5), dessen Auswirkungen auf die Vorgängerbauten schon seit geraumer Zeit eingehend erforscht sind.[26] Der Autor der Theodorvita im *Liber* möchte großzügigerweise diesem Papst auch das alleinige Verdienst für die Kirche *iuxta pontem Molbium*[27] zuschreiben, obwohl die *Notitia ecclesiarum* dem teilweise widerspricht. Eigentlich liefert der Text jedoch keine völlig falsche Information, denn es ist offensichtlich, dass Theodor ein Vorhaben seines Vorgängers Honorius, das weit hinter dem Zeitplan zurückgeblieben war, zu Ende führen wollte. Bedeutsam ist außerdem, dass Honorius' Biographie keinerlei Hinweis auf die unfertige Basilika an der Via Flaminia enthält. Daher kann der große Einsatz für Bau, Weihe und Ausstattung – *et ipse dedicavit et dona multa optulit* – zu Ehren Valentins in der Tat auf Theodor zu-

25 CTCR, II, 73, 118.

26 Palombi 2008, S. 222–223; Palombi 2009, S. 479–481.

27 LP, I, 333.

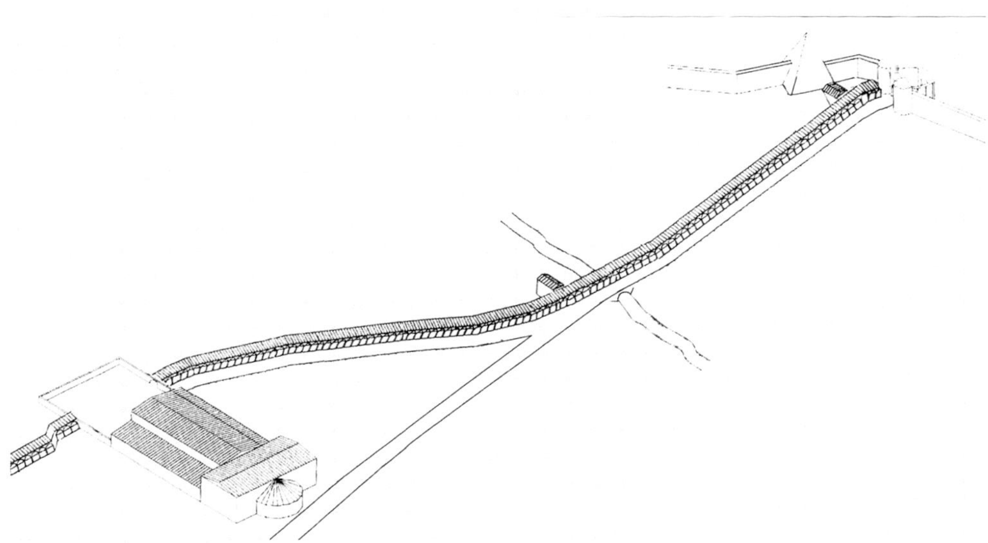

Abb. 6: Rom. Via Ostiense, Rekonstruktion der Verbindungsportikus zwischen Porta S. Paolo und der Basilika St. Paul vor den Mauern.

rückzuführen sein. Infolge der Umgestaltung im 7. Jahrhundert präsentierte sich die große Kirche nunmehr als dreischiffige Aula mit Apsis, gestützt von wertvollen Spoliensäulen aus Marmor, deren bedeutende Überreste im Zuge der Urbanisierung Roms im 19. Jahrhundert ans Licht kamen und heute noch teilweise an der Ecke zwischen Viale Tiziano und Viale Maresciallo Pilsudski zu sehen sind. Diese Prachtentfaltung lässt erneut an die *largesses* des Honorius denken. Für Theodor war es sicherlich eine komplexe, kostspielige Baustelle, wenn noch Leo III. über ein Jahrhundert später Geld für die Wiederherstellung des Daches ausgeben musste.[28]

Von Theodor stammen laut seines Biographen auch der Bau und die Ausschmückung eines Oratoriums an der Via Ostiense für den Märtyrer Euplius aus Catania, *foris porta(m) beati Pauli Apostoli*, d. h. in der Nähe der Cestius-Pyramide gelegen, am Anfang der spätantiken Portikus, die zu St. Paul führte (*porticus quae ducit ad beatum Paulum*) (Abb. 6). Es handelte sich um eine wichtige religiöse Infrastruktur, die Hadrian I. (772–795) vermutlich 782/783[29] von Grund auf restaurieren ließ; sie war mit mehreren *stationes* und Oratorien ausgestattet: Neben der für Euplius gab es weitere Kapellen für den Ägypter Mena/Minas und zur Erinnerung an die Begegnung zwischen Petrus und Paulus.[30]

28 LP, II, 9.

29 Geertman 1975, S. 14.

30 LP, II, 508. Spera 2002, S. 694–698; Spera 2011, S. 1326.

Das kleine Euplius-Oratorium lag wohl westlich der Straße, also rechter Hand nach Durchschreiten des Tores in Richtung St. Paul. Es wurde behauptet, der ursprüngliche Bau könne ein einschiffiger Raum mit Apsis und Gräberkrypta gewesen sein. Diese Hypothese entstand durch eine (wahrscheinlich falsche) geographische Überlagerung der Kapelle mit der nahegelegenen mittelalterlichen Kirche S. Salvatore de Porta (1849 zerstört). Robert Coates-Stephens hielt die Umwandlung eines antiken Mausoleums für möglich, wie im Falle von S. Passera an der Via Portuense – eine ansprechende Idee, denn sie würde Theodors Bauprojekten auch die Umgestaltung antiker Strukturen hinzufügen.[31] Leider zwingen uns sowohl die große Unsicherheit der topographischen Koordinaten des Oratoriums als auch die Unmöglichkeit einer präzisen Bestimmung anhand der äußerst spärlichen Quellen diesbezüglich zu größter Zurückhaltung.[32]

Wir können uns dennoch die Frage nach dem Grund für die Verehrung dieses unter Diokletian zum Märtyrer gewordenen Euplius aus Catania stellen, die vielleicht gerade unter Theodor einen entscheidenden Impuls erfuhr:[33] Man könnte an die wachsende strategische Bedeutung Siziliens (mit dem stärksten griechischsprachigen Bevölkerungsanteil byzantinischer Gebiete in Italien) denken oder auch an die territorialen Interessen der römischen Kirche auf der Insel mit entsprechender Präsenz von Sizilianern in Rom. Vielleicht gibt es jedoch noch präzisere Anhaltspunkte. Gregor I. berichtet, in Messina sei die Verehrung von Euplius mit der von Stephanus verknüpft gewesen; letzterer, wie wir gesehen haben, stand auch bei dem aus Jerusalem stammenden Theodor hoch in der Gunst.[34] Eine direkte Verbindung zwischen Theodor bzw. seiner Familie und Sizilien ist nicht nachweisbar, allerdings gibt es Beispiele wie bei Papst Konon (686–687), der aus Kleinasien stammte und in Sizilien aufwuchs, bzw. Sergius I., dessen Familie aus Antiochia kam und der in Sizilien geboren wurde, wie der *Liber* berichtet. Die Insel muss daher als bevorzugte Zwischenetappe für die Griechischsprachigen betrachtet werden, die auf dem Weg nach Rom dorthin gelangten.

Außerordentlich problematisch erscheint der Hinweis im *Liber pontificalis* auf eine ansonsten unbekannte Sebastianskapelle *intro episcopio Lateranense*, die Theodor erbaut und mit Stiftungen ausgestattet haben soll.[35] Die Repräsentationsräume bzw. die Reliquienrepositorien in der Residenz des Patriarchen sind oft von einem undurchdringlichen Schweigen umgeben. Wie Antonella Ballardini jedoch zu Recht bemerkte, lastete der Unterhalt des Bischofspalasts bis zur ersten Hälfte des 8. Jahrhunderts nicht

31 Coates-Stephens 1997, S. 183.

32 Spera 2004, S. 229.

33 Spera 2004, S. 229.

34 Greg. Ep., II, 9.

35 LP, I, 332; Real 2004, S. 98.

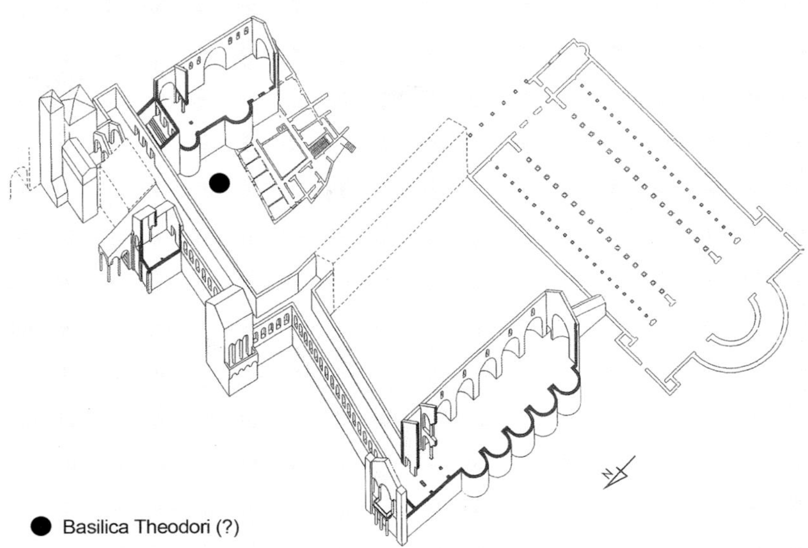

Abb. 7: Rom. Episcopium lateranense, axionometrische Rekonstruktion.

auf der Staatskasse.[36] Dies erklärt den Mangel an Informationen im *Liber*, mit Ausnahme der Kapelle zu Ehren des heiligen Venantius und der Märtyrer von Salona, die Johannes IV. anlegen ließ.

Es ist kein Zufall, dass die (schwierig zu lokalisierende) sogenannte Basilika von Papst Theodor im Lateran (Abb. 7) in seiner Biographie völlig fehlt. Erst in der Vita von Sergius I. tritt die *basilica quae dicitur domni Theodori papae* auf, um dann wieder bei Zacharias (741–752) genannt zu werden, der sie vielleicht restaurieren lässt, in jedem Fall aber ein *triclinium* davor baut, und bei Stefan III. (768–772), der dort den Truppen des *primicerius* Christophorus entgegentreten musste.[37] Die Erwähnungen einer *Basilica Theodori* brechen im 12. Jahrhundert endgültig ab. Die Lage dieser Aula innerhalb der mittelalterlichen Patriarchenresidenz erforschen seit einiger Zeit vor allem Antonella Ballardini, Paolo Liverani, Manfred Luchterhandt und Ulrich Real. Dank dieser Studien darf inzwischen als fast gesichert angenommen werden, dass dieser Repräsentations- und Kultraum sich in der Nähe der päpstlichen Gemächer und des Zugangsbereichs zum Bischofspalast befand.[38] Er stand unter dem Schutz der Heiligen Petrus und Paulus, deren Bildnisse über dem Eingang angebracht waren (Abb. 8). Hier beschränke ich

36 Ballardini 2015, S. 897.

37 LP, I, 374, 432, 479.

38 Liverani 1999, S. 538–541; Real 2004, S. 106; Luchterhandt 2015, S. 85; Ballardini 2015, S. 907.

mich auf eine Nennung der Basilika Theodors als ein eng mit der Papstresidenz zusammenhängendes Bauprojekt. Ich möchte nicht ausschließen, dass Theodor dort einen Teil der großen Zahl von Reliquien und Andenken unterbringen wollte, die zu jener Zeit aus dem inzwischen muslimisch besetzten Palästina nach Rom gelangten. Ebenso halte ich es für wahrscheinlich, dass Theodor, und nicht Honorius I., das Haupt des zur Zeit der persischen Besatzung 614–628 in Jerusalem gemarterten Anastasius nach Rom überführen ließ. Die Reliquie wurde in Rom schon gegen Mitte des Jahrhunderts im syrisch-hellenophonen Kloster Ad Aquas Salvias an der Via Laurentina verehrt.[39]

Obwohl Theodor der Verehrung von Heiligen- und Märtyrerreliquien pflichtschuldig Aufmerksamkeit schenkte, wie die verlorene Inschrift von S. Stefano al Celio bestätigte, entschied er sich gegen die von Honorius eingeleitete nachträgliche Ausstattung der suburbanen Heiligtümer, und die gewissenhafte Pflege dieser Stätten wurde erheblich eingeschränkt.[40] Die Frage nach den tieferen Gründen ist noch offen, aber über mindestens drei Punkte lohnt es sich nachzudenken.

1. Niedergang und mangelnde Sicherheit in den suburbanen Bezirken Roms: Diese beiden Aspekte werden oft zur nächstliegenden Begründung des Kurswechsels seitens der kirchlichen Autoritäten in der Mitte des 7. Jahrhunderts angeführt. Diese Behauptung ist zwar schwer zu widerlegen, sie kann jedoch das noch im Anfangsstadium befindliche Phänomen der Reliquienüberführungen nicht hinreichend erklären. Die Itinerarien geben den heiligen Stätten *extra moenia* noch breiten Raum. In politischer Hinsicht zeigte der Aufstand des *chartularius* Mauritius, dass der *exercitus romanus* nach wie vor eine starke Kontrolle über das Herzogtum ausübte. Im Übrigen herrschte eine Art militärische Stagnation zwischen dem Exarchat und den Langobarden unter Rothari (636–652). Die ungewissen Auswirkungen der Schlacht am Fluss Scultenna (November 643), die den Exarchen Isaak das Leben kostete, veranlassten die Langobarden, trotz ihres Siegs auf einen direkten Angriff auf Ravenna und das römische Herzogtum zu verzichten.[41]
2. Vermutlich spielten wirtschaftliche Faktoren die entscheidende Rolle: Johannes IV. hatte für diplomatische Unternehmungen in Dalmatien einen Großteil des Schatzes ausgegeben, der schon zur Zeit der Bauvorhaben von Honorius I. stark geschrumpft war. Außerdem benötigte der an sich schon kostspielige Unterhalt der Katakomben und *memoriae* im *suburbium* eine funktionierende Infrastruktur und ein effizientes Straßennetz, worauf Theodors Kirchenverwaltung vermutlich nicht mehr zählen

39 Die Quellenanalyse führt Flusin 1992, II, S. 354–356 zu der Annahme, Anastasius' Reliquien seien um 650 nach Rom gelangt, was jedoch ein Datum zur Zeit Theodors nicht grundsätzlich ausschließt.

40 Spera 2002; Geertman 2004, S. 106.

41 Bertolini 1968, S. 65–68.

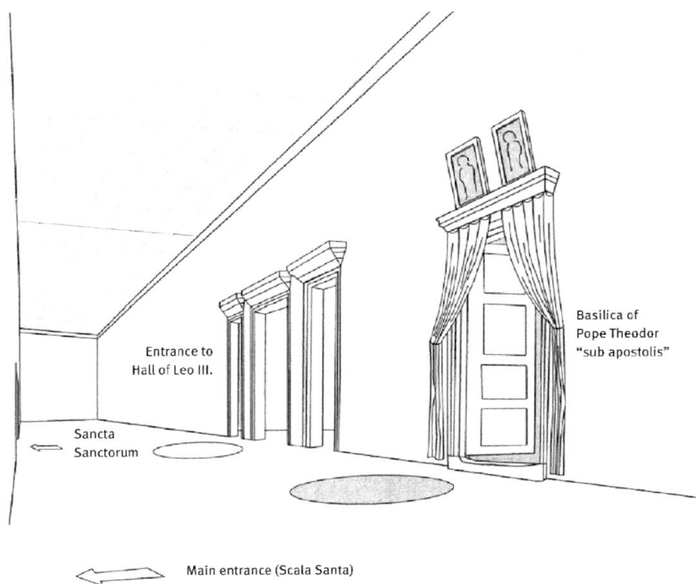

Abb. 8: Rom. Episcopium lateranense, hypothetische Rekonstruktion des Zugangs zur Basilica Theodori.

konnte. Mit anderen Worten: Der Verfall der Gegenden außerhalb der Stadtmauern könnte die Kirchenhierarchie entmutigt oder zumindest zu einer Verringerung ihrer Ambitionen im *suburbium* veranlasst haben. Zu Theodors Zeit fehlte es an jener ausgezeichneten Verflechtung zwischen Stadt und Außenbezirken, die die Entfaltung von Honorius' Mäzenatentum erst möglich gemacht hatte.

3. Es gibt jedoch einen weiteren Aspekt, der leicht übersehen wird, nämlich die besondere Beschaffenheit der orientalischen Gemeinde in Rom. In einer neuen Synthese der viel debattierten historiographischen Frage nach dem ›griechischen Rom‹ hat Vera von Falkenhausen die Grundzüge der orientalischen Präsenz in der *Urbs* von der Zeit Justinians bis zum Ende der byzantinischen Herrschaft (und darüber hinaus) scharfsichtig nachgezeichnet.[42] Die Rede ist von zweisprachigen Klerikern, aber auch (viel schlechter dokumentierbaren) Laienfunktionären und ihren Familien, mit kürzerer oder längerer Einwanderungsgeschichte. Obwohl Theodor zur höchsten Ebene der römischen Hierarchie aufgestiegen war, blieb er doch ein vollberechtigtes Mitglied seiner Ursprungsgemeinschaft. Diese Gruppe stellte zahlreiche Verwal-

42 Falkenhausen 2015.

tungsbeamte und zum Teil nicht-autochthone Militärs und setzte auf die Permeabilität der kirchlichen Rangordnung auch für jüngst eingewanderte Orientalen. Daher schlug diese Gemeinschaft vor allem im urbanen Umfeld Wurzeln, während ihr Interesse für die Vorstadt gering war. Ausnahmen gab es natürlich: Man denke nur an die bedeutenden, nicht-lateinischen monastischen Vorposten, wie das genannte Kloster Ad Aquas Salvias an der Via Laurentina, das mit der Verwaltung riesiger Ländereien betraut war, oder an die eher spärlichen Anzeichen für griechischsprachige Siedlungen in der Campagna, wie die Erforschung einiger Ortsnamen nahelegt.

Im Hintergrund der Maßnahmen Theodors bleibt das ›griechische‹ Rom mit seinem Klerus, seinen Kirchen und Klöstern – ein enges Netz an Institutionen, das schon lange gut funktioniert, als Theodor den Papstthron besteigt, denn es hat sich im Laufe der Zeit als Gegenstück zu den weltlichen Einrichtungen (Exarchat einerseits, Herzogtum und dessen Lokalbeamte andererseits) im Rahmen des *indirect rule* des oströmischen Reiches in Italien entwickelt. Es bleibt die Frage nach dem Beitrag Theodors zum Gesicht der Stadt. Wahrscheinlich war dieser doch erheblicher als die knappen Angaben im *Liber pontificalis* annehmen lassen. Vermutlich schweigt sich der *Liber* über mehrere seiner Aufträge aus, die von Griechen besiedelte Stadtgebiete an der *Ripa Graeca* bzw. auf dem Aventin betrafen, sodass auch die Erinnerung daran für immer verloren gegangen ist.

Aus den kargen Zeilen der Biographie dieses Papstes lassen sich immerhin drei interessante Aspekte herauslesen: die Pflege von Stätten zur Heiligenverehrung, wie im Falle des Euplius-Oratoriums an der Via Ostiense, die Preisgabe diverser Bauwerke, die schwer zu kontrollieren bzw. instand zu halten waren, wie die abseits gelegene Basilika von Nomentum, und schließlich die Vollendung prachtvoller und sehr beliebter Heiligtümer, wie die *memoria* Valentins an der Via Flaminia – drei eindeutige Indizien für eine zahlenmäßig eher beschränkte Bautätigkeit, aber mit eindeutig »pragmatischem« Ansatz.

Bibliographie

Abkürzungen

CTCR: Codice Topografico della Città di Roma, hg. von R. Valentini und G. Zucchetti, Rom 1940–1953.

Greg. Ep.: Grégoire le Grand, Registre des lettres. Introduction, texte, traduction, notes et appendices par Pierre Minard (Sources chrétiennes, 370–371), Paris 1991.

LP: Le Liber Pontificalis, texte, introduction et commentaire par l'abbé L. Duchesne, Paris 1955.

LTUR Suburbium: Lexicon Topographicum Urbis Romae. Suburbium, hg. von A. La Regina et al., Rom 2001–2008.

Theoph. *Chron.*: Theophanes, Chronographia, recensuit Carolus De Boor, Leipzig 1883–1885.

Literatur

Andaloro 1987 Maria Andaloro: Aggiornamento scientifico e bibliografia a G. Matthiae, Pittura romana del medioevo, I, Rom 1965, Rom 1987.

Ballardini 2015 Antonella Ballardini: »In antiquissimo ac venerabili Lateranensi palatio«: la residenza dei pontefici secondo il Liber Pontificalis, in: Le corti nell'alto medioevo, Atti della LXII Settimana di studio del CISAM (Spoleto 2014), Spoleto 2015, S. 889–927.

Basile 2000 Giuseppe Basile: Il restauro del mosaico absidale della Cappella dei Santi Primo e Feliciano in Santo Stefano Rotondo a Roma, in: Santo Stefano Rotondo in Roma. Archeologia, storia dell'arte, restauro. Atti del convegno internazionale (Rom 1996), hg. von Hugo Brandenburg und József Pál, Wiesbaden 2000, S. 151–153.

Bertolini 1968 Ottorino Bertolini: Il patrizio Isacio esarca d'Italia, in: Ottorino Bertolini. Scritti scelti di storia medioevale (Università degli Studi di Pisa. Pubblicazioni dell'Istituto di Storia della Facoltà di Lettere, 3), hg. von Ottavio Banti, Livorno 1968, Bd. I, S. 65–68.

Booth 2014 Phil Booth: Crisis of Empire. Doctrine and Dissent at the End of Late Antiquity (Transformation of the Classical Heritage, 62), Berkeley/Los Angeles/London 2014.

Brandenburg 2000 Hugo Brandenburg: S. Stefano Rotondo. Der letzte Großbau der Antike in Rom. Die Typologie des Baus. Die Ausstattung der Kirche. Die kunstgeschichtliche Stellung des Kirchenbaues und seiner Ausstattung, in: Santo Stefano Rotondo in Roma. Archeologia, storia dell'arte, restauro. Atti del convegno internazionale (Rom 1996), hg. von Hugo Brandenburg und József Pál, Wiesbaden 2000, S. 35-65.

Capitani 1992 Ovidio Capitani: Le relazioni tra le vite di Teodoro I e Martino I del »Liber Pontificalis« e gli Atti del Concilio Lateranense del 649: nuove prospettive, in: Studi e ricerche sull'Oriente cristiano 15, 1992, S. 5–14.

Ceschi 1982 Carlo Ceschi: Santo Stefano Rotondo (Atti della Pontificia Accademia Romana di Archeologia. Serie III. Memorie, 15), Rom 1982.

Coates-Stephens 1997 Robert Coates-Stephens: Dark Age Architecture in Rome, in: Papers of the British School at Rome 65, S. 177–232.

Davis-Weyer 1988 Cäcilia Davis-Weyer: Das Apsismosaik von S. Stefano Rotondo in Rom, in: Kirchen am Lebensweg. Festgabe zum 60. Geburtstag und 20. Bischofsjubiläum für seine Eminenz Friedrich Kardinal Wetter, Erzbischof von München und Freising (Jahrbuch des Vereins für Christliche Kunst in München e.V.; 17), hg. von Lothar Altmann und Hans Ramisch, München 1988, S. 385–408.

Davis-Weyer 1989 Cäcilia Davis-Weyer. S. Stefano Rotondo in Rome and the oratory of Theodore I, in: Italian Church decoration of the middle ages and early Renaissance. Functions, forms and regional traditions, hg.von William Tronzo, Bologna 1989, S. 61–80.

De Rossi 1888 Giovanni Battista de Rossi: Inscriptiones Christianae Vrbis Romae, septimo saecvlo antiqviores, II.1, Rom 1888.

Ekonomou 2007 Andrew J. Ekonomou: Byzantine Rome and the Greek popes. Eastern Influences on Rome and the Papacy from Gregory the Great to Zacharias, AD. 590–752, Lanham, MD 2007.

Falkenhausen 2015 Vera von Falkenhausen: Roma greca. Greci e civiltà greca a Roma nel medioevo, in: Roma e il suo territorio nel medioevo. Le fonti scritte fra tradizione e innovazione. Atti del Convegno internazionale di studio dell'Associazione italiana dei Paleografi e Diplomatisti (Rom, 25.–29.10.2012), hg. von Cristina Carbonetti, Santo Lucà und Maddalena Signorini, Spoleto 2015, S. 39–72.

Flusin 1992 Bernard Flusin: Saint Anastase le Perse et l'histoire de la Palestine au début du VIIe siècle), Paris 1992.

Gambuti 2014–2015 Emanuele Gambuti: Porticus Ecclesiae Sanctae Agnetis: lo scalone di accesso alla basilica onoriana, in: Quaderni dell'Istituto di Storia dell'Architettura n.s. 63, 2014–2015, S. 5–18.

Gandolfo 2004 Francesco Gandolfo: Il ritratto di committenza nella Roma medievale, Rom 2004.

Geertman 1975 Herman Geertman: More veterum. Il Liber Pontificalis e gli edifici ecclesiastici di Roma nella tarda Antichità e nell'Alto Medioevo, Groningen 1975.

Geertman 2004 Herman Geertman: Hic fecit basilicam. Studi sul Liber Pontificalis e gli edifici ecclesiastici di Roma da Silvestro a Silverio, hg. von Sible de Blaauw, Leuven/Paris/Dudley 2004.

Gianandrea 2012 Manuela Gianandrea: Il »doppio papa« nelle decorazioni absidali del Medioevo romano, in: Le plaisir de l'art du Moyen Âge: commande, production et réception de l'œuvre d'art. Mélanges en hommage à Xavier Barral i Altet, hg. von Rosa Alcoy et al., Paris 2012, S. 663–669.

Liverani 1999 Paolo Liverani: Dalle Aedes Laterani al Patriarchio lateranense, in: Rivista di Archeologia Cristiana 75, 1999, S. 521–549.

Luchterhandt 2015 Manfred Luchterhandt: Vom Haus des Bischofs zum Locus Sanctus: Der Lateranpalast im kulturellen Gedächtnis des römischen Mittelalters, in: The Emperor's House: Palaces from Augustus to the Age of Absolutism (Urban Spaces, 4), hg. von Michael Featherstone et al., Berlin [u. a.] 2015, S. 73–92.

Marin 2009 Emilio Marin: Il mosaico della cappella di S. Venanzio al battistero lateranense. Status quaestionis, in: Il cristianesimo in Istria tra tarda Antichità e alto Medioevo, novità e riflessioni, Atti della giornata tematica del Seminario di Archeologia Cristiana (Rom 2007), Vatikanstadt 2009, S. 209–215.

Matthiae 1965 Guglielmo Matthiae: Pittura romana del Medioevo, Rom 1965.

Minasi 2012 Mara Minasi: Nuove acquisizioni dai restauri delle pitture altomedievali della catacomba romana di Ponziano, in: Martiri, santi, patroni. Per una archeologia della devozione. Atti del X Congresso Nazionale di Archeologia Cristiana (Università della Calabria 2010), hg. von Adele Coscarella und Paola De Santis, Arcavacata di Rende 2012, S. 567–579.

Palombi 2008 Cinzia Palombi: S. Valentini basilica, ecclesia, coemeterium, in: LTUR Suburbium, V, S. 219–225.

Palombi 2009 Cinzia Palombi: Nuovi studi sulla basilica di San Valentino sulla Via Flaminia, in: Rivista di Archeologia Cristiana 85, 2009, S. 469–540.

Passigli 1985 Susanna Passigli: Una questione di topografia cristiana: l'ubicazione della basilica dei SS. Primo e Feliciano sulla Via Nomentana, in: Rivista di Archeologia Cristiana 61, 1985, S. 311–332.

Piazza 2006 Simone Piazza: Pittura rupestre medievale. Lazio e Campania settentrionale (secoli VI–XIII), Rom 2006.

Price 2014 The Acts of the Lateran Synod of 649, translated with notes by Richard Price (Translated Texts for Historians; 61), Liverpool 2014.

Ravegnani 2011 Giorgio Ravegnani: Gli esarchi d'Italia, Rom 2011.

Spera 2002 Lucrezia Spera: Luoghi di culto di carattere »rievocativo« nel suburbio, in: Ecclesiae Urbis, Atti del congresso internazionale di studi sulle chiese di Roma (IV–X secolo) (Rom 2000), hg. von Federico Guidobaldi und Alessandra Guiglia Guidobaldi, Vatikanstadt 2002, Bd. I, S. 691–712.

Spera 2004 Lucrezia Spera: S. Eupli oratorium, ecclesia, in: LTUR Suburbium, II, S. 228–230.

Spera 2011 Lucrezia Spera: Osservazioni sulle »porticus« dei complessi martiriali a Roma: assetti architettonico-urbanistici e questioni cronologiche, in: Marmoribus vestita. Miscellanea in onore di Federico Guidobaldi (Studi di antichità cristiana, 63), hg. von Olof Brandt und Philippe Pergola, Vatikanstadt 2011, Bd. II, S. 1299–1330.

Spera 2012 Lucrezia Spera: I santuari di Roma dall'antichità all'altomedioevo: morfologie, caratteri dislocativi, riflessi della devozione, in: I santuari di Roma, hg. von Sofia Boesch Gajano et al., Rom 2012, S. 32–58.

Susi 2000 Eugenio Susi: Teodoro I, in: Enciclopedia dei Papi (Istituto della Enciclopedia Italiana), Rom 2000, Bd. I, S. 594–598.

Taddei 2016 Alessandro Taddei: Il VII secolo. Da Sabiniano (604–606) a Sergio I (687–701), in: La committenza artistica dei papi a Roma nel Medioevo, hg. von Mario D'Onofrio, Rom 2016.

Thunø 2015 Erik Thunø: The apse mosaic in early medieval Rome: time, network, and repetition, Cambridge 2015.

Das Papsttum und Rom im 8. Jahrhundert

Neudeutung der institutionellen ›Wende‹ anhand der archäologischen Dokumentation

Lucrezia Spera

Die geläufigsten und bewährtesten Interpretationsmodelle der Entwicklung von Kirchengeschichte und Papsttum zwischen Spätantike und Mittelalter bescheinigen den Jahrzehnten zwischen dem Ende des 7. und der Mitte des 8. Jahrhunderts (in manchen Fällen sogar bis zur Karolingerzeit) eine Serie von außergewöhnlichen Neuerungen im Profil von Institutionen und Handlungsmöglichkeiten der römischen Bischöfe.[1] An diesen Neuerungen machen viele die endgültige Gestaltung der weltlichen Macht der Kirche fest, insbesondere die Schaffung des *Stato pontificio* und der *Repubblica di San Pietro*, um mit den Titeln der lesenswerten Bücher von Girolamo Arnaldi und Thomas Noble zu sprechen. Vor dem Hintergrund komplexer, von interagierenden Faktoren geprägter Szenarien (Verhältnis zu Byzanz, wechselnde Rolle des Exarchats, Kontakte zu den Langobarden und zu dem entstehenden Frankenreich, Bedrohung durch den Islam) zeichnet sich die Gestalt des Papstes in dieser Zeit durch eine nie dagewesene Dynamik aus, geprägt von zunehmender, meist endgültiger Aneignung von Funktionen und Bereichen, die ihm ursprünglich nicht zukamen, die jedoch auf natürliche Weise einbezogen oder auch programmatisch beansprucht wurden. Dies beruhte fast immer auf der Notwendigkeit, von der ›staatlichen‹ Macht hinterlassene Leerräume wieder zu füllen. So spielte der Papst letztendlich eine wesentliche Rolle in der Diplomatie, weit über die oft wiederkehrenden lehramtlichen Debatten hinaus. Er besitzt eine Autorität in zivilen und militärischen Angelegenheiten, insbesondere, aber nicht nur, für Rom und sein Herzogtum, natürlich erst seit Errichtung desselben.[2] Anlässlich der Wahl Pauls I. können der wiedererstandene Senat und das römische Volk im berühmten Brief

---

1 Zu berücksichtigen sind vor allem die insgesamt stets überzeugenden Ausführungen von Ottorino Bertolini, Thomas Noble, Girolamo Arnaldi, David Miller: Bertolini 1941, Noble 1984 (mit Noble 1995), Arnaldi 1987; unter den Studien Millers bes. Miller 1974 und Miller 1975.

2 Vgl. auch Bertolini 1966, Ullmann 1955, Ullmann 1972, Richards 1979, Delogu 2000b, Marazzi 1991 und Delogu 2010, S. 213–230; zu verschiedenen ›genetischen‹ Aspekten, mit einer recht kontroversen Deutung, s. Sessa 2012. Zu den Problemen der Schaffung des Herzogtums von Rom s. Bertolini 1941, S. 369–371, Bavant 1979, Arnaldi 1987, S. 25–28, 110, Delogu 2010, bes. S. 220–222.

an Pippin sich mit einer bedeutsam erneuerten Formulierung bezeichnen als »*firmi ac fideles servi sanctae Dei ecclesiae et* [...] *ter beatissimi et coangelici spiritalis [patris vestris, domni nostri Pauli] summi pontificis et universalis papae*.[3]

Die Wende im Verhältnis des Papsttums zur *Urbs*, über welche die Päpste ab der Karolingerzeit umfassende Regierungsmacht ausübten[4], lässt sich an zahlreichen archäologischen Indikatoren ablesen. Wie wir sehen werden, geben diese in ihrer Gesamtheit ein Bild ab, das sich vollständig mit den Belegen der Schriftdokumente deckt. Anhand direkter und ausschließlicher Blickpunkte bietet die Archäologie klar erkennbare materielle ›Zeichen‹ für die entsprechenden Entwicklungen, mit der Möglichkeit, bestimmte Elemente zu revidieren bzw. zu präzisieren.

Die Parameter zur Wertung der grundlegenden, bedeutenden Veränderungen in Gewichtung und Rolle des Papstes in Rom sind wie folgt zu bestimmen: Wahl der Residenz, Verantwortung für Verwaltung und Instandhaltung städtischer Infrastrukturen und des öffentlichen Raumes, Übernahme besonderer, ausschließlicher Kompetenzen der Staatsmacht (Münzprägung, verantwortliche Leitung der mit Bautätigkeit zusammenhängenden Produktionsbereiche), Aufbau von Hilfseinrichtungen für die Bürger.

Zum letztgenannten, eminent wichtigen Aspekt, der im Übrigen auf einem Kernelement der frühen Kirche gründet, nämlich der Fürsorge und Unterstützung für die *pauperes*,[5] gibt es schon eingehende Studien, in denen Zeiten und Modalitäten einer komplexen und effizienten ›Unterstützungsmaschinerie‹ hinreichend dargelegt sind. Sie wurde von den grundlegenden Maßnahmen Gregors des Großen vorweggenommen[6] und in der ersten Hälfte des 8. Jahrhunderts nachdrücklich institutionalisiert durch die Einrichtung von Diakonien[7] und den *domuscultae* genannten Zentren zur direkten Nahrungsmittelversorgung, einer revolutionären Neuerung im Vergleich zu den althergebrachten Landwirtschafts- und Vertriebsstrukturen.[8] Außerdem kam es vermutlich zu einer Potenzierung der sozialen Funktion des Episkopiums, da dieses ja über Lagerhallen (*paracellarium*)[9] und das entsprechende Personal verfügte, das Papst

3 Codex Carolinus, 13, MGH, *Epist.* III, 508–510. Zum Senat im Mittelalter s. Arnaldi 1982 und Arnaldi 1997.

4 Zum karolingischen Rom s. vor allem Krautheimer 1981, S. 143–178, Bauer 2001a, Bauer 2001–2002, Bauer 2004, Christie 2005, Barresi, Pensabene 2007, Cecchelli et al. 2007, Delogu 2010, S. 259–287, Goodson 2010, Luchterhandt 2010.

5 Im Wesentlichen Mazza 1989 und Mazza 2006; Fiocchi Nicolai 2007.

6 Arnaldi 1986; Pilara 2007 und Stasolla 2007 mit neueren Gesichtspunkten; vgl. auch Arnaldi 1987, S. 45–47 und Delogu 2010, bes. Anm. 2 S. 213–214. Zu den Räumen für karitative Tätigkeiten s. Giuntella 2001.

7 Bertolini 1947, Marazzi 1991, Falisiedi 1995, Hermes 1996, Dey 2008, Cecchelli 2010, Milella 2010; einige Ideen des immer noch wichtigen Durliat 1990 wurden in letzter Zeit in Frage gestellt.

8 Marazzi 1985, Arnaldi 1987, S. 91–93, De Francesco 1996, Marazzi 2001–2002, De Francesco 2004, S. 244–284.

9 Das Wort ist ein *terminus technicus* aus dem *Liber pontificalis*: Man findet es in der Vita Hadrians I. als Bezeichnung für ein Nahrungsmittellager (*vinum ... seu diversa legumina*), das aus den landwirtschaftlichen

Zacharias darüber hinaus mit einer häufigen Verteilung (*crebris diebus*) von Grundnahrungsmitteln an die bei St. Peter ansässigen Armen und alle Bedürftigen der Stadt betraute.[10] Laut der Biographie Hadrians I. empfing der Patriarch jeden Tag um die hundert Bedürftige zur Nahrungsmittelverteilung, *in portico quae est iuxta scala que ascendit in patriarchio, ubi et ipsi pauperes depicti sunt*, d.h. sogar die Bildausstattung ließ die vorwiegende Nutzung dieses Areals erahnen.[11] Im Papstpalast kam also der Bischof seinen Verpflichtungen zur Versorgung der Bevölkerung nach, und so entstand ein neues Zentrum städtischen Lebens, eine höchst geeignete Stätte für die Spendenrituale, die in direkter Linie auf die römischen Kaiser zurückgingen. Die Vita Gregors des Großen liefert dazu interessante Anhaltspunkte durch eine detaillierte Beschreibung der Schenkungen des Papstes zu Monatsbeginn einerseits an die Armen (lebenswichtige Güter wie *frumentum, vinum, caseum, legumen, lardum, manducabilia animalia, pisces, oleum*) und andererseits an die *primores* der Stadt (*pigmenta et alia delicatiora commercia*, also exquisite und exotische Waren).[12] Der Brauch, zu besonderen Feiertagen wie Ostern oder dem Fest der Heiligen Petrus und Paulus in der Vigilius-Basilika *aurei* bzw. *solidi*, aber auch *peregrina vestimenta*[13] an Bischöfe, Priester, Diakone und Würdenträger zu verteilen, folgte ohne Zweifel dem Beispiel der ehemaligen kaiserlichen *largitiones*.[14]

In den hier untersuchten Jahrzehnten traten verschiedene Schlüsselfiguren auf, deren Pontifikate ganz offensichtliche Veränderungen brachten, vor allem im Konsolidierungsprozess der Herrschaft über die Stadt. Bezüglich der Gestaltung der Bischofsresidenz als wahres, erkennbares ›Machtzentrum‹ im ausgehenden 8. und Anfang des 9. Jahrhunderts, insofern als sie allen für kaiserliche *palatia* festgestellten Maßstäben genügte[15], stellt das kurze Pontifikat von Johannes VII. (705–707) im Wesentlichen eine Phase des Übergangs und einen Reifeprozess dar. Dieser Papst ging vor allem wegen seiner gespannten Beziehungen zu Justinian II. im Zusammenhang mit der Billigung der Akten des *Quinisextium* in die Geschichte ein.[16] Bekanntlich verknüpft der Autor

---

Betrieben der Kirche bestückt wurde; der Biograf Gregors IV. (LP II, 81) erinnert an die Restaurierung einer Treppe *qui paracellarium respicit* und eines *balneum ›iuxta paracellarium‹*. S. Grisar 1901, S. 483, und D'Onofrio 2002, S. 233.

10 LP I, 435; vgl. auch LP I, 502. In der Organisation der Armenversorgung spielte wohl auch die territoriale Gliederung der Kirche eine Rolle, wie man ebenfalls der Vita Zacharias' entnehmen kann (dazu Spera 2010 und Spera 2013).

11 LP I, 502; s. Ballardini 2015, S. 913–914.

12 Vita Gregorii Magni II, 26.

13 Vita Gregorii Magni II, 25.

14 Allgemein Leader-Newby 2004, S. 11–59. Zu einer Bewertung der Maßnahmen s. auch Arnaldi 1987, S. 48.

15 Augenti 2003.

16 Caspar 1933, S. 630–637, Bertolini 1941, S. 410–412, Breckenridge 1972, Sansterre 1982, Sansterre 1987, Noble 1998, S. 47–49, Berto 2000.

seiner Biographie im *Liber pontificalis* die Bauarbeiten in S. Maria Antiqua mit der Errichtung eines Bischofspalastes (*episcopium quantum ad se construere maluit super eandem ecclesiam*), wo der Papst bis zu seinem Tod residierte (*illicque pontificati sui temporis vitam finivit*).[17] Obwohl diese im Allgemeinen für exzentrisch und persönlich gehaltene[18] Entscheidung des Papstes unterschiedlich ausgelegt werden kann, ist ihre außerordentliche politische Bedeutung klar verständlich.[19] In gewisser Hinsicht erklärt sie sich aus dem familiären Hintergrund und den daraus resultierenden Beziehungen zum ›Kaiserhügel‹, denn sein Vater Platon war *cura(tor) palatii*[20] gewesen. Bertolini begründet sie mit einem Bedürfnis nach größerer Distanz zur Unzufriedenheit in ›Laterankreisen‹, die mit Johannes' Position zum *Quinisextum* verbunden waren.[21] Sansterre, Arnaldi und Luchterhandt hingegen erklären sie mit der isolierten Lage und dem schlechten Schutz des Bischofspalasts am Lateran[22], d.h. mit der Wahl einer zentraler gelegenen Stätte[23], was wiederum laut Llewelyn und Verzone von einer konstruktiven Zusammenarbeit mit der weltlichen Macht zeugt.[24]

Die Errichtung des Episkopiums am Ort der berühmtesten römischen Herrscherwohnung belegt jedoch vor allem die klare Absicht, eine stete Präsenz des Papstes auf dem Palatin zu konsolidieren. Wobei der *Liber pontificalis* schon früher konstante Beziehungen zu diesem Hügel angegeben hatte. Man denke nur an die Wahl von Sergius I. im Oratorium S. Cesario[25], also in der Stadt: eine bedeutsame Geste des dauerhaften Siedelns an diesem äußerst symbolhaften Ort, an dem die weltliche Macht, von den Ereignissen unter Justinian II. und den Querelen um das Verhältnis zwischen Byzanz und dem Exarchat in Italien schon erheblich geschwächt[26], dem Bischof von Rom einen spezifischen und erkennbaren Raum zuerkennt.

---

17 LP I, 385.

18 Ballardini 2015, S. 897, und zuletzt Berto 2000, S. 640: diesbezüglich im Einklang mit der innovativen Entscheidung des Oratoriums in St. Peter als Grablege (Ballardini 2011). So auch Delogu 2010, S. 223.

19 Noble 1998, bes. S. 48.

20 Wie aus der bekannten Inschrift des 16. Jahrhunderts in S. Anastasia hervorgeht (ICh II 152; vgl. L. Duchesne, in LP I, 386 Anm. 1 und Augenti 1996, S. 46); de Rossi 1883, S. 494, und Ballardini 2015, S. 898.

21 Bertolini 1941, S. 412.

22 Sansterre 1982, S. 386, Arnaldi 1987, S. 74, Luchterhandt 2010, S. 326.

23 Delogu 2010, S. 223 und 229; er erkennt auch Anzeichen einer anfänglichen Veränderung des öffentlichen Raums in der Stadtmitte durch das Papsttum.

24 Verzone 1976, S. 39, und Llewelyn 1979, S. 41. Vgl. jedoch den Einwand von Sansterre 1982, S. 386–387.

25 LP I, 371; vgl. Falkenhausen 2000, aber auch Liverani 2003, bes. S. 151. Das spätantike Oratorium wurde lange Zeit südlich des Ostperistyls der *Domus Augustana* verortet, wo Bartoli 1929 allerdings nur mittelalterliche Malereien fand (vgl. Augenti 1996, S. 41–42). Besonders beachtenswert ist die Hypothese von Coarelli 2012, S. 421–450, bes. S. 432, der eine Verbindung zu den *Aedes Caesarum* vorschlägt.

26 Geschichtlicher Bezugsrahmen in: Bertolini 1941, S. 410–412, Breckenridge 1972, Sansterre 1982, Noble 1998, S. 47–49.

Der Versuch einer Annäherung unter rein archäologischen Gesichtspunkten kann bezüglich der fraglichen Baumaßnahme weitere Klärungen bieten: Den wenigen Worten des Biographen nach zu urteilen, handelte es sich eher um einen Neubau als nur um einen Umzug in einen Bereich der schon bestehenden Kaiserresidenz. Der allgemeine Hinweis *super* der Kirche S. Maria Antiqua ließ ihn mit größerer Plausibilität auf der Seite der *Domus Tiberiana* vermuten.[27] In der Tat konnten in allen Bereichen dieses Komplexes, die in den vergangenen Jahrzehnten über und unter der Erde erforscht wurden – im Süden und in den Verbindungen zur *area sacra*[28], bei der Bastione Farnesiano[29], entlang des Nordabhangs[30] und im Mittelbereich des großen Peristyls[31] –, klare und unmissverständlich übereinstimmende Indikatoren dafür gefunden werden, dass die Anlage ab der zweiten Hälfte des 5. Jahrhunderts verlassen wurde: weitläufige Abfallhalden vor allem für Bauschutt, Grabstätten, Spuren der Gewinnung von Spolien, Niveauverschiebungen wegen fehlender Instandhaltung. Alle diese Indizien lassen eine allgemeine und sehr frühe Aufgabe der *Domus Tiberiana* vermuten.[32] Wahrscheinlich hatte sie schon in antoninischer Zeit eine ›Zurückstufung‹ erfahren, hauptsächlich wohl nach dem Brand von 191, welcher der *Domus Augustana* zur endgültigen Durchsetzung als organisch strukturiertem und daher für eine Palastarchitektur geeignetem Modell verholfen hatte.[33] Unter dieser Voraussetzung konnte das Areal besser für das Vorhaben von Johannes VII. verwendet werden. Eine Grabung von 2007, deren Ergebnisse Francesca Carboni erst vor Kurzem veröffentlicht hat, lieferte endlich einen bedeutenden archäologischen Beleg: Die Erforschung des Bereichs mit dem Peristyl über der mittleren Kryptoportikus in den Farnesischen Gärten, wo noch zur Zeit von Maxentius gebaut wurde, bestätigt das Verlassen des kaiserlichen Baukomplexes in der zweiten Hälfte des 5. Jahrhunderts und beleuchtet zum einen den Abbau von Spolien sowie die Anlage von Deponien bis ins 7. Jahrhundert, zum anderen die darauf folgende Errichtung (oberhalb dieser Schicht und unter Wiederverwendung von Teilen des noch

27 Augenti 1996, S. 56–60, R. Santangeli Valenzani, in Meneghini/Santangeli Valenzani 2004, S. 209–210, Ballardini 2015, S. 897–898, Carboni 2016, Spera 2016, S. 104–105. Laut de Rossi 1883, bes. S. 495, befand sich der Bischofspalast von Johannes VII. eher im Areal der Kirche S. Sebastiano in Pallara. Gesamtbibliografie zur *Domus Tiberiana* in: Tomei/Filetici 2011.

28 Coletti 2004, Coletti/Celant/Pensabene 2006, Coletti/Margheritelli 2006, Coletti 2015.

29 Martin 2001, Ciceroni/Martin/Munzi 2004, S. 131–136,

30 Fontana/Munzi 2001, Munzi et al. 2004, bes. S. 92–93, Carboni 2011, S. 49–50.

31 Carboni/Sforza 2011, S. 207–208, Carboni 2016, S. 90. Eine weitere Information ergibt sich aus der Zerstörung von Mühlsteinen, die vermutlich zwischen dem 3. und dem 5. Jahrhundert an den Abhängen im Gebrauch waren: Sie wurden zerlegt und für Fußböden wiederverwendet. Einer davon wird ins 6. Jahrhundert datiert (Wilson 2003).

32 So schon Augenti 1996, S. 17–37, bes. S. 22–24, S. 29–30, Santangeli Valenzani in Meneghini/Santangeli Valenzani 2004, S. 209–210.

33 Krause 1995, bes. S. 197; Coarelli 2012, S. 467.

erhaltenen Mauerwerks) eines recht komplexen Gebäudes. Davon waren noch Reste eines großen, L-förmigen Raums (ca. 10 × 14 m) und einer viereckigen Konstruktion, einer Umgestaltung der Nordseite der Portikus, erhalten. Letztere besaß eine mit Backsteinen ausgekleidete Latrine. Beide Bauten waren in *opus mixtum* unter Verwendung von Spolien errichtet.[34] Innerhalb der Westportikus könnte eine Reihe kleinerer, weniger sorgfältig ausgeführter Räume, deren Mauern vielleicht aus ungebranntem Ton und deren Fußböden aus *opus signinum* bestanden, unter Umständen aus einer anderen, bescheideneren Bauphase stammen (Abb. 1).[35] Die Lage des Gebäudes, seine gesicherte Datierung nach dem 7. Jahrhundert und seine kurze Nutzungsdauer, wie insbesondere der Fund von glasierter Keramik (*ceramica in vetrina pesante*) in den Abfallschichten der Latrine anzeigt[36], lassen den u. a. von Francesca Carboni geäußerten Vorschlag, es handele sich um Überreste der im *Liber pontificalis* erwähnten Residenz von Johannes VII. auf dem Palatin, als sehr plausibel erscheinen. Obwohl sich nur kärgliche Mauerspuren erhalten konnten – das Gros wurde durch Spolienabbau und Gartenanlage in moderner Zeit unwiederbringlich ruiniert –, sind doch noch ein paar zusätzliche Beobachtungen möglich: Mindestens zwei der ausgegrabenen Räume, nämlich die L-förmige Aula und der viereckige Bereich im Norden, erscheinen aufgrund der parallel laufenden Wände und der Bauweise miteinander verwandt und waren wohl Teile eines erheblich umfangreicheren Komplexes. Es ist vorstellbar, dass dieser sich gegen den Nordwesthang des Hügels ausdehnte und ein Areal von bis zu 10.000 m² bedeckte, also nicht unähnlich dem *Patriarchium* in seiner größten Ausdehnung.[37] Auch die Charakteristiken des Mauerwerks sollten beachtet werden: Es wurde aus unterschiedlichem, wiederverwendetem Material erbaut (kleine Tuffblöcke, Marmor und anderer Stein, Ziegel); sie waren ohne Ordnung zusammengesetzt und wiesen eigentümliche Serien von schräg gesetzten Tuffblöcken auf. Alle diese Besonderheiten sind bei Gebäuden aus dem 7. und 8. Jahrhundert weit verbreitet, also aus der Zeit vor der erneuten Qualitätssteigerung in den karolingischen Bauhütten. Bedeutsam sind in diesem Zusammenhang – aufgrund der engen Analogie zum frühmittelalterlichen Mauerwerk auf dem Palatin – die im Komplex von St. Paul vor den Mauern ausgegrabenen Ruinen, die wohl zum dortigen Kloster gehörten und recht präzise in das Pontifikat von Gregor II. (715–731) datiert werden (Abb. 2).[38]

34 Carboni 2016.

35 Laut der Beschreibung in Carboni 2016, S. 92, lässt sich dies aus dem offensichtlichen Unterschied zwischen diesen Anlagen und Sockelleisten »aus Backsteinfragmenten, Steinen und wiederverwendeten, von einem Tongemisch zusammengehaltenen Marmorstücken« erahnen.

36 Carboni 2016, S. 92–94.

37 Am Lateran lässt sich die vom Bischofskomplex beanspruchte Grundfläche auf ca. 100 × 150 m errechnen. Zum *Patriarchium* s. unten Anm. 62 mit Bibliographie.

38 Spera/Esposito/Giorgi 2011.

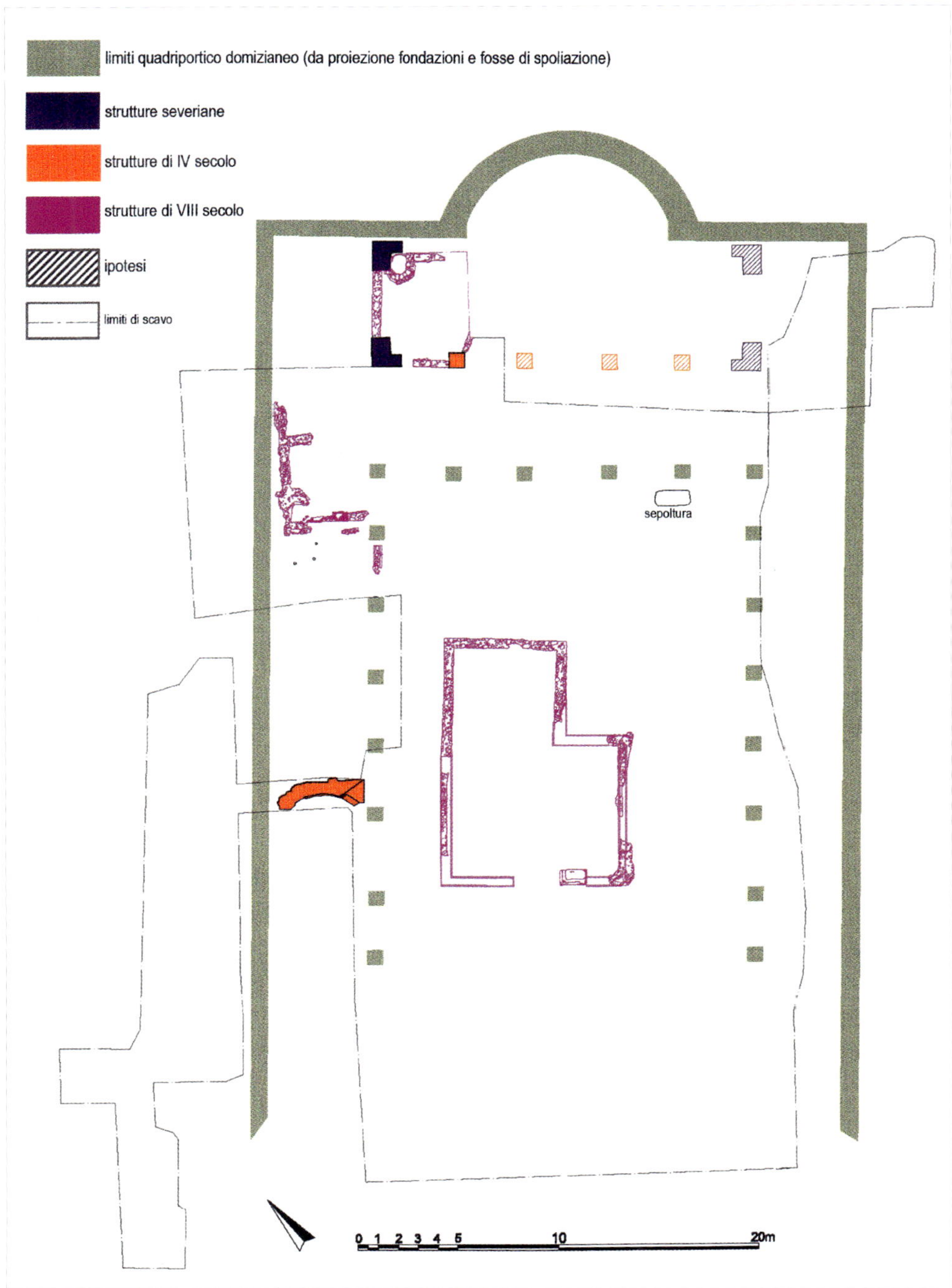

Abb. 1: *Domus Tiberiana*: Plan der beim zentralen Peristyl aufgefundenen Mauerreste.

Abb. 2: Mauerwerk im Vergleich: a–b) frühmittelalterliche Strukturen im Bereich der *Domus Tiberiana*; c) Klosterareal im Komplex von St. Paul vor den Mauern.

Mit dem Bau eines zweiten bischöflichen Palais auf dem Palatin als Alternative zum Lateran hatte Johannes VII. auf dem Hügel einen bislang unbekannten Dualismus eingeführt, weil sich nun das neue bischöfliche Zentrum neben dem offiziellen Sitz der weltlichen Macht befand – mit gesicherter Kontinuität in der *Domus Augustana*.[39] Nicht zuletzt wurden die Verbindungen zwischen Palatin und Forum Romanum an der Nordwestseite reaktiviert, namentlich über S. Maria Antiqua und dank anzunehmender Baumaßnahmen an den Abhängen.[40] Über dem Niveau des ehemaligen *Atrium Vestae*, in einem im Mittelalter zum Forum und zu S. Maria Liberatrice hin erbauten Raum, wurden die beiden Ziegel entdeckt, von denen Giovanni Battista de Rossi wohl nicht ganz zu Unrecht annahm, sie seien von oben heruntergebrochen. Sie tragen Stempel mit griechischen Schriftzeichen und Kreuz und werden der Zeit von Johannes VII. zugeordnet.[41] Das macht sie zu einem plausiblen Beleg der ersten Ziegelherstellung in Rom unter bischöflicher Leitung.[42]

Die Maßnahmen von Johannes VII. im mittleren Bereich lassen sich jedoch auch weitergehend deuten, falls die Schaffung des kirchlichen Archivs für die Verwaltung der nicht in das *patrimonium Sancti Petri* inkludierten Güter ebenfalls auf diesen Papst zurückgeht, wie die eingehende Studie von Wilhelm Kurze dargelegt hat.[43] Dieses Projekt würde gut zur Einstellung dieses Papstes passen, der schon 686 *curator* des *patrimonium Appiae* geworden war[44], und zu bestimmten Ereignissen seines Pontifikats (namentlich der Gewährung des Patrimoniums der *Alpes Cottiae*, das Rothari der Kirche entzogen hatte)[45]. Verschiedene Dokumente in der *Collectio Canonum* von Deusdedit bezeugen die Existenz dieses Archivs schon in der Zeit von Johannes VII. und seine ununterbrochene Nutzung bis ins 11. Jahrhundert mit dem Namen *Chartularium*.[46] Rodolfo Lanciani hat überzeugend ausgeführt, dass dieses dem *Testamentum* entsprach,

39 In der allgemeinen Wertung der monumentalen und literarischen Zeugnisse wurde das Siegel des Exarchen Paulus (723–726), das Bartoli »sul piano antico« entdeckte, ebenfalls als unbestreitbares Anzeichen von Kontinuität gesehen (Bartoli 1950, S. 272–275, Augenti 1996, 48).

40 Es ist allerdings recht unwahrscheinlich, dass mit den in Platons Inschrift (s. oben Anm. 20) genannten Restaurierungen einer monumentalen Treppe die Rampe bei S. Maria Antiqua gemeint ist, wie auch de Rossi 1883, S. 404, dachte; eine Baumaßnahme an der Südseite, zu S. Anastasia hin, ist eher anzunehmen (Spera 2016, S. 102).

41 De Rossi 1883. Im selben Raum, 1,60 m oberhalb des *Atrium Vestae*, wurden über 800 Münzen entdeckt, sowie zwei Beschläge mit einer Widmung für Papst Marinus II., was eine besondere Verwendung nahelegt (de Rossi 1883, Augenti 1996, S. 139–140). Zu den gestempelten Backsteinen: CIL XV, 1, 1594 (vgl. Augenti 1996, S. 140).

42 Steinby 1986, S. 115–116, s. aber auch unten.

43 Kurze 1990.

44 Wie der Inschrift in S. Anastasia (s. oben Anm. 20) zu entnehmen ist: Berto 2000, S. 638.

45 Arnaldi 1987, S. 75.

46 Kurze 1990, bes. S. 29–31; vgl. Deusdedit, *Collectio Canonum*, hg. von P. Martinucci, Venedig 1869, S. 193–194, S. 357.

Abb. 3: Reste der *Turris Chartularia* am Abhang des Palatins.

einer monumentalen Anlage, die in einer der Routen des *Itinerarium Einsidlense* beim Titusbogen angegeben ist.[47] Der Standort ist identisch mit der *Turris Chartularia*, die im 12. Jahrhundert der Frangipane-Familie gehörte und die sicherlich ihren Namen von der Nähe oder sogar ursprünglichen Zugehörigkeit zu diesem Komplex hatte (Abb. 3).[48] Bisher beruhte die Identifizierung des *Chartularium-Testamentum* vor allem auf den Überresten des viereckigen Baus am Palatinabhang, die lange Zeit als Bestandteil des Tempels für Jupiter Stator aufgefasst wurden[49], aber vielleicht eher das Fundament eines monumentalen Aufgangs zum Hügel aus severianischer Zeit waren. Von außerordent-

47 Valentini/Zucchetti 1942, S. 196 (mit Anm. 2). Zur Identifizierung mit dem *Chartularium:* Lanciani 1889, Sp. 499–500, Augenti 1996, S. 72–73, Del Lungo 2004, S. 103.

48 Bartoli 1912, de Rossi 1883, S. 495–497, Augenti 1996, S. 90–92, S. 142–143. Der Turm ist auf verschiedenen Veduten zu sehen, so z. B. auf denen von Cock (H. Cock, Praecipua aliquot Romanae antiquitatis ruinarum monumenta, Antwerpen 1551, Taf. Z. 195.) und Du Pérac (E. Du Pérac, Vestigi delle antichità di Roma, Rom 1575, Taf. XV): Augenti 1996, S. 90–95.

49 Zusammenfassung in Augenti 1996, S. 73.

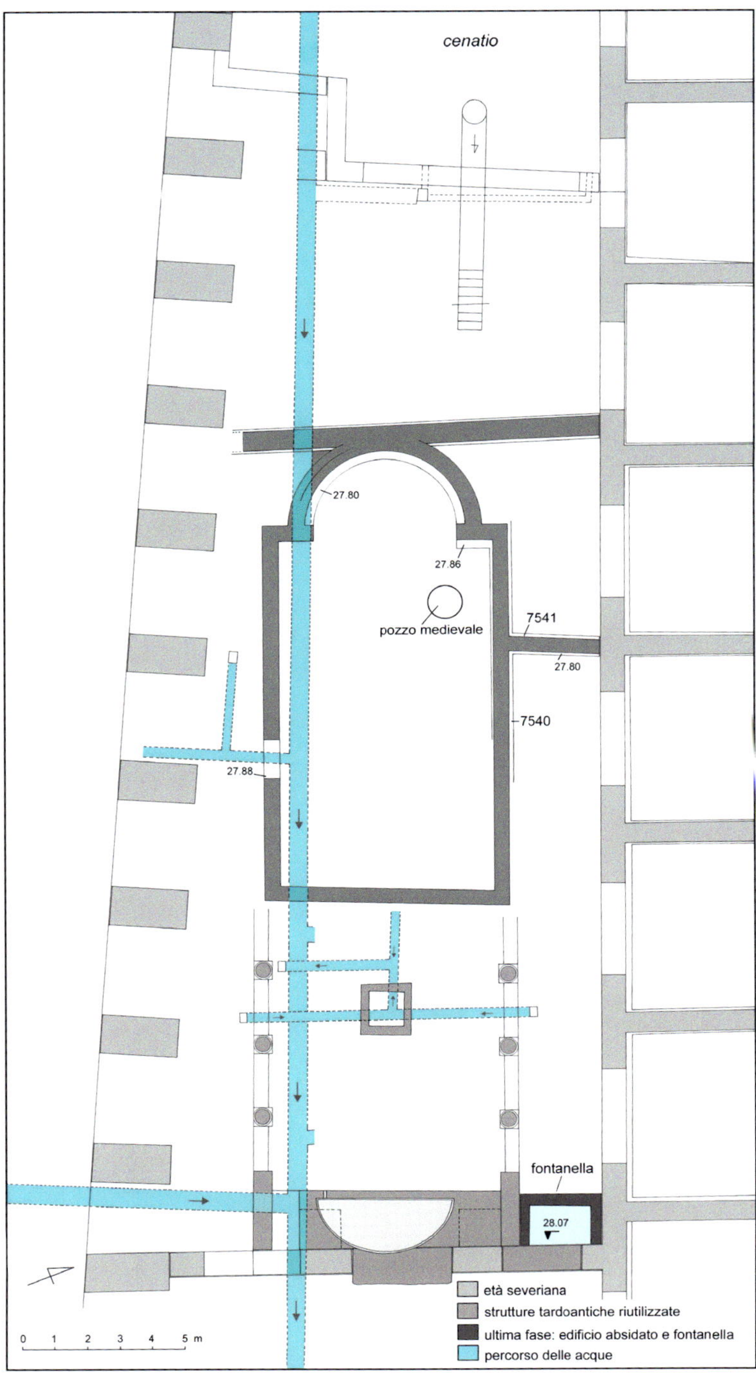

Abb. 4: Aula mit Apsis in den sogenannten Thermen des Elagabal.

lichem Reiz ist jedoch die Annahme, das Kirchenarchiv[50] sei in die sogenannten Thermen des Elagabal integriert worden – sowohl unter Wiederverwendung existierenden Mauerwerks als auch östlich davon. In diesem Bereich haben nämlich die jüngsten Grabungen von Clementina Panella und Lucia Saguì verschiedene Überreste nachantiker Gebäude freigelegt, Backsteinmauern aus spätantiker Zeit, die zu einem recht umfangreichen Bau im östlichen Bezirk gehörten[51], wo auch ein byzantinisches Siegel aus der Mitte des 9. Jahrhunderts entdeckt wurde (ein bedeutsamer Fund, obwohl er im Material zwischen modernen Schichten angetroffen wurde).[52] Außerdem wurde im Hof der sogenannten Thermen, in Wirklichkeit ein spätkaiserlicher Bankettsaal[53], eine kleinere (ca. 8 × 11 m) Aula mit Apsis ausgegraben, die mit Nebenräumen verbunden war. Sie entstand erst nach der Aufgabe des antiken Komplexes im 6. Jahrhundert, und ihre Mauern weisen einen erheblichen Anteil wiederverwendeter Materialien auf[54] (Abb. 4). Dieses Gebäude wurde von Lucia Saguì als das von Paul I. neu gegründete Oratorium der Heiligen Petrus und Paulus gedeutet[55], das jedoch vermutlich weiter westlich, nahe der Kirche der Heiligen Kosmas und Damian lag.[56] Es handelte sich jedenfalls um einen vielgestaltigen und raumgreifenden Komplex, und es könnten in der Tat die Räumlichkeiten des Kirchenarchivs gewesen sein, die logischerweise auch eine Kapelle umfassten, nämlich die genannte kleine Aula, die einen Teil der früheren Kolonnaden als Atrium nutzte, wie schon in einem anderen Zusammenhang erläutert wurde.[57] In der Route des frühmittelalterlichen Itinerars flankierte sie den schon früh von der *Via sacra* weg geleiteten Weg mit direktem Abstieg zum Kolosseum.[58]

Die von Johannes VII. eingeführte Neuerung auf dem Palatin markiert zweifelsohne einen wesentlichen Wendepunkt im Verhältnis zwischen dem Papsttum und Rom. Zu-

50 Die Annahme, es habe eine Verbindung zu einem byzantinischen Archiv bestanden, ist unbegründet (so Bartoli 1950, S. 269–270, Bison 2010, S. 253–254).

51 Bison 2010, bes. S. 255 zur Auffindung der Mauerreste. Die typologische Bestimmung habe ich aus einer mündlichen Anmerkung Lucia Saguìs abgeleitet. Diese Mauern sind in den veröffentlichten Plänen nicht auffindbar; es wäre interessant, etwaige Korrelationen hinsichtlich Ausrichtung und Niveau mit den späteren Aufbauten am Standort der sog. Thermen des Elagabal zu erforschen.

52 Bison 2010.

53 Saguì/Cante 2015, S. 51–63.

54 Saguì/Cante 2015, S. 64–67.

55 Saguì/Cante 2015, S. 64–65.

56 Zum Gebäude: Episcopo 1999; die beste Lokalisierung gründet auf ein Zeugnis von Torrigio, wonach es bis ins 16. Jahrhundert in der Nähe von Ss. Cosma e Damiano eine Apostelkirche gab, die unter Paul III. abgerissen wurde, um den Platz zu erweitern (Torrigio 1644, S. 73–75, Grisar 1896, S. 465, Ferrua 1943). Hülsen 1927, S. 422, hegt, allein auf der Grundlage der Quellen, daran keinen Zweifel.

57 Spera 2016, S. 105–106.

58 Diese Veränderung der antiken Wegführung in der Nähe des Titusbogens wurde auch von Lanciani 1889, Sp. 496 vermutet und ist im Plan von Leonardo Bufalini deutlich eingezeichnet. Dort verläuft der Abstieg am Podium des Tempels von Venus und Roma, wo der Turm der Annibaldi lag (Colagrossi 1913, S. 152).

nächst gibt es gute Gründe für die Hypothese, dass die Päpste das Episkopium ›über‹ S. Maria Antiqua weit über den Tod seines Erbauers hinaus – ja bis zum Pontifikat Gregors III. (731–741) – bewohnten, und dies trotz des persönlichen Charakters dieser Baumaßnahme, den der Biograph mit der Wendung *quantum ad se* andeutet. Diese Vermutung wurde von mehreren Historikern quasi stillschweigend vorausgesetzt (Duchesne, Bertolini, Sansterre, Arnaldi, Miller)[59], nicht zuletzt unter dem Eindruck eines Ereignisses, in das sein Nachfolger Konstantin verwickelt war: Dieser musste rasch eingreifen, um die Unruhen zu besänftigen, die sich bei der Ankunft des von Philippikos Bardanes ernannten neuen Herzogs Pietro auf der *Via Sacra* ereigneten.[60] Bei der Rückkehr des Papstes in den Lateran, wobei eine außerordentliche Aufwertung des alten Bischofspalasts geplant war, fand (*invenerat*) Zacharias (741–752) das *Patriarchium in magnam penuriam*[61] vor, vielleicht weil es seit Langem fast ungenutzt war.

Vor allem wird durch den Umzug auf den ›Kaiserhügel‹ deutlich, dass sich die Papstresidenz endgültig die Charakteristika der Palastarchitektur aneignet. Weitere prägende Veränderungen erfolgten in der Karolingerzeit, unter Hadrian I. und Leo III.[62] Dies geht aus den Merkmalen des Bauprojekts von Papst Zacharias hervor, womit eine die Bischofsresidenz betreffende Baumaßnahme zum ersten Mal Eingang in den *Liber pontificalis* findet aufgrund ihrer Bedeutung als Manifest der Selbstdarstellung[63]: Im Rahmen einer vollständigen Renovierung (*omne patriarchium paene a novo restauravit)* veranlasste dieser Papst eine erhebliche Erweiterung des Episkopiums, dank der Finanzmittel, die aufgrund der Vierteilung der Kircheneinkünfte dem Bischof zustanden (so zumindest die allgemeine Auslegung der Wendung *suam substantiam omnem per manus Ambrosii primicerii notariorum introduci mandavit*)[64]. Es kamen verschiedene neue Elemente hinzu: eine Portikus mit Turmanbau, Bronzetüren mit Reliefbildern des Erlösers und zwei *triclinia* – eine bemerkenswerte Fortführung der antiken *basilicae*. Nicht nur verwendet der Biograph eine neue Sprache (der *terminus* tritt im *Liber pon-*

59 Bertolini 1941, S. 421, Arnaldi 1987, S. 74, Sansterre 1982, S. 386. Ich stimme letzterem zu in der Vermutung, dass das Petrusoratorium *in patriarchio* (LP I, 402) wohl nicht auf Gregor II. zurückgeht. Es handelt sich im Übrigen um einen problematischen Aspekt, da von dieser Gründung sonst keine Spur erhalten ist. Zu Papst Konstantin vgl. Duchesne in LP I, 395 und Miller 2000, S. 646, außerdem de Rossi 1883 und Lauer 1900, S. 91.

60 LP I, 392 (Arnaldi 1987, S. 77, Noble 1998, S. 51, Miller 2000, S. 645).

61 LP I, 432.

62 Lauer 1900, Lauer 1911, Della Giovanpaola 1999, Luchterhandt 1999, D'Onofrio 2002, Liverani 2003, D'Onofrio 2004, Luchterhandt 2006, Ballardini 2010, Liverani 2012.

63 Bauer 2004, S. 63–66, Ballardini 2010, S. 906–913. Zu einem Überblick s. Osborne 2003. Man beachte, dass die Autoren des *Liber pontificalis* ab diesem Zeitpunkt die Baumaßnahmen der Päpste im Bischofspalais vermerken; zuvor waren zwar die verschiedenen Bauwerke mit spezifischen Toponymen bezeichnet worden, aber die entsprechenden Vorhaben wurden quasi als päpstliche Privatinitiative eingestuft.

64 LP I, 432. Zur Aufteilung der Einkünfte in die vier Ausgabenbereiche s. im Wesentlichen Arnaldi 1987, S. 49.

tificalis hier zum ersten Mal auf)[65]: Neu sind auch architektonische Modelle mit einer erweiterten Bedeutung, die selbstverständlich einem veränderten Protokoll angepasst sind, und neu sind die prachtvoll geschmückten Säle (*diversis marmorum et vitro metallis atque musibo et pictura ornavit*), besonders jener *super eandem turrem* (auch in Bezug auf die zugrunde liegenden ideologischen Werte, die aus einem aus der Antike überlieferten, gut lesbaren Repertoire schöpften), der mit einem Fresko des *Orbis terrarum* ausgestattet war (*et per ascendentes scalas in superioribus super eandem turrem triclinium et cancellos aereos construxit, ubi et orbis terrarum descriptione depinxit atque diversis versiculis ornavit*)[66].

Wenig nützlich erscheint eine Debatte darüber, ob die Vorbilder für das neue Episkopium von Papst Zacharias in Byzanz zu suchen sind oder – wie ebenfalls vertreten wurde – von seinem Aufenthalt in Pavia am Hof Liutprands herrühren.[67] Dessen Residenz, die archäologisch nicht bezeugt ist, beschreiben die Quellen hingegen als bewundernswert.[68] Die Sprache frühmittelalterlicher Bauwerke der Macht ist – wie man weiß – das Ergebnis einer langen Reihe von Anpassungen und Wanderungen, die vom Palatin ausgehen und nach einschneidenden Umgestaltungen in Konstantinopel in den Westen zurückkehren.[69] Auf dieser ›Reise‹ werden sie um viele Zeichen und Funktionen bereichert. In dieser Hinsicht könnte der erste von Papst Zacharias im *Patriarchium* gebaute Turm auch von der veränderten, vor allem norditalienischen Herrschaftsarchitektur mit ihren Befestigungen beeinflusst sein (z.B. der in der *Iconografia rateriana* für Verona bezeugte Bau).[70] Zweifellos ist die Umgestaltung des *Patriarchiums* im Zusammenhang mit der mehrfach gestärkten Autorität zu sehen, mit der Zacharias die politische Szene

65 Zur Bewertung der verwendeten Sprache s. den Beitrag von Jussen in diesem Band.

66 Bertolini 1951; die Verwendung der Kartographie in der römischen Welt als Machtausdruck ist in Nicolet 1991 gut erforscht. Eine Reihe konstruktiver Anhaltspunkte findet sich in Conti 2016; s. außerdem Gregory 2003 und Zumthor 2005. Die Bedeutung der universalen Macht des Papsttums wird aus verschiedenen Briefen Hadrians I. ersichtlich (E 57 und 57: PL 96, Sp. 1216, 1233). S. auch Ballardini 2010, S. 911–912.

67 Hallenbeck 1982 (mit Nobel 1998, S. 73–75).

68 Hudson 1987, Brogiolo 2000, S. 146.

69 Baldini Lippolis 2014, auch zum frühen Bezug auf Konstantinopel in Ravenna mit dem dortigen Triklinium Leos.

70 Der als *Palatium* bezeichnete Bau weist einen Bogen zwischen zwei Türmen auf und könnte den Zugang zur Residenz jenseits der Etsch darstellen (Brogiolo 2000, S. 139; mit anderer Meinung Lusuardi Siena 2012, bes. S. 62 Anm. 7 zu jüngeren Interpretationsfragen: aufgrund der ähnlichen Anlage bevorzugt diese Forscherin eine Deutung als Stadttor). Brogiolo 2000 liefert eine Reihe von Anhaltspunkten und die bekannte Dokumentation auch für die Königspaläste Pavia und Monza (letzterer mit Turmstrukturen) sowie einen Verweis auf die Szene auf der Helmplatte Agilulfs, eingerahmt von zwei Türmen, die vielleicht auf das Palais anspielen. Einige Jahrhunderte später nimmt das Episkopium in Genua die Gestalt des *Patriarchium lateranense* mit Türmen wieder auf (Cagnana 1997). Vgl. auch Marano 2007 mit Informationen zu Interferenzen in der architektonischen Ausformulierung der *episcopia*.

betritt: Er ist der erste ohne Billigung von Byzanz bzw. Ravenna gewählte Papst[71], er besitzt direkte Kontrolle über das Heer, wie die Kampagne von 742 gegen Trasamund, *dux* des Herzogtums Spoleto, beweist.[72] Sogar der *dux* von Rom, Stefan, dem Zacharias die Leitung der Stadt während seiner Reise nach Ravenna anvertraut, scheint vom Papst abhängig.[73] Ferner erwirkt Zacharias die Rückgabe von Ländereien im römischen Herzogtum und in der Pentapolis, wobei er zu den *perditae oves* des Papsttums auch Bevölkerungsgruppen zählte, die voll und ganz zu den byzantinischen Provinzen gehörten.[74] Schließlich organisiert er die öffentliche Fürsorge neu, ebenso die direkte Verteilung durch Gründung der *domuscultae*.

In den Jahrzehnten davor, von Johannes VII. bis Zacharias, war der Prozess der päpstlichen Machtzunahme begleitet von deutlichen Anzeichen einer vermehrten Übernahme von Verantwortung gegenüber der ›weltlichen Stadt‹. Der Raum, den diese neue Art des säkularen Engagements (veranlasst durch eine natürlich-paternalistische Tendenz zur Unterstützung und zum Schutz der Einwohner) in den Biographien einnimmt, lässt diesbezüglich keine Zweifel.[75]

Die Renovierung der Stadtmauern und neue Produktionsstätten für die entsprechenden Bauhütten sind von größter Bedeutung, nicht nur wegen einer realen Notwendigkeit der Instandhaltung des Verteidigungssystems, sondern auch im Hinblick auf die Rolle dieser wichtigen Infrastruktur zur Bestimmung des Stadtbilds. In seinem nur zwanzig Tage währenden Pontifikat hatte Papst Sisinnius, der sich laut seines Biographen in erster Linie um die *habitatores* [...] *Civitatis* kümmern wollte, Kalkstein *pro restauratione murorum*[76] vorbereiten lassen. Wenige Jahre später wurde dieses (offensichtlich genauso dringende wie repräsentative) Projekt von Gregor II. aufgegriffen, bedeutsamerweise auch hier gleich zu Beginn seines Pontifikats (*exordio pontificatus*), aber ebenso rasch aus verschiedenen Gründen wieder aufgegeben.[77] Erst Gregor III. wird es fast gänzlich fertigstellen (*plurima pars murorum* [...] *restaurata est*) unter Einsatz von Eigenmitteln (*de proprio*) für die Bewirtung der Arbeiter (*alimonia artificum*) und für den Kauf von Kalk.[78] Offenbar konnte aufgrund der starken Nachfrage für die Großbaustellen die Lieferung des benötigten Kalks nicht aus eigener Kraft bewältigt

71 Delogu 2000c, S. 656.

72 So schon Gregor II.: Delogu 2000a, S. 650, Delogu 2000c, S. 656.

73 LP I, 429, 431. Delogu 2000b, S. 658.

74 Arnaldi 1987, S. 105–108, Noble 1998, S. 72–78.

75 Spera 2011b, S. 335–340. In manchen Fällen ist die Beschreibung der Bauwerke von ausführlichen Hinweisen auf deren rasche Ausführung begleitet: so LP I, 388.

76 LP I, 388.

77 LP I, 396.

78 LP I, 420. S. im Wesentlichen Coates-Stephens 1999, S. 210–214 und Dey 2011, S. 63–69 zu den frühmittelalterlichen Bauphasen der Mauer.

werden.[79] Gregors Biographie enthält weitere interessante Hinweise bzw. Anzeichen für eine fortschreitende Normalisierung der Ausgaben und der zentralisierten Organisation der weltlichen Baustellen.

Die umfassenden Ergebnisse dieser Entwicklungen finden (zusammen mit ein paar zusätzlichen Elementen) gleichsam eine Zusammenfassung in der Gestalt Hadrians I. (772–795), der unsere Aufmerksamkeit auf das ausgehende 8. Jahrhundert lenkt.[80] Dieser Papst steht für die Übernahme der vollen Jurisdiktion über die Stadt, die ihren Ausdruck findet in der Ausübung aller Kompetenzen der öffentlichen Verwaltung, die zwar schon früher erworben wurden und sich konsolidiert hatten, damals jedoch logischerweise mit gelegentlicher Vollmacht durch die weltliche Gewalt. Hadrians Pontifikat kennzeichnete sich durch: Entstehung einer päpstlichen Münzanstalt mit Prägung von Silberdenaren (die bronzenen *siliqua*-Ausgaben mit Monogramm von Sergius I. waren nur als vereinzelte Emissionen aufgrund kaiserlicher Konzession vorgesehen)[81], Renovierung von *muri* und *turres* (mit hohen Kosten von 100 Goldpfund, vor allem für Lohn und Nahrung der Arbeitskräfte und Kalk)[82], direkte Verwaltung der antiken Denkmäler, über die der Pontifex auch zum ›industriellen‹ Abbau von Materialen für andere Bauten verfügte[83], Herstellung von Ziegeln und Backsteinen, wie die an verschiedenen Stätten aufgefundenen Stücke mit Papstmonogramm belegen (Abb. 5)[84], und *cura aquarum*. Hinsichtlich der Verwaltung der Wasserversorgung war die Kirche in den Jahrhunderten davor gewiss der Hauptabnehmer gewesen: Man denke nur an die

79 Es ist hingegen nicht ausgeschlossen, dass dies auf weniger bedeutenden Baustellen der Fall war, so z. B. im Kloster von St. Paul vor den Mauern, wo aufschlussreiche Belege zur Mörtelverarbeitung ans Licht kamen. Zwar wurde kein Kalk aus den frühmittelalterlichen Bauphasen gefunden, aber doch Anzeichen einer Kalkproduktion vor Ort (Spera/Esposito/Giorgi 2011). In jenen Jahrzehnten spielte die Kalkherstellung in ›industriellem‹ Maßstab in Rom eine wichtige Rolle: Santangeli Valenzani 2015a, bes. S. 338. Zu allgemeinen Produktions- und Vertriebsproblemen seit der Römerzeit s. Traini 2013, S. 31–48 und S. 49–59.

80 Bertolini 2000, Bauer 2001–2002, Bauer 2004, S. 43–46.

81 Travaini 1989, S. 40, Rovelli 1998, S. 84–84, Rovelli 2001, bes. S. 829–830, Bauer 2004, S. 45. Vgl. Marazzi 1991, S. 247–248.

82 LP I, 501. Coates-Stephens 1999, S. 211–213, Bauer 2001–2002, Dey 2011, S. 250–269.

83 LP I, 507 sowohl zur Zerstörung des *monumentum de tubertinus* im Hinblick auf die Erweiterung von S. Maria in Cosmedin, als auch zu den *plus quam XII milia tufos a litore alvei fluminis*, die zum Wiederaufbau der *porticus Sancti Petri* wiederverwendet wurden (s. dazu auch Santangeli Valenzani 2015a, S. 339). Besonders interessant ist, dass der päpstliche Zuständigkeitsbereich sich auch auf andere Gegenden erstreckte: Beispielhaft sei hier die Genehmigung für Karl d. Gr. genannt, Material (*musiva et marmora*) aus dem Kaiserpalast von Ravenna zu entnehmen (MGH, *Epist. Mer. et Kar.*, I, n. 81, 614), wie in Einhards Karlbiographie bestätigt wird (Einhard, Vita Karoli Magni, hg. von G. Waitz, 6. Aufl., MGH, *Script. Rer. Germ.*, Hannover, 1911, 31: *ad cuius structuram cum columnas et marmora aliunde habere non posset, Roma atque Ravenna devehenda curavit*); vgl. auch Ranaldi/Novara 2014, S. 115.

84 CIL XV, 1, 1677. S. Crostarosa 1896, S. 63–64, Steinby 1973–74, S. 117, Steinby 1986, S. 115; Bauer 2001b; außerdem Bruzzesi 2009 und Spera 2011b, S. 337.

Abb. 5: Ziegelstempel, vermutlich aus der Zeit Hadrians I.

bedeutenden Wasserleitungen zur Speisung von Baptisterien bzw. *balnea*, die der *Liber pontificalis* z.B. für das Pontifikat von Papst Symmachus in erheblicher Zahl verzeichnet.[85] Vermutlich wurden zu bestimmten Zeiten besondere Vollmachten genutzt, wie einige *fistulae* aus dem 5./6. Jahrhundert zeigen[86]. Die *cura aquarum* muss jedoch laut den Bestimmungen der *pragmatica sanctio*[87]noch im Zuständigkeitsbereich der weltlichen Macht gewesen sein, wenn sich Gregor I. im Jahr 602 durch Vermittlung des ravennatischen Subdiakons Johannes an den Präfekten des Prätoriums wenden musste, damit der *vir clarissimus Augustus* die nötige Instandhaltung der Aquädukte veranlassen konnte.[88] Hadrians Biograph berichtet ausführlich über die Restaurierung der vier damals genutzten Aquädukte. Schon Honorius I. hatte ja die Leitung der *aqua Traiana* für eine neue

85 LP I, 262, 263.

86 L. Spera in Palombi/Spera 2015, S. 53–54.

87 Pragmatica sanctio pro petitione Vigilii, 25 (MGH, *Leges*, V, 174): *Consuetudines et privilegia Romanae civitatis vel publicarum fabricarum reparationi, vel albo Tiberino vel foro aut portui Romano, sive reparationi formarum concessa, servari pre cipimus: ita videlicet, ut ex hisdem tantummodo titulis, ex quibus delegata fuerunt, praestentur.*

88 *Epist.* 12.6.

Mühle auf dem Gianicolo instand setzen lassen.[89] Die Maßnahmen werden im Detail dargestellt, und für drei der vier Leitungen (also ohne die *aqua Iovia*) erfahren wir auch etwas über die Nutzungen, die solche Renovierungen erforderlich machten: Atrium der Basilika und *balneum* im Vatikan (neben der oben genannten Mühle) für die *aqua Sabbatina-Traiana*, *balneum* und Baptisterium im Laterankomplex sowie römische Südstadt für die *aqua Claudia*, wofür sogar Arbeitskräfte aus Kampanien angeworben wurden, um die Fertigstellung zu beschleunigen, sowie *poene tota civitas* für die *aqua Virgo*.[90] Aufschlussreich präzisierte der Autor dieser Vita, dass große Mengen an Blei für die lange Leitung der *Sabbatina* nach St. Peter benötigt wurden, denn aufgrund erheblicher Vernachlässigung war viel davon entwendet worden.[91]

Der politisch-ideologische Wert dieser neuen Qualifikationen tritt nicht zuletzt in den wiederholten technischen Angaben zu den Bauhütten zutage, die in den Biographien der Päpste des 8. Jahrhunderts auftauchen. Diese Informationen ergänzen die früheren Huldigungen, die sich zwar in einer stets knappen Auflistung von Baumaßnahmen, aber vor allem in Beschreibungen von Schenkungen an Edelmetallen und kostbaren Stoffen bzw. in Details zu prachtvollen Dekorationen ergingen.[92] Zur häufigen Erinnerung an den technologischen wie finanziellen Aufwand für den Austausch der Holzbalken zur Dachrenovierung[93] gesellen sich nun – mit ähnlicher Absicht – mehrere Hinweise auf die Standfestigkeit der Bauwerke (*fabricis fortissimis*, *fortissime construere fecit* wird in der Vita Gregors III. betont)[94], auf Metallverstärkungen (*chartis plumbeis cooperuit* steht schon in der Biographie von Sergius I., aber auch in späteren)[95], auf eine sehr reichliche Verwendung von Kalk (*cum calce abundantissimo*: Gregor III. z.B. veranlasste Arbeiten in S. Maria *ad martyres*)[96], Kriterien, die die äußerst qualitätvollen Ergebnisse dieser Bauvorhaben betonen.

Im frühmittelalterlichen Rom ist praktisch ausschließlich der Bischof in der Lage, die kostspieligen Bauvorhaben auf höchstem technischem Niveau durchzuführen und

89 LP I, 324 (mit L. Duchesne, *ad comm. LP*, 327 Anm. 20). Die Jurisdiktion über die Stadt stand damals logischerweise noch unter direkter byzantinischer Kontrolle, weswegen der Papst die förmliche Genehmigung zur Wiederverwendung des Bronzedachs vom Tempel der Venus und Roma für St. Peter von Heraklius bekam (LP I, 323). Informationen zur Restaurierung der Wasserleitungen zwischen Spätantike und Frühmittelalter in: Coates-Stevens 1999, S. 215–223 und Marcelli/Munzi 2007, S. 35–41.

90 LP I, 504, 503–504, 504–505, 506.

91 LP I, 503–504. Bauer 2004, S. 188.

92 Saxer 1996–97, Delogu 2010, S. 289–308.

93 LP I, 508, 510, 512; LP II, 1, 2, 9, 11–12, 14, 25, 26, 28–29, 32, 33. Pani Ermini 1992.

94 LP I, 419.

95 LP I, 375; vgl. auch 419 zu Gregor III.

96 LP I, 420.

Abb. 6: Mauerreste, vermutlich aus der Zeit Hadrians I., südlich der Basilika von St. Paul vor den Mauern.

ihre Qualität zu gewährleisten, während anderswo die Bauqualität stark zurückgeht.[97] Einige der erhaltenen Bauwerke weisen in diese Richtung; darüber hinaus ließen detaillierte Analysen an manchen Stätten die Qualitätsmerkmale der Bauverfahren erkennen. So wurden z. B. in dem jüngst erforschten Bezirk südlich der Basilika von St. Paul vor den Mauern bedeutsame Anzeichen für die Verwendung sorgfältig ausgewählter Materialien ausgemacht, vor allem für die Mörtelherstellung. Bestenfalls verfügte man über ausgezeichnete Rohstoffe und über ausreichende Arbeitskräfte; an den uns bekannten römischen Baustellen scheinen keine von den anderswo verwendeten *machinae* ein-

97 Neben dem Kirchenbau und anderen von religiösen Institutionen durchgeführten Bauvorhaben (dazu Hinweise in Spera/Esposito/Giorgi 2011; zum Mauerwerk in Kirchen ein Überblick bei Krautheimer 1937–1980) sind hauptsächliche Gebäude (teilweise ohne Fundamente) dokumentiert, die mit äußerst heterogenem Spolienmaterial fast ohne Bindemittel bzw. sogar aus verderblichen Stoffen errichtet wurden; zu einem Überblick der zahlreichen Belege: Meneghini/Santangeli Valenzani 2004; vgl. auch Santangeli Valenzani 2015a.

gesetzt worden zu sein.[98] Am selben Ort konnten verschiedene Monumentalanbauten des 8. Jahrhunderts (mit Bauwerken aus dessen erster Hälfte unter Gregor II. und Gregor III. sowie weiteren aus der Zeit Hadrians I.)[99], und insbesondere der Vergleich zwischen diversen Mauerwerken, eine deutliche Verfeinerung in der Wiederverwendungspraxis erkennen lassen: Während für die früheren Strukturen extrem heterogenes Material (kleine Tuffblöcke und Backsteine, Marmor- und Tuffstücke aus unterschiedlichen Manufakten) in ungeordneter Manier wiederverwertet wurde, weisen die Mauern aus dem Jahrhundertende eine gezielte Auswahl des Baustoffs auf, wobei es sich überwiegend um unbeschädigte Backsteine und Tuffblöcke handelt – ein nicht unbedeutendes Indiz für einen organisierten Spolienabbau[100] und für geregelte Lagerungs- und Verteilungsverfahren, die in spezifischen Forschungen noch näher zu untersuchen sind (Abb. 6).

So wird Mitte des 9. Jahrhunderts der zügige Mauerbau um die *civitas* Leos IV. nicht nur die Bedeutung einer Vollendung jener *imitatio imperii* annehmen, die bis an das Gründungzeremoniell der nach dem Stifter benannten Städte reichte:[101] Sie kann ebenso als überzeugendster Beleg für die verbesserte Organisationsfähigkeit und Verwaltung komplexer Bauprojekte gelten, die für das frühmittelalterlichen Papsttum kennzeichnend sind.[102]

---

98 Spera/Esposito/Giorgi 2011. Zur Kalkherstellung und -verwendung und zu einzelnen *machinae* genügen die Beiträge in Bianchi 2011.

99 Zu diversen vorläufigen Ergebnissen vgl.: Spera 2009, Spera 2011a, Spera 2011c, Spera/Esposito/Giorgi 2011.

100 Vgl. auch oben Anm. 83. Zu einigen dieser Aspekte s. auch Santangeli Valenzani 2015b, S. 67.

101 Marazzi 1992, Marazzi 1994, Noble 2001.

102 Zum Mauerbau durch Leo IV. und zur Baustellenorganisation, mit Details aufgrund literarischer und epigrafischer Quellen, im Wesentlichen Gibson/Ward-Perkins 1979, Gibson/Ward-Perkins 1983, Marazzi 1994, S. 262–264, Pani Ermini 2000, S. 409–412, Pergola 2002, Meneghini in Meneghini/Santangeli Valenzani 2004, S. 63–65 (Der Autor nimmt an, dass der vollständige Abbau der Fußbodenplatten im Trajansforum mit dem Kalkbedarf dieser Großbaustelle bzw. jener zur Renovierung der Aurelianischen Stadtmauer zusammenhängen könnte).

Bibliographie

Arnaldi 1982 Girolamo Arnaldi: Rinascita, fine, reincarnazione e successive modifiche del senato romano (secoli V–XII), in: Archivio della Società romana di storia patria 105, 1982, S. 7–56.

Arnaldi 1986 Girolamo Arnaldi: L'approvvigionamento di Roma e l'amministrazione dei «Patrimoni di S.Pietro» al tempo di Gregorio Magno, in: Studi Romani 34, 1986, S. 25–39.

Arnaldi 1987 Girolamo Arnaldi: Le origini dello Stato della Chiesa, Turin 1987.

Arnaldi 1997 Girolamo Arnaldi: Il senato in Roma altomedievale (secoli VI, fine – X), in: Il Senato nella storia, Bd. II, Rom 1997, S. 95–105.

Augenti 1993 Palatia. Palazzi imperiali tra Ravenna e Bisanzio. (Ausstellung Ravenna, Biblioteca Classense, 14.10.2002–4.01.2003), hg. von Andrea Augenti, Ferrara 2003.

Augenti 1996 Andrea Augenti: Il Palatino nel Medioevo. Archeologia e topografia. Secoli VI–XIII, Rom 1996.

Baldini Lippolis 2014 Isabella Baldini Lippolis: Palatia, praetoria ed episcopia: alcune osservazioni, in: La villa restaurata e i nuovi studi sull'edilizia residenziale tardoantica, hg. von Patrizio Pensabene und Carla Sfameni, Bari 2014, S. 163–170.

Ballardini 2011 Antonella Ballardini: Un oratorio per la Theotokos: Giovanni VII (705–707) committente a San Pietro, in: Medioevo: i committenti, Atti del Convegno internazionale di studi (Parma, 21.–26.9.2010), hg. von Arturo Carlo Quintavalle, Mailand 2011, S. 94–116.

Ballardini 2015 Antonella Ballardini: «In antiquissimo ac venerabili lateranensi palatio»: la residenza dei pontefici secondo il Liber pontificalis, in: Le corti nell'alto medioevo, LXII Settimana di Studio della Fondazione Centro Italiano di Studi sull'Alto Medioevo (Spoleto, 24.–29.4.2014), Spoleto 2015, S. 889–927.

Barresi/Pensabene 2007 Paolo Barresi und Patrizio Pensabene: La «rinascita carolingia» del IX secolo: reimpiego, architettura, progettazione, in: La cristianizzazione in Italia tra Tardoantico e Altomedioevo, Atti del IX Congresso Nazionale di Archeologia Cristiana (Agrigent, 20.–25.11.2004), hg. von Rosa Maria Carra Bonacasa und Emma Vitale, Palermo 2007, Bd. I, S. 483–498.

Bartoli 1912 Alfonso Bartoli: Ultime vicende e trasformazioni cristiane della Basilica Emilia, in: Rendiconti dell'Accademia nazionale dei Lincei 21, 1912, S. 758–766.

Bartoli 1950 Alfonso Bartoli: L'ultimo relitto dell'archivio imperiale sul Palatino, in: Atti della Pontificia accademia romana di archeologia, Rendiconti 23–24, 1947–1948, 1948–1949 (1950), S. 269–275.

Bauer 2001–2002 Franz Alto Bauer: Il rinnovamento di Roma sotto Adriano I alla luce del Liber Pontificalis. Immagine e realtà, in: Mededelingen van het Nederlands Instituut te Rome 60–61, 2001–2002, S. 189–202.

Bauer 2001a Franz Alto Bauer: Roma in epoca carolingia, in: Carlo Magno a Roma (Ausstellung Vatikanstadt, Musei Vaticani 16.12.2000–31.3.2001), Vatikanstadt/Rom 2001, S. 81–96.

Bauer 2001b Franz Alto Bauer: Tegola bollata di Adriano I, in: Carlo Magno a Roma (Ausstellung Vatikanstadt, Musei Vaticani 16.12.2000–31.3.2001), Vatikanstadt/Rom 2001, S. 152–153.

Bauer 2004 Franz Alto Bauer: Das Bild der Stadt Rom im Frühmittelalter. Papststiftungen im Spiegel des Liber Pontificalis von Gregor dem Dritten bis zu Leo dem Dritten, Wiesbaden 2004.

Bavant 1979 Bernard Bavant: Le duché byzantin de Rome. Origine, durée et extension géographique, in: Mélanges de l'École française de Rome. Moyen Âge – Temps Modernes 91/1, 1979, S. 41–88.

Berto 2000 Luigi Andrea Berto: Giovanni VII, in: Enciclopedia dei papi. Bd. I, Rom 2000, S. 638–640.

Bertolini 1913 Gian Lodovico Bertolini: Qualche chiarimento su l'Orbis Pictus di Papa Zaccaria, in: Bollettino della Reale Società Geografica italiana s. V, II, 1913, S. 542–550.

Bertolini 1941 Ottorino Bertolini: Roma di fronte a Bisanzio e ai Longobardi, Bologna 1941.

Bertolini 1947 Ottorino Bertolini: Per la storia delle diaconie romane nell'alto medioevo sino alla fine del secolo VIII, in: Archivio della Società romana di storia patria 70, 1947, S. 1–145.

Bertolini 1966 Ottorino Bertolini: Gli inizi del governo temporale dei papi sull'esarcato di Ravenna, in: Archivio della Società romana di storia patria 89, 1966, S. 25–35.

Bertolini 2000 Ottorino Bertolini: Adriano I, in: Enciclopedia dei papi. Bd. I, Rom 2000, S. 681–695.

Bianchi 2011 Dopo la calcara: la produzione della calce nell'Altomedioevo. Nuovi dati da Lazio e Toscana fra ricerca sul campo, archeologia sperimentale e archeometria, hg. von Giovanna Bianchi, in: Archeologia dell'Architettura 16, 2011.

Bison 2010 Giulia Bison: Un sigillo bizantino dallo scavo delle pendici nord-orientali del Palatino, in: Mélanges de l'École française de Rome. Moyen Âge 122, 2, 2010, S. 245–259.

Breckenridge 1972 James Douglas Breckenridge: Evidence for the Nature of Relations Between Pope John VII and the Byzantine Emperor Justinian II, in: Byzantinische Zeitschrift 65, 1972, S. 364–374.

Brogiolo 2000 Gian Pietro Brogiolo: Capitali e residenze regie nell'Italia longobarda, in: Sedes Regiae (anni 400–800), hg. von Gisela Ripoll und José Maria Gurt, Barcelona 2000, S. 135–162.

Bruzzesi 2009 Marco Bruzzesi: Frammento di tegola con bollo di Adriano I, in: San Paolo in Vaticano: la figura e la parola dell'apostolo nelle raccolte pontificie, hg. von Umberto Utro, Todi 2009, S. 155.

Cagnana 1997 Aurora Cagnana: Residenze vescovili fortificate e immagini urbane nella Genova dell'XI secolo, in: Archeologia dell'architettura 2, 1997, S. 75–100.

Carboni 2011 Francesca Carboni: Scavi nel fronte lungo la via Nova, in: Domus Tiberiana. Scavi e restauri 1990–2011, hg. von Maria Antonietta Tomei und Maria Grazia Filetici, Mailand 2011, S. 40–51.

Carboni 2016 Francesca Carboni: Un complesso altomedievale nel cuore della Domus Tiberiana, in: Santa Maria Antiqua tra Roma e Bisanzio (Ausstellung Rom, Santa Maria Antiqua 17.3.–30.10.2016), hg. von Maria Andaloro, Giulia Bordi und Giuseppe Morganti, Mailand 2016, S. 86–95.

Carboni/Sforza 2011 Francesca Carboni und Fiammetta Sforza: Saggi di scavo sul piano degli Orti, in: Domus Tiberiana. Scavi e restauri 1990–2011, hg. von Maria Antonietta Tomei und Maria Grazia Filetici, Mailand 2011, S. 206–209.

Caspar 1933 Erich Caspar: Geschichte des Papsttums von den Anfängen bis zu Höhe der Weltherrschaft. Bd. II Das Papsttum unter byzantinischer Herrschaft, Tübingen 1933.

Cecchelli 2010 Margherita Cecchelli: Temi di approfondimento sul problema del servizio assistenziale, in: Diakonia, diaconiae, diaconato. Semantica e storia nei Padri della Chiesa. XXXVIII Incontro di studiosi dell'antichità cristiana (Rom, 7.–9.5.2009), Rom 2010, S. 539–573.

Cecchelli et al. 2007 Margherita Cecchelli et al.: L'assetto cultuale della Roma carolingia, in: La cristianizzazione in Italia tra Tardoantico e Altomedioevo, Atti del IX Congresso Nazionale di Archeologia Cristiana (Agrigent, 20.–25.11.2004), hg. von Rosa Maria Carra Bonacasa und Emma Vitale, Palermo 2007, Bd. I, S. 411–420.

Christie 2005 Neil Christie: Charlemagne and the Renewal of Rome, in: Charlemagne. Empire and society, hg. von Joanna Story, Manchester 2005, S. 167–182.

Ciceroni/Martin/Munzi 2004 Marina Ciceroni, Archer Martin und Massimiliano Munzi: I contesti tardoantichi e altomedievali del Bastione Farnesiano nella domus Tiberiana, in: Roma dall'antichità al medioevo II. Contesti tardoantichi e altomedievali, hg. von Lidia Paroli und Laura Vendittelli, Mailand 2004, S. 129–161.

Coarelli 2012 Filippo Coarelli: Palatium. Il Palatino dalle origini all'Impero, Roma 2012.

Coates-Stephens 1999 Robert Coates-Stephens: Le ricostruzioni altomedievali delle Mura Aureliane e degli acquedotti, in: Roma dal IV all'VIII secolo: quale paesaggio urbano? Dati da scavi recenti, Atti della seduta dei Seminari di archeologia cristiana (Roma, 13.3.1997), in: Mélanges de l'École française de Rome, Moyen Âge, 111, 1999, S. 209–225.

Colagrossi 1913 Pietro Colagrossi: L'Anfiteatro Flavio nei suoi venti secoli di storia, Florenz/Rom 1913.

Coletti 2010 Fulvio Coletti: Note su alcuni vasi invetriati dai contesti medio e tardo imperiali del santuario di Cibele sul Palatino, in: Archeologia Classica 55, 2004, S. 413–447.

Coletti 2015 Fulvio Coletti: Un impianto manifatturiero per la lavorazione dei tessuti e i sistemi sanitari di approvvigionamento idrico del lato meridionale della Domus Tiberiana, in: Scienze dell'antichità 21, 1, 2015, S. 118–137.

Coletti/Celant/Pensabene 2006 Fulvio Coletti, Alesssandra Celant und Patrizio Pensabene: Ricerche archeologiche e paleoambientali sul Palatino tra l'età arcaica e la tardoantichità, in: Atti del Convegno di Caserta (Febr. 2005) dell'Associazione Nazionale di Archeometria, Bologna 2006, S. 557–564.

Coletti/Margheritelli 2006 Fulvio Coletti und Lucia Margheritelli: Ultime fasi di vita, abbandono e distruzione dei monumenti dell'area sud-ovest del Palatino: contesti stratigrafici e reperti, in: Scienze dell'antichità 13, 2006, S. 465–497.

Conti 2016 Simonetta Conti: Il lungo cammino della Cartografia. Dal Paradiso Terrestre alla realtà del lontano oriente (secc. VII–XV), in: La storia della cartografia e Martino Martini, hg. von Elena Dai Prà, Mailand 2016, S. 25–46.

Crostarosa 1896 Pietro Crostarosa: Inventario dei sigilli impressi sulle tegole del tetto di S. Maria Maggiore, in: Bullettino di Archeologia cristiana 2, 1896, S. 52–89.

De Francesco 1996 Daniela De Francesco: Considerazioni storico-topografiche a proposito delle «domuscultae laziali», in: Archivio della Società romana di storia patria 119, 1996, S. 5–47.

De Francesco 2004 Daniela De Francesco: La proprietà fondiaria nel Lazio, secoli IV–VIII. Storia e topografia, Rom 2004.

De Rossi 1883 Giovanni Battista de Rossi, in: Rodolfo Lanciani: L'Atrio di Vesta, in: Notizie degli scavi di antichità 1883, S. 487–497.

Del Lungo 2004 Stefano Del Lungo: Roma in età carolingia e gli scritti dell'Anonimo Augiense, Rom 2014.

Della Giovanpaola 1999 Irma Della Giovanpaola: Patriarchium, in: Lexicon topographicum Urbis Romae, Bd. IV, Rom 1999, S. 62–66.

Delogu 2000a Paolo Delogu: Gregorio II, santo, in: Enciclopedia dei papi, Bd. I, Rom 2000, S. 647–651.

Delogu 2000b Paolo Delogu: The papacy, Rome and the wider world in the seventh and eighth century, in: Early Medieval Rome and the Christian West. Essays in Honour of Donald A. Bullough, hg. von Julia M. H. Smith, Leiden 2000, S. 197–220.

Delogu 2000c Paolo Delogu: Zaccaria, in: Enciclopedia dei papi. Bd. I, Rom 2000, S. 656–660.

Delogu 2010 Paolo Delogu: Le origini del Medioevo. Studi sul settimo secolo, Rom 2010.

Dey 2008 Hendrik W. Dey: Diaconiae, xenodochia, hospitalia and monasteries: 'social security' and the meaning of monasticism in early medieval Rome, in: Early medieval Europe 16/4, 2008, S. 398–422.

Dey 2011 Hendrik W. Dey: The Aurelian Wall and the Refashioning of Imperial Rome, AD 271-855, Cambridge 2011.

D'Onofrio 2002 Mario D'Onofrio: Aspetti inediti e poco noti del Patriarchio lateranense, in Medioevo: i modelli, in: Atti del convegno internazionale di studi (Parma, 27.9.–1.10.1999), hg. von Arturo Carlo Quintavalle, Mailand 2002, S. 221–236.

D'Onofrio 2004 Mario D'Onofrio: Il Patriarchio nascosto, in: Giornata di studio tematica dedicata al Patriarchio Lateranense (École française de Rome, 10.5.2001), in: Mélanges de l'École française de Rome, Antiquité, 116, 2004, S. 141–160.

Durliat 1990 Jean Durliat: De la ville antique à la ville byzantine. Le problème des subsistances (Collection de l'École française de Rome, 136), Paris-Rom 1990.

Episcopo 1999 Silvana Episcopo: Ss. Petrus et Paulus, ecclesia, in: Lexicon Topographicum Urbis Romae, IV, Rom 1999, S. 83–84.

Falisiedi 1995 Ugo Falisiedi: Le diaconie: i servizi assistenziali nella Chiesa antica, Rom 1995.

Falkenhausen 2000 Vera von Falkenhausen: Sergio I, santo, in: Enciclopedia dei papi, Bd. I, Rom 2000, S. 633–637.

Ferrua 1943 Antonio Ferrua: Sulle orme di Pietro, in La Civiltà Cattolica, 94, 1943, S. 36–45.

Fiocchi Nicolai 2007 Vincenzo Fiocchi Nicolai: Carità e fraternità all'origine delle catacombe cristiane, in: La carità intellettuale. Percorsi culturali per un nuovo umanesimo. Scritti in onore di Benedetto XVI, Vatikanstadt 2007, S. 467–472.

Fontana/Munzi 2001 Stefano Fontana und Massimiliano Munzi: Palatino, Domus Tiberiana, Scavi nel settore nord-orientale, in: Roma dall'antichità al medioevo. Archeologia e storia nel Museo Nazionale Romano Crypta Balbi, hg. von Maria Stella Arena et al., Mailand 2001, S. 608–610.

Gibson/Ward-Perkins 1979 Sheila Gibson und Bryan Ward-Perkins: The surviving remains of the Leonine Wall, in: Papers of the British School at Rome 47, 1979, S. 30–57.

Gibson/Ward-Perkins 1983 Sheila Gibson und Bryan Ward-Perkins: The surviving remains of the Leonine Wall. Part II: the Passetto, in: Papers of the British School at Rome 51, 1983, S. 222–240.

Giuntella 2001 Annamaria Giuntella: Gli spazi dell'assistenza e della meditazione, in: Roma nell'alto medioevo. Settimane di studio del Centro italiano di studi sull'alto medioevo, XLVIII (27.4.–1.5.2000), Spoleto 2001, S. 639–691.

Goodson 2010 Caroline J. Goodson: The Rome of Pope Paschal I. Papal power, urban revation, church rebuilding and relic translation, 817–824, Cambridge 2010.

Gregory 2003 Tullio Gregory: Lo spazio come geografia del sacro nell'occidente altomedievale, in: Uomo e spazio nell'alto medioevo, L Settimana di Studi del Centro Italiano sull'Alto Medioevo (Spoleto, 4.–8.4.2002), Spoleto 2003, S. 27–60.

Grisar 1896 Hartmann Grisar: Archeologia, in: La Civiltà Cattolica 47, 1896, S. 458–478.

Grisar 1901 Hartmann Grisar: Note topografiche storiche sulla più antica residenza dei papi al Laterano, in: La Civiltà Cattolica 54, 1901, S. 474–485.

Hallenbeck 1982 Jan T. Hallenbeck: Pavia and Rome: The Lombard monarchy and the papacy in the 8th century (Transactions of the American Philosophical Society 72/ 4), Philadelphia 1982.

Hermes 1996 Raimund Hermes: Die stadtrömischen Diakonien, in: Römische Quartalschrift für christliche Altertumskunde und Kirchengeschichte 91, 1996, S. 1–120.

Hudson 1987 Peter Hudson: Pavia: l'evoluzione urbanistica di una capitale altomedievale, in: Storia di Pavia, Bd. II, Pavia 1987, S. 237–315.

Krause 1995 Clemens Krause: Domus Tiberiana, in: Lexicon Topographicum Urbis Romae, Bd. II, Rom 1995, S. 189–197.

Krautheimer 1937–1980 Richard Krautheimer: Corpus Basilicarum Christianarum Romae. Le basiliche cristiane antiche di Roma (saec. IV–IX), Bd. I–V, Vatikanstadt 1937–1980.

Krautheimer 1981 Richard Krautheimer: Roma, profilo di una città 312–1308, Rom 1981.

Kurze 1990 Wilhelm Kurze: Notizen zu den Päpsten Johannes VII., Gregor III. und Benedikt III. in der Kanonessammlung des Kardinals Deusdedit, in: Quellen und Forschungen aus italienischen Bibliotheken und Archiven 70, 1990, S. 23–45.

Lanciani 1889 Rodolfo Lanciani: L'Itinerario di Einsiedeln e l'ordine di Benedetto Canonico, in: Monumenti antichi dell'Accademia nazionale dei Lincei 1, 1889, S. 437–552.

Lauer 1900 Philippe Lauer: Les fouilles du Sancta Sanctorum au Latran, in: Mélanges d'archéologie et d'histoire 20, 1900, S. 251–287.

Lauer 1911 Philippe Lauer: Le Palais de Latran. Étude historique et archéologique, Paris 1911.

Leader-Newby 2004 Ruth E. Leader-Newby: Silver and Society in Late Antiquity. Functions and Meanings of Silver Plate in the Fourth to Seventh Centuries, Aldershot 2004.

Liverani 2003 Paolo Liverani: Dal palatium imperiale al palatium pontificio, in: Acta ad archaeologiam et artium historiam pertinentia 17, 2003, S. 143–163.

Liverani 2012 Paolo Liverani: The episcopium of the Lateran from its origins to the Early Middle Ages – L'episcopio lateranense dalle origini all'alto medioevo, in: Des domus ecclesiae aux palais épiscopaux, hg. von Sylvie Balcon-Berry et al., Turnhout 2012, S. 119–131.

Llewelyn 1979 Peter A.B. Llewelyn: Le premier développement du collège des cardinaux, in: Recherches de science religieuse 67, 1979, S. 31–44.

LP Le Liber Pontificalis. Texte, introduction et commentaire, hg. von Louis Duchesne, I–II, Paris 1886–1892.

Luchterhandt 1999 Manfred Luchterhandt: Päpstlicher Palastbau und höfisches Zeremoniell unter Leo III, in: 799: Kunst und Kultur der Karolingerzeit, Bd. 3 Beiträge zum Katalog der Ausstellung Paderborn 1999, hg. von Christoph Stiegemann und Matthias Wemhoff, Mainz 1999, S. 109–122.

Luchterhandt 2006 Manfred Luchterhandt: Stolz und Vorurteil. Der Westen und die byzantinische Hofkultur im Frühmittelalter, in: Visualisierungen von Herrschaft frühmittelalterliche Residenzen. Gestalt und Zeremoniell, Internationales Kolloquium Istanbul 3./4.6.2004, hg. von Franz Alto Bauer (Byzas, 5), Istanbul 2006, S. 171–211.

Luchterhandt 2010 Manfred Luchterhandt: Rinascita a Roma, nell'Italia carolingia e meridionale, in: Storia dell'architettura italiana. Da Costantino a Carlo Magno, Bd. II, Mailand 2010, S. 322–373.

Lusuardi Siena 2012 Silvia Lusuardi Siena: L'origine dell'archetipo e il problema del palatium: una cronologia di VI secolo?, in: La più antica veduta di Verona. L'Iconografia Rateriana. L'archetipo e l'immagine tramandata, Atti del seminario di studi (6.5.2011, Museo di Castelvecchio), Verona 2012, S. 59–69.

Marano 2007 Yuri A. Marano: Domus in qua manebat episcopus: Episcopal Residences in Northern Italy during Late Antiquity (4th to 6th centuries A.D.), in: Housing in Late Antiquity. From Palaces to Shops, hg. von Luke Lavan, Lale Özgenel und Alexander Sarantis, Boston 2007, S. 97–129.

Marazzi 1985 Federico Marazzi: Le domuscultæ papali della Campagna Romana: un problema storico, topografico e archeologico dell'alto medioevo, in: Romana gens 1985, S. 13–18.

Marazzi 1991 Federico Marazzi: Il conflitto fra Leone III Isaurico e il Papato fra il 725 e il 733, e il ‹definitivo› inizio del Medioevo a Roma: un'ipotesi in discussione, in: Papers of the British School at Rome 59, 1991, S. 231–257.

Marazzi 1992 Federico Marazzi: La costruzione della «Civitas Leoniana» e qualche considerazione sulla costruzione di «città nuove» papali nel secolo IX, in: Geoarcheologia 1992, S. 67–86.

Marazzi 1994 Federico Marazzi: Le «città nuove» pontificie e l'insediamento laziale nel IX secolo, in: La storia dell'Alto Medioevo Italiano (V–X secolo) alla luce dell'archeologia, hg. von Riccardo Francovich und Ghislaine Noyé, Florenz 1994, S. 251–278.

Marazzi 2001–2002 Federico Marazzi: Il Liber Pontificalis e le domuscultae, in: Mededelingen van het Nederlands Instituut te Rome 60–61, 2001–2002, S. 167–188.

Marcelli/Munzi 2007 Marina Marcelli und Massimiliano Munzi: Roma medievale e l'acqua, in: I giganti dell'acqua. Acquedotti romani del Lazio nelle fotografie di Thomas Ashby 1892–1925 (Ausstellung Rom, The British School at Rome 5.10.–6.11.2007) (British School at Rome archive, 7), hg. von Susanna Le Pera und Rita Turchetti, Rom 2007, S. 35–47.

Martin 2011 Archer Martin: Palatino, Domus Tiberiana, Scavi nel Bastione Farnesiano, in: Roma dall'antichità al medioevo. Archeologia e storia nel Museo Nazionale Romano Crypta Balbi, hg. von Maria Stella Arena et al., Mailand 2001, S. 607–608.

Mazza 1989 Mario Mazza: Deposita pietatis: problemi dell'organizzazione economica in comunità cristiane tra II e III secolo, in: Atti dell'Accademia Romanistica Costantiniana. IX Congresso Internazionale, Perugia 1989, S. 187–218.

Mazza 2006 Mario Mazza: Struttura sociale e organizzazione economica della comunità cristiana di Roma tra il II e III secolo, in: Origine delle catacombe romane. Atti della giornata tematica dei Seminari di Archeologia cristiana (Rom, 21.3.2005), hg. von Vincenzo Fiocchi Nicolai und Jean Guyon, Vatikanstadt 2006, S. 15–28.

Meneghini/Santangeli Valenzani 2004 Roberto Meneghini und Riccardo Santangeli Valenzani: Roma nell'alto medioevo. Topografia e urbanistica della città dal V al X secolo, Rom 2004.

Milella 2000 Alessandra Milella: Le diaconie romane tra il VI e l'VIII secolo, in: Cultura e promozione umana. La cura del corpo e dello spirito dai primi secoli cristiani al Medioevo. Contributi e attualizzazioni ulteriori (Collana di cultura e lingue classiche, 6), Troina 2000, S. 83–99.

Miller 1974 David H. Miller: The Roman Revolution of the Eighth Century: A Study of the Ideological Background of the Papal Separation from Byzantium and Alliance with the Franks, in: Medieval Studies 36, 1974, S. 79–133.

Miller 1975 David H. Miller: Byzantine-Papal Relations during the Pontificate of Paul I: Confirmation and Completion of the Roman Revolution of the Eighth Century, in: Byzantinische Zeitschrift 68, 1975, S. 47–62.

Miller 2000 David Miller: Costantino, in: Enciclopedia dei papi, Bd. I, Rom 2000, S. 641–647.

Munzi et al. 2004 Massimiliano Munzi et al.: Domus Tiberiana: contesti tardo antichi dal settore nord-orientale, in: Roma dall'antichità al medioevo II. Contesti tardoantichi e altomedievali, hg. von Lidia Paroli und Laura Vendittelli, Mailand 2004, S. 91–128.

Nicolet 1991 Claude Nicolet: Space, Geography and politics in the early Roman Empire, Michigan 1991.

Noble 1984 Thomas F. X. Noble: The Republic of St. Peter. The birth of the Papal State, 680–825, Philadelphia 1984.

Noble 1995 Thomas F. X. Noble: The papacy in the eighth and ninth centuries, in: The new Cambridge medieval history, Bd. 2: c. 700 – c. 900. hg. von Rosamond MacKitterick, Cambridge 1995, S. 563–586.

Noble 1998 Thomas F. X. Noble: La Repubblica di San Pietro. Nascita dello Stato pontificio (680–825). Übers. von Flavia Frangini und Marco Belli, Genua 1998.

Noble 2001 Thomas F. X. Noble: Topography, celebration, and power: the making of a papal Rome in the eighth and ninth centuries, in: Topographies of Power in the Early Middle Ages, hg. von Mayke de Jong, Frans Theuws und Carine van Rhijn (The Transformation of the Roman World 6), Leiden 2001, S. 45–91.

Osborne 2003 John Osborne: Papal court during the pontificate of Zacharias (AD 741–52), in: Court Culture in the Early Middle Ages: The Proceedings of the First Alcuin Conference, hg. von Catherine Cubitt (Studies in the Early Middle Ages, 3), Turnhout 2003, S. 223–234.

Palombi/Spera 2015 Cinzia Palombi und Lucrezia Spera: La banca dati e il GIS degli indicatori di produzione. Note topografiche e prime riflessioni di sintesi, in: L'archeologia della produzione a Roma. Secoli V–XV, Atti del Convegno Internazionale di Studi (Roma, 27.–29.3.2014), hg. von Alessandra Molinari, Riccardo Santangeli Valenzani und Lucrezia Spera, Bari 2015, S. 9–72.

Pani Ermini 1992 Letizia Pani Ermini: Renovatio murorum tra programma urbanistico e restauro conservativo: Roma e il ducato romano, in: Committenza e produzione artistico-letteraria nell'alto medioevo occidentale. Settimane di Studio del Centro Italiano di Studi sull'Alto Medioevo, XXXIX (4.–10.4.1991), Spoleto 1992, S. 485–530.

Pani Ermini 2000 Letizia Pani Ermini: Dai complessi martiriali alle ‹civitates›: formazione e sviluppo dello ‹spazio cristiano›, in: La comunità cristiana di Roma. La sua vita e la sua cultura dalle origini all'alto medioevo, hg. von Letizia Pani Ermini und Paolo Siniscalco, Vatikanstadt, S. 397–419.

Pergola 2002 Stefania Pergola: Il fenomeno del reimpiego nelle mura leonine, in: Archivio della Società romana di storia patria 125, 2002, S. 5–32.

Pilara 2007 Gianluca Pilara: La gestione dell'annona civile e militare a Roma durante il pontificato di Gregorio Magno, in: L'Orbis Christianus Antiquus di Gregorio Magno, Convegno di studi (Rom, 26.–28.10.2004), hg. von Letizia Pani Ermini, Rom 2007, Bd. II, S. 505–529.

Ranaldi/Novara 2014 Antonella Ranaldi und Paola Novara: Karl der Große, Ravenna und Aachen, in: Karl der Große. Orte der Macht. Essays, hg. von Frank Pohle, Dresden 2014, S. 114–121.

Richards 1979 Jeffrey Richards: The popes and the papacy in the early middle ages 476–752, London 1979.

Rovelli 1998 Alessia Rovelli: La circolazione monetaria a Roma nei secoli VII e VIII. Nuovi dati per la storia economica di Roma nell'alto medioevo, in: Roma medievale. Aggiornamenti, hg. von Paolo Delogu, Florenz 1998.

Rovelli 2001 Alessia Rovelli: Emissione e uso della moneta: le testimonianze scritte e archeologiche, in: Roma nell'alto medioevo, Settimane di studio del Centro italiano di studi sull'alto medioevo, XLVIII, Spoleto 2001, S. 821–852.

Saguì/Cante 2015 Lucia Saguì und Matilde Cante: Archeologia e architettura nell'area delle «terme di Elagabalo», alle pendici nord-orientali del Palatino. Dagli isolati giulio-claudii alla chiesa paleocristiana, in: Thiasos. Rivista di Archeologia e architettura antica 4, 2015, S. 35–75.

Sansterre 1982 Jean-Marie Sansterre: Jean VII (705–707): idéologie pontificale et réalisme politique, in: Rayonnement grec. Hommages à Charles Delvoye, Brüssel 1982, S. 377–388.

Sansterre 1987 Jean-Marie Sansterre: A propos de la signification politico-religieuse de certaines fresques de Jean VII à Sainte-Marie-Antique, in: Byzantion 57, 1987, S. 434–440.

Santangeli Valenzani 2015a Riccardo Santangeli Valenzani: Calcare ed altre tracce di cantiere, cave e smontaggi sistematici degli edifici antichi, in: L'archeologia della produzione a Roma. Secoli V–XV, Atti del Convegno Internazionale di Studi (Rom, 27.–29.3.2014), hg. von Alessandra Molinari, Riccardo Santangeli Valenzani und Lucrezia Spera, Bari 2015, S. 335–344.

Santangeli Valenzani 2015b Riccardo Santangeli Valenzani: L'uso del laterizio a Roma nella tarda antichità e nell'alto medioevo, in: Archeologia dell'architettura 20, 2015, S. 65–68.

Saxer 1996–97 Victor Saxer: Le informazioni del Liber Pontificalis sugli interventi dei papi nella decorazione tessile delle chiese romane: l'esempio di S. Maria Maggiore (772–844), in: Atti della Pontificia Accademia Romana di Archeologia, Rendiconti 69, 1996–1997, S. 219–232.

Sessa 2012 Kristina Sessa: The formation of Papal Authority in Late Antique Italy. Roman Bishops and the Domestic Sphere, Cambridge 2012.

Spera 2009 Lucrezia Spera: Il complesso paolino nel Medioevo, in: San Paolo in Vaticano. La figura e la parola dell'Apostolo delle Genti nelle raccolte pontificie, hg. von Umberto Utro, Todi 2009, S. 98–109.

Spera 2010 Lucrezia Spera: Regiones divisit diaconibus. Il ruolo dei diaconi negli apparati amministrativi della Chiesa di Roma e la questione delle regioni ecclesiastiche, in: Diakonia, diaconiae, diaconato. Semantica e storia nei Padri della Chiesa, XXXVIII Incontro di studiosi dell'antichità cristiana (Rom, 7.–9.5.2009), Rom 2010, S. 453–488.

Spera 2011 Lucrezia Spera: Le forme della cristianizzazione nel quadro degli assetti topografico-funzionali di Roma tra V e IX secolo, in: Postclassical Archaeologies 1, 2011, S. 309–331.

Spera 2011a Lucrezia Spera: Dalla tomba alla «città» di Paolo: profilo topografico della Giovannipoli, in: Paulo apostolo martyri. L'apostolo San Paolo nella storia, nell'arte e nell'archeologia, Atti della giornata di studi (Rom, Università Gregoriana 19.1.2009), hg. von Ottavio Bucarelli und Martin Maria Morales, Rom 2011, S. 119–161.

Spera 2011c Lucrezia Spera: Osservazioni sulle porticus dei santuari martiriali a Roma. Assetti architettonico-urbanistici e questioni cronologiche, in: Marmoribus vestita, Miscellanea in onore di Federico Guidobaldi, Vatikanstadt 2011, S. 1039–1070.

Spera 2013 Lucrezia Spera: Il vescovo di Roma e la città: regioni ecclesiastiche, tituli e cimiteri. Ridefinizione di un problema amministrativo e territoriale, in: Episcopus, civitas, territorium, Acta XV Congressus Internationalis Archaeologiae Christianae (Toleti, 8–12.9.2008), Vatikanstadt 2013, Bd. I, S. 163–186.

Spera 2016 Lucrezia Spera: La cristianizzazione del Foro romano e del Palatino. Prima e dopo Giovanni VII, in: Santa Maria Antiqua tra Roma e Bisanzio (Ausstellung Rom, Santa Maria Antiqua 17.3.–30.10.2016), hg. von Maria Andaloro, Giulia Bordi und Giuseppe Morganti, Mailand 2016, S. 96–109.

Spera/Esposito/Giorgi 2011 Lucrezia Spera, Daniela Esposito und Elisabetta Giorgi: Costruire a Roma nel medioevo: evidenze di cantiere dallo scavo a San Paolo fuori le mura, in: Archeologia dell'Architettura 16, 2011, S. 19–33.

Stasolla 2007 Francesca Romana Stasolla: Modi e luoghi dell'assistenza nelle opere di Gregorio Magno, in: L'Orbis Christianus Antiquus di Gregorio Magno, Convegno di studi (Roma, 26.–28.10.2004), hg. von Letizia Pani Ermini, Rom 2007, Bd. I, S. 223–280.

Steinby 1973–1974 Eva Margareta Steinby: Le tegole antiche di Santa Maria Maggiore, in: Atti della Pontificia Accademia Romana di Archeologia, Rendiconti 46, 1973–1974, S. 101–133.

Steinby 1986 Eva Margareta Steinby: L'industria laterizia di Roma nel tardo impero, in: Società romana e impero tardoantico, II. Roma. Politica, economia, paesaggio urbano, hg. von Andrea Giardina, Rom 1986, S. 99–164.

Tomei/Filetici 2011 Domus Tiberiana. Scavi e restauri 1990–2011, hg. von Maria Antonietta Tomei und Maria Grazia Filetici, Mailand 2011.

Torrigio 1644 Francesco Maria Torrigio: I Sacri Trofei Romani del trionfante San Pietro gloriosissimo, Rom 1644.

Toubert 2001 Pierre Toubert: Scrinium et Palatium: la formation de la bureaucratie romano-pontificale aux VIIIe–IXe siècles, in: Roma nell'alto medioevo, Settimane di studio del Centro italiano di studi sull'alto medioevo, XLVIII, Spoleto 2001, S. 57–117.

Traini 2013 Lino Traini: La lavorazione della calce dall'antichità al Medioevo. Roma e le province dell'Impero, Rom 2013.

Travaini 1989 Lucia Travaini: Le monete a Roma nel Medioevo (V–XV secolo), in: Studi Romani 37, 1989, S. 38–49.

Ullmann 1955 Walter Ullmann: The growth of papal government in the Middle Ages: A study in the ideological relation of clerical to lay power, London 1955.

Ullmann 1972 Walter Ullmann: A Short History of the Papacy in the Middle Ages, London 1972 (2. Auflage New York 2003).

Valentini/Zucchetti 1942 Roberto Valentini und Giuseppe Zucchetti: Codice topografico della città di Roma, Bd. II, Rom 1942.

Verzone 1976 Paolo Verzone: La distruzione dei Palazzi imperiali di Roma e di Ravenna e la ristrutturazione del Palazzo Lateranense nel IX secolo nei rapporti con quello di Costantinopoli, in: Roma e l'età carolingia, Atti delle Giornate di Studio (Rom, 3.–8.5.1976), hg. vom Istituto di Storia dell'Arte dell'Università di Roma, Rom 1976, S. 39–54.

Wilson 2003 Andrew Wilson: Late Antique watermills on the Palatine, in: Papers of the British School at Rome 71, 2003, S. 85–109.

Zumthor 2005 Paul Zumthor: La misura del mondo. La rappresentazione dello spazio nel Medio Evo, Bologna 2005.

Die Päpste in S. Maria Antiqua

Zwischen Rom und Konstantinopel

Giulia Bordi

Das ikonographische Programm der Apsiswand von S. Maria Antiqua auf dem Forum Romanum geht auf Papst Johannes VII. (705–707) zurück. Ihm liegt ein komplexes Bildsystem zugrunde, dessen Elemente sowohl einzeln als auch im Zusammenhang interpretiert werden können (Abb. 1). In Anlehnung an einen modernen Terminus der Literaturkritik und Informatik könnten wir diese Wand als einen aus unterschiedlichen ikonographisch-rhetorischen Teilen bestehenden ›Hypertext‘[1] bezeichnen. Seine Deutung erfordert vom Betrachter eine intertextuelle Kompetenz[2], die ihm das Erkennen und das Verständnis der komplexen Beziehungen der Texte zueinander und zu früheren Texten (›Hypotexten‹) ermöglicht. In S. Maria Antiqua vollzieht sich dieser Prozess durch Palimpseste in der Malerei.

Der ›Hypertext‹ an der Kirchenwand vermittelt heute verschiedene Botschaften gleichzeitig; manche von ihnen scheinen gegensätzlich, wie Per Jonas Nordhagen wiederholt erklärt hat. Da wir den Schlüssel zum Verständnis in vielen Fällen verloren haben, wurden letztendlich andere Inhalte als die ursprünglich beabsichtigten hineininterpretiert.

Die facettenreiche Dekoration, mit der Johannes VII. das Presbyterium ausstatten ließ, beeindruckt nicht nur als Malzyklus, der im frühen Mittelalter seinesgleichen sucht, sondern stellt außerdem ein einzigartiges historisches Dokument dar, dessen Entschlüsselung einen wesentlichen Beitrag zur (gegenwärtig noch bruchstückhaften) Kenntnis

1 In der Literaturkritik verbindet ein hypertextuelles Verhältnis einen früheren ›Hypotext‹ mit einem späteren, von ersterem abgeleiteten ›Hypertext‹ (Genette 1997, S. 7–13). In der Informatik hingegen ist ein ›Hypertext‹ – laut Nelsons Definition – ein organisiertes System von Text- und Nicht-Text-Informationen in einer nicht-linearen, nicht-rigiden und elastischen Struktur, die nicht in konventioneller Weise auf einer gedruckten Seite gezeigt werden kann, sondern die Fähigkeiten eines Computers benötigt, um sie dynamisch anzuzeigen und nutzbar zu machen (Nelson 1992).

2 Ausgehend von den Überlegungen der Literaturwissenschaftlerin Julia Kristeva (1978, S. 121) versteht man heute unter ›Intertextualität‹ den Ansatz, der die Gesamtheit der Beziehungen eines jeden Texts mit allen anderen Texten, aber auch mit den entsprechenden soziokulturellen Gegebenheiten berücksichtigt. Vgl. Bernardelli 2013.

Abb. 1: Apsiswand, Santa Maria Antiqua, Rom, 6.–9. Jahrhundert.

Abb. 2: Umzeichnung der Dekorationsphasen der Apsiswand von Santa Maria Antiqua zur Zeit Johannes' VII. In Gelb: Phase 705/707, in Rot: Phase des ersten Jahrzehnts des 7. Jahrhunderts (G. Bordi – V. Valentini).

der Gedankenwelt eines Papstes im frühen 8. Jahrhundert leisten würde. Die einzige verfügbare Quelle zu Johannes VII. ist der *Liber pontificalis.*[3]

Beginnen wir mit der Beschreibung dieser Wand ab dem oberen Register zwischen dem Scheitelpunkt des Apsisbogens und dem Ansatz der Kalotte (Abb. 1–2). Hier ist die majestätische Anbetung des gekreuzigten Christus zwischen Maria und Johannes gemalt; es umrahmt sie eine Schar von Engeln, Seraphinen und Cherubinen, gefolgt von einer langen Inschrift auf Griechisch mit einer Reihe von Bibelzitaten.[4] Weiter unten steht eine jubelnde Menge. Nach der jüngsten Rekonstruktion von Per Olav Folgerø wurde das Register mit einer Darstellung von aus Sarkophagen steigenden Seelen abgeschlossen (Abb. 2), also mit einer Auferstehung der Heiligen, die bei Christi Tod auf dem Golgotha in ihren Gräbern ruhten (Mt 27,52).[5]

Aufgrund der Deutung von Rushforth und Tea[6] hat Nordhagen mehrfach die These vertreten, die Anbetung des gekreuzigten Christus sei eine Umsetzung der Anbetung des apokalyptischen Lammes, quasi als Befolgung von Kanon 82 des *Concilium Quinisextum* (der Trullanischen Synode) von 692, die jede Abbildung des Erlösers als Lamm untersagt hatte.[7] Nordhagen vertritt die Ansicht, Johannes VII. habe mit diesem Bild eines jungen Jesus mit nacktem Oberkörper und Kraushaar – nach dem Typus, der zur selben Zeit auf den Solidi Justinians II. (705–711) auftauchte – dem Willen des Kaisers entsprochen.[8] Ganz anders als sein Vorgänger Sergius I. (687–701), der sich geweigert hatte, die Dokumente des Trullanums zu unterzeichnen, weil sie *capitula Romana ecclesiae contraria* enthielten.[9] Diese Deutung wurde später von anderen Forschern wieder aufgenommen bzw. in Frage gestellt: Laut Breckenridge war Kanon 82 die logische Folge der chalkedonischen Christologie, die vom VI. Ökumenischen Konzil (680–681) mit anti-monotheletischer Prägung bekräftigt wurde. Die Darstellung der menschlichen Züge Christi nahm nun mit Blick sowohl auf seine göttliche als auch auf seine menschliche Natur eine neue Bedeutung an. Breckenridge meint, dass die Anbetung Christi in S. Maria Antiqua ein Ergebnis des Kompromisses zwischen Justinian II. und Johannes VII. ist. Als ersterer 705 wieder an die Macht kam, zeigte er sich konzilianter als 692; damals hatte er erfolglos versucht, Sergius I. einzukerkern. Der Papst war seinerseits

3 LP 88, 385–387.

4 Nordhagen 1968, S. 42–54.

5 Folgerø 2010; Folgerø [im Druck].

6 Rushforth 1902, S. 61; Tea 1937, S. 66–68.

7 Nordhagen 1968, S. 95–98; Nordhagen 2000, S. 129–134; Nordhagen 2002, S. 1751–1759.

8 Nordhagen 2000, S. 132–134; Nordhagen 2002, S. 1755–1757.

9 Sansterre 1982, S. 377–378. Im *Liber pontificalis* steht: *Sed hic, humana fragilitate timidus, hos nequaquam emendans per suprafatos metropolitas direxit ad principem.* (Johannes VII., von seiner eigenen menschlichen Schwäche verängstigt, schickte dem Kaiser, der zum zweiten Mal den Versuch einer Unterzeichnung durch den Papst unternommen hatte, die Dokumente ohne seine Unterschrift zurück), LP 88, 386.

bereit, Kanon 82 zu akzeptieren und die auf den Münzen vermittelte Christus-Ikonographie zu übernehmen.[10] Sansterre hat hingegen als erster vorgeschlagen, das Bildprogramm des Apsisbogens als direkten Ausdruck der Christologie des VI. Ökumenischen Konzils anzusehen. Die Anbetung des Gekreuzigten und Kanon 82 würden sich demnach beide auf das anti-monotheletische Konzilsdogma beziehen, also auch ohne eine unmittelbare Annahme des Kanons 82 durch Johannes VII. als Voraussetzung.[11]

Mit den alttestamentlichen Zitaten in der wunderbaren griechischen Inschrift, die an der Wand prangt »wie die Seite eines riesigen, mit Silberlettern auf purpurgefärbtes Pergament geschriebenen Manuskripts«[12], befassten sich nach Nordhagen noch Brenk[13], Tronzo[14], Kartsonis[15] und Folgerø[16]. Sie erkennen in der Zitatenreihe typologische Hinweise auf die Passion und Kreuzigung Christi, die eng mit der im 7. Jahrhundert in Jerusalem gefeierten Karfreitagsliturgie verknüpft und in der Katechese XIII des heiligen Kyrill von Jerusalem erwähnt sind.[17]

Auch diese Anbetung Christi wurde mit liturgischem Bezug ausgelegt. Laut Anna Kartsonis zeigt sich der Leib des Erlösers am Kreuz sowohl als apokalyptisches, von Engeln und Menschen angebetetes Lamm wie auch als eucharistisches Brot (*amnos*-Lamm). Die kosmische Verehrung des lebendigen Christus am Kreuz über dem Altar offenbart sich dem Gläubigen als monumentale Ikone und Symbol der Erlösung durch die Eucharistie.[18] Kartsonis' Annahmen folgend interpretierte Charles Barber das Bild als zugleich historische und theoretische Darstellung der Eucharistie, als Produkt des VI. Ökumenischen Konzils und umfangreiche Auslegung des Kanons 82. Es stehe im Einklang mit dem christologischen Zyklus an den Wänden des Presbyteriums, der verdeutlichen soll, dass Christus sowohl im Leben als auch nach der Auferstehung göttlicher *und* menschlicher Natur ist.[19] Ursula Nilgen dagegen macht in der Anbetung zwei verschiedene Bedeutungsebenen aus: Sichtbarmachung der liturgischen Verehrung

10 Breckenridge 1959, S. 85; Breckenridge 1972, S. 374.

11 Sansterre 1987, S. 339–440.

12 Cavallo 1988, S. 487.

13 Brenk 1971, S. 394–395.

14 Tronzo 1985, S. 100.

15 Kartsonis 1994, S. 170.

16 Folgerø 2009, S. 47–59; Folgerø [im Druck]. Er behauptet außerdem, die Schar der Engelsgestalten und der anbetenden Menschen sei eine Spiegelung von Dan 7,10. Im Zusammenhang mit der Katechese XV des heiligen Kyrill von Jerusalem gedeutet, besäße die Anbetung von S. Maria Antiqua dann auch eine eschatologische Bedeutung (Folgerø 2009, S. 56–57).

17 PG 33, 771–822. Die Katechese XIII bereitete die Katechumenen auf die Karfreitagsfeier vor und erklärte ihnen die Beziehung zwischen dem geschichtlichen Tod Christi am Kreuz und dem Geheimnis der Eucharistie (Kartsonis 1994, S. 170).

18 Kartsonis 1994, S. 169–172.

19 Barber 2002, S. 47–52.

Abb. 3: Apsisbogen, linke Wand, Johannes VII. und Leo II. (?), Augustinus und Leo der Große (?), Santa Maria Antiqua, Rom, 705/707.

Abb. 4: Apsisbogen, rechte Wand, Agatho (?) und Martin I., Gregor von Nazianz und Basilius von Caesarea, Santa Maria Antiqua, Rom, 705/707.

durch die Himmelswesen, nach dem Vorbild der Bildprogramme antiker Bogenmonumente, und ›historische‹ Kreuzigung als *apex* der Erzählungen aus dem Leben Christi an den Presbyteriumswänden.[20]

Fahren wir mit der Beschreibung fort: Im unteren Bereich, an den Seiten der Apsis, sind vier Päpste dargestellt: links (Abb. 3) von der Kalotte Johannes VII. (705–707) mit dem Nimbus der Lebenden und ein Papst ohne Namen; rechts (Abb. 4) ein weiterer anonymer Papst und Martin I. (649–655). Darunter waren vier Kirchenväter gemalt, von denen jedoch nur noch wenige Fragmente erhalten sind: auf der linken Seite Augustinus, von dem nur der Name übrig ist (Abb. 3), gefolgt von einer inzwischen vollkommen verlorenen Gestalt; auf der rechten Seite Gregor von Nazianz, von dem als einzigem das Gesicht erhalten ist, und Basilius von Caesarea, durch seinen *titulus* ausgewiesen (Abb. 4).[21] Den Abschluss der Dekoration bildeten gemalte Vorhänge, darüber eine Inschrift, die nur auf der linken Wand erhalten ist: »S(an)C(t)A D(e)I (geni) T(ri)CI SEMP(erque virgini Mar)IAE« (Abb. 5).[22]

Im Laufe der Zeit wurden die zwei fehlenden Päpste und der Kirchenvater unterschiedlich identifiziert, was sich natürlich auch auf die von den Malereien vermittelte politische Botschaft auswirkte. Im Folgenden sind die Positionen kurz zusammengefasst.

Marucchi erkannte in einem der beiden Päpste Honorius I. (625–638), der wie Martin I. in den Monotheletismus-Streit verwickelt war.[23] Rushforth schlug als vierten Kirchenvater Leo den Großen (440–461) vor[24]. De Grüneisen nahm an, zwischen Martin I. und Johannes II. seien zwei zwischen 655 und 705 amtierende Päpste abgebildet, während der verlorene Kirchenvater seines Erachtens Ambrosius, Hieronymus oder Leo sein konnte.[25] Wilpert sprach sich für Silvester (314–335) und Gregor den Großen (590–604) sowie für Ambrosius als Kirchenvater aus.[26] Für Tea konnte es sich bei den

20 Nilgen stellt außerdem die Verknüpfung zwischen dieser Anbetung und dem Kanon 82 infrage. Sie bezweifelt die Darstellung der Anbetung des Lammes in einem griechischen Kontext in Rom, da es in der byzantinischen Malerei so etwas noch nicht gegeben hatte; in der Tat hängt die Darstellung ja mit der Offenbarung des Johannes zusammen, die damals von der griechischen Kirche noch nicht anerkannt war. Vgl. Nilgen 2004, S. 129–134.

21 S. Nordhagen 1968, S. 39–43.

22 Transkribiert in Nordhagen 1968, S. 39. Aufgrund einiger im Jahr 1900 noch sichtbarer Buchstabenspuren nahm Wilpert für die rechte Wand folgende Inschrift an: I(ohannes indignus episcopus fecit). S. Wilpert 1916, Bd. II, S. 667; Bd. IV, Pl. 207, 2.

23 Marucchi 1900, S. 299. Aufgrund des beim VI. Ökumenischen Konzil (680–681) über Honorius I. verhängten Kirchenbanns wurde diese Hypothese bald aufgegeben.

24 Rushforth 1902, S. 73.

25 Grüneisen 1911, S. 144 und 147.

26 Wilpert 1916, S. 669–670.

Abb. 5: Apsisbogen, linke Wand, Gregor von Nazianz und Leo der Große, Santa Maria Antiqua, Rom, 650/663.

Päpsten um Leo den Großen bzw. Gregor den Großen und um Ambrosius handeln.[27] In jüngerer Zeit hat Nordhagen – dank einiger Buchstaben links und rechts der Papstfigur: »S(an)c(tu)s LE[o] / P(a)p(a) [R]O[m]A[n]US« – die Gestalt neben Johannes VII. als Leo den Großen identifiziert,[28] er verzichtet jedoch auf weitere Hypothesen zu den Figuren ohne *titulus*. Nordhagen verdanken wir ebenfalls den ersten Deutungsversuch der gesamten Bildanlage in der Apsis, auf die er zwischen 1967 und 2002 immer wieder zurückgekommen ist.[29] Eine zentrale Rolle spielen in der Deutung des Bildprogramms Papst Martin I. (Abb. 4) und das Laterankonzil von 649:[30] Rushforth und Tea vertreten die Meinung,[31] die Erinnerung an beide sei in der früheren Ausmalung sozusagen auf der siebten Schicht des Palimpsests gewesen[32].

Auf den beiden Wandpartien zu Seiten der Apsis, unterhalb der vier *Patres* und der Vorhänge Johannes' VII., sind Leo der Große und Gregor von Nazianz (links, Abb. 5) bzw. Basilius von Caesarea und Johannes Chrysostomus (rechts, Abb. 6) auszumachen. Nach der Rekonstruktion Brightmans (1902) hält jeder eine Schriftrolle mit den Auszügen aus eigenen Werken, die beim Laterankonzil von 649 zur Widerlegung der monothelestischen Häresie angeführt wurden.[33] Diese Deutung wurde von allen späteren Forschern übernommen, und dementsprechend wurde die Malschicht mit den Kirchenvätern auf 649–653, also in das Pontifikat Martins I. (649–655), datiert.[34]

Nordhagen erkennt eine Übertragung zwischen einer Malschicht der Apsiswand und der nächsten, denn als Johannes VII. die beiden Felder mit den Kirchenvätern an den Seitenwänden (üblicherweise in die Zeit Martins I. datiert) neu verputzen und bemalen ließ, hielt er doch die Erinnerung daran in seiner neuen, wirkmächtigen Inszenierung wach (Abb. 2). In der Tat gründet das Interpretationssystem des norwegischen Wissenschaftlers für die Malereien in S. Maria Antiqua auf dem (?) Papstduo Martin I. und Johannes VII. Seine Deutung des Bildprogramms fokussiert auf den Dualismus zwischen pro- und anti-byzantinischen Botschaften an den beiden Seiten der Apsiswand.

27 Tea 1937, S. 68, 73. Zunächst fand auch ich – wie Wilpert und Tea – es plausibel, dass der fehlende Papst in der Reihe Gregor der Große sei, Bordi 2016, S. 49.

28 Nordhagen 1968, S. 42.

29 Nordhagen 1967; Nordhagen 1968; Nordhagen 1995; Nordhagen 2000; Nordhagen 2002.

30 Zum Laterankonzil und zum Monotheletismus-Streit s. zuletzt (mit Verweis auf frühere Literatur): Price 2014.

31 Rushforth 1902, S. 65–73; Tea 1937, S. 64–69.

32 Zur Schichtenfolge der Wand in S. Maria Antiqua s. zuletzt: Bordi 2016, S. 34–53, Abb. 8–9.

33 Rushforth 1902, S. 68–73; Nordhagen 1962, S. 58–61; Nordhagen 1978, S. 97–99.

34 Laut Beat Brenk und Eileen Rubery gab Papst Martin I. diese Malereien als anti-monotheletisches Manifest zwischen 650 und 652 in Auftrag, als der Exarch Olympius sich in Rom und Norditalien aufhielt. Dieser war von Konstans II. gesandt, den Papst zu verhaften, der ohne Bestätigung des Kaisers den Papstthron bestiegen hatte. Olympius jedoch lehnte sich gegen den Kaiser auf und schlug sich auf die Seite des Papstes. Brenk 2004, S. 78–79; Rubery 2012, S. 339–374.

Abb. 6: Apsisbogen, rechte Wand, Basilius von Caesarea und Johannes Chrysostomus, S. Maria Antiqua, Rom, 650/663.

Im oberen Register mit der Anbetung, in Anlehnung an Kanon 82 der Trullanischen Synode (692), folgt das Christusgesicht dem Typus der Münzprägungen aus der zweiten Herrschaftszeit Justinians II. (704–711); das Ganze scheint Ausdruck einer eindeutigen Befürwortung der Vorgaben aus Konstantinopel. Im Gegensatz dazu ist die Abbildung Martins I., eines Märtyrers der Orthodoxie, im unteren Register für Nordhagen ein beredtes Zeichen von Widerstand und Unnachgiebigkeit gegenüber dem Kaiser.[35]

Ein paar Jahre später schlug Sansterre vor, den namenlosen zweiten Papst mit Agatho (678–681) zu identifizieren; damit bringt er erneut das VI. Ökumenische Konzil (680–681) mit seiner Überwindung des Monotheletismus ins Spiel. Sansterre hält außerdem fest, dass Martin I. hier nicht besonders hervorgehoben wird, denn er ist nur Teil der Geschichte der römischen Kirche im langen, 649 begonnenen Streit gegen die Monotheletisten.[36]

Nordhagen kam 2000 auf dieses Bildprogramm zurück und bezeichnete es erneut als sehr widersprüchlich. Papst Martin wird die Auszeichnung päpstlicher Unbeugsamkeit gegenüber Byzanz zuerkannt, und Johannes VII. hätte sogar eine byzantinische Waffe gegen Byzanz angewendet: Die Abbildung Martins neben der eigenen scheint eine in Konstantinopel zahlreich dokumentierte Praxis aufzugreifen[37], während am Bogen eine Ikonographie geschaffen wird, die den Kanon 82 feiert und den Einfluss des Trullanums auf Rom belegt.[38]

2002 revidiert Nordhagen seine Meinung und deutete das Programm von Johannes VII. als Zeichen der Unterstützung im Streit, der die byzantinische Hauptstadt immer noch entzweite. Trotz aller Bemühungen Justinians II. war der Monotheletismus noch nicht besiegt, wie der Wiedereinführungsversuch durch Philippikos Bardanes wenige Jahre später bewies. Demzufolge erscheint Martins Darstellung nun weniger prorömisch und eher kaisertreu.[39]

In neuerer Zeit haben sich auch Ekonomou[40] und Börjesson[41] Sansterres Annahme angeschlossen und den dritten Papst in der Reihe als Agatho identifiziert (Abb. 4). Dieser ›geistige Vater‹ des VI. Ökumenischen Konzils führte die Wiedervereinigung von Rom und Konstantinopel unter dem Zeichen der Orthodoxie herbei. Börjesson nahm darüber

35 Nordhagen 1968, S. 95–98.

36 Sansterre 1982, S. 382.

37 Vor seinem Einzug in Konstantinopel 712 ließ Philippikos Bardanes die Bilder des VI. Ökumenischen Konzils, das den Monotheletismus verurteilt hatte, zerstören und die Bilder der von diesem Konzil mit dem Kirchenbann belegten Persönlichkeiten wiederherstellen: Neben sein Porträt ließ er das des Patriarchen Sergius malen. Nordhagen 2000, S. 129–130.

38 Nordhagen 2000, S. 131–134.

39 Nordhagen 2002, S. 1755–1760.

40 Ekonomou 2007, S. 268.

41 Börjesson [im Druck].

hinaus an, der Kirchenvater rechts von Augustinus sei Hilarius oder Ambrosius, also einer der beim V. Ökumenischen Konzil (553) heiliggesprochenen Päpste (Abb. 3).[42]

Die Bezugnahme auf das VI. Ökumenische Konzil durch Agatho lenkt das Augenmerk von den Konzilien im Lateran (649) und im *Trullum* (692) ab, denen zuvor eine zentrale Rolle zugestanden wurde, und wirft ein neues Licht auf das Programm von Johannes VII., das viel weniger zweideutig bzw. dualistisch ist als bisher angenommen, wie wir noch sehen werden. Außerdem wurde die Auftraggeberschaft Martins I. in S. Maria Antiqua (für die beiden Felder mit den vier Kirchenvätern) jüngst von Price in Frage gestellt: Der Philologe bewies, dass von den vier Texten auf den Schriftrollen der Kirchenväter (Abb. 5–6), die beim Laterankonzil von 649 Verwendung fanden, nur zwei, nämlich die *excerpta* aus dem *Tomus ad Flavianum* Leos des Großen und aus dem *Sermo in S. Thomam Apostolum* von Johannes Chrysostomus, sich explizit mit den beiden Handlungen in Christus befassen, während die anderen beiden, aus *De Spiritu* des heiligen Basilius von Caesarea bzw. aus der *Oratio* XXX,12 des heiligen Gregors von Nazianz, die Willenseinheit von Vater und Sohn thematisieren, die ja sowohl von Duo- als auch von Monotheletisten akzeptiert war.[43] Die Zitate wären also nicht zur Erhärtung der anti-monothelestischen Position gewählt worden, sondern zur Betonung der gemeinsamen Aspekte der Tradition in Rom und derjenigen in Konstantinopel, in einem Klima der Entspannung und Kompromissbereitschaft, das laut Price mit dem Rombesuch von Konstans II. im Jahr 663, also während des Pontifikats von Vitalianus (657–672), in Zusammenhang stehen könnte.[44]

Der neue, von Price vorgeschlagene Ansatz mindert das polemische Element in der Darstellung der vier Väter, die nun kein anti-monothelestisches Manifest mehr wäre; außerdem weckt er Zweifel an der Behauptung, Martin I. sei der Auftraggeber der Ausschmückung von S. Maria Antiqua gewesen.[45]

Kommen wir jedoch auf das VI. Ökumenische Konzil zurück. Mit der *divalis iussio* vom 12. August 678 forderte Konstantin IV. Papst Donus auf, Legaten zu einer theologischen Debatte zu entsenden, um die vom Monotheletismus verursachte Spaltung zwischen Rom und Konstantinopel beizulegen.[46] Als das Schreiben eintraf, war Donus schon tot, und Agatho, der erste griechische Papst, antwortete erst zwei Jahre später. Er veranstaltete am 27. März 680 eine Synode in Rom, zu der er die Bischöfe aus ganz

---

42 Die beim V. Ökumenischen Konzil als *auctoritates* anerkannten Väter waren: Athanasius, Hilarius, Basilius, Gregor von Nazianz (der Theologe), Gregor von Nyssa, Ambrosius, Augustinus, Theophilus, Johannes von Konstantinopel, Kyrill, Leo der Große und Proculus. Börjesson 2015, S. 217–218; Börjesson [im Druck].

43 Price 2014, 80–81, Anm. 55; Price [im Druck].

44 Ebd.; LP 78: 2–3, 343.

45 Bordi 2016, S. 46–49.

46 Mansi 1759ff., Sp. 195–202.

Italien und sogar eine Vertretung aus den Gebieten nördlich der Alpen einlud mit dem unmissverständlichen Ziel, der territorialen Dimension der römischen Kirche neuen Sinn zu verleihen. Nach der erfolgreichen Evangelisierung, angefangen bei den Angelsachsen durch Gregor den Großen, erstreckte sich das kirchliche Zuständigkeitsgebiet nun tatsächlich auch auf das christianisierte barbarische Abendland.[47] Auf diese Weise legte Agatho den Grundstein zu einer neuen Universalekklesiologie, in der die *gentes* zum Bestandteil des *imperium Christianum* wurden, in Einheit mit dem Ostreich unter der *sedes apostolica*.[48] Während der Synode wurden zwei Schreiben an den *basileus* verfasst – eines dogmatischer Art mit einem vom Papst unterzeichneten Glaubensbekenntnis, das andere mit den Unterschriften der 125 teilnehmenden westlichen Bischöfe.[49] Agatho wollte dem Kaiser zu verstehen geben, das von der römischen Synode produzierte Dokument sei das Ergebnis einer Mobilisierung des gesamten westlichen Episkopats, das solidarisch und geschlossen hinter dem Papst stand, und dass die kanonisch tradierten Lehren nicht zur Diskussion standen, sondern nur akzeptiert werden konnten.[50]

Das Konzil begann am 7. November 680; acht Tage danach wurden die Briefe Agathos und der römischen Synode verlesen. Trotz allen Respekts vor dem Amt des Kaisers, dem die Stabilität des Reichs von Gott anvertraut war und der als *vicarius Christi* und Gottes *coregnator* gefeiert wurde, äußerte Agatho in seinem Bekenntnis eine der kaiserlichen Ideologie entgegenstehende Auffassung, denn er präsentierte sich selbst, d. h. den Nachfolger Petri, als Träger des wahren, von den *auctoritates* tradierten Glaubens.[51] Gleichzeitig ist sich der Papst seines Primats innerhalb der Kirche und seiner Aufgabe als Verteidiger der Orthodoxie bewusst. Das Konzil endete am 16. September 681, acht Monate nach Agathos Tod († 10. Januar 681).[52]

Das VI. Ökumenische Konzil von Konstantinopel war für Rom, um mit Delogu zu sprechen, »ein wahrhafter Erfolg des Papsttums«[53] mit folgenden Auswirkungen: Überwindung des Monotheletismus und Aussöhnung mit Konstantinopel, verbunden mit der Anerkennung als ›erste Kathedra der Patriarchen‹ und der Identifizierung Agathos mit dem Apostelfürsten[54] aufgrund des Petrinischen Glaubensbekenntnisses

47 Maccarrone 1991, S. 87–88.

48 Maccarrone 1991, S. 88–90.

49 Arnaldi 2000, S. 616; Delogu 2001, S. 57.

50 Bertolini 1941, S. 379; Arnaldi 2000, S. 616.

51 Maccarrone 1991, S. 79–82; Ferrazza 2016, S. 91–99.

52 Arnaldi 2000, S. 616.

53 Delogu 2001, S. 65.

54 Im *Sermo prosphoneticus* des Konzils an den Kaiser heißt es: »Das alte Rom, o Basileus, überreichte dir ein mit Gottes Hand geschriebenes Bekenntnis, und der Tag der Glaubenswahrheit begann von Westen her. Scheinbar handelte es sich nur um Papier und Tinte, aber es war Petrus, der durch Agatho sprach« (Mansi 1759 ff., Sp. 665–666), Übersetzung bei Arnaldi 2000, S. 616.

(Mt 16,18–19).[55] Dennoch wurde der Papst nicht als einzige Quelle der Orthodoxie anerkannt, denn Konstantin IV. stellte im *Edictum* und im *Sermo prosphoneticus* den *basileus* als ersten Garanten der kirchlichen Einheit und des reinen Glaubens dar, gab ihm also einen höheren Rang als der gesamten Kirchenhierarchie, einschließlich des Pontifex.[56] Ein weiterer Tiefschlag war der Bann gegen Papst Honorius I.[57] Zum Nachfolger Agathos wurde Leo II. gewählt, der jedoch erst am 17. August 682 geweiht werden konnte, nach der Bestätigung durch den Kaiser.[58] Leo vollendete das Werk seines Vorgängers, indem er die Sendung des *basileus* im Jahr 682 mit den zu unterzeichnenden Konzilsakten annahm. In seiner Antwort an Konstantin vom 7. Mai 683 lobte er zwar die Arbeit des Kaisers, den er als neuen David und *filius defensor* des apostolischen Stuhls bezeichnete, vor allem aber betonte er die wesentliche Rolle der römischen Kirche in der Ausarbeitung der Konzilsbeschlüsse. Außerdem wies der Pontifex nachdrücklich darauf hin, dass Konstantins Triumph ebenfalls in Bezug auf die *sedes apostolica* anzusehen war und auf den ihr von Gott gegebenen Auftrag, die Reinheit des Glaubens auf der ganzen Welt zu erhalten und zu verbreiten.[59]

Damit bekräftigte Leo II., der *vicarius Petri* sei der einzige Bewahrer des Glaubens und der Orthodoxie, eine Stellung, die der Kaiser eigentlich für sich beanspruchte. Der Papst präzisierte darüber hinaus, seine Aufgabe sei die Bestätigung (und nicht nur die Unterzeichnung) der Konzilsakten. Da der Papst sie als mit dem rechten Glauben konform anerkannt hat, kann nur er – und nicht der Kaiser – ihnen Autorität verleihen.[60]

Um dem Anspruch auf die zentrale Rolle des Papsttums innerhalb des *imperium Christianum* Gewicht zu verleihen und zur Fortsetzung der Maßnahmen Agathos ließ Leo II. die Konzilsakten und -dokumente aus dem Griechischen ins Lateinische übersetzen.[61] So konnten die Bischöfe im Westen und damit der Klerus und die Gläubigen der jeweiligen Diözesen das Glaubenskenntnis unterzeichnen, wie aus zwei Schreiben an den Westgotenkönig Erwig bzw. an die Bischöfe seines Reiches hervorgeht.[62] Die

55 Das Petrusbekenntnis ist das Fundament der Auffassung, dass die Päpste eine besondere Autorität in lehramtlicher Hinsicht besitzen, da sie ihre Kenntnis durch Petrus direkt von Christus beziehen. Price 2014, S. 40.

56 Susi 2000, S. 617–618; Ferrazza 2016, S. 114.

57 Magi 1972, S. 251; Ferrazza 2016, S. 114–115.

58 Susi 2000, S. 617.

59 Bertolini 1941, S. 390–391.

60 Ferrazza 2016, S. 120.

61 Als erste wurden übersetzt: das Glaubensbekenntnis, die Huldigung an den Kaiser und das Edikt Konstantins IV., s. Bertolini 1941, S. 389. Giandomenico Ferrazza und seiner Dissertation (2016), deren Hauptergebnisse in Kürze veröffentlicht werden, verdanke ich ein tieferes Verständnis der wesentlichen Rolle Leos II. durch die Übersetzung und Verbreitung einiger Akten des VI. Ökumenischen Konzils.

62 Bertolini 1941, S. 389–390; Maccarrone 1991, S. 91–95; Ferrazza 2016, S. 123–128.

Unterschriften sollten danach an der *Confessio* von St. Peter niedergelegt werden.[63] Die diesem Vorhaben zugrunde liegende ekklesiologische Auffassung widersprach nicht nur derjenigen von Byzanz, wie Bertolini und Susi dargelegt haben, sondern ermöglichte gleichzeitig autonome Entwicklungen gegenüber oder sogar im Widerstreit mit Konstantinopel, denn die Barbarenstaaten wurden aufgefordert, ihre Differenzen beizulegen und sich in gottgewollter geistlicher Einheit mit der *sedes apostolica* im Mittelpunkt zu identifizieren.[64] Der Papst pochte also auf die Schlüsselrolle Roms und des Stellvertreters Petri als alleinige Garanten des rechten Glaubens und der Einheit der Kirche – wenn auch mit dem unentbehrlichen Beitrag des Kaisers.[65]

Zur Dekoration des Apsisbogens in S. Maria Antiqua zurückkehrend, treten daher Zweifel an der vorgeschlagenen Identifizierung der Päpste und Väter auf. Laut Nordhagen, dessen Meinung sich alle späteren Forscher anschlossen, wäre die Gestalt rechts von Johannes VII. (Abb. 3) in der Papstreihe Leo der Große, gefolgt von Agatho und Martin I. (Abb. 4) (nach Meinung von Sansterre, Ekonomou und Börjesson). Johannes VII. ließ Leo I. jedoch auch am Pfeiler rechts vom Eingang der Vierzig-Märtyrer-Kapelle abbilden (Abb. 7)[66], wo der Papst wie in der Malerei der Apsiswand (nach 649) eine Schriftrolle trägt mit denselben Zitaten aus dem *Tomus ad Flavianum*, die während der V. Sitzungsperiode des Laterankonzils verlesen[67] und im Glaubensbekenntnis des Konzils von 680 wiederholt wurden.[68] Leos Darstellung an der Fassade des Oratoriums ist meines Erachtens ein Indiz dafür, dass in S. Maria Antiqua sowohl die Malereien von 649/663 als auch die von Johannes VII. beauftragten Fresken Leo als *auctoritas* darstellen sollten, als Hauptperson des Konzils von Chalkedon, dessen *Tomus ad Flavianum* die Monophysiten besiegt und die Lehre der Doppelnatur Christi festschreibt.[69] Seine Bedeutung als hoch verehrter Vertreter des päpstlichen Primats war in diesem Rahmen eher zweitrangig. Daher halte ich eine Verschiebung Leos vom Kirchenvater zum Vorbildpapst innerhalb ein und desselben Bildprogramms für unwahrscheinlich. Im allgemeinen Rahmen der Freskenausstattung von S. Maria Antiqua war Leo vermutlich stets als Autor des *Tomus*, also als Held der Orthodoxie, abgebildet.

---

63 S. De Blaauw 1987, S. 271–274; Maccarrone 1991, S. 93–94; sowie den Beitrag von Dijkstra/Van Espelo in diesem Band.

64 Bertolini 1941, S. 390; Susi 2000.

65 Susi 2000.

66 Nordhagen 1968, S. 84. Die Figur ist heute fast gänzlich verschwunden, jedoch auf dem von Josef Wilpert aquarellierten Foto noch sichtbar (Wilpert 1914, IV, Pl. 167,1).

67 *Agit enim utraque forma cum alterius communione quod proprium est, Verbo scilicet operante quod Verbi est, et carne exequente quod carnis est. Unum horum coruscat miraculis, aliud succumbit injuriis. Et sicut Verbum ab aequalitate paternae gloriae non recedit, ita caro naturam nostri generis non relinquit.* (PL, LXXXVII, col. 1193B). S. auch Price 2014, S. 333–334.

68 Folgerø [im Druck].

69 Maccarone 1991, S. 82; Ekonomou 2007, S. 268.

Abb. 7: Leo der Große mit eine Schriftrolle (links), Eingang der Vierzig-Märtyrer-Kapelle, Rom, 705/707 (nach Wilpert 1914, IV, Pl. 167,1).

In der Gestalt der Papstreihe, die Nordhagen anhand des *titulus* als Leo identifiziert, möchte ich eher Leo II. (682–683) erkennen (Abb. 3), den der *Liber pontificalis* als »Vir eloquentissimus, in divinis scripturis sufficienter instructus, greca latinaque lingua eruditus« bezeichnet. Dieser Papst ging wegen seiner Übersetzung der Konzilsakten von 680–681 und deren Verbreitung in den Bistümern des Westens in die Geschichte ein. Er unterstützte die von Agatho entwickelte ›supranationale‹ Ekklesiologie, wonach die christianisierten *gentes* den Mittelpunkt ihrer Einheit in der *sedes apostolica* fanden, und erweiterte auf diese Weise den Einflussbereich der römischen Kirche.[70]

Das oben Gesagte gibt wiederum der Annahme De Grüneisens Recht, wonach die Lücke zwischen Martin I. und Johannes VII. von zwei Päpsten ausgefüllt war, die zwi-

70 Maccarone 1991, S. 89–90.

schen 655 und 705 amtierten.[71] Links von der Theophanie in der Apsis stehend, hätte Johannes – von rechts beginnend – die Päpste Martin I., Agatho (Abb. 4) und Leo II. (Abb. 3) abbilden lassen, und im unteren Register zwei griechische (Basilius von Caesarea, Gregor von Nazianz, Abb. 4) und zwei lateinische Kirchenväter (Leo der Große, Augustinus, Abb. 3). Bei der Ausmalung von 649/663 (Abb. 5–6) wurde Johannes Chrysostomus durch Augustinus ersetzt, vielleicht in der Absicht, ein Gleichgewicht zwischen Ost und West herzustellen. Die vier *venerabili Patres* sollten jetzt wohl den Sieg über den Monotheletismus beim VI. Ökumenischen Konzil von 680–681 anstatt die Lateransynode von 649 verkörpern. Diese vier wurden aus der im *Liber pontificalis* genannten Neunergruppe der *venerabili Patres* ausgewählt als *auctoritates* für die Durchsetzung der Doktrin über die zwei Willen und zwei Handlungen in Christus, die 680 die Oberhand gewonnen hatte.[72] Zu erwähnen ist außerdem, dass in Agathos Schreiben an Kaiser Konstantin IV. die Textstellen aus den Werken des Bischofs von Hippo (*Contra Maximinum haereticum Arianorum Episcopum* bzw. *Contra Julianum*) eine ebenso große Bedeutung besaßen wie der *Tomus* von Leo dem Großen.[73]

In der Papstreihe hingegen, und angesichts der neuen Aufstellung, wurde Martin I. von Johannes VII. weder als Märtyrer der Orthodoxie noch in pro-kaiserlicher Funktion dargestellt, wie es Nordhagen zu unterschiedlichen Zeiten postuliert hatte, sondern als der Papst, der mit dem Konzil von 649 die Orthodoxie in seiner Eigenschaft als Petrusnachfolger verteidigt hatte. In S. Maria Antiqua steht Johannes in einer Reihe mit den Päpsten, die ab 649 die Vorrangstellung der *sedes apostolica et romana* über die anderen Patriarchate und ihre Rolle als geistige Mutter des Imperiums und alleinige Verteidigung der Orthodoxie aufgrund des Petrusbekenntnisses vertreten hatten.

Als Grieche musste sich Johannes VII. zwangsläufig auf seine Vorgänger Agatho und Leo zurückbesinnen, und er wollte in der Tat Mittler zwischen östlicher und westlicher Welt sein, fühlte er sich doch beiden zugehörig innerhalb einer universalen Ekklesiologie, in der nur die *sedes apostolica* den barbarischen Okzident und den kaiserlichen Orient zusammenhalten und die Reinheit des Glaubens bewahren konnte. Die Fokussierung auf das VI. Ökumenische Konzil von 680–681 zeigt einen radikalen Kurswechsel an: Zunächst wird eine als ambivalent empfundene Stellung des Papstes, zwischen Versöhnung mit dem Kaiser und Protest gegen ihn schwankend, vom Jubel über einen maßgeblichen Erfolg der Kirche abgelöst.[74] An der Apsiswand von S. Maria Antiqua

71 S. oben.

72 LP I, 352, c. 143.

73 PL 87, Sp. 1161–1214. Zu Augustinus und den zwei Willen in Christus s. zuletzt: Börjesson 2015; Börjesson [im Druck].

74 Die entscheidende Bedeutung des VI. Ökumenischen Konzils im Rahmen der Behauptung Roms als *sedes apostolica* und die Aktion der Päpste von Martin I. bis Agapitus wurde vor Kurzem von Rosamond

Abb. 8: 3D-Rekonstruktion des Oratoriums Johannes' VII. (Digitale Rekonstruktion von M. Carpiceci, Architekt, graphische Ausführung von G. Dibenedetto, Architekt).

zelebriert der Papst den dogmatischen Sieg der Kirche von Rom über den Monotheletismus; der wahre Erfolg ist allerdings die Durchsetzung der römischen Ekklesiologie.

In der Apsismitte war die Gottesmutter Maria zu sehen (Abb. 1). Wie ich schon an anderer Stelle in Bezug auf die Verputzschichten ausführte,[75] scheint sie unter Johan-

McKitterick bestätigt, die die Fortsetzung des *Liber Pontificalis* in den Pontifikat Agathos datiert, da er dazu dienen sollte, die Rolle des Papsttums in der Durchsetzung des orthodoxen christlichen Glaubens gegenüber Byzanz zu festigen. Der Plan der Kirche wird in der Reise Konstantins nach Konstantinopel 710 seine Vollendung finden. Vgl. McKitterick 2016, S. 255–273.

75 Bordi 2016, S. 49, Abb. 8–9.

nes VII. nicht übermalt worden zu sein. Der Papst hat demnach ein Marienbild vom Anfang des 7. Jahrhunderts verschont und sogar aufgewertet. Maria mit Kind war Teil eines Dreifigurenschemas (Abb. 2), denn sie wurde zwischen zwei Engeln gezeigt oder, besser, zwischen den Heiligen Petrus und Paulus,[76] wie in der ersten Ausmalung der Apsis aus dem 6. Jahrhundert bzw. wie in der Darstellung, die Johannes VII. an die Wand des Übergangs zwischen Kirche und Bischofspalast malen ließ.[77]

Auch in S. Maria Antiqua, wie in seiner Grabkapelle in St. Peter, stellt Johannes VII. die Mutter Gottes dar, denn sie verkörpert die Kirche Christi, als deren *servus* (Abb. 7)[78] sich der Papst erklärt: ein offensichtlicher Verweis auf das Attribut *servus Christi*, das Kaiser Justinian II. auf der Rückseite des während seiner ersten Amtszeit geprägten Solidus für sich in Anspruch nahm (685–695).[79] Laut Belting handelt es sich um eine polemische Anspielung: Der Papst, *de iure* noch Untertan von Byzanz, hätte auf diese Weise *de facto* erklärt, er wolle seine Souveränität im Auftrag der Gottesmutter allein ausüben.[80] Vernünftiger erscheint die Interpretation Opies, wonach Johannes VII. eher verdeutlichen wollte, dass der Papst die Jungfrau Maria vertritt, und daher die Kirche,[81] wie der Kaiser Christus auf Erden vertritt. Dies entsprach der damaligen Auffassung des Papsttums als Institution, die politisch, kulturell und spirituell immer noch dem Kaiserreich angehörte.[82]

Die hier dargelegte Deutung ergibt sich aus der immer stärkeren Überzeugung, dass Johannes VII. der erste Papst war, der in S. Maria Antiqua als Auftraggeber auftrat. Nachdem der Bischofspalast auf den Palatin verlegt worden ist[83], wird der Papst das am stärksten byzantinisch geprägte Gotteshaus zu seiner Palastkirche machen. Der völlig einzigartige ›Hypertext‹ im Presbyterium ist sowohl ein dogmatisches Manifest als auch und vor allem eine nachdrückliche Feststellung der römischen Ekklesiologie. In S. Maria Antiqua, wie in seiner Grabkapelle[84], erklärt sich der Grieche Johannes VII. als *vir eruditissimus et facundus eloquentia*, durch Bilder und Schrift: Δουλος της Θεωτοκου, *Servus Beatae dei Genitricis*, Diener der Kirche.

76 Bordi 2016, S. 46.

77 Nordhagen 1968, S. 80–81; Nordhagen 1982, S. 345–348.

78 Zum nicht erhaltenen Oratorium Johannes' VII. in S. Pietro und seiner 3D–Rekonstruktion s. Ballardini 2011, Ballardini 2013, Ballardini/Pogliani 2013, Ballardini 2016, S. 220–227. Ich danke Antonella Ballardini und Paolo Pogliani für die Erlaubnis, ihre 3D-Rekonstruktion des Oratoriums abzubilden.

79 Nach der Klassifizierung von Breckenridge handelt es sich um den Solidus vom Typ II, der zwischen 692 und 695 geprägt wurde (Breckenridge 1959, S. 63–65, 78, 90). Vgl. Cavallo 1988, S. 487; Belting 1991, S. 127; Opie 2002, S. 1827 Anm. 38.

80 Belting 1991, S. 127.

81 Opie 2002, S. 1827 Anm. 38.

82 Azzara 1997; Delogu 2001, S. 57–59.

83 Siehe dazu den Beitrag von Lucrezia Spera in diesem Band.

84 Ballardini 2016, S. 226.

Bibliographie

Arnaldi 2000 Girolamo Arnaldi: Agatone, santo, in: Enciclopedia dei papi, Bd. I, Rom 2000, S. 612–616.

Azzara 1997 Claudio Azzara: L'ideologia del potere regio nel papato altomedievale (secoli VI–VIII), Spoleto 1997.

Ballardini 2011 Antonella Ballardini: Un oratorio per la Theotokos: Giovanni VII (705–707) committente a San Pietro, in: Medioevo: i committenti, Atti del Convegno internazionale di studi (Parma, 21.–26.9.2010), hg. von Arturo Carlo Quintavalle, Mailand 2011, S. 94–116.

Ballardini 2016 Antonella Ballardini: Il perduto Oratorio di Giovanni VII nella basilica di San Pietro in Vaticano: architettura e scultura, in: Santa Maria Antiqua tra Roma e Bisanzio (Ausstellung Rom, Santa Maria Antiqua, 17.3.–30.10.2016), hg. von Maria Andaloro, Giulia Bordi und Giuseppe Morganti, Mailand 2016, S. 220–227.

Ballardini/Pogliani 2013 Antonella Ballardini und Paolo Pogliani: A reconstruction of the oratory of John VII (705–7), in: Old Saint Peter's, Rome, hg. von Rosamond McKitterick et al., Cambridge 2013, S. 190–213.

Barber 2002 Charles Barber: Figure and likeness. On the limits of representation in Byzantine iconoclasm, Princeton 2002.

Belting1994 Hans Belting: Likeness and Presence. A History of The Image before the Era of Art, Chicago/London 1994.

Bergmeier 2014 Armin F. Bergmeier: The Crucifixion as Theophany: Divine Visions in a Sermon by Anastasius Sinaita and on the Apse Wall of Santa Maria Antiqua, in: Journal of late antiquity 7, 2014, S. 65–85.

Bernardelli 2013 Andrea Bernardelli: Che cos'è l'intertestualità, Rom 2013.

Berto 2000 Luigi Andrea Berto: Giovanni VII, in: Enciclopedia dei papi, Rom 2000, S. 638–640.

Bertolini 1941 Ottorino Bertolini: Roma di fronte a Bisanzio e ai Longobardi, Bologna 1941.

Bordi 2016 Giulia Bordi: Santa Maria Antiqua attraverso i palinsesti pittorici, in: Santa Maria Antiqua tra Roma e Bisanzio (Ausstellung Rom, Santa Maria Antiqua, 17.3.–30.10.2016), hg. von Maria Andaloro, Giulia Bordi und Giuseppe Morganti, Mailand 2016, S. 34–53.

Börjesson 2015 Johannes Börjesson: Augustine on the Will, in: The Oxford Handbook of Maximus the Confessor, hg. von Pauline Allen und Bronwen Neil, Oxford 2015, S. 212–234.

Börjesson [im Druck] Johannes Börjesson: The Cult of Augustine in the Byzantine Church of the First Millennium, in: Santa Maria Antiqua. The Sistine Chapel of the Middle Ages (Studies in Medieval and Early Renaissance Art History), International Conference held at the British School at Rome (December 4–6, 2013), hg. von Eileen Rubery, Giulia Bordi und John Osborne, Turnhout [im Druck].

Breckenridge 1959 James Douglas Breckenridge: The numismatic iconography of Justinian II (685–695, 705–711 A.D.), New York 1959.

Breckenridge 1972 James Douglas Breckenridge: Evidence for the Nature of Relations between Pope John VII and the Byzantine Emperor Justinian II, in: Byzantinische Zeitschrift 65, 1972, S. 364–374.

Brenk 1971 Beat Brenk: Rezension von: Per Jonas Nordhagen, The Frescoes of John VII (A.D. 705–707) in: Santa Maria Antiqua in Rome, Rom 1968, in: Byzantinische Zeitschrift 64, 1971, S. 392–396.

Brenk 2004 Beat Brenk: Papal Patronage in a Greek Church in Rome, in: Santa Maria Antiqua al Foro Romano cento anni dopo, hg. von John Osborne, J. Rasmus Brandt und Giuseppe Morganti, Rom 2004, S. 67–81.

Cavallo 1988 Guglielmo Cavallo: Le tipologie della cultura nel riflesso delle testimonianze scritte, in: Bisanzio, Roma e l'Italia nell'alto medioevo, XXXIV Settimana di Studio della Fondazione Centro Italiano di Studi sull‹Alto Medioevo (Spoleto, 3.–9.4.1986), Spoleto 1988, S. 467–516.

De Blaauw 1987 Sible De Blaauw: Cultus et decor. Liturgie en architectuur in laatantiek en middeleeuws Rome, Basilica Salvatoris Sanctae Mariae Sancti Petri, Delft 1987.

De Grüneisen 1911 Wladimir de Grüneisen: Sainte-Marie-Antique, Rom 1911.

Delogu 2001 Paolo Delogu: Il papato tra l'impero bizantino e l'Occidente tra il VII e l'VIII secolo, in: Il Papato e l'Europa, hg. von Gabriele De Rosa und Giorgio Cracco, Soveria Mannelli (CZ) 2001, S. 55–79.

Ekonomou 2007 Andrew J. Ekonomou: Byzantine Rome and the Greek Popes: Eastern Influences on Rome and the Papacy from Gregory the Great to Zacharias A.D. 590–752, Plymouth 2007.

Ferrazza 2016 Giandomenico Ferrazza: La questione del "papato greco" (678–752). Categorie, contesti e testimonianze. Tesi di laurea in Storia medievale, Dipartimento di Studi Umanistici dell'Università degli Studi Roma Tre 2014–2015 (2016).

Folgerø 2004 Per Olav Folgerø: Traces of Palestinian Liturgy in the Old Testament Catena on the Apsidal Arch of S. Maria Antiqua in Rome, in: Bollettino della Badia greca di Grottaferrata, ser. III, 1, 2004, S. 63–67.

Folgerø 2009 Per Olav Folgerø: The text-catena in the frescoes in the sanctuary of S. Maria Antiqua in Rome (705–707 A.D.): a note on its links to the catechetical lectures of Cyril of Jerusalem, in: Bollettino della Badia Greca di Grottaferrata 3, 6, 2009, S. 45–66.

Folgerø 2010 Per Olav Folgerø: The Lowest, Lost Zone in the Adoration of the Crucified Scene in S. Maria Antiqua in Rome: A New Conjecture, in: Journal of the Warburg and Courtauld Institutes 72, 2009 (2010), S. 207–219.

Folgerø [im Druck] Per Olav Folgerø: Expression of Dogma. Text and Imagery in the Triumphal Arch Decoration in the Sanctuary of S. Maria Antiqua in Rome (705–707 A.D.), in: Santa Maria Antiqua. The Sistine Chapel of the Middle Ages (Studies in Medieval and Early Renaissance Art History), International Conference held at the British School at Rome (December 4–6, 2013), hg. von Eileen Rubery, Giulia Bordi und John Osborne, Turnhout [im Druck].

Genette 1997 Gérard Genette: Palinsesti. La letteratura al secondo grado, Turin 1997.

LP Le Liber Pontificalis. Texte, introduction et commentaire, hg. von Louis Duchesne, I–II, Paris 1886–1892.

Kartsonis 1986 Anna Kartsonis: Anastasis. The Making of an Image, Princeton 1986.

Kartsonis 1994 Anna Kartsonis: The emancipation of the crucifixion, in: Byzance et les images, Paris 1994, S. 151–187.

Maccarrone 1991 Michele Maccarrone: Romana Ecclesia, cathedra Petri, hg. von Piero Zerbi, Raffaello Volpini und Alessandro Galuzzi, Rom 1991.

Mansi 1759 ff Johannes Domenicus Mansi: Sacrorum conciliorum nova et amplissima collectio, Florenz 1759–1827.

Marucchi 1900 Orazio Marucchi: La chiesa di S. Maria Antiqua nel Foro Romano, in: Nuovo Bullettino di archeologia cristiana 6, 1900, S. 285–320.

McKitterick 2016 Rosamond McKitterick: The Papacy and Byzantium in the seventh and early eight-century sections of the Liber Pontificalis, in: Papers of the British School at Rome 84, 2016, S. 241–273.

Nilgen 2004 Ursula Nilgen: The Adoration of the Crucified Christ at Santa Maria Antiqua and the Tradition of Triumphal Arch Decoration in Rome, in: Santa Maria Antiqua al Foro Romano cento anni dopo, hg. von John Osborne, J. Rasmus Brandt und Giuseppe Morganti, Rom 2004, S. 129–135.

Nordhagen 1962 Per Jonas Nordhagen: The earliest Decorations in Santa Maria Antiqua and their Date, in: Acta ad archaeologiam et artium historiam pertinentia I, 1962, S. 53–72.

Nordhagen 1967 Per Jonas Nordhagen: John VII's adoration of the Cross in Sta Maria Antiqua, in: Journal of the Warburg and Courtauld Institutes 30, 1967, S. 388–390.

Nordhagen 1968 Per Jonas Nordhagen: The Frescoes of John VII (D.C. 705–707) in S. Maria Antiqua in Rome, in: Acta ad archaeologiam et artium historiam pertinentia III, 1968.

Nordhagen 1979 Per Jonas Nordhagen: S. Maria Antiqua. The Frescoes of the Seventh Century, in:

Acta ad archaeologiam et artium historiam pertinentia VIII, 1979, S. 89–142.

Nordhagen 1982 Per Jonas Nordhagen: "The harrowing of hell" as imperial iconography. A note on its use, in: Byzantinische Zeitschrift 75, 1982, S. 345–348.

Nordhagen 2000 Per Jonas Nordhagen: Constantinople on the Tiber: the byzantines in Rome and the iconography of their images, in: Early medieval Rome and the Christian West. Essays in honour of Donald A. Bullough, hg. von Julia M.H. Smith, Leiden 2000, S. 113–134.

Nordhagen 2002 Per Jonas Nordhagen: Early medieval church decoration in Rome and "the battle of images", in: Ecclesiae Urbis, Atti del congresso internazionale di studi sulle chiese di Roma (IV–X secolo), Rom, 4.–10.9.2000 (Studi di antichità cristiana, 59), hg. von Federico Guidobaldi und Alessandra Guiglia Guidobaldi, Vatikanstadt 2002, S. 1749–1769.

Opie 2002 John Lindsay Opie: Agnus Dei, in: Ecclesiae Urbis, Atti del Congresso Internazionale di studi sulle chiese di Roma (IV–X secolo), Rom, 4.–10.9.2000, (Studi di antichità cristiana, 59), hg. von Federico Guidobaldi und Alessandra Guiglia Guidobaldi, Vatikanstadt 2002, I, S. 1813–1840.

Price 2014 Richard Price: The Acts of the Lateran Synod of 649, translated with notes by Richard Price with contributions by Phil Booth and Catherine Cubitt, Liverpool 2014.

Price [im Druck] Richard Price: The frescoes in Santa Maria Antiqua, the Lateran Synod of 649 and pope Vitalian, in: Santa Maria Antiqua. The Sistine Chapel of the Middle Ages, International Conference held at the British School at Rome (December 4–6, 2013), hg. von Eileen Rubery, Giulia Bordi und John Osborne, Turnhout [im Druck].

Rubery 2012 Eileen Rubery: Conflict or Collusion? Pope Martin I (649–654/5) and the Exarch Olympius in Rome after Lateran Synod of 649, in: Studia Patristica 2012, S. 339–374.

Rushforth 1902 Gordon McNeil Rushforth: The Church of S. Maria Antiqua, in: Papers of the British School at Rome 1.1, 1902, S. 1–119.

Sansterre 1982 Jean-Marie Sansterre: Jean VII (705–707): idéologie pontificale et réalisme politique, in: Rayonnement grec. Hommages à Charles Delvoye, Brüssel 1982, S. 377–388.

Sansterre 1987 Jean-Marie Sansterre: A propos de la signification politico-religieuse de certaines fresques de Jean VII à Sainte-Marie-Antique, in: Byzantion 57, 1987, S. 434–440.

Susi 2000 Eugenio Susi: Leone II, santo, in: Enciclopedia dei Papi, Bd. I, Rom 2000, S. 617–620.

Tea 1937 Eva Tea: La basilica di Santa Maria Antiqua, Mailand 1937.

Tronzo 1985 William Tronzo: The prestige of Saint Peter‹s: observations on the function of monumental narrative cycles in Italy, in: Studies in the History of Art 16, 1985, S. 93–112.

Wilpert 2016 Josef Wilpert: Die Römischen Mosaiken und Malereien der Kirchlichen Bauten von IV–XIII Jahrhundert, Bd. I–III, Freiburg i. Br. 1916.

Die Aula Gotica von Santi Quattro Coronati – Kosmos, Antike und Tugenden im Selbstverständnis der Kurie

Dieter Blume

Im zweiten Viertel des 13. Jahrhunderts spitzte sich die Auseinandersetzung zwischen dem Papst und Kaiser Friedrich II. (1194–1250) dramatisch zu. Gregor IX. (1227–1241) formulierte ebenso wie sein Nachfolger Innozenz IV. (1243–1254) in diesem Zusammenhang einen deutlich gesteigerten Machtanspruch der Kurie. Auch militärisch schien der Konflikt zu eskalieren. Kaiserliche Truppen lagen im Umland von Rom. Daher fühlte sich Innozenz IV. bedroht, und anstatt im Juni 1244 in Narni mit dem Kaiser zu Verhandlungen zusammenzutreffen, floh er über seine Heimatstadt Genua nach Lyon. Von dort aus rief er für den Sommer 1245 ein Konzil nach Lyon ein, auf dem er am 17. Juli 1245 die Absetzung Friedrich II. verkündete.[1]

Aus diesen kritischen Jahren besitzen wir eine demonstrative Zurschaustellung päpstlicher Weltsicht in einem Zentrum kurialer Macht, die im Medium der Wandmalerei realisiert wurde und zu den raren Beispielen profaner Bildprogramme zählt, die zumindest soweit erhalten sind, dass sich der ursprüngliche Sinnzusammenhang noch erschließen lässt. Es handelt sich um die Ausmalung des Kardinalspalastes im Kloster von Santi Quattro Coronati in Rom. Dieser Palast wurde von Stefano Conti errichtet, die zugehörige Kapelle im Erdgeschoß am 22. März 1247 dem heiligen Silvester geweiht.[2] Zudem transferierte man Reliquien der ersten Päpste und versprach einen Ablass von 40 Tagen für den Besuch an bestimmten Festtagen. Nichts könnte deutlicher machen, dass von Anfang an auch eine öffentliche Nutzung dieser Kapelle vorgesehen war.

Stefano Conti, ein Neffe von Innozenz III. (1198–1216), war ein hochrangiges Mitglied der Kurie. 38 Jahre war er als *uditore del tribunale della curia* eine zentrale Figur in der Rechtsprechung. Zudem agierte er als Vermittler in zahlreichen Streitfällen und führte wichtige Verhandlungen im Auftrage des Papstes. Am 13. September 1245 wurde er von dem abwesenden Papst Innozenz IV. zum *vicarius urbis*, zum Stellvertreter des Papstes in Rom, eingesetzt. Er behielt dieses Amt bis 1249. Nach der Rückkehr des

1 Zu diesen Ereignissen siehe den Überblick bei Stürner 2000, S. 509–547, und Abulafia 1991, S. 351–358.

2 Grundlegend dazu Sohm 1997.

Papstes begab er sich 1251 an dessen Hof nach Perugia, wo er unter anderem wieder als *uditore del tribunale* tätig war.[3]

Den Palast bei Santi Quattro Coronati ließ Stefano Conti ausbauen, als er *vicarius urbis* wurde. Er wählte sehr bewusst diesen Ort in der Nähe des Lateran, um dort sein Amt auszuüben und Recht zu sprechen. Denn das Kloster auf dem Celio ließ sich sehr viel besser verteidigen.

Im Erdgeschoss ließ er die erwähnte Silvesterkapelle erbauen, die für einen öffentlichen Publikumsverkehr konzipiert wurde. An den Wänden wurde ein großformatiger Bilderzyklus angebracht, der erstmalig und in aller Ausführlichkeit die Konstantinische Schenkung zeigt und so den Machtanspruch des Papstes sowie den beanspruchten Vorrang vor dem Kaiser demonstrativ untermauert.[4] Im Vorraum malte man einen liturgischen Kalender an die Wände, wie es sonst auf den Seiten eines Sakramentars üblich ist. Dies findet sich zwar in Rom zu dieser Zeit mehrfach, doch handelt es sich hier um ein sehr frühes, wenn nicht sogar das erste Beispiel. Der Ablauf des Kirchenjahres und die an diesem Ort zu begehenden Feste werden damit jedem Besucher vor Augen gestellt. Das Totengedenken für zahlreiche Päpste nimmt hier einen breiten Raum ein, und auch der Vater des Erbauers Riccardo Conti wird genannt.[5] Die ehrwürdige Tradition der römischen Kirche wird in der Abfolge dieser Feste mit Nachdruck beschworen.

Darüber errichtete man im ersten Stock einen großen, repräsentativen Saal in modernen gotischen Formen, die damals in Rom noch gar nicht geläufig waren. Er besteht aus zwei kreuzgewölbten Jochen und zeichnet sich durch große Höhe (11,50 m) und beachtliche Dimensionen (17,30 × 9,20 m) aus. Der Hauptzugang erfolgte wohl über einen südlich angrenzenden Vorraum, die sogenannte *sala delle pentafore*. In diesem Saal, der heute zur Klausur des Nonnenklosters gehört, wurde zwischen 1996 und 2006 eine Ausmalung mit einem allegorischen Bildprogramm freigelegt, die zeitlich mit dem erwähnten Weihedatum der Kapelle zusammengeht (Abb. 1 und 7). Andreina Draghi hat diese Fresken publiziert und sorgfältig beschrieben.[6] Mir geht es jetzt, ähnlich wie auch Marius B. Hauknes, um den Versuch einer zusammenfassenden Interpretation.[7]

Wir haben es mit einem komplexen und ausgesprochen intellektuellen Bildprogramm zu tun, das die Zweiteilung der Architektur aufnimmt und in den beiden Jochen

3 Zur Biographie von Stefano Conti s. Maleczek 1983.

4 Sohm 1997, Mitchell 1981, Andaloro/Romano 2012, S.191–208.

5 Sohm 1997, S. 14–20, Maddalo 2007, Andaloro/Romano 2012, S. 180–190. Weitere monumentale Kalender finden sich in S. Maria sull'Aventino, der Abbazia Tre Fontane und in San Pellegrino in Bominaco/Abruzzen.

6 Draghi 2006 und Draghi 2012; zur Architektur Moretti 2006, Monciatti 2005, S. 76–84, und Barelli/Falconi 2000.

7 Hauknes 2016. Marius Hauknes hat mir freundlicherweise die Fahnen seines Aufsatzes überlassen, so dass ich hier noch einige Verweise einfügen konnte. Beide Arbeiten sind unabhängig voneinander entstanden, verfolgen aber im Wesentlichen eine verwandte Argumentation.

Abb. 1: Südwand des südlichen Joches, SS. Quattro Coronati, Aula Gotica, Rom, c. 1247.

ganz unterschiedliche Akzente setzt. Es ist zu vermuten, dass diese Situation auch auf die Nutzungsbedingungen rekurriert. Die figürlichen Zyklen befinden sich ausschließlich im Gewölbebereich oberhalb der Kapitellzone und damit hoch über den Köpfen der Betrachter.

Das Eingangsjoch im Süden präsentiert dem Besucher ein Abbild der irdischen Welt unter dem Sternenhimmel. In der Lünettenzone zieht sich ein Zyklus der Monatsarbeiten gegen den Uhrzeigersinn um den Raum. Er besitzt ein ausgesprochen monumentales Format, was bei diesem Thema eher ungewöhnlich ist. Entstanden ist diese Ikonographie im Kontext liturgischer Handschriften, wo sie der Gliederung des Kirchenjahres die Zeiterfahrung des natürlichen Jahreslaufes entgegensetzte. Seit dem 12. Jahrhundert begegnen uns die Monatsarbeiten vielfach im skulpturalen Schmuck von Portalen und Fassaden an Kirchen.[8] Sie sind dort aber immer den religiösen Themen nachgeordnet und treten eher als ergänzende Nebensache auf. In der Aula Gotica aber werden sie zur Hauptsache. Das ist eine bemerkenswerte Akzentverschiebung.

8 Webster 1938, vgl. auch Blume 2009, S. 527–533.

Abb. 2: Januar, SS. Quattro Coronati, Aula Gotica, Rom, c. 1247.

Die Personifikationen der einzelnen Monate sind in mehr oder weniger direkter Weise an den charakteristischen Tätigkeiten beteiligt. Mit einer Reihe von Begleitfiguren werden diese Handlungsmotive zu genrehaften Szenen ausgestaltet. Die in der ikonographischen Tradition nur versatzstückartig und recht isoliert vorkommenden Elemente werden hier zu einem szenischen Ganzen verbunden, das offenbar ganz bewusst den repräsentativen Charakter einer allegorischen Personifikation mit der lebendigen Dramatik einer Handlung zu verbinden sucht.

Der Januar besitzt die traditionelle Doppelgesichtigkeit, die den Jahreswechsel thematisiert, doch ist der Bifrons hier zu einem Trifrons erweitert, um so die frontale Ausrichtung der Figur zu wahren (Abb. 2). Es handelt sich um eine thronende Herrschergestalt, gekleidet in einen Mantel mit goldener Schmuckborte. Statt einer Krone trägt sie aber den breitkrempigen Hut der Landarbeiter, und anstelle eines Zepters hält sie einen Stab mit einer aufgespießten Wurst. Neben ihr hängt der Wurstkessel über einem lodernden Feuer, ein Diener schöpft Wurstsuppe daraus in eine Schale. Ein weiterer Gehilfe reicht der Monatspersonifikation einen Teller mit eben dieser Suppe sowie ein Gefäß mit Wein. Davon spricht auch die gut lesbare Inschrift in der unteren Rahmenleiste: *Ienuarius vinumque cibaria que(ret)* (Der Januar verlangt Speisen und Wein).

Abb. 3: März, SS. Quattro Coronati, Aula Gotica, Rom, c. 1247.

Dass dies nicht nur für Menschen gilt, demonstriert eine Maus, die auf der Stange, an der die Würste und Schinken trocknen, einen solchen Schinken zu erreichen sucht. Die Situation eines Schlachtfestes ist detailreich eingefangen, und die Gegenüberstellung der Herrschergestalt mit dem Wurstzepter und der bedächtig agierenden Maus bringt ein ironisches Element ins Spiel.

Höchst bemerkenswert ist auch die Darstellung des Monats März (Abb. 3). Das Motiv des Dornausziehers (*Spinario*) vertritt diesen Monat in Italien sehr häufig. Es ist ein Symbol der *Voluptas*, die im Monat März in der Natur erwacht, und der Dorn steht für das Laster, das jeden verwundet, der vom rechten Pfad abweicht. Statt der üblichen Einzelfigur sehen wir hier aber eine anrührende Szene zwischen Mann und Frau.[9] Der weitgehend nackte Mann sitzt mit vor Schmerz verzerrtem Gesicht auf einer Bank, das

9 Nur in Sessa Aurunca findet sich um 1200 ebenfalls eine zweifigurige, aber vollkommen anders gestaltete Gruppe; dazu und zu den möglichen byzantinischen und hellenistischen Vorlagen Glass 1991, S. 180–181. – Die antike Bronzefigur des Dornausziehers stand im Mittelalter auf dem Platz vor dem Lateran, der auch als Campo Martis bezeichnet wurde. Dies dürfte zur Identifizierung mit dem Monat März geführt haben. Magister Gregorius identifiziert sie als Priapus. Bober/Rubinstein 1986, Nr. 203, S. 235–236.

verwundete Bein hat er weggestreckt. Eine Frau in einem reich geschmückten Gewand hilft ihm und entfernt den schmerzenden Dorn. Dabei benutzt sie ihren Kopfschleier, um das Blut zu stillen, und hebt demonstrativ den entfernten Dorn empor. Die Konfrontation der beiden Geschlechter ist nicht frei von erotischen Konnotationen. Auch die Inschrift spielt darauf an: *Mens hebet ob spinas.* (Der Geist ist schwach gegen die Dornen). Doch die Frau wird hier nicht als Objekt der Begierde präsentiert, sie tritt als Helferin auf, die den Schmerz lindert. Dies erinnert an eine Rolle der Frau oder *Donna* in der höfischen Lyrik. Mit ihrer Zuwendung, so hofft der Dichter, möge sie seine Liebesqual lindern.[10]

Generell benennen die gut lesbaren Inschriften die spezifische Tätigkeit des jeweiligen Monats, erwähnen zumeist aber auch die Früchte, die zu diesem Zeitpunkt geerntet werden.[11] Für den April stehen zwei Hirten mit ihrer Herde unter blühenden Bäumen. Im Mai sehen wir einen vornehmen Reiter mit Blütenzepter und zwei Knaben bei der Kirschenernte. Nach der detailliert wiedergegebenen Getreideernte im Juni und der Tätigkeit des Dreschens im Juli folgt der August als ein älterer Mann, der ermattet von der Hitze unter einem Feigenbaum sitzt und dem ein leicht bekleideter Jüngling eine Schale mit Trauben anbietet. Zwei halbnackte Knaben, die nur ihre Hemden tragen, ernten im Baum die Feigen (Abb. 1). Im September sehen wir Küfer bei der Arbeit und im Oktober die Weinernte samt der Kelter. Im November erfolgen das Pflügen der Felder sowie die Aussaat des Wintergetreides. Die Personifikation des Dezembers schließlich überwacht das Schlachten der Schweine, auf das dann im Januar das Kochen der Würste erfolgen kann. Diese Szenenfolge stellt höchst anschaulich und detailreich die jahreszeitlich bedingten Tätigkeiten dem Betrachter vor Augen und ruft auf diese Weise den wiederkehrenden, immer gleichen Kreislauf des irdischen Lebens auf.

In einem oberen Register in der Spitze der Lünetten treten dann die *Artes liberales* auf, die sieben freien Künste. Oberhalb des Januars beginnt es mit der Grammatik, woran sich sogleich die Geometrie anschließt, denn der Schwerpunkt liegt ganz offensichtlich auf den mathematischen Wissenschaften des Quadriviums. Besonders hervorgehoben wird aber die Astronomie, die auf der Ostwand ein ganzes Bildfeld allein zugewiesen bekommt. Viele dieser Darstellungen sind nur fragmentarisch erhalten, doch ist noch zu erkennen, dass neben den weiblichen Personifikationen, welche die jeweilige Wissenschaft auch aktiv praktizieren, noch gelehrige Schüler auftreten, die assistierende Tätigkeiten übernehmen, sowie thronende Vertreter der einzelnen Disziplinen, die zusätzliche Inschriften halten. So ist auch hier deutlich ein narratives Element präsent.

10 Aus der Fülle der Literatur sei hier auf die Überblickswerke von Picone 2003, Friedrich 1964, S. 16–84, und Contini 1960 verwiesen.

11 Sämtliche Inschriften sowie detaillierte Beschreibungen bei Draghi 2006.

Die Geometrie hantiert mit einem großen Zirkel und diskutiert mit einem Gelehrten, wahrscheinlich Euklid. Die Musik bedient ein Glockenspiel und blickt zu einem Schüler herab, der eine Orgel spielt. Neben ihr thront vermutlich Tubalkain, der ein Saiteninstrument hält und sich so an diesem kleinen Konzert beteiligt (Abb. 1). Die Astronomie wendet sich gleichfalls einem Vertreter zu, in dem wir Ptolemaios vermuten dürfen. Ein Schüler läuft mit erhobenen Armen auf ihn zu.

Die Wissenschaften sind das Erkenntnismittel der Menschen, mit deren Hilfe sie die Welt verstehen können. Ihr Wissen vermag so über das Augenscheinliche und den immer gleichen Jahreslauf hinaus bis zu den Sternen zu gelangen. Das ist hier offensichtlich gemeint.

Das Kreuzgratgewölbe dieses Joches haben die Maler in eine Kuppel uminterpretiert, um ein veritables Abbild des Himmelsgewölbes zu präsentieren. Zwar sind hier die Zerstörungen sehr weitreichend, aber es ist für eine Rekonstruktion doch noch genügend erhalten (Abb. 4 bis 5). In den Zwickeln stehen die Personifikationen der Jahreszeiten, umgeben von jeweils drei Winden, die das kosmologische Element der Himmelsrichtungen einbringen. Die Anordnung der Jahreszeiten ist mit der Folge der Monatsarbeiten weiter unten an den Wänden korreliert, sodass sich eine stimmige Zuordnung ergibt. Oberhalb dieser Zwickel, die von der Malerei wie Pendentifs aufgefasst werden, setzt sich die Ausmalung in konzentrischen Bildstreifen fort. Leider sind aber die ausführlichen Inschriften auf den trennenden Rahmenstreifen nur sehr fragmentarisch erhalten und entziehen sich von daher einer Interpretation. Als erstes folgt eine phantasiereiche Meereslandschaft mit Fischen, Vögeln, Seekentauren und fischenden Knaben. Dargestellt ist offenbar die Grenze der bewohnbaren Welt, jener unüberschaubare Ozean, der nach mittelalterlicher Vorstellung die bevölkerte Erde umgibt. Darüber sind vor einem blauen, sternenübersäten Grund die Tierkreiszeichen zu sehen. Erhalten haben sich allein der Wassermann, der hintere Teil des Steinbocks, der Körper des Stiers und der Stachel des Skorpions. Der Wassermann ist eine gebückte Gestalt, die einen ledernen Wassersack entleert, den sie über der Schulter trägt (Abb. 4). Die Enden eines langen Tuchs, das auf der Schulter das Gewicht abpolstert, wehen dekorativ nach beiden Seiten. Der aus einer unzerschnittenen Tierhaut hergestellte Wassersack ist ein Element der bäuerlichen Alltagskultur, das hier an die Stelle der sonst üblichen Vase oder Urne tritt. Im Unterschied zu der astronomischen Überlieferung ist der Stier nicht als Büste, sondern als Ganzfigur wiedergegeben. Auch der Steinbock begegnet als normales Tier und nicht als Mischwesen mit Fischschwanz, wie er sonst durchweg dargestellt wird.[12]

12 Das Tierkreiszeichen Capricornus oder Steinbock findet es sich nur äußerst selten in Form eines normalen, kompletten Steinbockes. Vereinzelt findet es sich in ungenauen Darstellungen des Frühmittelalters, wie Basel, Univ.-Bibl. Ms. F II 15a, fol. 23r, Blume/Haffner/Metzger 2012, S. 41–42, Abb. 966, 977. Ein weiteres Beispiel aus einer liturgischen Handschrift ist Stuttgart, Württemberg. Landesbibl., Cod. Hist. 2° 415,

Abb. 4: Winter und Wassermann, SS. Quattro Coronati, Aula Gotica, Rom, c. 1247.

Abb. 5: Frühling und Stier, SS. Quattro Coronati, Aula Gotica, Rom, c. 1247.

Die Maler sind offenbar mit ihren Vorlagen und der wissenschaftlichen Genauigkeit eher großzügig umgegangen. Auch die Anordnung des Tierkreises ist auf die Jahreszeiten und die weiter unten dargestellten Monate abgestimmt, sodass der Raum in der Tat wie ein Modell des Kosmos funktioniert.[13]

Vom nächsten Bildstreifen hat sich nur noch ein Fragment erhalten, es zeigt die nackten Beine der Andromeda.[14] Neben ihr sind noch die Füße von Perseus zu erkennen (Abb. 4). Ohne Frage war hier der gesamte Sternenhimmel dargestellt und zwar offensichtlich nach Art einer Planisphaere. Die Vorbilder finden sich in astronomischen Handschriften. Derartige Himmelskarten sind ein fester Bestandteil der astronomischen Himmelsbeschreibung in der Aratos-Übersetzung des Germanicus, die seit dem 9. Jahrhundert häufig im klösterlichen Ausbildungsbetrieb benutzt und kopiert wurde[15] (Abb. 6). Die Anlage in konzentrischen Ringen ist gut vergleichbar, doch der Tierkreis bildet hier nicht den äußeren Rahmen, sondern ist als farbig unterlegtes Band leicht versetzt darüber gelegt und bildet von daher die astronomischen Gegebenheiten präziser ab.[16] Ein gleichfalls versetzter, goldener Reif bezeichnet zudem die Milchstraße. Aber auch in den Planisphaeren sind in der Nachbarschaft des Wassermannes Andromeda und Perseus zu sehen. Die römischen Maler haben die Struktur dieser Himmelskarten stark vereinfacht und zudem die Figuren in den einzelnen Streifen aufgerichtet, um das Ganze übersichtlicher zu gestalten. Die erkennbare Ähnlichkeit zu den Sternen am Nachthimmel ist so natürlich nicht mehr gegeben. Ganz offensichtlich ging es bei der Ausmalung nicht um astronomische Genauigkeit im Einzelnen, sondern nur um den Gesamteindruck.

In den Planisphaeren hat man schon aus Platzgründen die Bilder der Konstellationen immer weniger komplex gestaltet. So wurde Andromeda in der Regel ohne die

---

fol. 17v, Draghi 2006, Fig. 48, Hauknes 2016, Fig. 9. In den ab ca. 1300 kursierenden Illustrationen der Sterntafeln findet sich zuweilen gleichfalls der Steinbock und nicht der Ziegenfisch, ohne dass dies aber zu einer größeren Verbreitung geführt hätte; siehe Oxford, Bodleian Library, Ms. Rawl. C 117 und Rom, Bibl. Vaticana, Cod. Urb. Lat. 1399, Blume/Haffner/Metzger 2016, S. 426–440, Abb. 462, 476.

13 Hauknes 2016, S. 21, beschreibt, dass der Tierkreis im Uhrzeigersinn verläuft. Dies ist falsch! Die Ordnung verläuft gegen den Uhrzeigersinn wie bei den Monaten. Nur der Stier und der Steinbock sind in die gegenläufige Richtung orientiert; dies ist beim Stier die Regel, beim Steinbock jedoch nicht.

14 Die Namensinschrift »...ROMEDA« lässt an der Identifizierung keinen Zweifel.

15 Zu dieser Bildtradition Blume/Haffner/Metzger 2012; abgebildet wird hier aufgrund der besseren Erkennbarkeit die Planisphaere aus Bern, Burgerbibliothek, Ms. 88, fol. 11v, dazu ebd. S. 214–218, Abb. 112.

16 Himmelsbeschreibungen in der Tradition der sogenannten *Recensio interpolata* besitzen zudem eine Darstellung der Büsten von Sol und Luna im Rund des Tierkreises, beispielsweise St. Gallen, Ms. 250, p. 215, Blume/Haffner/Metzger 2012, S. 77, 508–514. Das mag den römischen Malern eine zusätzliche Anregung gewesen sein. In der Handschrift Dijon, Bibliothéque muncipale, Ms. 488, fol. 64r, findet sich stattdessen der nördliche Himmelspol, markiert durch die beiden Bären und den Drachen in der Mitte des Tierkreises, ebd. S. 114, 227–233, Abb. 140.

Abb. 6: Planisphaere, Aratea des Germanicus, Bern, Burgerbiliothek, Ms. 88, fol. 11v.

seitlichen Felsen und mit abgeknickten Armen dargestellt. Auch das Gewand hat man oft fortgelassen, obwohl eigentlich nur die Arme und der Oberkörper entblößt sind. In den Fresken ist man ähnlich verfahren. Dort ist aus den seitlichen Felsen, an die Andromeda gekettet ist, eine Rahmung geworden, die eher vegetabil anmutet. Auch in den astronomischen Handschriften des Mittelalters mutieren die Felsen oft zu eigenartigen Gebilden, die an Pflanzen oder knorrige Baumstämme erinnern.[17]

Der Besucher steht also in diesem Joch in einem veritablen Kosmosmodell, das unterhalb des Sternenhimmels sowohl den Ozean als Grenze der bewohnbaren Welt wie die Winde als die zentralen Achsen und die Jahreszeiten präsentiert. Darunter kommen die menschlichen Tätigkeiten im Jahreslauf und sein Erkenntnisstreben zur Anschauung. Das Abbild des Sternenhimmels im Gewölbe eines Palastes ist zugleich auch ein literarischer Topos, der seit der Antike immer wieder aufgegriffen wurde. Ovid beschreibt derartiges am Palast des Sonnengottes Apoll, und es findet sich gleichfalls in mittelalterlichen Schilderungen vom Grab des Darius oder dem Palast des legendären Priesterkönigs Johannes.[18] Um 1100 verfasst dann Baldricus Bourgueilianus eine detaillierte Beschreibung des Schlafzimmers der Adela von Blois, die wohl gleichfalls als literarische Fiktion anzusehen ist.[19] Auch hier gibt es die Sterne an der Decke und am Boden sogar eine Weltkarte. An den Wänden sieht man die Taten der Menschen von der Schöpfung bis in die jüngste Gegenwart. Die sieben freien Künste umstehen hier als Statuen das Bett der Herzogin. Von daher gibt es eine Reihe von Parallelen zur Aula Gotica und das verweist deutlich darauf, welchen Anspruch Stefano Conti mit dieser Ausmalung verband. Er orientierte sich an den avancierten Leitbildern der höfischen Kultur.

Das Rahmensystem dieser Bilder entfaltet darüber hinaus ein reiches Spektrum antiker Dekorationskunst (Abb. 1 bis 3 und 7). Keines der aus der Spätantike überlieferten Motive sollte offenbar fehlen, und so wird die antike Tradition des christlichen Rom und der römischen Kirche auch im formalen Erscheinungsbild eindrücklich beschworen. In der Höhe der Kapitelle umgibt den Raum ein breites Band von Eroten mit Festons. Dazu kommen sirenenartige Mischwesen, die antike Vasen flankieren. Ein perspektivisch angelegter Konsolfries mit Vogelmotiven unterteilt die Lünetten. Ornamentalisierte Säulen trennen die Monatsarbeiten und tragen Arkadenbögen aus stilisierten Delphinen. Auf den Kämpferplatten dieser Säulen haben dann noch nackte Eroten

17 Als Beispiele seien genannt Dijon, Bibliothèque muncipale, Ms. 488, fol. 69r und Paris, Bibliothèque Nationale, Ms. lat. 8663, fol. 21v, siehe Blume/Haffner/Metzger 2012, S. 227–233, Abb. 150 und S. 430–435, Abb. 685.

18 Ovid, Metamorphosen II, 5–18; Walter von Châtillon, Alexanderreis, VII, 393–397; siehe Fenzi 1976, Lehmann 1945.

19 Hilbert 1979 Nr. 134 *Adelae comitissae*, S. 149ff., S. 303ff.; Otter 2001.

Abb. 7: Nordwand des nördlichen Joches, SS. Quattro Coronati, Aula Gotica, Rom, c. 1247.

Platz, die das Rankenwerk als Spielwiese nutzen. Der antikische Dekor prägt auch das zweite Joch, doch finden sich hier statt der nackten Eroten bekleidete junge Frauen, die ihre Kopfschleier variantenreich drapieren. Es wird ein spezifisch stadtrömischer Prunk entfaltet, der bezeichnenderweise in der gleichzeitigen Silvesterkapelle im Erdgeschoss vollkommen fehlt. Das markiert eine klare Differenzierung der Räume.

Die Bildwelt des nördlichen Joches besitzt einen grundlegend anderen Charakter, auch wenn wir die gleichen antiken Dekorationselemente wiederfinden. Der Betrachter ist umgeben von nahezu lebensgroßen Gestalten der Tugenden, die wehrhaft gerüstet in Kettenhemden auftreten (Abb. 7 und 8). Zu ihren Füßen kauern Laster und negative Beispielfiguren. Auf ihren Schultern tragen sie Heilige als Vertreter der Kirche. Die Kirche ruht hier wortwörtlich auf den Schultern der Tugenden! In der Mitte der Stirnwand als Fokus dieser Figurenansammlung sehen wir uns Salomon gegenüber, der als Herrscher und Richter zugleich auftritt und die rechte Hand im Weisegestus mahnend erhoben hat. Darunter dürften die Sitzbank der kurialen Richter sowie der Thron Stefano Contis gestanden haben. Das ist die Folie, vor der in diesem Saal Politik gemacht und Recht gesprochen wurde. Salomon wird als Leitbild päpstlicher Herrschaft und kurialer Rechtsprechung aufgerufen, und dieses alttestamentliche Leitbild wird wie ein antiker Kaiser vorgeführt.

Die Tugenden umgeben Salomon wie eine Leibwache, sie sind der militärische Arm des Rechts und vollziehen an den Lastern und den negativen Beispielfiguren die gerechte Strafe. Es handelt sich aber nicht um die üblichen sieben Kardinaltugenden, sondern wir haben es mit einer sehr spezifischen, genau überlegten Auswahl zu tun. Es handelt sich um zwölf Tugenden, so wird die Parallele zu den Monaten und zu den Aposteln gewahrt. Den Herrscher Salomon flankieren auf der einen Seite *Concordia* (Eintracht) und *Sobrietas* (Bescheidenheit, Mäßigkeit), auf der anderen Seite *Largitas* (Großzügigkeit, Freigiebigkeit) und *Vera Religio* (Mildtätigkeit). Es handelt sich um vier deutlich politische Tugenden, die aber eine starke religiöse Färbung besitzen.

An der rechten, östlichen Wand folgt dann *Caritas* (Nächstenliebe), die durch *Timor Dei* (Gottesfurcht), *Amor coelestis* (Himmlische Liebe) und *Aemulatio sancta* (Heiliger Eifer) weiter spezifiziert wird. Wir haben es mit einer zusammenhängenden Gruppe zu tun, welche die unterschiedlichen Seiten des christlichen Liebesverständnisses erläutert. Auf der linken, westlichen Wand ist dann *Humilitas* (Demut) zu sehen, die von *Patientia* (Geduld), vermutlich *Fides* (Glaube) und einer weiteren, heute zerstörten Tugendfigur begleitet wird. Auch hier gibt es deutlich erkennbar einen inneren Zusammenhang. Mit *Humilitas* und *Caritas* werden auf den Seitenwänden theologische Leittugenden aufgerufen, die mit Hilfe der benachbarten Personifikationen weiter entfaltet und spezifiziert werden. Alle Tugenden halten Schriftrollen mit passend ausgewählten Zitaten, die bis auf wenige Ausnahmen der Bibel entnommen sind.[20]

Die Heiligen auf den Schultern der Tugenden als beispielhafte Vertreter der Kirche entstammen sowohl dem Alten wie dem Neuen Testament als auch der nachbiblischen Zeit. Auf der linken, westlichen Seite finden sich mit Daniel, David und Hiob Vertreter des alten Bundes. Neben Salomon sieht man Paulus und Laurentius, an der rechten Wand dann Petrus auf den Schultern der *Caritas*. Hinzu kommen die Kirchenväter Augustinus und Hieronymus sowie die erst kürzlich heiliggesprochenen Gründer der Bettelorden Franziskus und Dominikus.[21] Damit reicht die Reihe der kirchlichen Vertreter, die von den Tugenden gestützt werden, bis an die Gegenwart heran und umfasst das gesamte Panorama der Heilsgeschichte. Die Zuordnung der Heiligen zu den einzelnen Tugenden ist immer inhaltlich begründet und bezieht sich auf das spezifische Profil dieser Vertreterfigur. So wird Hiob natürlich von *Patientia* getragen, Franziskus von *Amor coelestis* und Dominikus von *Aemulatio sancta* (Abb. 8).

Die Beispielfiguren der Laster, die geschlagen unter den Füßen der Tugenden kauern, sind allesamt historische Gestalten und viel zitierte Typen. Wir treffen auf Simon

20 Alle Inschriften mit den Textnachweisen bei Draghi 2006.

21 Die Namensinschrift des Augustinus ist aufgrund einer Fehlstelle weitgehend unleserlich, erhalten ist nur »...tin(us)«. Aufgrund der Mitra könnte man auch an den heiligen Martin denken, doch halte ich Augustinus für wahrscheinlicher; vgl. Draghi 2006, S. 271–272.

Abb. 8: Aemulatio Sancta mit Dominikus und Simon Magus, SS. Quattro Coronati, Aula Gotica, Rom, c. 1247.

Magus, Julian Apostata, Nero und Alexander sowie Judas und Mohamed. Auch ihre Zuordnung zu den einzelnen Lastern ist natürlich mit Bedacht gewählt.

Alles in allem handelt es sich nicht allein um eine sehr spezifische Auswahl, sondern auch um ein ausgesprochen dicht gewebtes Programm. Wir haben es mit einem gelehrten Bildtraktat über Ethik und Theologie zu tun, das eine wehrhafte Kirche triumphierend um die Idealgestalt des weisen Salomon gruppiert. Viele der Versatzstücke dieses Bilderreigens sind aus anderen Zusammenhängen bekannt und vertraut. Die Konfrontation der Tugenden mit den unterlegenen Lastern fußt auf der *Psychomachia* des Prudentius und ist weit verbreitet. Historische Beispielfiguren bei den freien Künsten oder den Tugenden finden sich gleichfalls sehr häufig. Auch die Evangelisten oder Apostel auf den Schultern der Propheten sind ein eingeführtes Motiv.[22] Doch die konkreten Kombinationen, die spezielle Auswahl ebenso wie die Verbindung all dieser Elemente sind neu und von großer Originalität.

Im oberen Teil der Schildwände des Nordjoches kommt noch ein weiteres, ganz erstaunliches Element hinzu. Hier treffen wir auf Versatzstücke antiker, heidnischer Ikonographie, die uns nicht in der Sockelzone, sondern in unmittelbarer Nachbarschaft zum Gewölbe oberhalb der Tugenden begegnen. Dort sehen wir zwei lagernde Flussgötter über Salomon, Sol und Luna in ihren Wagen und sogar Mithras, der den Opferstier tötet (Abb. 7, 9 und 10). Auffällig ist aber, dass es bei diesen Bildern keine Beschriftung oder Benennung gibt, denn ansonsten ist jede Figur dieser Ausmalung durch eine Inschrift eindeutig identifiziert. Darüber hinaus dominiert ein Moment der Symmetrie, wie es für ornamentale Kompositionen geläufig ist. In der Mitte der Lünetten ist immer eine große, prunkvolle Vase positioniert, die mit Früchten gefüllt ist. Die antik anmutenden Gestalten sind diesem dekorativen Mittelpunkt immer streng symmetrisch zugewandt. Weiterhin ist die antike Ikonographie auf eigentümliche Weise entschärft und ins Allgemeine verschoben, sodass eine genauere Bestimmung der Darstellungen nicht möglich ist. Die Flussgötter halten Füllhörner mit Früchten an Stelle von Gefäßen, aus denen Wasser fließt. Zudem weisen sie auf Körbe mit Blüten und Früchten. Damit variieren sie das Motivrepertoire der weiblichen Personifikation der Erde (Tellus), die oft in symmetrischer Anordnung mit Oceanus gezeigt wird.[23] Hier dürfte eine Anregung für die Maler gelegen haben, doch haben sie alle spezifischen Charakteristika offenbar bewusst vermieden. Sol und Luna halten Blütenzepter, die zu ihnen eigentlich nicht passen. Weder der Strahlenkranz der Sonne noch die Mondsichel, welche die Darstellungen der Luminaria ansonsten immer kennzeichnen, sind vorhanden. Die Differenzierung der Zugtiere, Rinder beim Mond und Pferde bei der Sonne, wird zwar beibehalten, aber

22 Zu möglichen Vorbildern vgl. Draghi 2006, S.17–107 und Hauknes 2016, S. 15–17.

23 Als Beispiel sei hier ein Sarkophag des 3. Jahrhunderts n. Chr. aus Santa Maria Antiqua in Rom genannt, Aust.-Kat. Santa Maria Antiqua 2016, Nr. 19, S. 346–347.

Abb. 9: Sol und Luna (?), SS. Quattro Coronati, Aula Gotica, Rom, c. 1247.

Sol lenkt immer eine Quadriga und nicht ein Zweigespann. Mithras, von dem nur eine Figur erhalten ist, wurde wohl gleichfalls symmetrisch wiederholt. Auch hier fehlen alle weiteren Elemente, die für das Verständnis so wichtig sind.[24]

Sehr wahrscheinlich sind diese Bilder nicht als inhaltliche Bestandteile des Programms gemeint, sondern hier soll noch einmal verstärkt *Antichitá* aufgerufen werden. Demonstrativ und unübersehbar wird die antike Tradition beschworen, in der die Kurie steht. Gemalt werden Versatzstücke, die jeder unmittelbar als antik erkennt, und die darüber hinaus mit der Motivik des Überflusses verbunden sind. Die *Ecclesia militans* des 13. Jahrhunderts, die uns in diesem Joch entgegentritt, steht in der ununterbrochenen Kontinuität der Antike und der von den Aposteln gegründeten Kirche. Interessanterweise sind diese antiken, römischen Elemente in der Ausmalung nicht gleichmäßig verteilt. In der Silvesterkapelle fehlen diese Motive ganz, im ersten, südlichen Joch des repräsentativen Saales beschränken sie sich auf das Dekorationssystem und damit auf untergeordnete Bereiche. Erst im zweiten Joch füllen sie dann sogar großformatige

24 Mithras findet sich auch auf den Kapitellen von Monreale, die 1174–1189 entstanden sind. *Varietas*, die Vielzahl verschiedener Themen, scheint hier ein bestimmendes Moment gewesen zu sein, Brenk 2001.

Abb. 10: Mithras, SS. Quattro Coronati, Aula Gotica, Rom, c. 1247.

Bildfelder. Dies weist auf eine Differenzierung hin, die vermutlich auf die Funktion und die unterschiedliche Zugänglichkeit der Räume Bezug nimmt. In dem Raumteil, in dem die Vertreter der Kurie thronen, nehmen die antik-römischen Bildmotive einen besonders prominenten Platz ein, der weit über alles hinausgeht, was wir sonst kennen. Diese Bilder signalisieren Überfluss und Kontinuität zu der großen Vergangenheit. Und genau dies soll offenbar auch dem Wirken des Stefano Conti und der päpstlichen Kurie zugeschrieben werden.

Leider sind die Fresken im Gewölbe dieses zweiten Joches vollständig zerstört. Kein einziges Fragment ist erhalten geblieben, das irgendwelche Rückschlüsse erlauben würde. Vorstellen könnte man sich eventuell eine Christusbüste, die vielleicht von Engeln umgeben war, so wie das zur gleichen Zeit in einigen Gewölben der Krypta des Domes von Anagni realisiert wurde.[25] Dann wäre der wahre, göttliche Himmel dem Sternenhimmel gegenübergestellt, der allein von den Menschen mit ihren irdischen Augen wahrgenommen werden kann. Denkbar wären jedoch auch die vier apokalyptischen Wesen als Symbole der Evangelisten oder sogar eine rein ornamentale, mit antiken Motiven arbeitende Dekoration.

25 Giammaria 2001.

Das Bildprogramm der Aula Gotica besteht aus der Kombination zweier Kuppelräume, die ganz unterschiedlich konzipiert, aber dennoch in vielerlei Hinsicht aufeinander bezogen sind. Die Konfrontation weltlich-profaner Themen, die als ein kohärentes Kosmosmodell inszeniert werden, mit einer theologischen Tugendallegorese ist, soweit ich sehe, einzigartig. Die Fülle der antiken Dekorationselemente und das bewusste Aufrufen der römischen Tradition bilden eine Art Klammer, die beide Teile noch einmal miteinander verzahnt. In den beiden Jochen sind zugleich auch grundlegende Aspekte des christlichen Weltverständnisses anschaulich gemacht. So steht der Kreislauf der Natur und der irdischen Welt dem über alle Wechselfälle der Geschichte erhabenen System der theologischen Tugenden gegenüber. Natur und Ethik bilden hier im Grunde zwei Pole, denen dann auch der Gegensatz von Zeit und Dauer, von Zeitlichkeit und Ewigkeit zugeordnet ist.

In der historischen Situation der vierziger Jahre des 13. Jahrhunderts muss man das wohl auch als einen Gegenentwurf zu dem intellektuellen Profil des Kaiserhofes von Friedrich II. in Süditalien sehen. Auch Friedrich II. griff bekanntlich sehr gezielt auf antike Formen und Symbolik zurück, um sein Verständnis des Kaisertums zu legitimieren. Mit dem Brückentor von Capua, das den nördlichen Eingang ins kaiserliche Herrschaftsgebiet programmatisch markierte, lässt sich ein einschlägiges Bildprogramm rekonstruieren, das antike und mittelalterliche Elemente subtil verband.[26] Die Förderung der Wissenschaften sowie ein Interesse an Astronomie und Astrologie sind für den Kaiserhof belegt.[27] Dem stellte Stefano Conti im militärisch bedrohten Rom ein eigenes Bildprogramm entgegen, das gleichfalls auf hohem Niveau Antike, die Wissenschaften und insbesondere die Astronomie aufruft, die damals als eine Art Leitwissenschaft fungierte. Doch lässt sich diese Ausmalung natürlich nicht auf die Propaganda gegen Friedrich II. reduzieren, aber sie konnte in diesem Zusammenhang doch eine gewisse Wirkung entfalten. Zugleich muss man sie aber auch als Ausdruck eines Austausches verstehen, der zwischen Papst- und Kaiserhof ungeachtet aller Streitpunkte geführt wurde. Gerade in einer für die Kurie schwierigen Situation war es offenbar wichtig, ein intellektuelles Profil zu zeigen. So führen uns die Fresken der Aula Gotica vor allem den intellektuellen Rang vor Augen, der in diesen Jahren an der päpstlichen Kurie anzutreffen war. Das päpstliche Rom war bereits in der ersten Hälfte des 13. Jahrhunderts ein intellektuelles Zentrum, an dem viele naturwissenschaftliche Texte kursierten und auch aktiv verbreitet wurden.[28] Das ist die eigentliche Basis für die in vielerlei Hinsicht höchst erstaunliche Bildausstattung im Kardinalspalast von Santi Quattro Coronati.

---

26 Willemsen 1953, Brenk 1991, Claussen 1993.

27 Blume 2000, S. 47–51.

28 Paravicini Bagliani 1991, Paravicini Bagliani 1995.

Bibliographie

Abulafia 1991 David Abulafia: Herrscher zwischen den Kulturen, Friedrich II. von Hohenstaufen, Berlin 1991.

Andaloro/Romano 2012 Maria Andaloro und Serena Romano: La pittura medievale a Roma, Corpus, Vol. 5 Il Duecento e la cultura Gotica 1198–1287, Mailand 2012.

Barelli/Falconi 2000 Lia Barelli und Maria Falconi: Il palazzo cardinalizio dei SS. Quattro Coronati a Roma al tempo di Federico II, in: Cultura artistica , città e architettura nell' età federiciana, Atti del convegno internazionale di studi a Reggio di Caserta 1995, hg. von Alfonso Gambardella, Rom 2000, S. 279–291.

Blume 2000 Dieter Blume: Regenten des Himmels. Astrologische Bilder in Mittelalter und Renaissance, Berlin 2000.

Blume 2009 Dieter Blume: Wissenschaft und Bilder. Vom Hof Karls des Großen zur Klosterreform, in: Karolingische und Ottonische Kunst (Geschichte der Bildenden Kunst in Deutschland , Bd. 1), hg. von Bruno Reudenbach, München 2009, S. 520–551.

Blume/Haffner/Metzger 2012 Dieter Blume, Mechthild Haffner und Wolfgang Metzger: Sternbilder des Mittelalters. Der gemalte Himmel zwischen Wissenschaft und Phantasie, Bd. I 800–1200, Berlin 2012.

Blume/Haffner/Metzger 2016 Dieter Blume, Mechthild Haffner und Wolfgang Metzger: Sternbilder des Mittelalters und der Renaissance. Der gemalte Himmel zwischen Wissenschaft und Phantasie, Bd. II 1200–1500, Berlin 2016.

Bober/Rubinstein 1986 Phyllis Pray Bober und Ruth Rubinstein: Renaissance Artists and Antique Sculpture, A Handbook of Sources, London 1986.

Brenk 1991 Beat Brenk: Antikenverständnis und weltliches Rechtsdenken im Skulpturenprogramm Friedrich II. in Capua, in: Musagetes, Festschrift für Wolfram Prinz, Berlin 1991, S. 93–103.

Brenk 2001 Beat Brenk: Zur Programmatik der Kapitelle im Kreuzgang von Monreale, in: Opere e Giorni, Festschrift für Max Seidel, hg. von Klaus Bergdolt und Giorgio Bonsanti, Venedig 2001, S. 43–50.

Claussen 1993 Peter Cornelius Claussen: Bitonto und Capua, Unterschiedliche Paradigmen in der Darstellung Friedrich II., in: Staufisches Apulien, Schriften zur Staufischen Geschichte und Kunst, Bd. 13, hg. von Gesellschaft für staufische Geschichte e.V. Göppingen, Göppingen 1993, S. 77–124.

Contini 1960 Gianfranco Contini: Poeti del Duecento, Mailand 1960.

Draghi 2006 Andreina Draghi: Gli affreschi dell'Aula gotica nel Monastero dei Santi Quattro Coronati. Una storia ritrovata, Mailand 2006.

Draghi 2012 Andreina Draghi: in: Maria Andaloro und Serena Romano: La pittura medievale a Roma, Corpus, Vol. 5 Il Duecento e la cultura Gotica 1198–1287, Mailand 2012, S. 136–176.

Fenzi 1976 Enrico Fenzi: Di alcune palazzi, cupole e planetari nella letteratura classica e medioevale e nell' Africa del Petrarca, in: Giornale Storico della Letteratura Italiana 153, 1976, S. 12–59, S.186–229.

Friedrich 1964 Hugo Friedrich: Epochen der italienischen Lyrik, Frankfurt 1964.

Giammaria 2001 Un universo dei simboli, Gli affreschi della cripta nella cattedrale di Anagni, hg. von Gioacchino Giammaria, Rom 2001.

Glass 1991 Dorothy F. Glass: Romanesque Sculpture in Campania. Patrons, Programs and Style, University Park, Pennsylvania 1991.

Hauknes 2016 Marius B. Hauknes: The Painting of Knowledge in Thirteenth-Century Rome, in: Gesta 55, 2016, S. 1–28.

Hilbert 1979 Karlheinz Hilbert: Baldricus Burgulianus, Carmina, Heidelberg 1979

Lehmann 1945 Karl Lehmann: The Dome of Heaven, in. Art Bulletin 27, 1945, S. 1 ff.

Maddalo 2007 Silvia Maddalo: Rappresentazione il tempo a Roma nel Duecento: i calendarii dipinti tra tradizione laico e riproposta cristiana, in: Medioevo: La chiesa e il palazzo, I convegni di Parma 8, hg. von Arturo Carlo Quintavalle, Mailand 2007, S. 583–597.

Maleczek 1983 Werner Maleczek: Stefano Conti, in: Dizionario Biografico Italiano, Bd. 38, Rom 1983, S. 475–478.

Mitchell 1981 John Mitchell: St. Silvester and Constantine at SS. Quattro Coronati, in: Federico II e l'arte del Duecento italiano, hg. von Angiola Maria Romanini, Bd. 2, Rom 1981, S. 15–32.

Monciatti 2005 Alessio Monciatti: Il Palazzo Vaticano nel Medioevo, Florenz 2005.

Moretti 2006 Giuseppina Filippi Moretti: Le vicende costruttive dell'Aula gotica nel complesso dei Santi Quattro Coronati, in: Andreina Draghi: Gli affreschi dell'Aula gotica nel Monastero dei Santi Quattro Coronati. Una storia ritrovata, Mailand 2006, S. 391–405.

Otter 2001 Monika Otter: Baudri of Bourgeil »To countess Adela«, in: The Journal of Medieval Latin 11, 2001, S. 60–141.

Paravicini Bagliani 1991 Agostino Paravicini Bagliani: Federico II e la corte dei Papi: Scambi culturali e scientifici, in: Medicina e scienze della natura alla corte dei papi nel Duecento, Spoleto 1991, S. 53–84.

Paravicini Bagliani 1996 Agostino Paravicini Bagliani: La Vita Quotidiana alla Corte dei Papi nel Duecento, Rom 1996.

Picone 2003 Michelangelo Picone: Percorsi della Lirica Duecentesca, Dai Siciliani alla Vita Nuova, Fiesole 2003.

Ausst.-Kat. Santa Maria Antiqua 2016 Santa Maria Antiqua tra Roma e Bisanzio (Ausstellung Rom, Santa Maria Antiqua, 17.3.–30.10.2016), hg. von Maria Andaloro, Giulia Bordi und Giuseppe Morganti, Mailand 2016.

Sohm 1997 Andreas Sohm: Bilder als Zeichen der Herrschaft. Die Silvesterkapelle in SS. Quattro Coronati (Rom), in: Archivium Historiae Pontificiae, Bd. 35, Rom 1997, S. 7–47.

Stürner 2000 Wolfgang Stürner: Friedrich II.. Teil 2 Der Kaiser 1220 bis 1250, Darmstadt 2000.

Webster 1938 James Carson Webster: The Labors of the Months in Antique and Medieval Art, Chicago 1938.

Willemsen 1953 Carl Arnold Willemsen: Kaiser Friedrichs II. Triumphtor zu Capua, Wiesbaden 1953.

III. Politik und Diplomatie

Anchoring authority in Saint Peter's grave

Imperial and ecclesiastical politics at the *confessio* from Antiquity to the early Middle Ages

Roald Dijkstra, Dorine van Espelo

Nowadays, the 'Vatican' is synonym for the Catholic Church, of which Saint Peter's basilica is the symbolical as well as physical landmark of Catholicism worldwide. Forming the core of the church, the grave of the apostle Peter is the unequalled anchor for religious authority in the Christian world. The periods of Late Antiquity and the early Middle Ages witnessed the development of this once modest site on the outskirts of Rome into the focal point for religious and political power.

It is most probable that the earliest veneration of Peter at the Vatican Hill, the place in Rome where he was allegedly buried, was generated spontaneously by Christians asking for mediation of the apostle. In the beginning of the fourth century, however, the Roman emperor Constantine (306–337) constructed a basilica at the very location, thus enhancing the cult site with an imperial stamp of approval. It was a conscious attempt of the emperor to use the grave of the most famous and most Roman apostle for his own political purposes, which does not deny a 'sincere' adherence to the Christian cult and the apostle.[1]

At the same time, the bishop of Rome, Sylvester (314–335), is also likely to have been involved in the building process of St. Peter's.[2] The Roman bishop may have advised the emperor on all kinds of practical matters. Sylvester certainly did not dispose of the funds necessary to construct such a huge building, let alone to decorate it, but undoubtedly had better knowledge of the theology and cultic practice of the Christian faith. Moreover, since the Roman emperor was only incidentally in Rome, we therefore may assume that the bishop was in charge of supervising the building and the activities

1 The date of the construction of old Saint Peter's (consistently called Saint Peter's in this contribution) is generally considered to have been between 321–329, see Krautheimer/Corbett/Frazer 1977, p. 272–278. Bowersock has argued that the basilica was not built by Constantine but by his son Constantius: Bowersock 2002.

2 See e.g. McKitterick 2013, p. 115, and Gem 2014, p. 61.

deployed in it.[3] It may even be suspected that Sylvester advised the emperor to decide on which saint should be selected as the dedicatee of the first Christian memorial.

Sylvester and his staff evidently had an obvious self-interest in the choice of Peter, since the growing ambitions of the Roman bishop were legitimized mainly by his claim to be the successor of the apostle as leader of the Christian Roman community. Peter's burial place thus functioned as a physical and symbolical anchor for political authority of the Roman episcopate. As the case of Saint Peter's makes clear from the start, the use of such an anchor was not exclusive: both emperor and bishop could profit from it, albeit for different reasons and with different motives.

After his imperial usurpation and a decade of unrest, Constantine was still working on establishing firm political ground for his rule and had to strengthen his position in view of his competitor reigning in the East, Licinius (308–324). Sylvester had to make clear to both secular and Christian Romans, including the authorities, that his own importance should not be ignored and that he should be considered the leader of the Christian community in Rome.[4] A few years earlier, the emperor and the then bishop Miltiades (310–314) had discovered their mutual interest in the construction of the first monumental church in Rome (and the world), the *Basilica Salvatoris* or *Constantiniana* (also called the Lateran). Adjacent to this church, an episcopal palace was built.[5] This pioneering cooperation between the imperial and episcopal administration demonstrated their capability of constructing a large, public monumental building near the centre of Rome in an innovative architectural form, with an equally innovative function. Now, emperor and pope joined forces once again as both realized the potential of the apostle Peter's most famous place of worship as a cornerstone for their own power.[6]

With an emperor possibly not (yet) profoundly interested in Christian doctrine and a bishop depending on external support, the two men could easily share their anchor. Things became more complicated, however, when Constantine left the empire to his sons. Although the emperors still visited Rome only occasionally, the fact that the em-

3 The Roman elites' influence in Saint Peter's was probably restricted since they mostly adhered to traditional, mostly pre-Christian, cults and were thus at this point not likely to be interested in the functioning of the basilica. Some of them were, however, as is most famously testified by the sarcophagus of Junius Bassus, prefect of Rome, who died in 359, found near the apostle's grave, see e.g. Cameron 2002. The role and interest of the elites (and also of the ordinary faithful) in Peter's basilica and the apostle's grave in particular will be discussed by Dijkstra in a contribution in the forthcoming volume *Through the Papal Lens* (Liverpool University Press).

4 Sylvester was even brought before an imperial tribunal *a sacrilegis accusatus* (*Constitutio Valentiniani imperatoris* 11, *Patrologia Latina* 13, p. 583); an event that is otherwise unknown, see Pietri 1976, p. 168.

5 Leadbetter 2002.

6 A lot more can be and has been said about potential motives and practical matters concerning the erection of Saint Peter's. In our opinion, however, the peculiar qualities of the burial place were the major decisive factor.

peror Constantius II (337–361) favoured Arian Christianity cannot but have damaged the relationship with the Roman bishop, as is illustrated by an intriguing incident crucially involving Peter's grave.[7] It concerns an open clash between the bishop and emperor and is mentioned by Athanasius in his *Historia Arianorum* (35–7). It is hardly a coincidence that this confrontation took place at Peter's tomb. At the same time, it is the first political event in the basilica of which a testimony remains, although the building must have been in use for a considerable period of time at that moment.[8]

Athanasius wrote at the end of 357 during his third exile, and not accidentally, at a time when Liberius was also banished. The *Historia Arianorum* is the continuation of Athanasius' *Apologia secunda contra Arianos*: in the second edition of the latter text Athanasius had tried to defend himself in order to avoid yet another exile. His attempts were in vain, and in his work Athanasius heavily criticizes the emperor Constantius. Given the tensions surrounding Athanasius and his well-known strength of character, the source has to be treated carefully, but it does reveal a particular role of Peter's grave.

Athanasius recounts a mission by the eunuch Eusebius to bishop Liberius (352–366) in 355. Eusebius, *praepositus sacri cubiculi* or grand chamberlain of the palace in Constantinople, acted on behalf of Constantius.[9] The bishop is asked to subscribe to the emperor's measures in favour of the Arians, and consequently, against Athanasius. Liberius refuses this request, however, in a probably fictive speech in which he refers to the apostle Peter twice (*Historia Arianorum* 36). Athanasius describes how the eunuch reacts furiously, and goes to Saint Peter's (§37):

> "And the eunuch was grieved not so much by the fact that *Liberius* did not sign, but because he found him hostile towards his heresy. He forgot that he stood for a bishop, threatened him fiercely and left with the gifts. And he committed an outrage, foreign to Christians and even more daring than (*is usual for*) eunuchs: indeed, in imitation of the transgression of Saul, after he had left for the shrine of Peter the apostle, he dedicated the gifts to him (ἀπελθὼν εἰς τὸ μαρτύριον Πέτρου τοῦ ἀποστόλου, τὰ δῶρα αὐτῷ ἀνέθηκεν). But when Liberius came to know this, he became very angry at the person who watched over the place (τὸν τηροῦντα τὸν τόπον) and had not hindered him (*the eunuch*): and he threw them (*the gifts*) away as an improper offering (ὡς ἄθυτον θυσίαν). And this infuriated the castrate even more".[10]

7 For the relationship between Liberius and Constantius see Pietri 1976, p. 237–268.

8 The only earlier event recorded to have taken place in Saint Peter's is a service in which Ambrose's sister Marcellina took the vow of virginity, in 353 (see Ambrose's *De virginibus* 3,1,1).

9 Date: Portmann 2006, p. 230 (note 222). Portmann offers a German translation of the text. In the passage cited below, he points to the Biblical parallel of 1 Samuel 13.7–13. The passage is briefly mentioned in Spera 1998, p. 5.

10 Translation: author (Dijkstra).

The intervention of Liberius makes clear that he either feared the power of the gifts placed in proximity to the apostle, or considered the gifts an intrusion of inimical objects in his territory. In other words: he realized the importance of Peter's *confessio*, just as the eunuch, who went to the apostle in the first place. Eusebius turned the gifts for the bishop to his ultimate predecessor Peter and thus tried to fundamentally undermine the bishop's authority, whose authority was based on his succession of that same apostle. Both bishop and emperor clearly realized the political and religious potential pertaining to the apostle's tomb.

The same is true for the narrator of the event, Athanasius. He enlarges the case to Biblical proportions by comparing the eunuch Eusebius – representative of the emperor – to King Saul. In 1 Samuel 13.7–13 it is described how Saul decides to make an offering to God in order to prevent his men from mutiny, although he had promised to wait for the prophet Samuel. When Samuel appears he reproaches the king: Saul cannot longer remain the king of Israel. With this comparison, Athanasius actually denies Constantius' right of emperorship.

Beside this rhetorical ornament, the story also includes information on some practical issues concerning the *confessio*. Apparently, the guard was not able to prevent the eunuch from leaving his gifts nor did he dare to remove them himself, probably because of the hierarchical difference between the two men.[11] Incidentally, this is the first reference to the personnel working at Saint Peter's, which, given the size of the basilica, must have been more numerous than the poor guard who fell victim to Liberius' anger.[12]

The event should not necessarily be taken as an indication of the weakness of the Roman bishop's power in administering the memorial, since the bishop had the authority to remove Eusebius' offerings.[13] Unfortunately, we are not informed as to how Liberius heard of them, nor about the exact spot where the gifts were deposited. Most likely, however, the gifts were left in front of the shrine, visible for other visitors and therefore all the more harmful to the bishop's image. Votive offerings at the grave of

11 Or otherwise he had not noticed what happened, which seems rather unlikely. In general, guards or priests in religious buildings seem to have had only little authority in late antiquity and did not watch visitors closely as is nicely illustrated in a poem probably from the fourth century (*Anthologia latina* 1,21), see Focardi 1998.

12 However, Sozomenos' *Historia ecclesiastica* 9,10,4 mentions only one φύλαξ τῆς ἐκκλησίας in the text of the *Sources Chrétiennes* (based on the edition in the GCS series no. 50). The older *Patrologia Graeca* edition (PG 67, colon 1617), apparently cited (in Latin!) by Thacker 2014, p. 141, has a plural.

13 *Pace* Thacker 2014, p. 141. McLynn 2004, p. 253–254 interprets the incident as an example of the uneasiness felt by bishops when an emperor entered a church. In his *Contra Parmenianum Donatistam* (2.4.1–2), Optatus of Milevis suggests that the catholic bishop could deny heretic adversaries to approach Peter's grave, but it is unclear whether Optatus' assumption is based on reliable testimony or mainly part of his rhetoric. The treatise is dated to 364–367.

Peter are attested from the period before the construction of the basilica already and they continued to be given in later times (see below).[14]

An even larger significance of the basilica in ecclesiastical politics is visible from the fifth century onwards, when Saint Peter's became an anchor for episcopal power in several elections. The two competing candidates tried to find the most suitable basis for power in Rome. In 418, after the death of Zosimus, Eulalius (418–419) held the Lateran, the official seat of the Roman bishop: Boniface (418–422) marched to Saint Peter's after his consecration, obviously in order to control access to the grave of the alleged founder of papal power. Later, when he had to leave Saint Peter's on orders of the emperor, Boniface went to that other grand memorial of a martyr-apostle closely associated with Peter, Paul. Even more striking is the case of Symmachus (498–514) and Laurentius (498–499), in which the former barricaded himself in Saint Peter's for several years (app. 501–506), while the latter was the officially recognized bishop.[15] From his Petrine home base, Symmachus succeeded in obtaining imperial support, and eventually Laurentius was removed from the papal See. A few years later, Symmachus made very clear that he understood the symbolical significance of the apostle Peter. In a letter to the emperor Anastasius (491–518), he condemned the imperial opposition to his authority by claiming Peter's personal intervention on his behalf and asked rhetorically whether Anastasius dared to withstand Peter's power, because he was an emperor.[16]

Meanwhile, the Roman emperors after Constantine also showed their interest in the *confessio*, although the sources are rather reticent on this aspect. At the one famous visit of an emperor that took place under the rule of the Constantinian dynasty – that of Constantius II in 357 – the emperor might have visited Saint Peter's and prostrated before the grave of the apostle, but this can only be inferred from two general remarks in John Chrysostom that suggest that around the year 390 such an act was normal.[17] Maybe even more important, and in a way more permanent, was an experiment by the emperor Honorius (395–423), who built an imperial mausoleum adjacent to the church.[18] It was one of the most direct imperial appeals on the authority of the apostle Peter, but given Honorius' absence from Rome it might not have influenced the bishop's control

---

14 Coins have been found in the grave, see Toynbee 1953, p. 18–19.

15 See Latham 2012 in particular, also Latham 2014, Wirbelauer 1994 and for Symmachus and Laurentius, Pietri 1966.

16 See *Epistula* 10, e.g. 10,7 (ed. Thiel, p. 703): *Meum cogistasti honorem repellere, quem interuentu suo beatus Petrus imposuit. An quia imperator es, contra Petri niteris potestatem?*

17 Liverani 2007, p. 91.

18 Concise overview in Johnson 2009, p. 167–174. Cf. Liverani 2014, p. 31, about the mausoleum of Honorius: "Through this imperial connection and through the authority of the apostle, the basilica of Saint Peter was also the place in which delicate political and religious questions could be raised that interested both the emperor and the Roman bishop."

of Peter's grave. Moreover, Honorius' example was not followed by other emperors. In fact, pope Leo I's (440–461) entombment in Saint Peter's, which constituted the first papal burial there, should be seen as an imitation of this imperial tradition.[19] Nevertheless, in the later eighth century the mausoleum became an emblematic focal point for the bond between the papacy and the Frankish rulers of the Carolingian dynasty when pope Paul I (757–767) turned it into an oratory for Petronilla, the alleged daughter of Peter. She was adopted as patron saint of the Carolingians, and in 758 Paul had the baptismal gown of Gisela, king Pippin's daughter, ritually placed there in order to confirm their spiritual bond of *compaternitas* or co-parenthood.[20] Significantly, Pippin's gift of a silver table was placed by the same pope *in sacram confessionem*, in order to creating an everlasting memorial for the Carolingian family in the basilica.[21]

One of the main reasons why the connection of the Vatican with the Roman emperors of the past remained alive was the fact that the basilica became part of the trajectory of triumphal processions from around the year 400 onwards.[22] By c. 500–550, an imperial visit to Peter's church did not particularly seem to raise a dust, and was perhaps even a common sight. Visiting Saint Peter's basilica prior to entering the city of Rome proper as part of the Roman *adventus* ritual was, however, a precedent created by the Ostrogoth king Theodoric (475–526) in 500.[23] The triumphal character of the imperial procession thus became infused with an element of pilgrimage.

Religious devotion also incited material contributions by the secular elite, including emperors and kings, whose gifts to the shrine, varying from precious jewels to various liturgical objects such as candlesticks, are also mentioned on occasion.[24] Emperor Valentinian III (425–455) especially had the *confessio* lavishly decorated in silver and had precious gifts placed over the shrine.[25] Quite a few popes of the late antique world donated substantially to Saint Peter's basilica and to the apostle's shrine, as is testified by

19 McKitterick 2013, p. 111–117; De Blaauw 2016, p. 93–95.

20 Story 2013, p. 269; Letter of Pope Paul I to Pippin, *Codex Carolinus*, nr. 14, p. 511–512. For the bond of *compaternitas* as a spiritual ritual and political tool, see Angenendt 1980.

21 Letter of Pope Paul I to Pippin, *Codex Carolinus*, nr. 21, 522–524. Van Espelo will comprehensively discuss the central role of Peter's *confessio* in the Carolingian-papal bond in a contribution in the forthcoming volume *Through the Papal Lens* (Liverpool University Press).

22 Fraschetti 1999, p. 252–266, also on imperial visits outside the context of the *adventus*; Liverani 1999, p. 34–35, and 34–40 for the accessibility of the Vatican.

23 Liverani 2007, p. 92–94, and Liverani 2014, p. 29–30.

24 For instance Duchesne, *Liber Pontificalis* (hereafter *LP*), Life of Hormisdas, I, ch. 10, p. 271–272 (from king Clovis, emperor Justin and king Theoderic). All English translations of the papal lives in the *LP* as given in this article are from Davis 2000 and 2007; the Latin editions used are from Duchesne 1886 and 1892.

25 Duchesne, *LP*, Life of Xystus III, I, ch. 4, p. 233.

their biographies in the so-called *Liber Pontificalis*. Some had the actual structure of the basilica and/or shrine thoroughly modified, such as the aforementioned Symmachus.[26]

The grave's architectural setting was most considerably changed by pope Gregory the Great, whose pontificate (590–604) is generally considered to mark the transition from late antiquity to the early middle ages, in order to accommodate the increasing quantities of visitors better in addition to allowing mass to be celebrated above Saint Peter's body (*super corpus beati Petri*).[27] Although pilgrimage to the Vatican was an important phenomenon in antiquity already, especially from the sixth century onwards the afflux of pilgrims augmented even further. The sanctuary's new setting probably also allowed relics to be created more effectively and large numbers of pilgrims to be effectively guided around the holy area.[28] From Gregory's correspondence with the Western royal aristocracy we learn that Peter's *confessio* and the apostle's relics proved suitable tools for Gregory to articulate of Roman pre-eminence, and this prelate emphatically employed Petrine relics in the diplomatic contacts between the papal See and the elite of the Christian world. Although he was not the first pope to send out relics to secular rulers, it was Gregory who universally adopted the practice.[29]

Another key element in Gregory's promotion of the Petrine primacy was the systematic practice of solemn oath-swearing at the apostle's tomb (*ante corpus*), a "ritualistic exercise of public submission at the very locus of papal power".[30] Invoking Peter's authority in this way was the highest card the pope could play to secure the utmost loyalty and dedication from his agents, such as his Sicilian *rectores*, but it was also employed as a means for delinquents to purge themselves before the apostle, thus proving their innocence.[31] Using Peter's sepulchre as a physical location to perform such an act, however, was not entirely unprecedented. Pope Boniface II's (530–532) biography reveals that this prelate, "driven by jealousy and malice" gathered a synod in Saint Peter's basilica, and had it approve of a decree which allowed the pope to select a successor of his own choice, the deacon Vigilius. This decree was, in the first instance, reinforced

26 Demacopoulos 2013, p. 102–116.

27 See e.g. Brenk 1995, De Blaauw 1995, and Dal Santo 2012, p. 79; Duchesne, *LP*, Life of Gregory, I, ch. 4, p. 312.

28 De Blaauw 1987, p. 530–534, and 632–633; Spera 1998, p. 49–51; Leyser 2000, p. 300; Alan Thacker notes, however, that Gregory's works may not have been as invasive as is usually assumed given that the altar probably had been directly above the grave since Jerome's time: Thacker 2007, p. 46–48.

29 Tom Noble has pointed out that Symmachus was probably the first pope to distribute Petrine relics: Noble 1994, 527. On Gregory's letters in relation to relics, see Demacopoulos 2013, p. 134–162, Leyser 2000, p. 300–302.

30 De Blaauw 1987, 316–317; quotation from Demacopoulos 2013, p. 140.

31 For instance in a letter to the Ravennese subdeacon John: nr. 11.16 (November 600), p. 277–278; cf. Demacopoulos 2010, p. 337; De Blaauw 1987, p. 316.

by the *sacerdotes* present at the synod, and "with an oath before the *confessio* of Saint Peter". Soon thereafter, however, doubts as to the document's licitness arose, and a second synod was held, ruling it unconstitutional. Then, "in front of the *confessio* of Saint Peter in the presence of all the *sacerdotes*, clergy, and senate, he [Boniface] destroyed the actual decree by fire" to render the decree null and void.[32] The oath performed by Boniface and the synod therefore served to validate their decision before the apostle, and, ultimately, God. It was also a means to verify the orthodox and canonical nature of the decree and the synod. In this instance, therefore, Peter's tomb functioned as a locus for authentication where the saint could be called upon as both a judge and witness. Similar uses of the *confessio* as a physical anchor for determining church tradition and orthodoxy can be found with other episcopal synods or clerical gatherings that were kept under the watchful eyes of Peter. Such councils occurred multiple times in papal history, such as the anti-iconoclastic synod held in the pontificate of Pope Gregory III (731–741), that gathered "in front of the most holy *confessio* of Saint Peter's most sacred body". It was attended not just by clerics, namely the various bishops, as well as priests, deacons, all the clergy, but was also assisted by "the noble consuls and the rest of the Christian people"[33]. The practice of oath swearing may have been an inspiration for Pope Leo III (795–816), who, after being accused of adultery and perjury in 799–800, purged himself in Saint Peter's with a pledge, although he did so in the *ambo* and not in front of the *confessio* specifically.[34] His act of purification was witnessed by a crowd of Frankish and Roman lay and clerical dignitaries, who would shortly thereafter witness Charlemagne's imperial coronation that famously took place in the same church in 800, by the hands of the indemnified Pope Leo.

Oath swearing in combination with placing written documents on Peter's *confessio* to have them validated also constituted a key element in the inauguration of bishops, as is testified by the *Liber Diurnus*, a collection of various textual models prepared for the composition of important official documents that date mostly from 680 to 790 and were used by the papal chancery. It contains circa one hundred formulae of which one in particular, probably datable to the late seventh century, is the profession of faith that was drawn up, signed, and read aloud in Saint Peter's after the new bishop was consecrated.[35] Additionally, special prayers were sung in front of the *confessio* during the ceremonial

32 *LP*, Life of Boniface II, ch. 3–4, p. 53.

33 *LP*, Life of Gregory III, ch. 3, p. 20; Duchesne, *LP*, I, p. 416. On the *LP*'s description of synods held in Saint Peter's as part of papal representation, see McKitterick 2013, p. 100.

34 Duchesne, *LP*, Life of Leo III, II, ch. 21–22, p. 6–7.

35 This specific profession was probably written shortly after the year 682: Duchesne 1891, p. 24–30. It reads: [...] *presentem nostrae professionis paginam per ill* notarium scriptum cum nostrae manus subscriptione coram omnibus relectam in confessione beati Petri apostolorum principis deposuimus, tamquam ipso testificante de puritate conscientiae nostrae* [...]. *Liber Diurnus*, ed. von Sickel, formula 84, p. 102–103.

consecration.[36] The bishop's oath was then deposited in Peter's *confessio*, as a testimony to the new prelate's purity of conscience. It is difficult to say when exactly this became common practice, but from the records in the *Liber Diurnus* it appears that it already was current around 700 at the latest, or that it was turning into standard practice around that time. When the Anglo-Saxon missionary Boniface (d. 754) was appointed bishop in Rome on November 30th of the year 722, he placed his own oath or *indiculum* with his own hands above Saint Peter's body (*supra sacratissimum corpus tuum).*[37]

Just how significant Peter's sanctuary was in this procedure, as a place where church tradition was safeguarded and the purity of mind was assessed, may be illustrated by an incident during the rule of Pope Constantine (708–715). The newly consecrated archbishop of Ravenna named Felix refused to provide the pope with the customary written *cautiones*, and wrote his own instead. Doubts that had risen in the Lateran as to the archbishop's righteousness were confirmed as the bonds were found "grimy as if charred by fire" a few days after they had been placed, according to custom, in Peter's *confessio*.[38] As a matter of course, the apostle had detected the impertinence, and Felix, who had lapsed in not following tradition and not sufficiently recognizing Petrine – *in extenso* papal – authority, was subsequently arrested and punished for his presumptuousness.

It would be safe to state that the apostolic *confessio*'s status as a symbolical as well as physical 'anchor' for authoritative tradition and as a *locus* where solemn promises were tested and formalized had gained prominence in the course of the centuries. As the early middle ages progress, we see the various aspects pertaining to the sanctuary's political-religious role touched upon above focalize in the papal representation of diplomatic relations between the Roman episcopate and the Carolingian dynasty of the Frankish realm, the same line of rulers that would produce the first emperor in the post-Roman West since 476, in the person of the aforementioned Charlemagne (768–814). From the earliest moments of rapprochement between the two, Saint Peter's grave was at the heart of the action. Pope Gregory, for instance, accompanied his written petition for military aid against the Lombards in 739 with the keys to the apostolic tomb, and when in 754 King Pippin (751–768) solemnly promised Stephen II (752–757) to restore lands to the papacy (in the so-called Donation of Pippin) that the Lombards had taken earlier from the papacy, the documents were reportedly placed in or on Saint Peter's tomb (*in confessione*), in order that the papal successors possess and dispose of the documents

36 Angenendt 1977, p. 65; Benz 1975, p. 358–359.

37 Boniface's episcopal oath: ed. Tangl, no. 16, p. 28–29.

38 *LP*, Life of Constantine, ch. 2, p. 92.

forever.[39] When Charlemagne triumphantly visited Rome twenty years later after definitively conquering the Lombard territories, he first went to Saint Peter's basilica to pay his respects at the *confessio* before being allowed to enter the city of Rome proper, and pope and king ratified their promises to each other *ad corpus beati Petri*. At a later stage, Charlemagne vowed to uphold his father Pippin's assertion as to the restoration of the papal territories, and written versions of the bestowal were placed in the *confessio*.[40]

Given the status of Peter's tomb and the place it had come to occupy in imperial presence in Rome and in the history of the papacy, the choice to stage Charlemagne's imperial inauguration ceremony at Peter's tomb during the celebration of mass on Christmas in the year 800 was premeditated. Pope Leo's biography describes how, immediately after the pope had personally placed a crown on Charlemagne's head:

> "all the faithful Romans seeing how much he [Charlemagne] defended and how greatly he loved the holy Roman church and its vicar, at God's bidding and that of Saint Peter, keybearer of the kingdom of heaven, cried aloud with one accord: 'To Charles, pious Augustus crowned by God, great and pacific Emperor, life and victory!' Three times this was said in front of Saint Peter's sacred *confessio* (*ante sacram confessionem beati Petri apostoli*), with the invocation of many saints, and by them all he was established as Emperor of the Romans"[41].

Afterwards followed an anointing by the hands of Pope Leo. The papal biographer did not fail to mention how the freshly invested emperor, following ancient custom, subsequently donated precious gifts, among others a silver table and golden objects, that were presented *in confessione* and *super altare(m)*.[42]

Never before had an emperor of the West been instated in Saint Peter's basilica in the presence of a Roman bishop, and Charlemagne's establishment as 'Emperor of the Romans' was thus essentially an innovation anchored in a longstanding institution. Yet

---

39 *LP*, Life of Stephen II, ch. 47, p. 71–72: "As for the keys, both of the city of Ravenna and of the various cities of the exarchate of Ravenna, along with the donation concerning them that their king had issued, he [Fulrad] placed them in Saint Peter's *confessio*; and he handed them over to this apostle of God and to his vicar the holy pope and to all his successor pontiffs for ever, for their possession and management [...]."

40 Duchesne, *LP*, Life of Hadrian I, I, ch. 35–43, p. 496–498.

41 *LP*, Life of Leo III, ch. 23–24, p. 187–189; Duchesne, *LP*, II, p. 7–8: *Tunc universi fideles Romani videntes tanta defensione et dilectione quam erga sanctam Romanam eccclesiam et eius vicarium habuit, unanimiter altisona voce, Dei nutu atque beati Petri clavigeri regni caelorum, exclamaverunt: 'Karolo, piissimo Augusto a Deo coronato, magno et pacifico imperatore, vita et victoria!'. Ante sacram confessionem beati Petri apostoli, plures sanctos invocantes, ter dictum est; et ab omnibus constitutus est imperator Romanorum.*

42 Duchesne, *LP*, II, ch. 24, p. 7–8. Charlemagne may have been following his father Pippin's example as years earlier, he too had donated a silver table that was placed in the *confessio* by Pope Paul: Angenendt 1977, and see note 21 above.

Leo's pontifical biography passed off the ceremonial as something essentially traditional, rooted in the Petrine cult. Under the aegis of the apostle, therefore, new traditions were established and rooted in his sanctuary that formed the heart of the Roman episcopate's headship of the Western Church.

Conclusion

Although the place of Peter's grave was probably first visited for devotional purposes by ordinary Christians without interference by formal institutions, in the fourth century it was definitely appropriated by both the Roman emperor and the Roman bishop. As such, it became a symbolical and physical anchor for legitimacy and authority. Occasionally, conflicts were fought out 'on' the grave, both between bishop and emperor and between competing bishops. Control of and access to the site became a politico-religious instrument of legitimization. As time went on, the apostle's grave more and more became a yardstick by which piety and divine approval were measured, and it came to occupy a central role in papal representation. This development is perhaps most visibly illustrated by the famous inauguration of Charlemagne as emperor in front of the *confessio*; the Petrine tomb was deemed to be the best place for the invocation of imperial tradition. Thereafter, Peter's grave would remain an anchor for authority for centuries to come, until the present day.

Bibliography

Sources:

Codex Carolinus, ed. Wilhelm Gundlach, MGH Epistolae III (Epistolae Merowingici et Karolini aevi; 1), Berlin 1892.

Letters from Gregory the Great, ed. Ludwig Hartmann, MGH Epistolae II (Gregorii I papae Registrum epistolarum; 2), Berlin 1899.

Letters from Boniface, ed. Michael Tangl, MGH Epistolae selectae I, Berlin 1916.

Liber Diurnus romanorum Pontificium ex unico Codice Vaticano, ed. Theodor von Sickel (SB der Kaiserlichen Akademie der Wissenschaften, Philosophisch-historische Klasse CX-II), Wien 1889.

Liber Pontificalis, ed. Louis Duchesne, *Le Liber Pontificalis. Texte, Introduction et Commentaire* I & II Paris 1886/1892, republished by Cyrille Vogel 1955/1957.

Raymond Davis: The Book of Pontiffs (*Liber Pontificalis*). The Ancient Biographies of the First Ninety Roman Bishops to AD 715 (Translated Texts for Historians; 6), Liverpool 2000.

Raymond Davis: The Lives of the Eighth-Century Popes (*Liber Pontificalis*). The Ancient Biographies of Nine Popes from AD 715 to AD 817 (Translated Texts for Historians; 13), Liverpool 2007 (2nd Ed.).

Werner Portmann: Athanasius. Zwei Schriften gegen die Arianer. Verteidigungsschrift gegen die Arianer. Geschichte der Arianer, Stuttgart 2006.

Andreas Thiel: Epistulae Romanorum Pontificum genuinae et quae ad eos scriptae sunt a S. Hilaro usque ad Pelagium II. Tomus I. A S. hilaro usque ad S. Hormisdam ann. 461–523, Braunsberg 1868.

Sozomène. Histoire ecclésiastique, tome IV. Livres VII–IX. Traduction du grec par André-Jean Festugière et Bernard Grillet (Sources Chrétiennes; 516), Paris 2008.

Literature:

Angenendt 1977 Arnold Angenendt: *Mensa Pippini Regis*. Zur liturgischen Präsenz des Karolinger in Sankt Peter, in: Hundert Jahre Deutsches Priesterkolleg beim Campo Santo Teutonico, ed. Erwin Gatz, Rom et al. 1977, p. 52–68.

Angenendt 1980 Arnold Angenendt: Das geistliche Bündnis der Päpste mit den Karolingern (754–796), Historisches Jahrbuch 100, 1980, p. 1–94.

Benz 1975 Karl Benz: '*Cum ab oratione surgeret*'. Überlegungen zur Kaiserkrönung Karls des Großen, Deutsches Archiv für Erforschung des Mittelalters 31, 1975, p. 337–369.

Bowersock 2002 Glen Bowersock: Peter and Constantine, in: 'Humana sapit': études d'Antiquité tardive offertes à Lellia Cracco Ruggini, ed. Jean-Michel Carrié und Rita Lizzi Testa, Turnhout 2002, p. 209–217.

Brenk 1995 Beat Brenk: Der Kultort, seine Zugänglichkeit und seine Besucher, in: Akten des XII. internationalen Kongresses für christliche Archäologie. Bonn, 22.–28.9.1991, ed. Ernst Dassmann und Josef Engemann, Münster 1995, Bd. 2, p. 69–122.

Cameron 2002 Alan Cameron: The Funeral of Junius Bassus, in: Zeitschrift für Papyrologie und Epigraphik 139, 2002, p. 288–292.

Dal Santo 2012 Matthew Dal Santo: Debating the Saints' Cult in the Age of Gregory the Great. Oxford Studies in Byzantium, Oxford 2012.

De Blaauw 1987 Sible de Blaauw: Cultus et decor. Liturgie en architectuur in laatantiek en middeleeuws Rome: Basilica Salvatoris, Sanctae Mariae, Sancti Petri, Delft 1987.

De Blaauw 1995 Sible de Blaauw: Die Krypta in stadtrömischen Kirchen: Abbild eines Pilgerziels, in: Akten des XII. internationalen Kongresses für christliche Archäologie. Bonn, 22.–28.9.1991, ed. Ernst Dassmann and Joseph Engemann, Münster 1995, Bd. 1, p. 559–567.

De Blaauw 2016 Sible de Blaauw: Die Gräber der frühen Päpste, in: Die Päpste. Amt und Herrschaft in Antike, Mittelalter und Renaissance (Die Päpste, Bd. 1; Publikationen der Reiss-Engelhorn-Museen, Bd. 74), ed. Bernd Schneidmüller et al., Regensburg 2016, p. 77–99.

Demacopoulos 2010 George Demacopoulos: Gregory the Great and the appeal to Petrine authority, in: Papers Presented at the Fifteenth International Conference on Patristic Studies held in Oxford 2007 (Studia Patristica; 48), ed. Jane Baun et al., Leuven 2010, p. 333–346.

Demacopoulos 2013 George Demacopoulos: The Invention of Peter. Apostolic Discourse and Papal Authority in Late Antiquity, Philadelphia 2013.

Duchesne 1891 Louis Duchesne: Le *Liber Diurnus* et les élections pontificales au VIIe siècle, Bibliothèque de l'école des Chartres 52, 1891, p. 5–30.

Focardi 1998 Gabriella Focardi: Il carme del pescatore sacrilego (Anth.Lat. 1, 21 Riese). Una declamazione in versi, Bologna 1998.

Fraschetti 1999 Augusto Fraschetti: La conversione da Roma pagana a Roma cristiana, Rom/Bari 1999.

Gem 2013 Richard Gem: From Constantine to Constans: the Chronology of the Construction of Saint Peter's Basilica, in: Old Saint Peter's, Rome, ed. Rosamond McKitterick et al., Cambridge 2013, p. 35–64.

Johnson 2009 Mark Johnson: The Roman Imperial Mausoleum in Late Antiquity, Cambridge et al. 2009.

Krautheimer/Corbett/Frazer 1977 Richard Krautheimer, Spencer Corbett und Alfred Frazer: Corpus basilicarum Christianarum Romae V, Vatikanstadt 1977.

Latham 2012 Jacob Latham: From Literal to Spiritual Soldiers of Christ: Disputed Episcopal Elections and the Advent of Christian Processions in Late Antique Rome, Church History 81, 2012, p. 298–327.

Latham 2014 Jacob Latham: Battling Bishops, the Roman Aristocracy, and the Contestation of Civic Space in Late Antique Rome, in: Religious Competition in the Third Century CE: Jews, Christians, and the Greco-Roman World, ed. Jordan Rosenblum, Lily Vuong and Nathaniel DesRosiers, Göttingen/Bristol (USA) 2014, p. 126–137.

Leadbetter 2002 Bill Leadbetter: Constantine and the Bishop: The Roman Church in the Early Fourth Century, Journal of Religious History 26, 2002, p. 1–14.

Leyser 2000 Conrad Leyser: The Temptations of Cult: Roman Martyr Piety in the Age of Gregory the Great, Early Medieval Europe 9, 2000, p. 289–307.

Liverani 1999 Paolo Liverani: La topografia antica del vaticano, Vatikanstadt 1999.

Liverani 2007 Paolo Liverani: Victors and Pilgrims in Late Antiquity and the Early Middle Ages, Fragmenta, in: Journal of the Royal Netherlands Institute in Rome 1, 2007, p. 83–102.

Liverani 2013 Paolo Liverani: Saint Peter's and the City of Rome between Late Antiquity and the Early Middle Ages, in: Old Saint Peter's, Rome, ed. Rosamond McKitterick et al., Cambridge 2013, p. 21–34.

McKitterick 2013 Rosamond McKitterick: The Representation of Old Saint Peter's basilica in the *Liber Pontificalis*, in: Old Saint Peter's, Rome, ed. Rosamond McKitterick et al., Cambridge 2013, p. 95–118.

McLynn 2004 Neil McLynn: The Transformation of Imperial Churchgoing in the Fourth Century, in: Approaching Late Antiquity: the Transformation from Early to Late Empire, ed. Simon Swain and Mark Edwards, Oxford 2004, p. 235–270.

Noble 1994 Thomas Noble: Michele Maccarrone on the Medieval Papacy, in: Catholic Historical Review 80, 1994, p. 518–533.

Pietri 1966 Charles Pietri: Le Sénat, le peuple chrétien et les partis du cirque à Rome sous le Pape Symmaque (498–514), in: Mélanges d'archéologie et d'histoire 78, 1966, p. 123–139.

Pietri 1976 Charles Pietri: Roma Christiana. Recherches sur l'Eglise de Rome, son organisation, sa politique, son idéologie de Miltiade à Sixte III (311–440), Rom 1976.

Spera 1998 Lucrezia Spera: *Ad limina apostolorum.* Santuari e pellegrini a Roma tra la tarda antichità e l'alto medioevo, in: La geografia della città di Roma e lo spazio del sacro. L'esempio delle trasformazioni territoriali lungo il percorso della Visita alle Sette Chiese Privilegiate, hg. von Claudio Ceretti, Rom 1998, p. 1–104.

Story 2013 Joanna Story: The Carolingians and the oratory of Saint Peter the Shepherd, in: Old Saint Peter's, Rome, ed. Rosamond McKitterick et al., Cambridge 2013, p. 257–273.

Thacker 2007 Alan Thacker: Rome of the Martyrs. Saints, cults and relics, fourth to seventh centuries, in: Roma Felix – Formation and Reflections of Medieval Rome, ed. Éamonn Ó Carragáin und Carol Neuman de Vegvar, Farnham 2007, p. 13–49.

Thacker 2013 Alan Thacker: Popes, Emperors and Clergy at Old Saint Peter's from the Fourth to the Eighth Century, in: Old Saint Peter's, Rome, ed. Rosamond McKitterick et al., Cambridge 2013, p. 137–156.

Toynbee 1953 Jocelyn Toynbee: The Shrine of St. Peter and its Setting, in: The Journal of Roman Studies 43, 1953, p. 1–26.

Wirbelauer 1994 Eckhard Wirbelauer: Die Nachfolgerbestimmung im römischen Bistum (3.–6. Jh.). Doppelwahlen und Absetzungen in ihrer herrschaftssoziologischen Bedeutung, in: Klio 76, 1994, p. 388–437.

Bildung und Umbildung kirchlicher Strukturen in Italien zwischen Spätantike und Frühmittelalter

Donatella Nuzzo

Die kirchlichen Strukturen im spätantiken und frühmittelalterlichen Italien waren bereits Gegenstand zahlreicher Studien, in denen diverse Aspekte mit verschiedenen Ansätzen analysiert wurden.[1] Das Thema bietet in der Tat zahlreiche Anhaltspunkte für Forschung und Vertiefung, auch im Hinblick auf die zeitliche und geographische Bandbreite. In diesem Beitrag wird es mit Blick auf die Tagung darum gehen, die Tätigkeit der Bischöfe von Rom in den Prozessen zur Schaffung und Entwicklung der Kirchenorganisation im Gebiet Italiens sowie die Beziehungen zu den Institutionen anderer Diözesen zu beleuchten. Im Hintergrund bleiben daher einige grundsätzliche Aspekte, wie die weitreichenden politischen Veränderungen dieser Epoche, die Beziehungen zum Kaiserreich und zu den Langobarden, die Auseinandersetzungen über die Kirchenlehre, die Verbreitung der Heiligenverehrung u. a. Exemplarisch seien die Fälle von Mailand, Ravenna und Süditalien herausgegriffen, an denen sich die Entwicklung der Kirchenstruktur seit der Spätantike (ab dem 4. Jahrhundert) ablesen lässt. Die Studie endet an der Schwelle zum 11. Jahrhundert, als sich eine neue Kirchenanordnung im Rahmen der reformierten *Ecclesia* herausgebildet hatte.

Bis zur Zeit Konstantins findet sich im Zusammenhang mit der territorialen Gliederung der Kirche keinerlei Hinweis auf Diözesen bzw. metropolitische Strukturen. Die früheste Auskunft über die Kirchenorganisation stammt aus dem 4. Jahrhundert; sie war das Ergebnis der Vorgaben des I. Ökumenischen Konzils, das Konstantin 325 in Nicäa einberufen hatte und das die Beziehungen zwischen der Gliederung der Reichsgebiete und derjenigen der Bischofskirchen auf der Grundlage von Diokletians Unterteilung in Provinzen regelte.[2] Nicäa bestimmte die Schaffung von Kirchenprovinzen und des

1 S. zuletzt Otranto 2014; Boesch Gajano 2014; Ronzani 2014 und Alzati 2014. Vgl. außerdem Nuzzo 2015, Nuzzo (im Druck) und Fonseca 2016.

2 Liebeschuetz 2001, S. 139–140; Pietri 1995, S. 554–555; Perrin 2010, S. 731–733; Alzati 2014, S. 914–915; Di Berardino 2014, S. 102–104; Fonseca 2016, S. 7–8.

metropolitischen Systems[3] sowie den Vorrang der Bischöfe von Alexandria, Antiochia und Rom in Anbetracht ihrer angestammten Autorität.[4]

Die von Konstantin veranlasste Unterteilung der Diözese Italien[5] in die beiden Einheiten *annonaria* und *suburbicaria*, jeweils geleitet vom *vicarius Italiae* (mit Sitz in Mailand) und vom *vicarius Urbis* (mit Sitz in Rom) wirkte sich besonders auf die Verwaltung der Kirche und die Bildung der entsprechenden Territorialbezirke aus. Die enge Abhängigkeit der kirchlichen von der kaiserlich-römischen, in Provinzen gegliederten Verwaltungsstruktur war von den kaiserlichen Behörden beabsichtigt, um beide in einem einzigen System zusammenzuführen; sie stellte sich aber besonders in Italien als sehr ungenau heraus.

Nach dem Versuch von Papst Damasus (366–384), die Jurisdiktion der *sedes apostolica* auf ganz Italien auszudehnen[6], wurde im ausgehenden 4. Jahrhundert unter Papst Siricius (384–399) die Unterteilung Italiens zwischen den Sitzen von Rom und Mailand an der Grenzlinie zwischen *Italia annonaria* und *Italia suburbicaria* festgelegt. Dennoch bestand Siricius in verschiedenen Schreiben an alle italienischen Bischöfe auf seinem Recht, Bischöfe zu weihen.[7]

Die Ansprüche des Bischofs von Rom gründeten bekanntlich auf der Doktrin des Papstprimats, dessen Kernpunkt die Auffassung der *sedes apostolica* als »una Petri sedes« ist, wie Damasus sie in einem der Epigramme für das vatikanische Baptisterium definiert.[8] Ab dem 5. Jahrhundert wird der Begriff *sedes apostolica* in der kirchlichen Terminologie allgemein gebräuchlich für die Autorität des römischen Pontifex über die anderen Bischöfe. Als Nachfolger und damit Stellvertreter des heiligen Petrus und kraft seines Amtes übte er die Leitung *totius ovilis dominici* aus, wie Papst Gelasius (492–496) ausführte.[9] In Petri Namen wurde also eine hierarchische Unterordnung aller Bischöfe gegenüber dem römischen Papst durchgesetzt. Noch Hadrian I. bekräftigte in

3 Laut Kanon 4 des Konzils von Nicäa sollte das Zuständigkeitsgebiet des Metropoliten mit der Provinz zusammenfallen; ein neuer Bischof sollte von allen Bischöfen der Provinz gewählt und vom Metropoliten bestätigt werden. Kanon 5 bestimmte den Ablauf der zwei Mal pro Jahr stattfindenden Bischofssynoden (Di Berardino 2006, S. 20–21).

4 Konzil von Nicäa, Kanon 6 (Di Berardino 2006, S. 22–23).

5 Giardina 1986, S. 5–10; Porena 2010, S. 539–540.

6 Carletti 2000. Zur Situation Italiens zu Damasus' Zeit und zu seinem Anspruch, die römische Jurisdiktion auf ganz Italien auszudehnen, vgl. auch Liebeschuetz 2005, S. 29–31.

7 Pietri 1976, S. 888–909; Siric. epist. 5 (PL 13, 1157A); epist. 6 (PL 13, 1165). Vgl. Cavalcanti 2000, S. 377–378.

8 ED 4. Vgl. Maccarrone 1960, S. 634–650.

9 Gelas. epist. V (PL 59, 30).

einem Schreiben von 785 an die oströmischen Kaiser den Primat der *sedes petrina in toto orbe terrarum*[10] mit Verweis auf die bekannte Bibelstelle Mt 16,17–19.

In dieser Hinsicht ist es interessant, die Epitaphe der spätantiken und frühmittelalterlichen Päpste nach Äußerungen über die apostolische Sukzession zu untersuchen: Coelestin I. (422–432) wird in seiner Grabinschrift als *praesul apostolicae sedis venerabilis* bezeichnet.[11] Über den 530 in St. Peter beigesetzten Felix IV. steht auf dem Grab: *sedis apostolicae crescere fecit opes*[12]; noch beeindruckender ist in der Grabinschrift seines Nachfolgers Bonifaz II. (530–532) dieser als Soldat des apostolischen Stuhls und als für die ganze Welt geweihter Bischof dargestellt.[13] Im Epitaph Johannes' II. (533–535) lesen wir, sein Nachfolger Agapitus habe als höchster Bischof der Stadt Rom die oberste Stufe (*culmen*) des heiligen apostolischen Stuhls inne.[14] Für Pelagius I. (556–561) wird u. a. gesagt, er habe als Bischof die ehrwürdigen, von den berühmten Vätern festgelegten Dogmen des apostolischen Glaubens mit neuen Licht erfüllt.[15] Das Epitaph von Deusdedit (615–618) bezeichnet dessen Pontifikat als *culmen apostolicum*[16], mit derselben Formulierung, die zur Zeit Coelestins, etwa zwei Jahrhunderte zuvor, für die Weiheinschrift des römischen *titulus* von S. Sabina geschaffen worden war.[17] Derselbe Begriff mit ebensolcher Bedeutung findet sich auf der Grabplatte für Bonifaz V. (619–625) und im 10. Jahrhundert für Sergius III. (904–911) und Benedikt VII. (974–983).[18] Von besonderer Bedeutung sind die Hinweise im Epitaph von Honorius I. (625–638), wonach er sich in der Leitung der *sedes apostolica* so verhielt wie ein Hirte, der seine Herde zu führen weiß.[19] Eine ähnliche Bestimmtheit wird Papst Agatho (678–681) bescheinigt: *sedis apostolicae foedera firma tenet.*[20] Ebenfalls auf die apostolische Herkunft des römischen Episkopats nimmt die Grabinschrift für Hadrian I. (772–795) Bezug, die von Karl dem Großen in Auftrag gegeben wurde und den Pontifex als *pastor apostolicus* definiert.[21] *Praesul apostolicus* wird hingegen im ausgehenden 9. Jahrhundert Papst Ma-

10 PL 96, 1215: *cuius (Petri) sedis in toto orbe terrarum primatu fungens, caput omnium Dei ecclesiarum constituta est, et quemadmodum beatus Petrus apostolus per Domini praeceptum regens ecclesiam, nihilo minus subsequenter et tenuit semper et retinet principatum.*

11 ICUR, IX 24833.

12 ICUR, II 4152.

13 ICUR, II 4153.

14 ICUR, II 4154.

15 ICUR, II 4155.

16 ICUR, II 4160.

17 Carletti 2008, 252–253.

18 IC II, 128–129, X (Bonifaz V.); 212, 59 (Sergius III.); Montini 1957, S. 161 (Benedikt VII.).

19 ICUR, II 4161.

20 IC II, 129, XI.

21 IC II, 226.

rinus I. (882–884) genannt.[22] In späterer Zeit ist die Verwendung des Begriffs *sedes apostolica* für die Grabinschriften von Stephan VI. (896–897) und Anastasius III. (911–913) dokumentiert.[23] Als Anspielung auf den petrinischen Ursprung der Kirche greift man Ende des 10. Jahrhunderts auf die Worte *cathedra apostolica* zur Bezeichnung des Pontifikats von Gregor V. (995–999) zurück.[24] Die Grabinschrift Silvesters II. (999–1003) schließlich verweist ausdrücklich auf den ersten Bischof der Stadt: Fünf Jahre lang übte er die Funktionen des heiligen Petrus aus (*vicem Petri*), bis der Tod ihn ereilte.[25]

Die *sedes apostolica* wird in den Briefen Gregors des Großen (590–604) im Zusammenhang mit der Verleihung des Palliums erwähnt. An Bischof Marinianus von Ravenna schreibt er beispielsweise: *Apostolicae sedis benivolentiae et antiquae consuetudinis ordine provocati fraternitati tuae, quam in Ravennati ecclesia gubernationis suscepisse constat officium, pallii usum pervidimus concedendum.*[26]

In Wirklichkeit gehen die ersten mit der Palliumverleihung einhergehenden Privilegien dem Pontifikat Gregors voraus. Ab dem Anfang des 6. Jahrhunderts wird das Pallium, »eine Art Stola, die während feierlicher Messen an bestimmten Festtagen über die anderen liturgischen Gewänder getragen wurde«[27], in der Tat zu einem bedeutenden Element der päpstlichen Autorität.[28]

Abgesehen von der Angabe im *Liber pontificalis* über Papst Markus (336) *constituit ut episcopus Hostiae* […] *palleum uteretur*[29] – vermutlich erst bei der Abfassung der Biographie entstanden[30] – sind andere Hinweise im *Liber* bedeutsamer: Felix IV. (526–530) soll Bonifaz das Pallium gegeben haben, um ihn als seinen Nachfolger zu designieren[31], und zum Zeichen der Absetzung von Papst Silverius 537 ließ Belisarius ihm das Pallium abnehmen.[32] Ende des 8. Jahrhunderts war im Triklinium Leos III. der

22 Montini 1957, S. 144.

23 IC II, 215, 81 (Stefan VI.); 217, 87 (Anastasius III.).

24 IC II, 217, 88 (Gregor V.).

25 Montini 1957, S. 165–168.

26 Greg. M. epist. V, 61 (CChr SL: CXL, 363).

27 Maccarrone 1960, S. 730; vgl. Berthod 2001, S. 15; Lobrichon 2003, S. 136–138. Die Herkunft und Verbreitung des Palliums erforschte auch Joseph Wilpert mit Bezug auf die vorhandene literarische und ikonographische Dokumentation (Wilpert 1898–1899, S. 13–35, S. 41–61); er betonte den Wert des Palliums als Element der Vereinigung zwischen der römischen Kirche und den Hauptkirchen des Orients und das Verhältnis zu den Metropolitensitzen (Wilpert 1898–1899, S. 57–58).

28 Weckwerth/Schrenk/Zanella 2015, S. 821–823 und S. 827–829.

29 LP I, 202.

30 Martí Bonet 1976, S. 9.

31 Es handelt sich um den *Praeceptum papae Felicis morientis*: […] *Cui etiam* […] *pallium tradidi* […] (LP I, 282). Vgl. Martí Bonet 1976, S. 9.

32 *Adhuc ea loquente, ingressus Iohannis, subdiaconus regionarius primae regionis, tulit pallium de collo eius et duxit in cubiculum; expolians eum induit eum vestem monachicam et abscondit eum* (LP I, 293). Vgl. Martí Bonet 1976, S. 9.

Abb. 1: Rom, Triklinium Leos III. Zeichnung von Alfonso Ciacconio. Petrus überreicht Leo III. das Pallium und Karl dem Großen die Insignien.

heilige Petrus auf der Kathedra dargestellt, wie er Leo III. das Pallium und Karl dem Großen die Insignien überreicht (Abb. 1).[33] Es handelte sich demnach um ein Kennzeichen des Papstamts, das jedoch – wie diverse Papstbriefe und später einige Wendungen im *Liber diurnus* belegen[34] – vom Papst aus verschiedenen Gründen an andere Bischöfe verliehen werden konnte als »Zeichen des ›Wohlwollens des apostolischen Stuhls‹ und Ausweis der Bischofswürde«[35]. Zunächst scheint nämlich die Verleihung des Palliums an die italienischen Bischöfe nicht notwendigerweise an ihre Funktion als Metropoliten geknüpft gewesen zu sein: Sie symbolisierte die Unterordnung der anderen Kirchen gegenüber der römischen Mutterkirche. So wird Bischof Secundus von Taormina das Pallium von Pelagius I. im Jahr 559 entzogen, weil sein Verhalten nicht dem Amt entsprach[36], während es ein Jahrzehnt später von Johannes III. an Petrus, Bischof von Ravenna, verliehen wird.[37] In den Briefen Gregors des Großen finden sich mehrere Hinweise auf die Konzession des Palliums:[38] Die Ehre wird nicht nur einigen sizilianischen Bischöfen (Syrakus[39], Messina[40] und Palermo[41]) sowie dem Bischof von Ravenna[42] zuteil (alle diese Diözesen gehörten zur römischen Jurisdiktion), sondern 593 auch Constantius, dem Bischof und Metropoliten von Mailand.[43] Gegenüber den Oberhirten von Ravenna bekräftigt Gregor, das Pallium dürfe nur vier Mal pro Jahr bei feierlichen Litaneien angelegt werden, und zwar an den Festtagen der Heiligen Johannes der Täufer, Peter und Paul sowie Apollinaris und am Jahrestag der Weihe des Ortsbischofs.[44]

Zur Zeit von Honorius I. besteht vermutlich noch der Brauch, den Bischöfen Siziliens das Pallium zu bewilligen[45]; außerdem verleiht der Papst selbst dieses Privileg an Primogenius, Bischof von Grado.[46] Dieser war ein römischer Subdiakon, und seine

33 Iacobini 1989, S. 189–196.

34 *Liber diurnus* XLV–XLVIII, S. 32–33.

35 Maccarrone 1960, S. 733.

36 Pelag. I epist. 41 (Gassò 1956, S. 114–115). Vgl. Martí Bonet 1976, S. 7.

37 Vgl. Greg. M. epist. III, 54 und Append. VII (CChr SL: CXL, 200–203 und 1100). Vgl. Martí Bonet 1976, S. 8.

38 Martí Bonet 1976, S. 11–22.

39 Greg. M. epist. VI, 18 (CChr SL: CXL, 388).

40 Greg. M. epist. VI, 8 (CChr SL: CXL, 377).

41 Greg. M. epist. XIII, 38 (CChr SL: CXL, 1041).

42 Greg. M. epist. III, 54; V, 11; V, 15; V, 61; VI, 31; IX, 168; Append. VI; Append. VII (CChr SL: CXL, 200–203; 277; 280–281; 363; 403–404; 726–727; 1097–1099; 1100).

43 Greg. M. epist. IV, 1 (CChr SL: CXL, 217–218).

44 Gregor d.Gr. gewährt Bischof Johannes (auf Zeit) und Bischof Marinianus (für immer) die Verwendung des Palliums bei feierlichen Litaneien (Greg. M. epist. V, 11 und V, 61: CChr SL: CXL, 277; 363).

45 Honor. I fragm. II (PL 80, S. 482–483). Vgl. Martí Bonet 1976, S. 57–58.

46 Honor. I epist. II (PL 80, S. 469–470). Vgl. Martí Bonet 1976, S. 58–59.

durch das Pallium aufgewertete Bischofswahl (628) sollte betonen, dass Grado der wahre, von Rom anerkannte Metropolitensitz von Aquileia war.[47]

In den folgenden Jahrhunderten, vermutlich seit der Karolingerzeit, setzte sich der Brauch der Verleihung des Palliums an die Metropoliten weitgehend durch; dies bedeutete nicht zuletzt, dass ihr Amt die Zustimmung des Papstes erforderte, wodurch das römische Papsttum wiederum als Spitze der gesamten Kirchenhierarchie auftrat.[48]

Um 400 schrieb Rufinus von Aquileia in der Übersetzung von Kanon 6 des Konzils von Nicäa, die Jurisdiktion des Bischofs von Rom könne nur über die Kirche des suburbikarischen Italiens ausgeübt werden: *Et ut apud Alexandriam, et in urbe Roma, vetusta consuetudo servetur, quia vel ille Aegypti, vel hic suburbicariarum Ecclesiarum sollicitudinem gerat.*[49] Es scheint, als habe Ende des 4./Anfang des 5. Jahrhunderts das Provinzensystem in Italien keinen richtigen Bezugspunkt in der kirchlichen Organisation dargestellt. Vorrangig waren andere Faktoren: die Unterteilung Italiens in *annonaria* und *suburbicaria*, das Prestige des jeweiligen Bischofssitzes und seiner Oberhirten und die politisch-institutionelle Rolle der Stadt.

Die Diözese Mailand

Während des Pontifikats von Damasus machte Ambrosius verschiedene Personen seines Vertrauens zu Bischöfen im annonarischen Italien. Die metropolitische Struktur konnte er dank seines persönlichen Ansehens und dank der wichtigen Rolle Mailands als Kaiserstadt durchsetzen. Ambrosius' Machtbereich entsprach dem Gebiet der *Italia annonaria* und nicht der weltlichen Provinz. Dort konnte er seine Vorrechte ausüben, also Provinzsynoden einberufen und Bischöfe weihen, auch in neu eingerichteten Diözesen.[50]

Die Liste der Bischöfe, die 451 (über ein halbes Jahrhundert nach Ambrosius' Tod) am Provinzkonzil von Mailand teilnahmen, dokumentiert eine starke Präsenz der Oberhirten aus der *provincia Liguria* und einiger Bischöfe aus der *Aemilia*, aber gleichzeitig das Fehlen von Vertretern derjenigen Städte, die früher eng mit der ambrosianischen Metropole verbunden waren (darunter Modena, Bologna und Imola).[51] Offenbar waren diese Bistümer in den Kontrollbereich der Kirche von Ravenna übergegangen,

47 Piussi 2000, S. 128.

48 Vgl. Martí Bonet 1976, S. 69–123.

49 Rufin. hist. 1, 6, 6 (PL 13, S. 475).

50 Alzati 1986; Alzati 2007; Alzati 2014, S. 916–923; vgl. auch Zangara 2000, S. 272–272, Anm. 33.

51 S. die *Epistula synodica* von Bischof Eusebius an Papst Leo d. Gr. (Leo M. *epist.* XCVII: PL 54, S. 945–950). Alzati 1986, S. 51–55; Marano 2010, S. 320–322; Cantino Wataghin 2013, S. 25.

deren metropolitische Autorität sich damals im Aufbau befand.[52] Dennoch, und trotz der Verlegung des Kaisersitzes nach Ravenna, hatte die Mailänder Kirche immer noch eine Vorrangstellung inne, was sich insbesondere an der Gestalt des Bischofs Eusebius[53] (Mitte 5. Jahrhundert) ablesen lässt.

Weitaus schwieriger stellte sich die Situation nach dem Umzug des Bischofs Honoratus (um 560–571) von Mailand nach Genua zur Zeit der Langobardeninvasion dar.[54] Diese Schwierigkeiten wurden offensichtlich in der päpstlichen Gewährung des Palliums an Bischof Constantius (593)[55] und im Einschreiten der Mailänder Kirche unter Gregor dem Großen während des Episkopats von Deusdedit.[56] In jenen Jahren hatte die Provinz sogar die Diözese Como verloren, die sich im Dreikapitelstreit für Aquileia entschieden hatte und deshalb in die Zuständigkeit des dortigen Metropoliten fiel.[57]

Zwar kam mit Johannes Bonus (641–659)[58] der Bischof von Mailand an seinen angestammten Sitz zurück, aber die metropolitische Provinz von Mailand nahm erst in der zweiten Hälfte des Jahrhunderts wieder Gestalt an, obwohl ihr Bischof das Recht auf Weihe des Oberhirten der Königsstadt Pavia an die römische Kirche verloren hatte.[59] In diesen Rahmen gehören die Episkopate von Mansuetus (672–681) und Benedikt (685–732), die sich wie Ambrosius in der ambrosianischen Basilika der Heiligen Gervasius und Protasius beisetzen ließen.[60] Zu Beginn des 8. Jahrhunderts scheiterte Benedikt allerdings im Streit mit Papst Konstantin I. (708–715) in seinem Bemühen, die Kirche von Pavia wieder in die Provinz Mailand zurückzuführen. Er pochte dabei auf das Recht jedes rechtmäßigen Metropoliten, den Suffraganbischof zu weihen.[61]

Ein deutlicher Beleg für den Aufschwung und die Vitalität der Mailänder Kirchenprovinz war das Episkopat des *sanctissimus archiepiscopus* Angilbert II. (824–859), der 842 ein Provinzkonzil in der ambrosianischen Basilika einberief.[62] Weitere Anzeichen dafür sind die Provinzkonzile von 860 bzw. 864 zur Zeit des Erzbischofs Tado (860–868).[63]

Die Bedeutung der Kirche von Mailand wurde von Bischof Anspert (868–881) weiter ausgebaut, insbesondere durch eine neuerliche Aufwertung des heiligen Ambrosius,

52 Zangara 2000, S. 273–275, S. 301–303; Savigni 2006, S. 49–52; Carlà 2010, S. 245–247.
53 Vgl. Anm. 51.
54 Alzati 2014, S. 929–933.
55 Greg. M. epist. IV, 1, anno 593 (CChr SL: CXL, 217–218).
56 Greg. M. epist. XII, 14, anno 602 (CChr SL: CXL, 988); XIII, 31, anno 603 (CChr SL: CXL, 1032).
57 Alzati 2014, S. 933 (mit Bibliografie).
58 Navoni 1990, S. 87–89; La Salvia 2000.
59 Alzati 2014, S. 933–935. Vgl. Lanzani 1995, S. 64–81.
60 Picard 1988, S. 84–85.
61 LP I, S. 391–392, und Alzati 2014, S. 935.
62 Navoni 1990, S. 102–104.
63 Navoni 1990, S. 105–106.

über den damals eine weitere Biographie verfasst wurde.[64] Auch Anspert wurde in der ambrosianischen Basilika beigesetzt; dort hatte er den Chorraum mit den Märtyrergräbern herrichten und ein Atrium bauen lassen, wie sein Epitaph belegt. Sein Streit mit Papst Johannes VIII. ist berühmt: Er hatte die Einberufung zu den päpstlichen Konzilen von 878 und 879 abgelehnt und wurde daraufhin exkommuniziert. Erst in seinem letzten Bischofsjahr (881) kam es zur Versöhnung.[65] Die Beziehungen zu Rom normalisierten sich unter seinem Nachfolger Anselm II. (882–896), und in der Folge unter Hilduin (931-936). Um seine Ernennung zu festigen, sandte dieser Raterius, den Bischof von Verona, nach Rom mit dem Auftrag, Johannes XI. um die Verleihung des Palliums zu bitten. Der Papst schickte daraufhin das Pallium nach Mailand – unter Umgehung der üblichen Praxis – und ersparte Hilduin den üblichen persönlichen Bittgang nach Rom.[66]

Die Bischöfe von Mailand übten das Metropolitenamt bis zur Zeit Ariberts (1018–1045) aus[67], also bis zum Wendepunkt durch die Kirchenreform.

Die Bischöfe von Rom und Ravenna

Gegen Mitte des 5. Jahrhunderts, mit dem Episkopat des Petrus Chrysologus zur Zeit Kaiser Valentinians III., begann die Kirche von Ravenna, wie schon angedeutet, eine metropolitische Autorität auszuüben. Aus dem *Sermo* des Chrysologus anlässlich der Weihe von Marcellinus in Voghenza lässt sich eine gewisse Unterstützung des laufenden Prozesses durch Papst (*decreto beati Petri, decreto principis christiani*)[68] und Kaiser ablesen. Wenig später berichtete Agnellus in seiner Biographie von Johannes I. (477–494) von einer Metropole, der 14 Diözesen unterstellt waren.[69]

Ein besonders wichtiger Zeitpunkt in der Geschichte des ravennatischen Bischofssitzes war der Amtsantritt Maximians (546–556), der mit dem Titel *archiepiscopus* ausgezeichnet wurde. Seine Ernennung entsprach dem Willen Justinians.[70] Wie Agnellus festhält, wurde er in Patras von Papst Vigilius geweiht; nach Erhalt des Palliums begab

64 Ambrosioni 2003, S. 234.

65 Ambrosioni 2003.

66 Picasso 1990, S. 146–147. Vgl. Martí Bonet 1976, S. 130.

67 Picasso 1990, S. 156–163.

68 Petr. Chrys. serm. 175: *Edicto Caesaris et pagani universorum Dominus obtemperaturus occurrit, et decreto beati Petri, decreto principis Christiani, servus adhuc aliquis irreverenter obsistit?* (PL 52, S. 656). Vgl. Zangara 2000, S. 298–304.

69 LPRav, 198 (CChr Continuatio Medievalis: 199): *usque in praesentem diem quattuordecim civitates cum episcopis sub Ravennae ecclesiae redactae sunt.*

70 S. Farioli Campanati 2005 zu Maximians Titel *archiepiscopus*. Carlà 2010, S. 257–261.

er sich nach Ravenna.[71] Im umfangreichen Bauprogramm, das Maximian zugeschrieben wird, ist vor allem die Vollendung der Kirche S. Apollinare in Classe von Bedeutung, die seine Vorgänger Ursicinus und Viktor begonnen hatten. Der Bau beherbergte die Reliquien des heiligen Apollinaris und war Teil eines größeren Programms zur Steigerung der lokalen Bischofstradition, die mit dem Namen des Heiligen verbunden war.[72] Maximian brachte angeblich auch den Bau der mit der bischöflichen Residenz verbundenen *Domus Tricoli* zum Abschluss: Deren Widmungsinschrift nennt zur Legitimierung die ganze Reihe der Bischöfe, die zu diesem Vorhaben beigetragen hatten; außerdem wurden sie in *imagines clipeatae* dargestellt.[73] Die Inschrift erinnert ebenfalls an Maximians Bedeutung als Bischof mit der Wendung *culmen apostolicum*, wenn auch »in der Form einer Tapinosis«[74].

Wie wir Agnellus' »stark anti-römisch geprägtem«[75] *Liber pontificalis* aus der ersten Hälfte des 9. Jahrhunderts entnehmen, verstärkte sich mit dem Ende der Herrschaft Justinians die Einmischung der römischen Päpste in die Wahl der ravennatischen Erzbischöfe: Der aus Rom stammende Johannes II. (578–595) wurde vermutlich von Pelagius II. ausgesucht.[76] Seitdem war die Basilika von S. Apollinare die Grablege der Oberhirten von Ravenna, quasi eine Nachahmung der schon über ein Jahrhundert währenden Tradition der Päpste, sich in St. Peter bestatten zu lassen.[77] Sein Nachfolger Bischof Marinian (595–um 606), der Mönch in S. Andrea am *Clivus Scauri* gewesen war, wurde in Rom von Gregor dem Großen geweiht.[78]

Erst gegen Mitte des 7. Jahrhunderts erhielt die Kirche von Ravenna einen höheren Rang dank der Bischöfe Maurus (644–673) und Reparatus (673–679), vor allem als 666 Kaiser Constans II. ihre Autokephalie bestätigte. In jenem Jahr sandte Bischof Maurus den Presbyter Reparatus nach Syrakus, wo Constans II. sich aufhielt, um die Unabhängigkeit Ravennas von Rom zu beantragen. Gregor, Exarch von Ravenna, befürwortete dieses Vorhaben und erläuterte in der Bittschrift, dass der Rang der Stadt als Metropo-

---

71 LPRav, 239 (CChr Continuatio Medievalis: 199): *Qui, excogitato consilio, iussit consecrari beatum Maximianum Polensem diaconum episcopum a Vigilio papa in civitate Patras aput Achaiam pridie Idus Octubris, ind. X, quinquies p. c. Basilii iunioris, anno nativitatis suae XLVIII, et dato pallio Ravennam misit.*

72 Rizzardi 2011, S. 146–165. Vgl. Carletti 2009, S. 339–340; Carlà 2010, S. 248–249.

73 LPRav, 243 (CChr Continuatio Medievalis: 199). Vgl. Cirelli 2008, S. 234; Carletti 2009, S. 340.

74 Carletti 2009, S. 340. Vgl. LPRav, 243 (CChr Continuatio Medievalis: 199): *Ipse autem factis propriis se non meruisse culmen apostolicum, sed pietate Dei.*

75 Savigni 1992, S. 331. Vgl. Brown 1990, S. 299; Mauskopf Deliyannis 2006, S. 10–11.

76 LPRav, 267 (CChr Continuatio Medievalis: 199): *Iste, ut dixi, Romae natus, ab ipsa sede hic missus doctrinam apostoli instanter praedicabat, et ut omnes a peccato se averterent.* An die römische Herkunft des Bischofs wird auch in der Weihinschrift der Kirche S. Severo in Classe erinnert (CIL, XI 301).

77 Picard 1988, S. 180–193.

78 LPRav, 268 (CChr Continuatio Medievalis: 199): *A beatissimo Gregorio Romae consecratus fuit et ab eo hic missus est.*

litensitz schon in einem Schreiben des Kaisers Valentinian III. verankert war; deshalb musste Ravenna von der römischen Jurisdiktion entbunden werden und sein Bischof das Recht haben, von drei Suffraganbischöfen geweiht zu werden und das Pallium vom oströmischen Kaiser zu erhalten.[79] Im römischen *Liber pontificalis* findet die Autokephalie Ravennas in der Vita des zeitgenössischen Papst Vitalianus (657–672) keine Erwähnung, und in der Tat intervenierte er nicht, im Gegenteil: Er widersetzte sich dieser Entscheidung erst beim Tod von Constans II. im Jahr 668 und beorderte Maurus zwei Mal nach Rom. Dieser jedoch leistete dem päpstlichen Befehl keine Folge.[80]

Die *iussio* von Constans II. oder besser die 675 von Kaiser Konstantin IV. Pogonatus gewährte Steuerfreistellung ist im berühmten Mosaik von S. Apollinare in Classe verewigt: Es zeigt Konstantin IV. mit seinen Brüdern Heraclius und Tiberius bei der Überreichung der *privilegia* an Bischof Reparatus (673–679), der von seinem Vorgänger Maurus begleitet wird (Abb. 2).[81] Die Trennung zwischen den beiden Kirchen endete erst während der Amtszeit von Reparatus' Nachfolger Theodor (679–693), der sich bei der römischen Synode von 680 dem Papst unterwarf.[82]

Eine neue Phase in der Konkurrenz zwischen Rom und Ravenna begann nach der endgültigen Ausweisung des Exarchen (751) durch den Langobardenkönig Aistulf, der eine Wiederherstellung der Autokephalie forderte.[83] Die Kirche von Rom bekräftigte jedoch mehrfach ihre Jurisdiktion über Ravenna und sein Umland. Nach der *promissio* von 774, mit der Karl der Große dem Papst die ursprüngliche Jurisdiktion über das Exarchat bestätigte, blieb unter Papst Hadrian I. (772–795) das Verhältnis zwischen Rom und Ravenna gespannt.[84] Belege dafür finden wir noch aus dem Pontifikat Leos III. (795–816), der 815 das Dach der Basilika S. Apollinare in Classe erneuern ließ, um die päpstliche Autorität über die Stadt zum Ausdruck zu bringen.[85] Den Ansprüchen der römischen Kirche widersetzte sich wiederum Bischof Georg von Ravenna (835–846), der den Versuch unternahm, König Lothars Unterstützung für die Wiederherstellung der Autokephalie seiner Kirche zu gewinnen.[86]

Nach Mitte des 9. Jahrhunderts wiesen die Bischöfe von Rom, insbesondere Nikolaus I. (858–867) und Johannes VIII. (872–882), immer wieder auf den Primat des apostolischen Stuhls hin. Das Konzil von 860–861 in Rom verstärkte indes den Gegensatz zwischen Johannes, Erzbischof von Ravenna, und dem Papst. Nach der Exkommunika-

79 Corsi 1983, S. 184–185; Pilara 2009, S. 386; Mauskopf Deliyannis 2010, S. 283–284.

80 Pilara 2009, S. 386–187.

81 Rizzardi 2011, S. 157–158; Cosentino 2014.

82 Pilara 2009, S. 397.

83 Savigni 1992, S. 331–332.

84 Savigni 1992, S. 336–340.

85 LPRav, 349 (CChr Continuatio Medievalis: 199). Vgl. Brown 1990, S. 302.

86 Savigni 1992, S. 344. Vgl. Scaravelli 2000, S. 344–345.

Abb. 2: Ravenna, S. Apollinare in Classe. Die Übergabe der Privilegien an Bischof Reparatus.

tion durch Nikolaus I., die wahrscheinlich auf doktrinalen Meinungsverschiedenheiten beruhte, wurde Johannes zu einem Eid gezwungen, wonach er den Forderungen des apostolischen Stuhls nachkommen würde: jedes Jahr nach Rom zu reisen und die Suffraganbischöfe erst nach Erhalt der päpstlichen *consecrandi licentia* zu weihen.[87]

Wenige Jahre später (877) wurde bei dem von Johannes VIII. einberufenen Konzil von Ravenna festgelegt, dass jeder Metropolit innerhalb von drei Monaten nach seiner Weihe dem Papst sein Treuebekenntnis zukommen lassen und das Pallium erbitten musste. Die Anlässe, zu denen es getragen werden konnte, waren von der *sedes apostolica* bestimmt, wie schon Gregor der Große bestätigt hatte.[88] Diese Anweisungen allgemeiner Art waren auch auf die Situation in Ravenna anzuwenden, wie die nachfolgenden Maßnahmen von Johannes VIII. hinreichend beweisen: Bischof Romanus wurde aufgefordert, sich zusammen mit seinen Suffraganbischöfen unverzüglich (*omni mora postposita*) nach Rom zu begeben, und er musste die Entscheidung des Papstes hinsichtlich der Bischofsernennungen für Sarsina und Faenza hinnehmen.[89]

Noch in ottonischer Zeit (998) verlieh Papst Gregor V. das Pallium an Gerbert von Aurillac, Bischof von Ravenna und künftiger Papst Silvester II. (999–1003), zum »Gebrauch nur zu den vorgesehenen Zeiten und Anlässen«[90].

Das suburbikarische Italien

In Süditalien hingegen konnte sich Rom ohne größere Widerstände durchsetzen und behielt die Kontrolle über die suburbikarischen Diözesen von der Mitte des 5. bis zum 6. Jahrhundert. Dies belegen die päpstlichen Briefsammlungen und die Synoden, die anlässlich des Weihetags des Papstes oder des Festtags der Heiligen Peter und Paul einberufen wurden und an denen die Bischöfe aus Süditalien teilnahmen.[91] In seiner Eigenschaft als Metropolit war der Bischof von Rom für die Ernennung der Bischöfe[92] und die Besetzung der Bischofssitze zuständig.

Wie man weiß, verfügte Papst Gelasius im ausgehenden 5. Jahrhundert eine eher sakramentale als territoriale Aufteilung, vor allem in Folge der Kontroversen zwischen benachbarten Bischöfen über die Grenzen ihrer Diözesen.[93] Dies war das Ergebnis der

87 Savigni 1992, S. 345–347; Bougard 2000, S. 7–9.
88 Martí Bonet 1976, S. 122–123; Savigni 1992, S. 349.
89 Savigni 1992, S. 350–352.
90 Savigni 1992, S. 359; Huschner 2000, S. 110. Vgl. Martí Bonet 1976, S. 130.
91 Pietri 1976, S. 917.
92 Diese Aufgabe ist im *Liber Pontificalis* immer wieder genannt: *Hic fecit … episcopos per diversa loca* (gefolgt von der Anzahl der Weihen).
93 Lauwers 2008, S. 31–32; Otranto 2009, S. 128–134; Ermini Pani 2013, S. 4–5; Nuzzo (im Druck).

Schaffung von Bischofssitzen, deren Anzahl – vor allem im 5. Jahrhundert – immer weiter zunahm, allerdings ohne jede systematische Planung. Die Briefsammlung beweist, dass es zu Gelasius' Zeit nicht an Anlässen für eine päpstliche Intervention zur Lösung von Problemen fehlte, die vom Mangel an Bischöfen und Presbytern in den diversen Diözesen verursacht waren.[94] Es kam immer häufiger zu Situationen – den späteren Briefen Gregors des Großen nach zu urteilen – wie Sedisvakanz und gravierende Finanzprobleme verschiedener Diözesen.

In der Tat scheint die Neuorganisation der Bistümer eines der Hauptanliegen Gregors des Großen im ausgehenden 6. Jahrhundert gewesen zu sein.[95] Seinen Briefen ist zu entnehmen, dass er im Falle einer Sedisvakanz nur selten zwei benachbarte Sitze unter die Leitung eines einzigen Bischofs stellte[96] und meistens als vorläufige Lösung die Ernennung von Visitatoren vorschlug[97], die bis zur Bischofswahl von höchst angesehenen Männern im Amt bleiben sollten.[98] Sofort nach ihrer Ernennung sollten die neuen Bischöfe einen Antrittsbesuch beim Papst machen.[99] Von einer Vakanz waren auch zahlreiche süditalienische Diözesen betroffen, und in der Tat befassten sich die meisten von Gregors juristischen Interventionen mit der Ernennung neuer Bischöfe. Gregors *Registrum* beweist den großen Einsatz dieses Papstes zum Erhalt der metropolitischen Vorrechte in einer Zeit, da neue politische Machtverhältnisse und doktrinale Differenzen die spätantike Kirchenstruktur Italiens endgültig in Unordnung gebracht hatten.

Die Bistumsgliederung in Süditalien, für deren Aufrechterhaltung Gregor sich engagiert hatte, änderte sich im Laufe des 7. Jahrhunderts grundlegend, allerdings: »Die Nicht-Erwähnung zahlreicher Bischofssitze in der äußerst kargen Dokumentation des 7.–8. Jahrhunderts bedeutet nicht notwendigerweise, dass sie aufgehoben wurden, vor allem wenn sie in Akten aus dem 9. Jahrhundert wieder auftreten«.[100] Obwohl es im *Liber pontificalis* für diese Zeit an Hinweisen auf den Papst als Metropoliten fehlt, wurde doch nach wie vor am Ende der meisten Papstviten die Anzahl der Bischofsweihen vermerkt.

94 Nuzzo (im Druck).

95 Boesch Gajano 2000, S. 558; Martin 2006, S. 241–242; Boesch Gajano 2014, S. 139–140.

96 S. Greg. M., epist. I, 8; II, 37, 42; III, 20; VI, 9 (CChr SL: CXL, 10; 121–122, 130–131; 165–166; 377–378).

97 S. Greg. M., epist. I, 15, 51; II, 9, 10, 14, 22, 23, 31, 32, 35; III, 13, 24; V, 13, 21, 48; VI, 21; VII, 16; IX, 60, 81, 100, 185; XI, 3 (CChr SL: CXL, 15, 64–65; 96–97, 100–101, 108–109, 117–119, 120; 159–160, 169–170; 279, 289, 341–342; 391–392; 467; 617, 635, 652–653, 741; 861).

98 S. Greg. M., epist. I, 55, 58, 78; II, 3, 33; III, 15, 35; IV, 39; V, 9, 22, 24; VII, 39; IX, 82, 101, 140, 141, 143, 167, 186; X, 19; XII, 4; XIII, 18; XIV, 11 (CChr SL: CXL, 67–69, 86; 91–92, 119; 162, 180–181; 260–261; 275–276, 290–291; 503; 636, 653, 691–695; 725–726, 742; 848–849; 972; 1018–1019; 1080–1081).

99 S. Greg. M., epist. IX, 139; X, 6, 7 (CChr SL: CXL, 690–691; 832–833).

100 Vitolo 1990, S. 85. Vgl. auch Vitolo 1999, S. 430–431.

Es scheint daher, als seien die Kirchen in Süditalien (mit Ausnahme derer im byzantinischen Territorium) noch bis Mitte des 10. Jahrhunderts vom römischen Bischofssitz abhängig gewesen und als habe der Papst, in seiner Eigenschaft als Metropolit, sein Recht, die Oberhirten dieser Bistümer zu weihen, beibehalten.[101]

Die neue Bistumsorganisation im Süden Italiens strukturierte sich mit der Zeit um die kirchlichen Zentren von Benevent, Capua und Salerno, die in der zweiten Hälfte des 10. Jahrhunderts zu Metropolitensitzen wurden.[102] Denselben Titel verliehen die Päpste in dieser Zeit auch den Diözesen von Neapel, Amalfi und Sorrent.[103]

Am Ende des 10. Jahrhunderts sprengte die Einsetzung von Metropoliten in Süditalien zwar die suburbikarische Kirchenprovinz, gleichzeitig wurde aber dadurch die Autorität der Kirche von Rom gefestigt.[104] Der von mindestens drei Suffraganbischöfen geweihte Erzbischof musste innerhalb von drei Monaten das Pallium vom Papst erbitten und in regelmäßigen Abständen dem Pontifex einen *ad limina*-Besuch abstatten.[105] Die Einsetzung neuer Metropoliten sollte außerdem die süditalienischen Bistümer gegen die Kontrolle des Patriarchats von Konstantinopel abschirmen: Im selben Zeitraum hatte dieses nämlich den Oberhirten von Reggio, Otranto, S. Severina, Tarent, Bari, Canosa und Trani den Rang und Titel eines Erzbischofs zuerkannt.[106]

Aufgrund der territorialen Umstrukturierung durch die Normannen erfuhr auch die Bistumsgliederung tiefgreifende Veränderungen. Die Eidesformel, die Robert Guiscard 1059 in Melfi vor Papst Nikolaus II. sprach, verpflichtete den Normannenfürsten, »Dei gratia et Sancti Petri dux Apuliae et Calabriae«, alle Kirchen in seinem Herrschaftsbereich der päpstlichen *potestas* zu unterstellen.[107]

Wenige Jahrzehnte später schrieb Gregor VII. in den *Dictatus papae* (1075–1076) fest, der Bischof von Rom sei der einzige, der als ›universal‹ bezeichnet werden konnte, und nur er habe u. a. das Recht, Bischöfe ab- und wieder einzusetzen und die Diözesangliederung umzugestalten.[108] Damit läutete er in der Organisation der kirchlichen Institutionen eine neue Phase ein[109] und untermauerte zugleich, was die römische Kirche in Petrus' Namen seit jeher vertrat.

101 Vitolo 1990, S. 116; Fonseca 2016, S. 21–27.

102 Kamp 1977, S. 165–166; Fonseca 1987, S. 13–20; Vitolo 1990, S. 116–119; Fonseca 1996, S. 3–17; Spinelli 1996; Ramseyer 2006, S. 125–145 (besonders für Salerno); Barone 2014, S. 194; Fonseca 2016, S. 24–27.

103 Vitolo 1990, S. 117.

104 Fonseca 2016, S. 27.

105 Vitolo 1990, S. 117. Vgl. Martí Bonet 1976, S. 131–138.

106 Vitolo 1990, S. 117; Vitolo 1996, S. 114.

107 Fonseca 1987, S. 79–80.

108 Greg. VII Registrum, Dict. Papae II und VII (MGH. Epistolae selectae, II, I, Berolini 1955², hg. von Erich Caspar, S. 202–203).

109 Capitani 2000; Capitani 2015, S. 31–88; Curzel 2015, S. 74–76; Mazel 2015, bes. S. 58–61.

Bibliographie

Alzati 1986 Cesari Alzati: Metropoli e sedi episcopali fra tarda antichità e alto medioevo, in: Chiesa e società. Appunti per una storia delle diocesi lombarde. Storia religiosa della Lombardia, I, Brescia 1986, S. 47–77.

Alzati 2007 Cesare Alzati: L'attività conciliare in ambito ecclesiastico milanese nel contesto dell'Italia Annonaria tra tarda antichità e alto Medioevo, in: Albenga città episcopale. Tempi e dinamiche della cristianizzazione tra Liguria di Ponente e Provenza. Convegno internazionale e tavola rotonda, Albenga, 21.–23.9.2006 (Istituto internazionale di studi liguri. Atti dei convegni: XII), hg. von Mario Marcenaro, Genova/Albenga 2007, S. 231–266.

Alzati 2014 Cesare Alzati: La Chiesa di Milano tra contesto italico ed ecumene al tramonto della tarda antichità, in: Chiese locali e chiese regionali nell'alto medioevo. LXI Settimana di studio della Fondazione Centro Italiano di studi sull'alto medioevo (Spoleto, 4.–9.4.2013), Spoleto 2014, S. 913–948.

Ambrosioni 2003 Annamaria Ambrosioni: «Atria vicinas struxit et ante fores». Note in margine a un'epigrafe del IX secolo, in: A. Ambrosioni, Milano, papato e impero in età medievale. Raccolta di studi, hg. von Maria Pia Alberzoni und Alfredo Lucioni, Mailand 2003, S. 229–244.

Barone 2014 Giulia Barone: La chiesa di Roma: tradizioni, realtà, orizzonti (secoli VIII–XI), in: Chiese locali e chiese regionali nell'alto medioevo. LXI Settimana di studio della Fondazione Centro Italiano di studi sull'alto medioevo (Spoleto, 4.–9.4.2013), Spoleto 2014, S. 189–225.

Berthod 2001 Bernard Berthod: Le pallium, insigne des évêques d'Orient et d'Occident, in: Bulletin du Centre international d'étude des textiles anciens 78, 2001, S. 15–25.

Boesch Gajano 2000 Sofia Boesch Gajano: Gregorio I, santo, in: Enciclopedia dei Papi, Bd. I, Rom 2000, S. 546–574.

Boesch Gajano 2014 Sofia Boesch Gajano: Gregorio Magno: primato, azione pastorale, esercizio del potere, in: Chiese locali e chiese regionali nell'alto medioevo. LXI Settimana di studio della Fondazione Centro Italiano di studi sull'alto medioevo (Spoleto, 4.–9.4.2013), Spoleto 2014, S. 117–155.

Bougard 2000 François Bougard: Niccolò I, santo, in: Enciclopedia dei Papi, Bd. II, Rom 2000, S. 1–22.

Brown 1990 Thomas S. Brown: Louis the Pious and the Papacy, a Ravenna Perspective, in: Charlemagne's Heir, New Perspectives on the Reign of Louis the Pious (814–840), hg. von Peter Godman und Roger Collins, Oxford 1990, S. 297–308.

Cantino Wataghin 2013 Gisella Cantino Wataghin: Vescovi e territorio nel Piemonte meridionale tardoantico: una prospettiva archeologica, in: Il viaggio della fede. La cristianizzazione del Piemonte meridionale tra IV e VIII secolo. Atti del convegno (Cherasco, Bra, Alba, 10.–12.12.2010), hg. von Silvia Lusuardi Siena, Edoardo Gautier di Confiengo und Bruno Taricco, Alba/Bra/Cherasco 2013, S. 23–51.

Capitani 2000 Ovidio Capitani: Gregorio VII, santo, in: Enciclopedia dei Papi, Bd. II, Rom 2000, S. 188–212.

Capitani 2015 Ovidio Capitani: Gregorio VII: il papa epitome della Chiesa di Roma, hg. von Berardo Pio, Spoleto 2015.

Carlà 2010 Filippo Carlà: Milan, Ravenna, Rome: Some Reflections on the Cult of the Saints and on Civil Politics in Late Antique Italy, in: Rivista di Storia e Letteratura Religiosa 46, 2010, S. 197–272.

Carletti 2000 Carlo Carletti: Damaso I, santo, in: Enciclopedia dei Papi, Bd. I, Rom 2000, S. 349–372.

Carletti 2008 Carlo Carletti: Epigrafia dei cristiani in Occidente dal III al VII secolo. Ideologia e prassi, Bari 2008.

Carletti 2009 Carlo Carletti: Epigrafia episcopale di Ravenna nei secoli V e VI. Note preliminari, in: Ideologia e cultura artistica tra Adriatico e Mediterraneo orientale (IV–X secolo). Il ruolo dell'autorità ecclesiastica alla luce di nuovi scavi e ricerche. Atti del Convegno Internazionale (Bologna-Ravenna, 26.–29.11.2007), hg. von Raffaella Farioli Campanati et al., Bologna 2009, S. 333–344.

Cavalcanti 2000 Elena Cavalcanti: Siricio, santo, in: Enciclopedia dei Papi, Bd. I, Rom 2000, S. 375–381.

Cirelli 2008 Enrico Cirelli: Ravenna: archeologia di una città, Florenz 2008.

Corsi 1983 Pasquale Corsi: La spedizione italiana di Costante II, Bologna 1983.

Cosentino 2014 Salvatore Cosentino: Constans II, Ravenna's Autocephaly and the Panel of the Privileges in St. Apollinare in Classe: A Reappraisal, in: Aureus. Volume dedicated to Professor Evangelos K. Chrysos, hg. von Taxiarchis G. Kolias und Konstantinos G. Pitsakis, Athen 2014, S. 153–169.

Curzel 2015 Emanuele Curzel: Vescovi e diocesi in Italia prima del secolo XII. Sedi, spazi, profili, in: La diocesi di Bobbio. Formazione e sviluppi di un'istituzione millenaria, hg. von Eleonora Destefanis und Paola Guglielmotti, Florenz 2015, S. 69–93.

Di Berardino 2006 Angelo Di Berardino: I Canoni dei Concili della Chiesa antica, I. I Concili greci (Studia Ephemeridis Augustinianum, 95), Rom 2006.

Di Berardino 2014 Angelo Di Berardino: Organizzazione delle comunità agli inizi del IV secolo, in: Costantino il Grande alle radici dell'Europa. Atti del Convegno Internazionale di Studio in occasione del 1700° anniversario della Battaglia di Ponte Milvio e della conversione di Costantino, hg. von Enrico Dal Covolo und Giulia Sfameni Gasparro, Vatikanstadt 2014, S. 79–104.

Ermini Pani 2013 Letizia Ermini Pani: Episcopus, civitas, territorium, in: Episcopus, Civitas, Territorium. Acta XV Congressus Internationalis Archaeologiae Christianae (Toledo, 8–12.9.2008) (Studi di antichità Cristiana, 65), hg. von Olof Brandt et al., Vatikanstadt 2013, S. 1–15.

Farioli Campanati 2005 Raffaella Farioli Campanati: Per la datazione della Cattedra di Massimiano e dell'Ambone di Agnello, in: Studi in memoria di Patrizia Angiolini Martinelli, hg. von Silvia Pasi, Bologna 2005, S. 165–168.

Fonseca 1987 Cosimo Damiano Fonseca: Particolarismo istituzionale e organizzazione ecclesiastica del mezzogiorno medioevale, Galatina 1987.

Fonseca 1996 Cosimo Damiano Fonseca: Longobardia e Longobardi nell'Italia meridionale: le istituzioni ecclesiastiche, in: Longobardia e Longobardi nell'Italia meridionale: le istituzioni ecclesiastiche. Atti del secondo Convegno internazionale di studi promosso dal Centro di cultura dell'Università cattolica del Sacro Cuore (Benevent, 29.–31.5.1992), hg. von Giancarlo Andenna und Giorgio Picasso, Mailand 1996, S. 3–17.

Fonseca 2016 Cosimo Damiano Fonseca: Gli ordinamenti territoriali ecclesiastici nell'antica Diocesi suburbicaria e la loro evoluzione in età medievale, in: Studi medievali 3ª ser., LVII, 2016, S. 1–32.

Giardina 1986 Andrea Giardina: Le due Italie nella forma tarda dell'impero, in: Società romana e impero tardoantico. I. Istituzioni, ceti, economie, hg. von Andrea Giardina, Bari 1986, S. 1–30.

Huschner 2000 Wolfgang Huschner: Gregorio V, in: Enciclopedia dei Papi, Bd. II, Rom 2000, S. 107–111.

Iacobini 1989 Antonio Iacobini: Il mosaico del Triclinio Lateranense, in: Fragmenta Picta. Affreschi e mosaici staccati del Medioevo Romano (Ausstellung Rom, Castel Sant'Angelo 15.12.1989–18.2.1990), hg. von Maria Andaloro et al., Rom 1989, S. 189–196.

Kamp 1977 Norbert Kamp: Vescovi e diocesi nell'Italia meridionale nel passaggio dalla dominazione bizantina allo Stato normanno, in: Il passaggio dal dominio bizantino allo Stato normanno nell'Italia meridionale. Atti del secondo Convegno di studi (Taranto-Mottola, 31.10.–4.11.1973), hg. von Cosimo Damiano Fonseca, Taranto 1977, S. 165–187.

Lanzani 1995 Vittorio Lanzani: L'età longobarda, in: Diocesi di Pavia, hg. von Adriano Caprioli, Antonio Rimoldi und Luciano Vaccaro, Brescia 1995, S. 45–84.

La Salvia 2000 Vasco La Salvia: Giovanni (Giovanni Bono, Giovanni il Buono), santo, in: Dizionario biografico degli italiani, 55, Rom 2000, S. 512–514.

Lauwers 2008 Michel Lauwers: Territorium non facere diocesim. Conflits, limites et représentation territoriale du diocèse V[e]–XIIIe siècle, in: L'espace du diocèse: genèse d'un territoire dans l'Occident médiéval, V[e]–XIIIe siècle. Actes de deux journées d'étude (Rennes, 15.5.2004 u. 9.4.2005), hg. von Florian Mazel, Rennes 2008, S. 23–65.

Liber diurnus 1889 Liber diurnus Romanorum Pontificum ex unico codice Vaticano, hg. von Theodor von Sickel, Vindobonae 1889.

Liebeschuetz 2001 John H. W. G. Liebeschuetz: The Decline and Fall of the Roman City, Oxford 2001.

Liebeschuetz 2005 John H. W. G. Liebeschuetz: From Synodal Petition to Imperial Constitution: Ambrose, epistula extra collectionem 7 and Collectio avellana 13, in: Atti dell'Accademia Romanistica Costantiniana. XV Convegno Internazionale in onore di Carlo Castello (Perugia-Spello, 8.–10.10.2001), Neapel 2005, S. 27–36.

Lobrichon 2003 Guy Lobrichon: Le vêtement liturgique des évêques au IXe siècle, in: Costume et société dans l'Antiquité et le haut Moyen Age, zusammengestellt von François Chausson und Hervé Inglebert, Paris 2003, S. 129–141.

Maccarrone 1960 Michele Maccarrone: La dottrina del Primato papale dal IV all'VIII secolo nelle relazioni con le Chiese occidentali, in: Le Chiese nei regni dell'Europa occidentale e i loro rapporti con Roma sino all'800. VII Settimana di studio del Centro Italiano di studi sull'alto medioevo (Spoleto, 7.–13.4.1959), Spoleto 1960, S. 633–742.

Marano 2010 Yuri Marano: L'edilizia cristiana in Italia settentrionale nel V secolo: la testimonianza dei complessi episcopali, in: Le trasformazioni del V secolo. L'Italia. I barbari e l'Occidente romano. Atti del Seminario di Poggibonsi (18.–20.10.2007), hg. von Paolo Delogu und Stefano Gasparri, Turnhout 2010, S. 285–341.

Martí Bonet 1976 José Martí Bonet: Roma y las Iglesias particulares en la concesión del palio al los obispos y arzobispos de occidente. Año 513–1143, Barcelona 1976.

Martin 2006 Jean-Marie Martin: Grégoire le Grand et l'Italie, in: Histoire et culture dans l'Italie byzantine. Acquis et nouvelles recherches (Collection de l'École française de Rome, 363), hg. von André Jacob, Jean-Marie Martin und Ghislaine Noyé, Rom 2006, S. 240–278.

Mauskopf Deliyannis 2006 Deborah Mauskopf Deliyannis: Introduction, in: Agnelli Ravennatis, Liber Pontificalis Ecclesiae Ravennatis (Corpus christianorum. Continuatio Medievalis, 199), hg. von Deborah Mauskopf Deliyannis, Turnhout 2006, S. 7–121.

Mauskopf Deliyannis 2010 Deborah Mauskopf Deliyannis: Ravenna in Late Antiquity, New York 2010.

Mazel 2015 Florian Mazel: Diocèse et territoire: enjeux historiographiques, questions de méthode et problématique historique dans la recherche française, in: La diocesi di Bobbio. Formazione e sviluppi di un'istituzione millenaria, hg. von Eleonora Destefanis und Paola Guglielmotti, Florenz 2015, S. 47–68.

Montini 1957 Renzo U. Montini: Le tombe dei Papi, Rom 1957.

Navoni 1990 Marco Navoni: Dai Longobardi ai Carolingi, in: Diocesi di Milano, hg. von Adriano Caprioli, Antonio Rimoldi und Luciano Vaccaro, Brescia 1990, S. 83–121.

Nuzzo 2015 Donatella Nuzzo: L'organizzazione delle Chiese nell'Italia tardo antica tra isole e terraferma, in: Isole e terraferma nel primo cristianesimo. Identità locale ed interscambi culturali, religiosi e produttivi. Atti dell'XI Congresso Nazionale di Archeologia Cristiana (Cagliari-Sant'Antioco, 23.–27.9.2014), hg. von Rossana Martorelli, Antonio Piras und Pier Giorgio Spanu, Cagliari 2015, S. 49–62.

Nuzzo [im Druck] Donatella Nuzzo: Roma e l'organizzazione delle Chiese dell'Italia suburbicaria da Damaso a Gregorio Magno, in: Costellazioni geo-ecclesiali da Costantino a Giustiniano: dalle chiese 'principali' alle chiese patriarcali. XLIII Incontro di studiosi dell'antichità cristiana (Rom, 7.–9.5.2015) [im Druck].

Otranto 2009 Giorgio Otranto: Per una storia dell'Italia tardoantica cristiana, Bari 2009.

Otranto 2014 Giorgio Otranto: Cristianizzazione del territorio, comunità locali e culti fino a Gregorio Magno fra sviluppi spontanei e spinte centralizzatrici, in: Chiese locali e chiese regionali nell'alto medioevo. LXI Settimana di studio della Fondazione

Centro Italiano di studi sull'alto medioevo (Spoleto, 4.–9.4.2013), Spoleto 2014, S. 51–112.

Perrin 2010 Michel-Yves Perrin: La «grande chiesa» dall'impero pagano all'impero cristiano, in: Storia d'Europa e del Mediterraneo. I. Il mondo antico. III. L'ecumene romana. VII. L'impero tardoantico, hg. von Giusto Traina, Rom 2010, S. 697–749.

Picard 1988 Jean-Charles Picard: Le souvenir des évêques. Sépultures, listes épiscopales et culte des évêques en Italie du Nord des origines au Xe siècle (Bibliothèque des Écoles françaises d'Athènes et de Rome, 268), Rom 1988.

Picasso 1990 Giorgio Picasso: La chiesa vescovile: dal crollo dell'impero carolingio all'età di Ariberto (882–1045), in: Diocesi di Milano, hg. von Adriano Caprioli, Antonio Rimoldi und Luciano Vaccaro, Brescia 1990, S. 143–166.

Pietri 1976 Charles Pietri: Roma christiana. Recherches sur l'église de Rome, son organisation, sa politique, son idéologie de Miltiade à Sixte III (311–440) (Bibliothèque des Écoles françaises d'Athènes et de Rome, 224), Rom 1976.

Pietri 1995 Luce Pietri: Une nouvelle chrétienté. Introduction, in: Histoire du christianisme des origines à nos jours. II. Naissance d'une chrétienté, hg. von Charles Pietri und Luce Pietri, Paris 1995, S. 553–555.

Pilara 2009 Gianluca Pilara: Mauro, in: Dizionario Biografico degli Italiani, Rom 2009, S. 385–387.

Piussi 2000 Sandro Piussi: Da Attila ai Longobardi, in: Patriarchi: quindici secoli di civiltà fra l'Adriatico e l'Europa centrale, hg. von Sergio Tavano und Giuseppe Bergamini, Mailand 2000, S. 125–129.

Porena 2010 Pierfrancesco Porena: L'amministrazione tardoantica, in: Storia d'Europa e del Mediterraneo. I. Il mondo antico. III. L'ecumene romana. VII. L'impero tardoantico, hg. von Giusto Traina, Rom 2010, S. 525–600.

Ramseyer 2006 Valerie Ramseyer: The Transformation of a Religious Landscape. Medieval Southern Italy, 850–1150, Ithaca 2006.

Rizzardi 2011 Clementina Rizzardi: Il mosaico a Ravenna. Ideologia e arte, Bologna 2011.

Ronzani 2014 Mauro Ronzani: L'organizzazione spaziale della cura d'anime e la rete delle chiese (secoli V–IX), in: Chiese locali e chiese regionali nell'alto medioevo. LXI Settimana di studio della Fondazione Centro Italiano di studi sull'alto medioevo (Spoleto, 4.–9.4.2013), Spoleto 2014, S. 537–561.

Savigni 1992 Raffaele Savigni: I papi e Ravenna. Dalla caduta dell'Esarcato alla fine del secolo X, in: Storia di Ravenna, II, 2, Dall'età bizantina all'età ottoniana. Ecclesiologia, cultura e arte, hg. von Antonio Carile, Venedig 1992, S. 331–368.

Savigni 2006 Raffaele Savigni: Vescovi e arcivescovi, in: Santi, banchieri, re: Ravenna e Classe nel VI secolo. San Severo il tempio ritrovato (Ausstellung Ravenna, Complesso di San Nicolò 4.3.–8.10.2006), hg. von Carlo Bertelli und Andrea Augenti, Mailand 2006, S. 49–52.

Scaravelli 2000 Irene Scaravelli: Giorgio, in: Dizionario biografico degli italiani, 55, Rom 2000, S. 344–345.

Spinelli 1996 Giovanni Spinelli: Il papato e la riorganizzazione ecclesiastica della Longobardia meridionale, in: Longobardia e Longobardi nell'Italia meridionale: le istituzioni ecclesiastiche. Atti del secondo Convegno internazionale di studi promosso dal Centro di cultura dell'Università cattolica del Sacro Cuore (Benevent, 29.–31.5.1992), hg. von Giancarlo Andenna und Giorgio Picasso, Mailand 1996, S. 19–42.

Vitolo 1990 Giovanni Vitolo: Vescovi e diocesi, in: Storia del Mezzogiorno III, Neapel 1990, S. 75–151.

Vitolo 1996 Giovanni Vitolo: L'organizzazione della cura d'anime nell'Italia meridionale longobarda, in: Longobardia e Longobardi nell'Italia meridionale: le istituzioni ecclesiastiche. Atti del secondo Convegno internazionale di studi promosso dal Centro di cultura dell'Università cattolica del Sacro Cuore (Benevent, 29.–31.5.1992), hg. von Giancarlo Andenna und Giorgio Picasso, Mailand 1996, S. 101–147.

Vitolo 1999 Giovanni Vitolo: Vescovi e diocesi nel Mezzogiorno medievale: lo stato delle ricerche, in: Munera parva. Studi in onore di Boris Ulianich, hg. von Gennaro Luongo, Neapel 1999, Bd. I, S. 427–441.

Weckwerth/Schrenk/Zanella 2015 Andreas Weckwerth, Sabine Schrenk und Francesco Zanella: Pallium, in: Reallexikon für Antike und Christentum, Bd. XXVI, Stuttgart 2015, S. 803–831.

Wilpert 1898–1899 Giuseppe Wilpert: Un capitolo di storia del vestiario. Tre studii sul vestiario dei tempi poscostantiniani, I–II, Rom 1898–1899.

Zangara 2000 Vincenza Zangara: Una predicazione alla presenza dei principi: la Chiesa di Ravenna nella prima metà del sec. V, in: Antiquité tardive 8, 2000, S. 265–304.

›Reich‹ – ›Staat‹ – ›Kirche‹?

Worüber verhandelten die Päpste mit den fränkischen Herrschern?

Bernhard Jussen

Eine Generation ist vergangen, seit eine Gruppe seinerzeit sehr einflussreicher deutscher Mediävisten ihrem Lehrer Gerd Tellenbach zum 80. Geburtstag eine Festschrift gewidmet hat mit dem Titel *Reich und Kirche vor dem Investiturstreit.*[1] Als Leitwort für die makrohistorische Strukturierung der westeuropäischen Geschichte hatte das Schlüsselwort ›Investiturstreit‹ seit dem Ende des ersten Weltkriegs eine rasante Karriere in der deutschsprachigen Geschichtswissenschaft und ihren Popularisierungsmedien gemacht, stetig häufiger verwendet im Verlauf der 20er, 30er und 40er Jahre bis zum Zenit in den 1950er Jahren. Danach sank der Stern dieses Schlüsselwortes über mehrere Jahrzehnte wieder. Als die Festschrift im Jahr 1985 erschien, galt ›Investiturstreit‹ als ›Epochenbegriff‹, als Leitvokabel für ein ›Zeitalter‹, ganz in der Linie der damals aktuellen neunten Auflage des *Gebhardt. Handbuch der deutschen Geschichte* aus dem Jahr 1970. Dort hieß der vierte Teil (gebunden 1970) bzw. vierte Band (dtv 1973, zehn Auflagen bis 1999) *Investiturstreit und frühe Stauferzeit.*[2]

Inzwischen ist dieses Schlüsselwort der 1920er bis 1950er Jahre als Epochenbegriff in die Disziplingeschichte verabschiedet worden. Spätestens seit der Jahrtausendwende wird es zwar noch für einen konkreten historischen Ereigniszusammenhang benutzt (wie »Canossa 1077« oder »Worms 1122«), aber als Strukturierungswort für makrohistorische Darstellungen (»Das Zeitalter des …«) ist es weitgehend ausgemustert. Das über viele Jahrzehnte prominente Schlüsselwort ist von den Überschriften abgesunken in die Fließtexte der Handbücher und Synthesen, und auch dort ist es nicht mehr prominent.[3]

1 Schmid 1985.

2 Jordan 1973.

3 Diese Gebrauchsgeschichte des Konzepts ›Investiturstreit‹ erschließt sich leicht durch vergleichendes Lesen von Synthesen und Handbüchern der letzten rund 100 Jahre und durch gezielte Suche nach dem Terminus; sie wird zudem empirisch bestätigt durch die (natürlich noch vorläufige, mit unpräzisen Korpora arbeitende, keine Auflagenhöhen berücksichtigende usw.) Auswertung durch den *Google NGram Viewer* (books.google.com/ngrams). In dem Literaturkorpus *German (2009)* ist die oben geschilderte Entwicklung der Gebrauchshäufigkeit deutlich zu erkennen. Es gibt keinen Grund für die Annahme, dass zukünftige, präziser kontrollierte Korpora diese Beobachtung in Frage stellen würden.

Exemplarisch zumindest für die deutschsprachige Situation ist das derzeit wohl am weitesten verbreitete akademische Lehrbuch der Geschichtswissenschaft, das *Oldenbourg Lehrbuch Geschichte Mittelalter* (seit 2007). Obgleich das Inhaltsverzeichnis feinteilig aufgefächert ist, kommt es – immerhin ein Überblickswerk für das Studium des ›Mittelalters‹ – ohne das Schlüsselwort ›Investiturstreit‹ aus. Auf den wenigen Seiten, die die Konflikte zwischen Kaiser und Papst zusammenfassen, muss sich das ehemalige Leitwort deutscher Mediävistik Anführungszeichen gefallen lassen.[4] Die Argumentation des knappen Kapitels verschiebt – wie inzwischen fast alle Darstellungen – das Gewicht drastisch. Über ›Investiturstreit‹, ›Canossa‹ und über einen Papst, der den Kaiser exkommuniziert, sprechen die Handbücher nur noch als Nebenthema. Im Zentrum des Erklärungsinteresses steht etwas anderes: die beginnende Auseinandersetzung zwischen Königen und Fürsten um eben jene politischen Tektonik, die mit der Entstehung eines ›Reiches‹ seit dem 12. Jahrhundert eine Form fand. Ob man knappe oder umfangreiche historische Darstellungen zur Hand nimmt, das Konzept ›Investiturstreit‹ strukturiert das historische Denken nicht mehr.[5]

Weniger Aufmerksamkeit hat die Geschichtswissenschaft dem ersten, nicht minder zeitgebundenen Teil des Festschriftentitels von 1985 gewidmet – »Reich und Kirche …«. Man mag zunächst feststellen, dass die Formel ›Reich und Kirche‹ weitgehend abwesend ist in heutigen Publikationen zur fränkischen Zivilisation (also den poströmischen Jahrhunderten bis zur Jahrtausendwende).[6] Sie gehört erst für die Zeit seit etwa dem 12. Jahrhundert zur gängigen Sprache geschichtswissenschaftlicher Darstellungen. Zumindest implizit gilt diese Formel anscheinend als ungeeignet für Aussagen über die Zeit ›vor dem Investiturstreit‹. Nur in alter Literatur findet man sie häufig für die fränkische Zeit. Diese Beobachtung ist zunächst einmal merkwürdig. Warum vermeidet die Forschung die Formel ›Reich und Kirche‹, obgleich kaum jemand ein Problem damit hat, das erfolgreichste nachrömische politische System – das ›fränkische‹ – als ›Reich‹ zu bezeichnen? Versuche, für diese Frage Sensibilität zu schaffen, gibt es schon seit den frühen 1980er Jahren.[7]

4 Meinhardt/Ranft/Selzer 2007, hier im von Ludger Körntgen verfasste Abschnitt *Vom Reich der Franken zum Reich der Deutschen* zum Konflikt mit den Päpsten S. 53–56 mit dem Abschnitt *Kaiser und Papst vor dem ›Investiturstreit‹*.

5 In Frank Rexroths sehr kondensiertem Buch *Deutsche Geschichte im Mittelalter* verschwindet der Konflikt in einer kleinen Passage des Kapitels *Herrscherdynastie und Fürstenversammlung (1075–1152)*; vgl. Rexroth 2005; in umfassenderen Darstellungen wie zum Beispiel Borgolte 2002 findet man den Konflikt oft nur über das Register (hier bes. S. 73–74).

6 Zum Kontext der hier skizzierten Deutung jener Zivilisation vgl. Jussen 2014.

7 Johannes Fried hat wiederholt versucht, eine Forschungsdiskussion über methodisch vertretbare Benennungen der nachrömischen politischen Systeme zu entfachen, so besonders: Fried 1982; Fried 1994; Fried 2005.

Politische Sprache vor der Trennung des Religiösen und des Politischen

Zunächst eine Skizze des Unstrittigen: Als die römischen Kaiser sich seit Mitte des 5. Jahrhunderts zunehmend in den griechischen Teil des Mittelmeers zurückzogen und sich für den nordalpinen Raum des alten Imperiums kaum noch engagierten, blieb den nordalpinen – nun postimperialen – Teilen der griechisch-römischen Mittelmeerwelt nur eine einzige Institution, die stabile politische Strukturen bereitstellen konnte. Während am Bosporus das alte römische Imperium mit Senat und Zirkusspielen noch für viele Jahrhunderte weiterlebte, verschwanden seine Institutionen im lateinischen Teil. Hier, in den vom Imperium zurückgelassenen Räumen, blieb als einzige Institution mit großflächiger Infrastruktur und vergleichsweise funktionierenden Verfahren die *ecclesia* zurück. Die Geschichte der poströmischen politischen Kulturen im lateinischen Europa ist über weite Strecken eine Geschichte von politischen Magnaten in Bischofspositionen – besonders in jener Kultur, die sich ›fränkisch‹ nannte. Am Bosporus hingegen, wo das römische Imperium fortlebte, haben politische Magnaten sich nicht für Bischofssitze interessiert. Wir sind auch gewohnt, dass die Geschichte der fränkischen politischen Kultur eine Geschichte der permanenten engen Kommunikation zwischen Päpsten und Herrschern war, zugleich aber eine Geschichte des stets unscharf bleibenden, ungeklärten Rangverhältnisses dieser beiden Exponenten. Demgegenüber gelten die Patriarchen der griechischen Kirche weiterhin, trotz verschiedener Relativierungen, als eine Art von ›Hofbischöfen‹ der römischen Kaiser am Bosporus.

Mit anderen Worten: Es ist zunächst Wiederholung von Unstrittigem, wenn der *ecclesia* die zentrale Funktion für die Entstehung neuer, stabiler politischer Kulturen im poströmischen Lateineuropa zugeschrieben wird. Die knappe Skizze deutet zunächst an, dass es im griechischen Teil des Imperiums nach dem Ende des lateinischen Teils noch für viele Jahrhunderte einen politischen Raum *außerhalb* der Kirche gab, einen Raum des Zirkus und des Senats. Im lateinischen, poströmischen Teil hingegen reorganisierten die vom Imperium zurückgelassenen Protagonisten das Feld politischen Handelns *innerhalb* jener Institution, die das Verhältnis der Menschen zum Jenseits zu betreuen hatte – innerhalb der *ecclesia*.

Diese grundsätzliche Einigkeit der Geschichtswissenschaft endet allerdings bei dem Versuch, die Grundlagen politischen Handelns in den neuen, poströmischen Kulturen präziser zu fassen. Jedes politische Handeln ist von Intentionen und Rechtfertigungsstrategien geleitet. Rechtfertigende Erzählungen, Repräsentationen und intentionale Handlungen kommen nicht ohne einen Denkrahmen aus, ohne eine normative Ordnung, auf die sie sich beziehen.[8] Jede heutige Deutung arbeitet implizit oder explizit mit

8 Vgl. dazu die Aufsatzbände Forst 2010 und Fahrmeir 2013.

einer Hypothese zu dieser normativen Ordnung. Jede Deutung beantwortet implizit oder explizit die Frage, wie die Protagonisten der nachrömischen Zivilisationen das politische Ganze gedacht und ausgedrückt haben, auf das sich ihr regierendes Handeln bezog. Haben sie sich auf einen ›Staat‹ bezogen, wie bisweilen behauptet wird?[9] Oder auf ein ›Reich‹, wie es zumeist heißt? Oder dachten sie viel weniger abstrakt und bezogen sich auf Gefüge von verflochtenen personalen Beziehungen, auf ›Personenverbände‹?

Gegenwärtig findet man verschiedene Deutungsrichtungen. Eine stark von der anthropologischen und gruppensoziologischen Forschung inspirierte Richtung deutet die frühen nachrömischen Gesellschaften bis etwa zur Jahrtausendwende in der Tradition von Leitformeln wie ›Gesellschaften ohne Staat‹ oder ›Face-to-face Gesellschaften‹ als ›Königsherrschaft ohne Staat‹. Entworfen werden Kulturen, die auf personalen Beziehungen in direkter Interaktion gründen. Aus dieser Perspektive sind insbesondere symbolisch-rituelle Kommunikation und die ihr vorgängigen Entscheidungsprozesse konstitutiver Teil des politischen Systems.[10] Eine andere Richtung argumentiert, dass die fränkische Welt zwar keinen herausragenden Traktat zur politischen Theorie hinterlassen habe, man ihr gleichwohl eine ›Staatstheorie‹ unterstellen müsse. Eine solche implizite Theorie von ›Staat‹ sei etwa aus den narrativen Texten – besonders der hofnahen Annalistik – herauszulesen. Insbesondere begriffsgeschichtliche Fragen sind für diese Perspektive zentral, etwa danach, was die Zeitgenossen mit dem Terminus *regnum* ausgedrückt haben. Ein ›Reich‹? Einen ›Staat‹? Eine ›Herrschaft‹?[11] Eine weitere Position vertritt die Auffassung, dass es nur einen einzigen Bezugsrahmen politischen Handelns gegeben habe, und zwar *ecclesia*. Dies bedeutet, dass sowohl das Handeln der Päpste und Bischöfe als auch das Handeln der Könige und Großen auf den Deutungsrahmen *ecclesia* bezogen waren und durch diesen legitimiert wurden. Ein Wort wie *regnum* bezeichnet nach dieser Deutung nicht einen institutionellen Rahmen für herrscherliches Handeln, sondern ein Attribut des Herrschers.[12]

Vor einigen Jahren haben zwei Sammelbände bereits im Buchtitel Position bezogen: *Staat im frühen Mittelalter* (2006) und *Der frühmittelalterliche Staat* (2009). Die Bücher konturieren in einigen Beiträgen eine weitere Argumentationslinie.[13] Sie reklamieren, dass die Diskussion – wie sie paradigmatisch um das Wort *regnum* geführt wird – obsolet sei, da sie die Existenz eines Staates oder eines Reichs von der Existenz

9 Vgl. besonders die Bände Airlie/Pohl/Reimitz 2006 und Pohl/Wieser 2009; mit Blick auf das Römische Imperium: Lundgreen 2014.

10 *Königsherrschaft ohne Staat* ist der programmatische Untertitel von Althoff 2000; zu den jeder rituellen Kommunikation vorgeschalteten Entscheidungsprozessen vgl. Althoff 2016; eine kondensierte Lehrbuchversion dieses Ansatzes mit weiterer Literatur bietet: Althoff 2007.

11 So besonders Hans-Werner Goetz; vgl. z. B. Goetz 2006 und Goetz 2009.

12 So bes. Fried (wie Anm. 7); vgl. Jussen (wie Anm. 6) S. 78–100.

13 Vgl. Anm. 9; vgl. besonders die Diskussion des Forschungsstandes von Walter Pohl (Pohl 2006).

eines Konzeptes von ›Staat‹ oder ›Reich‹ abhängig mache. Stattdessen müsse bei den Handelnden und Autoren mit jener Art von ›praktischem‹ Wissen gerechnet werden, das man mit Pierre Bourdieu »Wissen ohne Konzept« oder mit Michael Polanyi »implizites Wissen« (*tacit knowledge, tacit knowing*) nennt.[14] Die begriffsgeschichtliche Exegese eines Terminus wie *regnum* sei mithin sinnlos.

Die methodische Blickverschiebung auf implizites statt explizites Wissen ist in der Tat produktiv. Allerdings wird die Beweislast durch diese Verschiebung eher erschwert. Denn wer annimmt, dass ein ›Wissen ohne Konzept‹ das Regierungshandeln eines Herrschers und seines Hofes gesteuert habe, muss zwar kein explizites Konzept, dafür aber ein implizites Wissen nachweisen. Dies ist viel schwieriger. Üblicherweise sucht man implizites Wissen in der Semantik, in spezifischen Ausdrucksweisen von Autoren, und zwar in solchen, die als Gewohnheitsformulierungen erkennbar sind. Wer nachvollziehen will, wie man in Rom oder in Aachen um das Jahr 800 politisches Handeln konzipierte, wer beobachten will, mit welcher politischen Sprache sich der päpstliche und der fränkische politische Apparat verständigten, kommt nicht um die Untersuchung von Worten oder Wortgruppen umhin. Nur dadurch lässt sich das ›implizite Wissen‹ offenlegen, das die Regierenden (oder die erzählenden Autoren) leitete – im Lateran in Rom nicht anders als im fernen Aachener Palast des fränkischen Königs.

Was gilt es zu klären? Oft hat sich die Diskussion auf die Interpretation des Wortes *regnum* konzentriert, und dies ist trotz der genannten Kritik zielführend. Nicht zielführend ist eine Konzentration auf einige wenige Formulierungen, die besonders aussagekräftig zu sein scheinen, zumindest dann nicht, wenn implizites Wissen zu untersuchen ist. Denn wenn Autoren über ein Problem nachdenken, etwa im Interesse einer Definition, dann weichen sie oft signifikant von den üblichen Ausdrucksgewohnheiten ab, auch von ihren eigenen. Wer der erfolgreichsten poströmischen Zivilisation, der fränkischen, einen ›Staat‹ unterstellt oder auch nur ein ›Reich‹ – sei es auf der Grundlage einer erzählerisch implizit entfalteten ›Staatstheorie‹, sei es als Wissen ›ohne Konzept‹ – deutet *regnum* in Texten der fränkischen Zivilisation als Terminus für eine vom König unabhängige politische Institution, *innerhalb* derer dem König eine Funktion zukommt: Der König, *rex*, muss dann als Funktion in einem abstrakten institutionellen Subjekt, einem ›Reich‹ oder ›Staat‹, sichtbar werden. Die Gegenposition möchte *regnum* im Sinn von ›Königtum‹, ›Herrschaftsbereich‹ oder ›Königsmacht‹ verstehen, also *regnum* als ein Attribut des *rex*, das sich auf die Räume und Menschen bezieht, in und bei denen der König seine *potestas* (Macht/Herrschaft) geltend machen konnte: *regnum* ist demnach die Reichweite des königlichen Zugriffs.

14 So Walter Pohl ebd.; Bourdieu 1979, S. 543; Polanyi 1985; von »praktischem Wissen« spricht Patzold 2006.

regnum im Codex Carolinus

Um die Verwendung des Wortes *regnum* exemplarisch zu beobachten, sei im Folgenden ein Konvolut von Briefen der Päpste an die fränkischen Könige aus den Jahren 739 bis 791 herangezogen. Die ursprünglich auf Papyrus geschriebenen Briefe sind im Jahr 791 am fränkischen Königshof in einen Pergamentcodex übertragen worden, ausdrücklich um sie vor dem Verfall zu bewahren. Seit dem 17. Jahrhundert heißt er *Codex Epistularis Carolinus*.[15] In diesen päpstlichen Briefen, die Karl der Große hat konservieren lassen, ist das Wort *regnum* in 223 Situationen gebraucht worden. In rund zwei Drittel dieser Gebrauchssituationen geht es um das Diesseits, in einem Drittel um das Jenseits. In weit mehr als der Hälfte der Situationen ist *regnum* als Genitivattribut gebraucht (146 mal), kein Mal brauchte ein Autor *regnum* als Subjekt.[16]

regnum im Jenseits: besitzen, nicht betreten

Wo es um *regnum* im Jenseits geht, wird dies durchweg mit den Attributen *coelum* und *caelestis* ausgedrückt – *regnum coelorum*, *regnum coeli* und *regnum caelestis*. Meist ist von nur einem *regnum* im Jenseits die Rede, bisweilen aber auch von mehreren (*regna caelestia*).[17] Selten nur fassen die Päpste das Jenseits als *regnum Dei*, kaum als *regnum Domini*.[18] Wie im Neuen Testament ist der Himmel oder das Jenseits also oft ein Plural – die Jenseitse, die Himmel; und es gibt dort mehr als nur ein *regnum*.

Der bei weitem häufigste Gebrauchszusammenhang in den am fränkischen Hof gesammelten Briefen bezieht sich auf den heiligen Petrus, den Türwächter (*ianitor*) und Inhaber der Schlüssel (*claviger*) des himmlischen *regnum*.[19] Zwar sind diese Formeln in Papstbriefen wenig überraschend, auffällig aber ist die Art, wie sie verwendet werden.

---

15 Eine umfassende Analyse des Codex bietet Hack 2006; vgl. ferner Van Espelo 2013; Edition: Gundlach 1892, S. 469–657, S. 476: *denuo memoralibus membranis summo cum certamine renovare ac rescribere decrevit*.

16 Jenseits des hier untersuchten Corpus taucht *regnum* in Papstbriefen bisweilen passivisch auch im Nominativ auf, z. B. *quoniam ipsorum est regnum caelorum* (Zacharias VI,80, Epp III,80 im Rückgriff auf Mt 5,3 *Beati pauperes spiritu, quoniam ipsorum est regnum caelorum*); in den heiligen Texten fanden die Autoren der Briefe natürlich auch den Gebrauch von *regnum* als aktives Subjekt, etwa Mt 3,1; 4,17; 10,7: *appropinquavit enim regnum caelorum*, sie haben dies aber nicht in ihre Sprachgewohnheiten übernommen.

17 Rund 40 Gebrauchssituationen insgesamt; Plural bei Constantinus II. (VIII, 99): *caelestia regna*; Paulus I. (VIII, 27): *in celestibus regnis*.

18 In sieben Gebrauchssituationen *regnum Dei*, in nur einer *regnum Domini*.

19 39 Gebrauchssituationen von *claviger regni caelorum/caelestis*, 10 von *ianitor*; auf eine sprachliche Unterscheidung der verschiedenen Päpste (Paul I. verwendet *ianitor*, Hadrian I. *claviger*) kann hier verzichtet werden.

Die Rede vom Türwächter, vom Schlüsselbesitzer und vom Ausschluss aus dem himmlischen *regnum* legt einen geschlossenen Raum nahe, in den man eintritt. Die Päpste dürften die Passagen der Evangelien auswendig gekannt haben, in denen Jesus die Formel »ins himmlische *regnum* eintreten« verwendet.[20] Doch sie haben ihren Adressaten in diesem Briefkonvolut nicht ein einziges Mal einen Eintritt ins himmlische *regnum* in Aussicht gestellt. *Intrare* oder etwas ähnliches, irgendein Verb, das räumlich funktioniert, gibt es in den Briefen als Bezugsverb des himmlischen *regnum* nicht. Diese Beobachtung mag zunächst in Erinnerung rufen, dass biblische Formeln nicht als Elemente des naheliegenden Ausdrucksfundus vorausgesetzt werden können. Was die Autoren in der Liturgie endlos repetiert haben, muss nicht in die eigenen Ausdrucksgewohnheiten übertragen worden ein. Hier wie insgesamt haben diese bibelfesten Zeitgenossen nur einiges von dem, was sie aus Bibel, Liturgie und Bibelkommentaren an Sprachfiguren und Metaphern kannten, in den eigenen Ausdrucksvorrat übernommen.

Wozu also, wenn nicht zum Hindurchtreten, war diese Türe gut, die der heilige Petrus als Türsteher bewachte und die Petri Nachfolger den fränkischen Königen allein in diesem überschaubaren Briefkorpus rund 50 Mal brieflich ins Gedächtnis geschrieben haben? Einige Wendungen mögen sich noch gut mit dem Bild des Eintretens verbinden lassen, so besonders »von den himmlischen *regna* ausgeschlossen sein« (*alienare, separare, alienus esse*).[21] Doch das Konvolut der oft wiederholten Verben ist eindeutig, es hat nichts mit ›eintreten‹ zu tun. Gott möge, so wünschten die Päpste, den königlichen Adressaten die himmlischen *regna* »zum Besitz übertragen« (*celestia vobis regna tribuat possidenda*),[22] sie »zu Teilhabern des himmlischen *regnum* machen«[23] und ihnen »die Steuerräder des *regnum* übergeben«.[24] Hilfreich für die Deutung dieser Passagen mag ein Brief Papst Hadrians I. an Karl den Großen sein. Hadrian, der als einziger in dieser

20 Etwa Mt. 5,20: *dico enim vobis quia nisi abundaverit iustitia vestra plus quam scribarum et Pharisaeorum non intrabitis in regnum caelorum;* Mt. 7, 21: *non omnis qui dicit mihi Domine Domine intrabit in regnum caelorum sed qui facit voluntatem Patris mei qui in caelis est ipse intrabit in regnum caelorum;* Mt 18,3: *et dixit amen dico vobis nisi conversi fueritis et efficiamini sicut parvuli non intrabitis in regnum caelorum;* Mt 19,23: *Iesus autem dixit discipulis suis amen dico vobis quia dives difficile intrabit in regnum caelorum,* und öfter; zitiert nach www.bibelwissenschaft.de (Bibelportal der deutschen Bibelgesellschaft).

21 Z. B. Gregor III. (VIII, 2): *sic non tibi ipse princeps apostolorum claudat celestia regna;* Stephan II (VIII, 9): *non sitis alieni a regno Dei,* (VIII, 10): vos *alienare … a regno Dei et vita aeterna;* Stephan III. (VIII, 45): *non sitis alieni a regno Dei.*

22 Constantin II (VIII, 99): *celestia vobis regna* […] *tribuat possidenda;* Paul I. (VIII, 33): *celeste regnum vobis* […] *tribuat possidendum.*

23 Paul I. (VIII, 28): *celestis regni participes faciat;* Paul I. (VIII, 43): *cum egregio illo ac praecipuo David rege et eximio prophetarum in celestibus regnis participem te esse;* Hadrian I. (VII, 52): *et celestis regni gaudiis vos faciat esse per infinita saecula participes;* Hadrian I. (VIII, 55): *etiam et celestis regni gaudiis vos faciat esse participes;* statt regni participes stellt Constantin II. (VIII, 98) ihnen in Aussicht, *aeternae beatitudinis participes* zu sein.

24 Hadrian I. (VIII, 53): *caelestis regni gubernacula tribuens vobis.*

Sammlung häufig von der Adoption der Könige und insgesamt der Getauften durch Gott sprach, hat in einem Brief eine Formel Augustins aufgegriffen. Augustin hatte zur Deutung des himmlischen *regnum* die Adoption herangezogen, also das soziale Feld der Verwandtschaft: »Ihr seid ins *regnum* Gottes adoptiert.«[25] Die Formulierung steht in einem reichen, kaum standardisierten Pool von Ausdrücken um die Worte ›Adoption‹ und ›adoptieren‹, etwa »zu Söhnen Gottes adoptiert« oder »die Herrlichkeit der *adoptio*« haben. Augenscheinlich fasste Hadrian mit *regnum* kein territoriales Konzept, in das man durch eine Türe eintritt, sondern eine Rechtsfigur, die das Macht-, Autoritäts-, und Zugehörigkeitsverhältnis zwischen Personen regelt, hier zwischen Gott und den Gerechtfertigten. Zur Zeit des Augustinus, auf den Papst Hadrian sich rund 400 Jahre später bezog, gab es das römische Rechtsinstitut der Adoption noch, Augustinus bediente sich für seine Vorstellungen vom Jenseits also einer Metapher. Zur Zeit Karls des Großen und Papst Hadrians war das Rechtsinstitut der Adoption längst verschwunden, des Augustinus Metapher von der Adoption durch Gott war zur eigentlich Bedeutung des Wortes *adoptio* geworden.[26] Die zitierten Phrasen lassen sich nicht harmonisieren mit dem Bild der Türe, die der heilige Petrus bewacht, und die in den Evangelien auch ausdrücklich zum Hindurchtreten gedacht ist. Kurzum, *regnum* ist etwas, das die königlichen Adressaten der päpstlichen Briefe im Jenseits besitzen (*possidere*), lenken (*gubernare*), annehmen (*accipere, percipere*),[27] bekommen (*tribuere, concedere*), an dem sie teilhaben (*participes esse*).

regnum im Diesseits: eine Variante von *regalis*

In rund zwei Dritteln der Gebrauchssituationen von *regnum* sprechen die Päpste über das Diesseits. Auch in diesen Situationen findet sich nichts, das auf *regnum* als ein institutionelles Subjekt (ein ›Reich‹) verweist, nichts, das einen Referenzrahmen oder Bezugspunkt für königliches Handeln ausdrücken würde. Der König und sein Handeln werden nicht auf *regnum* bezogen, der König erfüllt nicht eine Funktion im *regnum*. Das Nomen *regnum* ist nur eine Variante von *regere*, *regnare* oder *regalis*, kurz, es ist nicht Akteur, sondern Attribut. Es ist bezeichnend, dass die bei weitem häufigste

25 Hadrian I. (VIII, 95): *Unde et beatus Augustinus, egregius doctor, in sermone de natale domini inquit: Audite filii lucis, adoptati in regnum Dei* (vgl. Augustinus, Sermo 144 In Natali Domini 1, 1, ed. Migne PL 38, Paris 1845, S. 1015).

26 Vgl. zur Adoption Jussen 1991.

27 Stephan II (VIII, 11): *et accipite regnum vobis ab origine mundi praeparatur.*

Phrase, nämlich *regni vestri*, ein an den König gebundenes Genitivattribut ist.[28] In der häufigen Formel »der Thron des/eures *regnum*« (*solium regni, solum regni vestri*) ist *regnum* offensichtlich ›Herrschaft‹.[29] Gott bewahrt (*conservare*), vermehrt oder erweitert (*dilatare*), gewährt (*largiri, concedere*) dem König »den Thron Eurer Herrschaft«.

Gott ist generell im Gros der Sätze, in denen *regnum* auftaucht, Subjekt der Handlung, so auch in der Standardphrase »Gott erweitere die Grenzen eures *regnum*« (*terminos regni vestri dilatet*).[30] Dass auch in dieser Phrase, in der *regnum* mit Grenzen in Verbindung gebracht wird, *regnum* ein Attribut von *rex* ist, verdeutlichen die Varianten: Paul I. und Stephan III. ersetzen *regnum* in dieser Phrase durch *regalis*: »Gott erweitere die königlichen (*regales*) Grenzen eurer Macht«, an anderen Stellen wird *regnum* weggelassen (»eure Grenzen erweitert) oder *terminos* gestrichen.[31] Nomen und Adjektiv – *regnum* und *regalis* – sind als Attribute des *rex* austauschbar, es ist signifikant, dass die Päpste in dieser Briefsammlung häufiger zum Adjektiv *regalis* greifen als zum Nomen *regnum*. Die häufige Nähe von ›Grenze‹ (*terminus*) und *regnum*, mithin ein gewisser Raumbezug, verschiebt die Semantik von *regnum* nicht in Richtung eines institutionellen Subjektes, eines ›Reiches‹, auch hier geht es um ›Macht‹ und ›Reichweite königlichen Zugriffs‹. Ein Raum und eine Grenze machen noch kein institutionelles Subjekt. Auch die Macht eines Warlords ist auf einen begrenzten Raum bezogen, und auch dort, wo es um Zuständigkeit geht, um Kompetenz, wird Kompetenzüberschreitung mit dem Wort ›Grenze‹ (*terminus*) ausgedrückt. ›Grenze‹ ist oft, aber nicht immer, irgendwie räumlich. Aus dem karolingischen Korpus der Papstbriefe sei ein Brief Hadrians I. herangezogen, der die »Überschreitung der Grenzen der Kirchenväter« anprangert.[32]

Häufig ist schließlich eine Phrase,[33] in der das Genitivattribut *regni* auf ›Steuerruder‹ (*gubernacula*) bezogen wird. Am wenigsten Komplikationen bereitet es, die Phrase als eine Form semantischer Redundanz zu fassen, einer im Lateinischen vertrauten rhetorischen Gewohnheit. Im Rahmen des bislang Zusammengetragenen sind *regni gubernacula* die ›Steuerruder der Königsmacht‹. Bis zur Jahrtausendwende gibt es wohl kaum

---

28 *Regni vestri* kommt im Codex Carolinus 34 mal vor; niemand außer Papst Constantin II. (der Verlierer) hat die Formel erweitert zu *regni vestri Francorum* (VIII, 99: *regni vestri a Deo confortati Francorum terminos dilatet*; VIII, 98: *a Deo protecti regni vestri Francorum*); in drei weiteren Briefen ergänzte ein Papst das Attribut *regni* mit *Francorum*.

29 Die Phrase findet sich elf Mal im Briefkorpus.

30 Die Phrase wird im Briefkorpus sieben Mal in der zitierten Form verwendet, vier weitere Male ähnlich.

31 Stephan III. (VIII,4) und Paul I. (VIII,42): *terminos regales vestrae potentiae dilatet*; Hadrian I. (VIII, 61): *ut amplius vestrum dilatet regnum et victorias tribuat*; Stephan III. (VIII, 44) und Paul I. (VIII, 42 u. VIII, 39): *terminos vestros dilatet*; für diese letzte Phrase vgl. die biblischen Referenzen: Exodus 34, 24 (*tulero gentes a facie tua et dilatavero terminos tuos*); Deuteronomium 12, 20 (*dilataverit Dominus Deus tuus terminos tuos*).

32 Hadrian I. (VIII, 94): *terminos antiquorum patrum transgredientes*.

33 Sie wird in 29 Zusammenhängen gebraucht.

einen Zusammenhang, in dem eine Übersetzung wie ›Regierung des Reiches‹ sinnvoll wäre. Auch im Jenseits durften die Könige auf diese Steuerruder ihrer Macht hoffen, jedenfalls wünschte Papst Hadrian I., »dass unser Erretter die Steuerruder der himmlischen Königsmacht (*caelestis regni gubernacula*) Euch zu genießen gewährt«.[34]

Zum Vergleich: Die »Königlich-fränkischen Annalen«

Knapp sei das Konvolut der päpstlichen Briefe mit einem Annalenwerk verglichen, das in besonderer Nähe der fränkischen Regierenden geschrieben worden ist. Der anonyme und ohne Titel überlieferte Text ist von ca. 790 bis 814 vermutlich von fünf Schreibern verfasst worden. In der internationalen Forschung wird er als »Königlich-fränkische Annalen« bezeichnet (englisch *Royal Frankish Annals*, französisch *Annales royales des Francs*, niederländisch *Koninklijke Frankische Annalen* oder *Annalen van de Frankische koningen*). Der in Deutschland immer noch verwendete Titel *Reichsannalen*, der im reichsseligen 19. Jahrhundert erfunden wurde, ist zu Recht international isoliert. Er projiziert in den Text eine im 19. und frühen 20. Jahrhundert populäre Phantasie, die einer semantischen Untersuchung nicht standhält.

Das päpstliche Briefkorpus und das hofnahe Annalenwerk repräsentieren unterschiedlich funktionierende Textsorten, unterschiedliche Perspektiven der Funktionsträger, unterschiedlich funktionierende Orte, Höfe und kulturelle Prägungen. Der Blick auf den Gebrauch des Wortes *regnum* führt trotzdem zum gleichen Befund. Das bislang beobachtete ließe sich auch an diesem Text zeigen. Besonders instruktiv ist aber, was das Annalenwerk zusätzlich preisgibt: die Art, wie die Autoren die politischen Führungsgruppen syntaktisch mit *regnum* verbinden.

Der syntaktische Einbau der Führungsgruppen

Mehr oder weniger intuitiv spricht die Forschung von den ›Großen des Reiches‹, ganz so, wie sie von ›Reichstagen‹ spricht, wenn in den Texten nur von ›Versammlungen‹ (*placitum, conventus, congregatio*) die Rede ist. Eine unglückliche Rolle spielt für dieses Weiterschleppen längst obsoleter Reichsphantasien die Übersetzung der *Königlich-fränkische Annalen* in der *Freiherr von Stein Gedächtnisausgabe* aus dem Jahr 1955, in der Termini wie *placitum* oder *conventus* seriell als ›Reichstag‹ übersetzt werden: »763. König Pippin hielt seinen Reichstag (*placitum suum*) ...«; oder: »822. Hierher

34 Hadrian I. (VIII,51): *redemptor noster caelestis regni gubernacula vos perfrui annuat.*

schrieb er einen Reichstag aus (*generali conventu congregatio*) ....«; oder: »[825] Dann löste er den Reichstag auf (*dimissoque conventu*) ...«, und öfter.[35] Nicht anders fällt der Befund mit Blick auf die ›Großen des Reiches‹ aus, die bis in die Gegenwart durch viele Publikationen geistern, oder gar mit Blick auf den ›Reichsadel‹. Die Autoren der *Königlich-fränkischen Annalen* haben nicht ein einziges Mal von *primores regni* oder *principes regni* oder ähnlichem gesprochen. Die *primores* werden nahezu immer auf eine *gens* bezogen (*primores* der Franken, der Dänen), nur zweimal auf den Herrscher (*primores sui*), aber nie auf *regnum*.

Der Terminus *optimates* wird anders verwendet als *primores*, er wird kaum einmal auf eine *gens* bezogen (*optimates Francorum*), sondern entweder ohne nähere Bestimmung verwendet oder auf den König bezogen (*optimates sui*). Der Codex der Papstbriefe zeigt das gleiche Bild. Erst um die Wende zum 10. Jahrhundert – drei Generationen nach dem Abbruch des Annalenwerkes – taucht die Formel von den Großen des *regnum* in annalistischen Texten auf, und zwar sehr selten.[36] Nicht vor dem 12. Jahrhundert werden Wendungen wie *principes regni* zur festen Sprechweise, also erst in dem Moment, in dem sich mit der Etablierung eines eigenen politischen Bereiches neben dem religiösen die Bedeutung von *regnum* verändert – von einem Attribut des Königs zu einem abstrakten institutionellen Subjekt. Erst in diesem Moment wird *regnum* zu einem ›Reich‹, innerhalb dessen der König eine Funktion hat, nicht anders als die *principes* dieses abstrakten Subjektes.

Vom konkreten zum abstrakten Denken? Ein Vergleich mit dem Gebrauch von *ecclesia*

Der Gebrauch des Terminus *regnum* und die damit verbundene politische Theorie bekommt ein noch deutlicheres Profil im Vergleich mit dem Gebrauch eines Wortes, mit dem tatsächlich ein abstraktes institutionelles Subjekt ausgedrückt wurde: *ecclesia*. Wenn die Schreiber und Autoren von *ecclesia* sprachen, dann sprachen sie *ecclesia* all das zu, was sie bei der Verwendung von *regnum* vermissen lassen: *Ecclesia* hat Eigenschaften – *sancta ecclesia*. Vergleichbares finden wir bei *regnum* nicht, bei *imperium*

35 Diese drei Beispiele (S. 21, 131, 142) stehen für rund 40 weitere, vgl. Rau 1977.

36 Wenn Ludwig der Deutsche (MGH Epp 6) von den *primates regnorum nostrorum* spricht, ist nicht *regnum* der Akteur, sondern der Autor, *regnum* wie in den behandelten Fällen ein Attribut Ludwigs; die Anrede in einem Brief des Papstes Johannes VIII. (in MGH Epp 7, No. II, 140) ist eines der wenigen frühen Funde auf der Suche nach dieser Formulierung: *Ugoni, Teutderico et Bernardo illustrissimis regni Francorum*.

erst im 12. Jahrhundert.[37] *Regnum* hat in den Briefen des *Codex Carolinus* und in den *Königlich-fränkischen Annalen* nie Eigenschaften. *Ecclesia* hat ihre eigenen Angelegenheiten oder Streitfälle – *causae ecclesiae*. Diese Formel – *causa ecclesiae* – hatte seit den Kirchenvätern einen festen Platz im Formulierungsvorrat der Autoren,[38] aber kaum einem Autor vor dem späten 11. Jahrhundert kam die Formulierung *causa regni* in den Sinn. Außerdem sprechen die Autoren beider Korpora ganz selbstverständlich vom Personal der *ecclesia* – vom *clerus ecclesiae* oder den *legati ecclesiae*. *Regnum* hat in diesen beiden Korpora nie Personal, nur der *rex* hat Personal und (selten) die *gens*. Wenn Hadrian I. von den »Gesandten Eurer königlichen Macht« (*missis vestrae regalis potentiae*) spricht, dann ist dies exemplarisch.[39] Legaten (*missi, legati*) werden nie vom *regnum* gesandt, wohl aber von der *ecclesia*.

Der Unterschied ist augenfällig. Es ist leicht zu erkennen, wie die Autoren sprachen, wenn sie eine Institution als Subjekt bezeichneten. Der Vergleich mit *ecclesia* ist deshalb besonders wichtig für die wissenschaftliche Diskussion, weil es in der Forschung die Tendenz gibt, eine makrohistorische Entwicklung zu unterstellen vom frühmittelalterlichen *konkreten Denken* in personalen Beziehungen zum hochmittelalterlichen *abstrakten Denken* von politischen Institutionen. Diese Deutung kann nur vertreten, wer nicht mit theologischen Konzeptionen des Politischen rechnet, also Ekklesiologie nicht als Form politischer Theorie wahrnimmt. Der Gebrauch des Wortes *ecclesia* zeigt, dass die Autoren der langlebigsten poströmischen politischen Kultur keine Schwierigkeit hatten, eine komplexe abstrakte politische Institution zu denken, und sie haben es andauernd gemacht, wenn sie über *ecclesia* sprachen. Mit mangelnder Abstraktions*fähigkeit*, mit einem Denken in ›konkreten‹ personalen Beziehungen, sind die beobachteten Ausdrucksgewohnheiten von *regnum* nicht zu erklären.

Das Buch der Könige: *Liber regnorum* oder *Liber regum*?

Um das Profil von *regnum* im Vergleich mit dem Gebrauch von *ecclesia* weiter zu schärfen, bietet sich eine Gewohnheit der Autoren an, die bislang für die Deutung der fränkischen politischen Kultur nicht herangezogen worden ist. In der Präambel zu jenem Rechtstext, den die Forschung *Admonitio Generalis* nennt, beruft Karl sich auf den

37 Vgl. Weinfurter 2005; insgesamt wird auch *imperium* vor dem 12. Jahrhundert nicht als institutionelles Subjekt verwendet, sondern sehr ähnlich wie *regnum*.

38 Rund 250 Belege in Migne's Patrologia Latina bis zum 10. Jahrhundert von *causa ecclesiae* und *causa ecclesiastica*.

39 Hadrian I (VIII, 56): *unde nos ilico, secundum qualiter missis vestrae regalis potentiae decet, omnem praeparationem seu et caballos in obviam eorum direximus.*

jüdischen König Josia. Dieser Rückbezug wird eingeleitet mit dem Hinweis auf das alttestamentliche *Buch der Könige*, in dem dieser König Josia vorkommt. In Karls Text aber steht für das *Buch der Könige* nicht *regum liber*, sondern *regnorum liber*, also *regnum* statt *rex*: »In den Büchern der Königtümer lesen wir nämlich ...«.

Die Edition von Hubert Mordek und Klaus Zechiel-Eckes kommentiert lakonisch: »*regnorum* statt *regum* nicht ungewöhnlich«.[40] Dem ist zuzustimmen. Aber was bedeutet diese Feststellung? Das *Buch der Könige* wurde in den patristischen Texten, bei Augustinus, Hieronymus oder Ambrosius, weit öfter *liber regnorum* genannt als – wie nach unserer Gewohnheit – *liber regum*. Im 8. und 9. Jahrhundert veränderte sich das Verhältnis zwar zusehends; *liber regum* wurde nun häufiger, aber der Titel *liber regnorum* blieb ein ganz gewöhnlicher. Solange in den poströmischen politischen Systemen Isidors Definition »*regnum* kommt von *rex*« dem Sprachgebrauch der Autoren weitgehend entsprach, so lange war es nicht wichtig, ob das *Buch der Könige* ein *liber regum* oder ein *liber regnorum* war.[41] Äußerst zaghaft änderten sich die Formulierungen seit der Wende zum 10. Jahrhundert. Je mehr seit dem späten 11. Jahrhundert der Terminus *regnum* das politische Ganze bezeichnete, innerhalb dessen dem *rex* seine Position zugewiesen war, desto problematischer wurde der Titel *liber regnorum* für das *Buch der Könige*. In den Texten des 12. und 13. Jahrhunderts wurde der Titel *liber regnorum* kaum noch gebraucht. Gegen die Autorität der Kirchenväter haben die Autoren des 12. und 13. Jahrhunderts den Titel *liber regnorum* fallen gelassen, denn inzwischen waren die Bedeutungen von *rex* und *regnum* deutlich verschieden.

Von *regnum et sacerdotium* zu *regnum et ecclesia*

Was die *Königlich-fränkischen Annalen* und die päpstlichen Briefe im *Codex epistularis Carolinus* gezeigt haben, ließe sich an vielen weiteren Texten verschiedener Gattungen wiederholen: Mit dem Wort *regnum* bezeichneten die Autoren nicht das politische Ganze, auf das sich Regierungshandeln bezog. *Regnum* war nicht Terminus für etwas, das den König einschloss. Deutungssicherheit haben nicht etwa Definitionen gegeben, die man sporadisch finden mag, auch nicht besonders ausführliche Formulierungen, sondern habitualisierte Ausdrucksweisen, die sich nicht zuletzt in der Syntax entdecken lassen: die Kasus des Wortes *regnum*, die Subjekte der Sätze, die Verben, mit denen diese Subjekte mit *regnum* verbunden sind, die syntaktischen Bezüge der Führungsgruppen,

40 Mordek/Zechiel-Eckes/Glatthaar 2012, S. 183, Anm. 16; Text S. 182, Z. 30 f.; Mordek und Zechiel-Eckes übersetzen »Königreiche« statt wie hier »Königtümer«.

41 Isidor von Sevilla, Ethymologien 9,3,1, Lindsey 1911: *regnum a regibus dictum*.

der Vergleich mit einem ganz anders gebrauchten Wort wie *ecclesia* und – nicht zuletzt – die Beliebigkeit, mit der das *Buch der Könige* benannt wurde.

Ob im Lateran oder im Aachen des 8. und 9. Jahrhunderts, die Architekten der erfolgreichsten nachrömischen Zivilisation im lateinischen Westen haben den normativen Rahmen ihres Regierungshandelns deutlich artikuliert. Mit der Formel der eingangs zitierten Festschrift – ›Reich und Kirche‹ – ist dieser normative Rahmen verfehlt, denn von einem ›Reich‹ (oder gar einem ›Staat‹) ist auch dann nichts zu finden, wenn wir im Sinne der aktuellen Diskussionen nach ›Wissen ohne Konzept‹, nach ›implizitem‹ oder ›praktischem‹, *tacit* oder *silent* Wissen suchen.[42] Die politische Theorie jener Jahrhunderte war nicht implizit, praktisch und *tacit*, sondern explizit und elaboriert: Sie war Ekklesiologie, politische Theologie. In aller Deutlichkeit zeigt dies der systematisch unterschiedliche Gebrauch der Worte *regnum* und *ecclesia*.

Der Raum des Politischen war der Raum des Religiösen. *Regnum* als ›Reich‹, als institutionelles Subjekt und abstrakter Akteur, gewann erst Kontur, als sich seit dem späten 11. Jahrhundert ein eigener Bereich des Politischen *neben* dem Bereich des Religiösen entwickelte, als man mit Formeln wie ›Reich und Kirche‹ zwei verschiedene Institutionen zu bezeichneten begann, deren Verhältnis zueinander ausgedrückt werden musste.[43] Jetzt erst werden Wendungen wie »Angelegenheiten des *regnum*« (causae *regni*) und »die Großen des *regnum*« (principes *regni*) gängig. Noch viel später, als sich seit dem 16. Jahrhundert die Republik als politische Alternative zum Königtum etablierte und theoretisch reflektiert wurde, entstand zunächst nur für diese – die Republik – das Konzept ›Staat‹, als Gegenkonzept zu ›Monarchie‹.[44] Mögen sich die Konzepte von ›Staat‹ und ›Reich‹ seither noch oft gewandelt haben, und mag es in den historischen Geisteswissenschaften auch endlos viele Definitionsversuche geben, so bleibt doch die Deutung der fränkischen Welt bis etwa zum Jahr 1000 gleich: Wer die Wörter ›Reich‹ oder ›Staat‹ für die fränkische Welt verwendet, arbeitet unausweichlich mit einer Zweiheit. Selbst wenn die »enge Verschränkung« von ›Reich‹ und ›Kirche‹ betont wird, ist das Kind schon in den Brunnen gefallen. Denn verschränkt kann nur sein, was verschieden ist.

In diesem Sinne sei abschließend daran erinnert, dass die Zeitgenossen im Briefkorpus und im Annalenwerk nicht ein einziges Mal die beiden Schlüsselworte durch »und« verbunden haben, nie »*ecclesia et regnum*« geschrieben haben. Bis ins 11. Jahrhundert

---

42 Vgl. oben zu Anm. 13 und 14.

43 Wenn zuvor hier und dort einmal ein Autor das Wort *regnum* zum Subjekt eines Satzes machte und dieses *regnum* agieren ließ, fallen diese Sätze aus semantischer Perspektive unter das Stichwort »Varianz«. In Reginos Chronik zum Beispiel findet sich eine solche Gebrauchssituation unter rund 270 Einsätzen des Wortes *regnum*. Für die Beobachtung von Diskursen und diskursiven Veränderungen aber ist entscheidend, wann solche Varianzen diskursmächtig geworden sind.

44 Dies erklärt Skinner 2012.

sollte es so bleiben. In kaum einer Situation war es sinnvoll, eine abstrakte Institution (*ecclesia*) und einen ihrer internen Aufgabenbereiche (*regnum*) in einem Atemzug (*ecclesia et regnum*) zu nennen. Wer die Formel *regnum et ecclesia* (oder umgekehrt) in den großen Textsammlungen sucht, findet die Karriere dieser Phrase erst seit dem späten 11. Jahrhundert. Zuvor griff man zu einer anderen Phrase: »Königtum und Priestertum« (*regnum et sacerdotium*). Die Karriere der Formel *regnum et ecclesia* seit dem späten 11. Jahrhundert ist ein deutlicher semantischer Indikator für die Trennung des Politischen und des Religiösen. Drückt die frühere Formel – in den Jahrhunderten der politischen Theologie – zwei Aufgabebereiche innerhalb desselben politischen Ganzen (*ecclesia*) aus, so die neue Formel das Nebeneinander zweier institutioneller Subjekte.

Bibliographie

Airlie/Pohl/Reimitz 2006 Staat im frühen Mittelalter (Forschungen zur Geschichte des Mittelalters 11), hg. von Stuart Airlie, Walter Pohl und Helmut Reimitz, Wien 2006.

Althoff 2000 Gerd Althoff: Die Ottonen. Königsherrschaft ohne Staat (Urban TB 473), Stuttgart [u. a.] 2000 [weitere Auflagen 2005, 2013].

Althoff 2007 Gerd Althoff: Herrschen ohne Staat. Ressourcen und Rituale, in: Oldenbourg Geschichte Lehrbuch Mittelalter, hg. von Matthias Meinhardt, Andreas Ranft und Stephan Selzer, München 2007 (2. Aufl. 2009), S. 101–102.

Althoff 2016 Gerd Althoff: Kontrolle der Macht. Formen und Regeln politischer Beratung im Mittelalter, Darmstadt 2016.

Borgolte 2002 Michael Borgolte: Europa entdeckt seine Vielfalt 1050–1250 (Handbuch der Geschichte Europas Bd. 3), Stuttgart 2002.

Bourdieu 1979 Pierre Bourdieu: La distinction. Critique sociale du jugement, Paris 1979.

Fahrmeir 2013 Rechtfertigungsnarrative. Zur Begründung normativer Ordnung durch Erzählungen (Normative Orders 7), hg. von Andreas Fahrmeir, Frankfurt am Main 2013.

Forst 2010 Die Herausbildung normativer Ordnungen. Interdisziplinäre Perspektiven, hg. von Rainer Forst, Frankfurt am Main 2010.

Fried 1982 Johannes Fried: Der karolingische Herrschaftsverband im 9. Jahrhundert zwischen »Kirche« und »Königshaus«, in: Historische Zeitschrift 235, 1982, S. 1–43.

Fried 1994 Johannes Fried: ›gens‹ und ›regnum‹. Wahrnehmungs- und Deutungskategorien politischen Wandels im früheren Mittelalter. Bemerkungen zur doppelten Theoriebindung des Historikers, in: Sozialer Wandel im Mittelalter. Wahrnehmungsformen, Erklärungsmuster, Regelungsmechanismen, hg. von Jürgen Miethke und Klaus Schreiner, Sigmaringen 1994, S. 74–104.

Fried 2005 Johannes Fried: Um 900 – Warum es das Reich der Franken nicht gegeben hat, in: Die Macht des Königs. Herrschaft in Europa vom Frühmittelalter bis in die Neuzeit, hg. von Bernhard Jussen, München 2005, S. 83–89.

Goetz 2006 Hans-Werner Goetz: Die Wahrnehmung von Staat und Herrschaft im frühen Mittelalter, in: Staat im frühen Mittelalter (Forschungen zur Geschichte des Mittelalters 11), hg. von Stuart Airlie, Walter Pohl und Helmut Reimitz, Wien 2006, S. 41–68.

Goetz 2009 Hans-Werner Goetz: Erwartungen an den »Staat«. Die Perspektive der Historiographie in spätkarolingischer Zeit, in: Der frühmittelalterliche Staat – Europäische Perspektiven (Forschungen zur Geschichte des Mittelalters 16), hg. von Walter Pohl und Veronika Wieser, Wien 2009, S. 471–485.

Gundlach 1892 Codex epistolaris carolinus (MGH Epistolae 3. Epistolae Merowingici et Karolini aevi 1), hg. von Wilhelm Gundlach, Berlin 1892, S. 469–657.

Hack 2006 Achim Thomas Hack: Codex Carolinus. Päpstliche Epistolographie im 8. Jahrhundert (Päpste und Papsttum 35), Stuttgart 2006.

Jordan 1973 Karl Jordan: Investiturstreit und frühe Stauferzeit 1056–1197 (Gebhardt Handbuch der deutschen Geschichte, 9. Aufl., Bd. 4), München 1973 [zehn Auflagen bis 1999].

Jussen 1991 Bernhard Jussen: Patenschaft und Adoption im frühen Mittelalter. Künstliche Verwandtschaft als soziale Praxis (Veröffentlichungen des Max-Planck-Instituts für Geschichte, 98), Göttingen 1991.

Jussen 2014 Bernhard Jussen: Die Franken. Geschichte, Gesellschaft, Kultur (C. H. Beck Wissen), München 2014.

Lindsey 1911 Isidori hispalensis episcopi etymologiarum sive originum libri XX, hg. von Wallace Martin Lindsey, 2 Bde, Oxford 1911.

Lundgreen 2014 Staatlichkeit in Rom? Diskurse und Praxis (in) der römischen Republik, hg. von Christoph Lundgreen, Stuttgart 2014.

Meinhardt/Ranft/Selzer 2007 Oldenbourg Geschichte Lehrbuch Mittelalter, hg. von Matthias Meinhardt, Andreas Ranft und Stephan Selzer, München 2007 [2. Aufl. 2009].

Mordek/Zechiel-Eckes/Glatthaar 2012 Hubert Mordek, Klaus Zechiel-Eckes und Michael Glatthaar: Die Admonitio generalis Karls des Grossen (Monumenta Germaniae historica. Fontes iuris Germanici antiqui in usum scholarum separatim editi, 16), Hannover 2012.

Patzold 2006 Steffen Patzold: Die Bischöfe im karolingischen Staat. Praktisches Wissen über die politische Ordnung im Frankenreich des 9.Jahrhunderts, in: Staat im frühen Mittelalter (Forschungen zur Geschichte des Mittelalters 11), hg. von Stuart Airlie, Walter Pohl und Helmut Reimitz, Wien 2006, S. 181–200.

Pohl 2006 Walter Pohl: Staat und Herrschaft im Frühmittelalter. Überlegungen zum Forschungsstand, in: Staat im frühen Mittelalter (Forschungen zur Geschichte des Mittelalters 11), hg. von Stuart Airlie, Walter Pohl und Helmut Reimitz, Wien 2006, S. 9–38.

Pohl/Wieser 2009 Der frühmittelalterliche Staat – Europäische Perspektiven (Forschungen zur Geschichte des Mittelalters 16), hg. von Walter Pohl und Veronika Wieser, Wien 2009.

Polanyi 1985 Michael Polanyi: Implizites Wissen (Suhrkamp Taschenbuch Wissenschaft 543), Frankfurt am Main 1985 [2. Aufl. 2016].

Rau 1955 Reinhold Rau: Quellen zur karolingischen Reichsgeschichte 1. Die Reichsannalen. Einhards Leben Karls des Großen. Zwei Leben Ludwigs. Nithards Geschichte (Ausgewählte Quellen zur deutschen Geschichte des Mittelalters 5), Darmstadt 1955 [2. Aufl. 1977].

Rexroth 2005 Frank Rexroth: Deutsche Geschichte im Mittelalter (C. H. Beck Wissen), München 2005.

Schmid 1985 Reich und Kirche vor dem Investiturstreit. Vorträge beim wissenschaftlichen Kolloquium aus Anlass des 80. Geburtstags von Gerd Tellenbach, hg. von Karl Schmid, Sigmaringen 1985.

Skinner 2012 Quentin Skinner: Die drei Körper des Staates (Historische Geisteswissenschaften 2), Göttingen 2012.

Van Espelo 2013 Dorine Van Espelo: A testimony of Carolingian rule? The Codex epistolaris carolinus, its historical context, and the meaning of imperium, in: Early Medieval Europe 21, 2013, S. 254–282.

Weinfurter 2005 Stefan Weinfurter: Um 1157 – Wie das Reich heilig wurde, in: Die Macht des Königs. Herrschaft in Europa vom Frühmittelalter bis in die Neuzeit, hg. von Bernhard Jussen, München 2005, S. 190–204.

Päpstliche Textilgeschenke des späten 13. Jahrhunderts – Objekte, Akteure, Funktionen

Christiane Elster

Ein bis heute im Schatz der Lateranbasilika erhaltenes und in die erste Hälfte des 14. Jahrhunderts datierendes Pluviale (Abb. 1) wird in einem Inventar aus dem Jahr 1640 einer Schenkung durch einen »San Calisto Papa« zugeschrieben, bei dem es sich entweder um den Märtyrerpapst Calixt I. (217–222) oder um Papst Calixt II. (1119–1124) handeln dürfte, der in der in S. Giovanni in Laterano begraben war.[1] Durch die Bezeichnung des Papstes als Heiligen wird der Wert des Pluviales für das ihn besitzende Kollektiv enorm gesteigert, da sie ihm quasi den Status einer Sekundärreliquie sicherte.

Ähnlich wie in diesem Beispiel finden sich in vielen spätmittelalterlichen und neuzeitlichen Inventaren von Kirchen in Rom und dem ehemaligen Kirchenstaat in den Bestandslisten der liturgischen Textilien immer wieder Einträge, die Paramente beschreiben, die während des Mittelalters als päpstliche Geschenke an die klerikalen Institutionen gelangt waren. Über lange Zeiträume hinweg, bis weit in die Neuzeit hinein, wurden diese Textilien mit den Namen der päpstlichen Schenker verknüpft und in Erinnerung gehalten.

Die Päpste des Mittelalters verschenkten häufig kostbare liturgische Textilien, Geräte und Handschriften an kirchliche Institutionen innerhalb und außerhalb Roms. Diese Schenkungen führten zu einer an Träger, Raum und Handlung gebundenen Neukontextualisierung der mobilen Gaben und dienten der Etablierung einer auf das römische Papsttum ausgerichteten Kultur delegierter Repräsentation, politischer Loyalität und der Memoria.

1 »Vn Piviale Antichiss.mo tessuto con oro Perle et seta […], quale si giudica esser di san Calisto Papa.« Inventario della Sacristia della S.o S.ta Chiesa Lateranense […] 1640; Lateran, Archivio Capitolare, AAA 5, S. 41. Es handelt sich um das im römischen Volksmund so genannte *Piviale di San Silvestro*, das einer Legende zufolge angeblich durch Papst Bonifaz VIII. (1294–1303) während der Verkündung des Ablasses zum Heiligen Jahr 1300 getragen worden sein soll. Diese Überlieferung ist jedoch nicht haltbar, da das Pluviale erst nach dem Pontifikat Bonifaz' VIII. entstanden ist, es wird zwischen 1320 und 1340 datiert. Vgl. Christie 1938, S. 149–152, Kat.-Nr. 78; Andaloro 1990, S. 282–285.

Dieser Beitrag wird sich innerhalb der Gesamtheit an materieller Kultur, die von den Päpsten des Mittelalters als Gabe eingesetzt wurde, auf das textile Medium konzentrieren und insbesondere päpstliche Gewand- und Mantelschenkungen des späten 13. Jahrhunderts in den Blick nehmen.[2] Nach einer historischen Einordnung des Phänomens werden zwei Fallbeispiele vorgestellt, die exemplarisch zeigen, wie päpstliche Schenkungen liturgischer Paramente um 1300 als beziehungsstiftende Akte eingesetzt werden konnten. Als den Schenkvorgang maßgeblich prägender Akteur ist dabei neben dem päpstlichen Schenker (römische Kirche) und den Empfängerinstitutionen auch die textile Gabe selbst in den Blick zu nehmen. Die Wirkmächtigkeit (›agency‹) der liturgischen Textilgeschenke dürfte abgesehen von ihrem materiellen Wert wesentlich aus ihrer Farbigkeit und Bildsprache (figürliche Darstellungen oder Muster), aus ihrem durch ihre Funktion als Bekleidung der Zelebranten und sonstigen Requisiten der christlichen Liturgie begründeten Status als Sakralobjekte, sowie aus ihrer auf den päpstlichen Schenker bezogenen memorialen Aufladung resultiert haben.[3]

Die päpstlichen Textilgeschenke des Mittelalters sind innerhalb eines Spannungsfeldes vielfältiger Formen und Typen von Textil- und Kleiderschenkungen der europäischen Vormoderne zu verorten, nämlich dem Schenkungs- und Stiftungswesen an die Kirche, dem höfischen Geschenkwesen und der Armenfürsorge.[4] Möglicherweise bildete die Rezeption und Adaption einer rituellen Geste der Herrschaftsdemonstration aus dem profanen Kontext den Ausgangspunkt der päpstlichen Textilschenkungen des Mittelalters. Denn es stellt sich die Frage, ob sie möglicherweise die zeremonielle Praxis herrschaftlicher Kleidergaben in der römischen Spätantike, die einen Teil des medienübergreifenden Systems kaiserlicher Ehrengaben bildeten, und am kaiserlichen Hof in Byzanz imitierten.[5] Denkbar ist, dass sich dieser Rezeptionsprozess in Folge der Pippinischen Schenkung an Papst Stephan II. (752–755) vollzog, als sich die weltliche Macht der römischen Kirche zu konstituieren begann.

Dass die Tradition von Schenkungen kostbarer liturgischer Textilien durch Päpste in der Tat bis ins 8. Jahrhundert zurückgeht, ist aus den Viten der Päpste des 8. und 9. Jahrhunderts im *Liber pontificalis* ersichtlich. Die karolingischen Päpste bemühten

2 Grundlegend für den Beitrag ist meine 2013 an der Universität Köln abgeschlossene Dissertation, die 2017 im Michael Imhof-Verlag erscheinen wird (im Folgenden zitiert als Elster 2017b).

3 Bei der Verwendung der Begriffe ›Akteur‹ und ›agency‹ orientiere ich mich an Latour 2007 [2005]. Zur theologischen Deutung der liturgischen Paramente in der mittelalterlichen Liturgieallegorese (Liturgiekommentare und Messerklärungen, Ankleidegebete, Ordinationsriten) vgl. Miller 2014a, S. 51–95.

4 Vgl. Elster 2017b, Kapitel 4.2.

5 Vgl. Bauer 2010 (besonders S. 17); Woodfin 2012, S. 159–161. Franz Alto Bauer hat gezeigt, dass die Gabe in der römischen Spätantike mit der personalen Aura des (sakral überhöhten) kaiserlichen Schenkers aufgeladen war, d. h. sie vergegenwärtigte ihn und speicherte in ihrer spezifischen Materialität seine personale Wirkmächtigkeit. Spätantike Ehrengaben dienten also der Verbreitung kaiserlicher Präsenz. Vgl. Bauer 2009, S. 59–65.

Abb. 1: Pluviale mit Szenen aus den Viten Marias und Christi sowie aus Heiligenmartyrien, Metall- und Seidenstickerei auf Leinengrund, England, 1. Hälfte 14. Jahrhundert. Rom, San Giovanni in Laterano, Tesoro.

sich nicht nur um die Restaurierung und Neuausstattung der bedeutenden frühchristlichen Kirchen in Rom, sondern beschenkten diese und Kirchen außerhalb Roms auch großzügig mit liturgischen Geräten und Textilien. Aus Stiftungslisten, welche die päpstlichen Gaben minutiös aufführen, geht hervor, dass es sich bei den Textilien ausschließlich um Paramente zur Dekoration des Kirchenraumes und Presbyteriums handelte. Genannt werden im Wesentlichen *vestes*, *vela* und *cortinae*, d.h. Altarparamente und Behänge für die bogenförmigen Öffnungen des Altarziboriums oder der das Presbyterium abschließenden Arkaden.[6] Bei einem großen Teil der in den verschenkten Paramenten verarbeiteten Gewebe dürfte es sich um aus Byzanz, Ägypten, Syrien und Persien stammendes Importgut gehandelt haben.[7] Es haben sich zwar keine päpstlichen Textilgeschenke dieser Zeit erhalten, doch aus den Beschreibungen des *Liber pontificalis* und den aus dem Reliquienschatz der *Sancta Sanctorum* stammenden, zu Beginn des

6 Vgl. Liber pontificalis, Duchesne 1955, Bd. 1, S. 486–523; Bd. 2, S. 1–139; dazu Martiniani-Reber 1999, S. 290–291; Andaloro 2003. Zur Selektivität der Stiftungslisten im *Liber pontificalis* und der damit verbundenen Problematik ihrer statistischen Auswertung vgl. Bauer 2004, S. 27–38.

7 Die geographisch verankerten Bezeichnungen einiger der im *Liber pontificalis* genannten Gewebe lassen Rückschlüsse auf ihre Herkunft und Fertigungsorte zu. Vgl. Saxer 1996/1997.

20. Jahrhunderts geborgenen Textilien[8] ist zu schließen, dass es sich um kostbare Seidengewebe handelte, die meist mit profanen Bildmotiven gemustert waren. Der *Liber pontificalis* nennt zahlreiche Behänge mit stilisierten Tieren, die in eine Struktur aus kreisförmigen Medaillons (*rotae*) eingeschrieben waren. Unter den Textilgeschenken Papst Leos III. (795–816) werden *vestes* mit der Darstellung von Vögeln, Greifen, Elefanten und Raubtieren beschrieben.[9] Die aus dem Osten stammenden Gewebe erreichten Rom vermutlich in Form loser Stoffbahnen und wurden in dort ansässigen Werkstätten zu Paramenten weiterverarbeitet – dies würde die Hinzufügung christlicher Bildinhalte und ihre teils präzise Abstimmung auf die Patrozinien der römischen Empfängerkirchen erklären. So schenkte Papst Gregor IV. (827–844) der Kirche S. Marco mit Greifen und Löwen gemusterte Altarbehänge, auf denen sich gestickte Applikationen mit der Darstellung der Geburt Christi und der Auferstehung befanden. Greif und Löwe wurden hier entsprechend des im 3. Jahrhundert n. Chr. zusammengestellten Tierkatalogs des *Physiologus* christlich ausgedeutet.[10]

Päpstliche Schenkungen liturgischer Gewänder sind dagegen erst ab der Mitte des 12. Jahrhunderts belegbar. Laut der *Descriptio Lateranensis Ecclesiae* schenkte Papst Anastasius IV. (1153–1154) der Lateranbasilika eine weiße Kasel mit einem kostbaren Besatz.[11] Hier kommt innerhalb der päpstlichen Textilschenkungen zum ersten Mal die Gattung der Kleidung ins Spiel. Das relativ späte Aufkommen päpstlicher Kleiderschenkungen macht Maureen Miller an der Rezeption weltlicher Herrschaftsgewandung im Kontext der *imitatio imperii*-Bestrebungen des Reformpapsttums Gregors VII. (1073–1085) fest. Der päpstliche Ornat und die priesterliche liturgische Gewandung allgemein nahmen ab dem späten 11. Jahrhundert einen monarchischen Charakter an. In Rom wurden die Gewänder des Klerus vermutlich erst seit dieser Zeit aus kostbaren Materialien wie Seide, Gold und Silber gefertigt und avancierten damit zu teuren Luxusgütern, die sie als päpstliche Textilgeschenke, analog zu den seidenen Altarparamenten und Behängen, interessant machten.[12] Davon abgesehen lässt das kulturenübergreifende Phänomen herrschaftlicher Kleidergaben darauf schließen, dass verschenkte Gewänder in

---

8 Heute in den Vatikanischen Museen. Vgl. Volbach 1942, S. 34–54, Kat.-Nr. T 100–T171; Andaloro 2003, S. 63–66.

9 Vgl. Liber pontificalis, Duchesne 1955, Bd. 2, S. 1–48.

10 […] *sepe iamdictus venerabilis papa obtulit in praenominata ecclesia [ecclesia beati Marci] vestem cum chriphis et chrisoclabo per circuitum, habentem in medio Nativitatem domini nostri Iesu Christi;* […] *obtulit vero praenominatus pontifex vestem aliam cum leonibus, habentem Resurrectionem Domini de chrisoclabo*; […]. Liber pontificalis, Duchesne 1955, Bd. 2, S. 75. Dazu Martiniani-Reber 1999, S. 298.

11 *Ad ornamentum etiam sacrosancti dominici altaris plurima dona optulit,* […]. *Exinde quintodecimo die casulam unam albam et optimam pretioso aurifrigio circumdatam ad celebrationem missae.* Descriptio Lateranensis Ecclesiae, Valentini/Zucchetti 1946, Bd. 3, S. 351 f.

12 Vgl. Miller 2014b, S. 45–46.

besonderer Weise mit der Präsenz des Gebers aufgeladen waren.[13] Denn Kleidung weist als eine zweite Haut, die den Individualkörper seiner sozialen Rolle gemäß ›verkleidet‹, aufgrund ihres engen Bezugs zum menschlichen Körper naturgemäß eine besondere Fähigkeit auf, personale Wirkmächtigkeit zu speichern. Mit der Gabe kostbarer liturgischer Gewänder an geistliche Einrichtungen adaptierten die Päpste zudem die seit dem frühen Mittelalter weit verbreiteten Schenkungen von Herrscher- und Krönungsmänteln weltlicher Herrscher an die Kirche.[14]

Eine wichtige Quelle für das päpstliche Schenkungswesen im 13. Jahrhundert stellt die in den *Gesta Innocentii Tertii* enthaltene Geschenkliste dar, die ganz in der Tradition der Stiftungslisten der karolingischen Päpste im *Liber pontificalis* steht.[15] Wie seine karolingischen Vorgänger engagierte sich Papst Innozenz III. (1198–1216) für die Erneuerung, Restaurierung und Ausstattung von Kirchen und geistlichen Einrichtungen innerhalb und außerhalb Roms. Der Papst beschenkte sie regelmäßig mit liturgischen Geräten, Handschriften und Textilien. Letztere waren folglich Bestandteile einer medienübergreifend angelegten Schenkpolitik der Päpste. Alle von den Päpsten des 13. Jahrhunderts als Gaben eingesetzten Artefakte waren Gebrauchsgegenstände, die in der Liturgie der geistlichen Empfängerinstitutionen praktisch verwendet werden konnten.

Bei den Textilien, welche die Päpste des späten 13. Jahrhunderts verschenkten, kamen sowohl Neuware als auch aus dem päpstlichen Schatz stammende Gebrauchttextilien zum Einsatz.[16] Bei letzteren handelte es sich um liturgische Paramente einschließlich Gewänder, die vor den Schenkungen vermutlich innerhalb der päpstlichen Liturgie genutzt worden waren. Der vormalige Eigengebrauch und die damit einhergehende körperliche Berührung dürfte zu einer besonders starken Aufladung der textilen Gaben mit der Präsenz des päpstlichen Schenkers geführt haben.[17]

---

13 Dafür spricht auch, dass solche Kleidergaben häufig mit einem Investiturritual verbunden waren. Eine kulturenübergreifende Untersuchung des Phänomens der herrschaftlichen Kleidergabe findet sich bei Gordon 2001.

14 Vgl. Keupp 2014, S. 70, 72; Schramm 1957.

15 Gesta Innocentii III, in: PL 214 (1890), Kap. CXLV, Sp. 203–211, Kap. CXLIX, Sp. 226–228. Dazu vgl. Bolton 1999.

16 Die päpstlichen Schenkungen liturgischer Textilien des späten 13. Jahrhunderts sind im Kontext der für die gesamte Kurie charakteristischen Schenkpraktiken zu sehen. Bei vielen Kardinälen der Zeit ist ein ähnliches Schenkverhalten feststellbar wie bei den an dieser Stelle behandelten Päpsten.

17 In der christlichen Tradition spielte die Berührung eine wesentliche Rolle für die Aufladung von Artefakten mit Präsenz und Wirkmacht. Bereits von Christus selbst ist überliefert, dass seine besonderen Heilskräfte auf seine Kleidung übergingen. Dies verdeutlicht die Episode von der Heilung der Blutflüssigen, die im Moment der Berührung des Gewandes Christi durch die Kranke erfolgt (Mk 5,25–34). Auf dem gleichen Prinzip basierte die Wirkmächtigkeit von Kontaktreliquien, die sich in Folge der Berührung eines Heiligenkörpers –

Abb. 2: Pluviale mit Greifen, Doppeladlern und Papageienpaaren, Gold- und Seidenstickerei auf Samit, Zypern oder Sizilien (?), 2. Viertel 13. Jahrhundert (?). Anagni, Kathedrale, Museo del Tesoro.

Im Hinblick auf Form und Farbigkeit, Provenienz, Material und Techniken, Bildsprache und figürliche Programme waren die liturgischen Textilien, welche die Päpste des späten 13. Jahrhunderts verschenkten, sehr vielfältig. Diese Diversität dürfte der Verschiedenartigkeit und Internationalität der Paramente, die sich um 1300 im päpstlichen Schatz befanden und die in den päpstlichen Schatzinventaren von 1295 und 1311 beschrieben werden, entsprochen haben.[18] So waren die Paramente und Textilien aus Geweben und Stickereien unterschiedlichster Provenienz und Machart gefertigt, die in den Inventaren als »opera« genau klassifiziert und dokumentiert werden. Es handelte sich um Luxusgüter, die aus den bedeutendsten Textilzentren der Zeit in Europa, dem Mittelmeerraum, Byzanz und sogar dem mongolischen Großreich stammten. Die Textilbestände des päpstlichen Schatzes muten wie eine vormoderne Sammlung an, die das politische Beziehungsnetz und den Universalanspruch des Papsttums um 1300 widerspiegelte.[19] Diese Sammlung speiste sich sowohl aus von den Päpsten selbst in Auftrag gegebenen bzw. angekauften Stoffen und Gewändern als auch aus diplomatischen

sowohl zu dessen Lebzeiten als auch nach seinem Tod – mit dessen Präsenz aufluden und seine Heilskräfte an beliebige Orte fernab des Heiligengrabes transportieren konnten. Vgl. Bauer 2009, S. 63.

18 Vgl. Inventar päpstlicher Schatz 1295, Molinier 1882–1888; Inventar päpstlicher Schatz 1311, Regesti Clementis Papae V 1892.

19 Zu den Textilbeständen des päpstlichen Schatzes um 1300 und ihrer schriftlichen Überlieferung in den päpstlichen Inventaren von 1295 und 1311 vgl. Elster 2017a (im Druck).

Abb. 3: Kasel (Vorderseite) mit Greifen, Doppeladlern und Papageienpaaren, Gold- und Seidenstickerei auf Samit, Zypern oder Sizilien (?), 2. Viertel 13. Jahrhundert (?). Anagni, Kathedrale, Museo del Tesoro.

Geschenken an die römische Kirche, etwa denen des englischen Königshauses oder der byzantinischen Kaiser.[20]

Im Folgenden werden zwei Beispiele vorgestellt, die exemplarisch die Vielfalt päpstlicher Textilgeschenke des späten 13. Jahrhunderts widerspiegeln. Es handelt sich in beiden Fällen um liturgische Gewänder, die aus dem päpstlichen Schatz und damit aus dem liturgisch-zeremoniellen Gebrauch der Päpste stammten.

Zunächst wird es um eine Auswahl der liturgischen Paramente gehen, die sich aus Schenkungen Bonifaz' VIII. (1294–1303) im Domschatz von Anagni erhalten haben. Die Gruppe von vier liturgischen Gewändern mit Gewebe imitierenden Gold- und Seidenstickereien auf einem roten Samit besteht aus einem Pluviale, einer Kasel und zwei Dalmatiken (Abb. 2, 3).[21] Der fingierte Musterrapport wird durch mit Greifen, Doppeladlern und Papageienpaaren gefüllten Rundmedaillons gebildet (Abb. 4). Der Auftragskontext dieser Paramente ist nicht bekannt; es ist aber überliefert, dass sie sich zu Beginn des Pontifikats Bonifaz' VIII. im päpstlichen Schatz befanden.[22] Ihre Beschreibung in einem um 1300 zu datierenden Inventar der Schenkungen Bonifaz' VIII. an die Kathedrale von Anagni dokumentiert zudem ihre Zugehörigkeit zu dem von Bonifaz an die Domkirche seiner Heimatstadt gestifteten Konvolut an liturgischen Textilien und Geräten.[23]

Während das Pluviale in der von Bonifaz VIII. nach Anagni geschenkten Form erhalten geblieben ist, handelt es sich bei den übrigen drei Gewändern um im späten 16. Jahrhundert vorgenommene Zweitverarbeitungen. Im Zuge dieser zwischen 1573 und 1576 zu datierenden Umarbeitungen wurde ein radmantelförmiges Parament, das in gleicher Art wie das Pluviale geschnitten und bestickt war, auseinandergeschnitten und diente als Materiallieferant zur Herstellung einer Kasel und zweier Dalmatiken, wobei in letztere auch Teile weiterer Paramente eingearbeitet wurden.[24] Die Zugehörigkeit der in der heutigen Kasel verarbeiteten Teile sowie der Rückenteile der Dalmatiken zu einem einzigen, radmantelförmigen Parament geht aus der Bindung und Beschaffenheit

20 Zu päpstlichen Ankäufen und Aufträgen von Textilien vgl. Jacoby 2014, S. 108–109. Diplomatische Textilgeschenke an die Päpste des Mittelalters sind z. B. aus England und Byzanz überliefert. Sowohl der englische König Eduard I. (1272–1307) als auch sein Nachfolger Eduard II. (1307–1327) schenkten wiederholt kostbare Paramente in *opus anglicanum* an Päpste und Kardinäle. Vgl. Christie 1938, S. 3; Brel-Bordaz 1982, S. 15. Zur Rolle des *opus anglicanum* in der englisch-päpstlichen Diplomatie des 13. Jahrhunderts vgl. Gardner 2000. Zu byzantinischen Seiden im päpstlichen Schatz vgl. unten, S. 298 mit Anm. 36, 37.

21 Vgl. Ausst.-Kat. Rom 2000, S. 240, Kat.-Nr. 1; Mortari 1963. Eine neue und ausführliche Bearbeitung der Paramente findet sich in Elster 2017.

22 Vgl. Inventar päpstlicher Schatz 1295, Molinier 1885, S. 25–26, 29–30, Nr. 890–895, 945; Inventar päpstlicher Schatz 1311, Regesti Clementis Papae V 1892, S. 419, 420, 427.

23 Vgl. Inventar Schenkungen Bonifaz' VIII. Anagni, Fenicchia 1979, Nr. 9, 18, 38, 65.

24 Die Umarbeitungsmaßnahmen bestanden außerdem in der Entfernung der auf den Besätzen der Paramente applizierten Perlen und Metallapplikationen. Vgl. Elster 2017b, Kapitel 5.3.1.

Abb. 4: Detail des Pluviales in Anagni (Abb. 2).

des Grundstoffes (einem Samit mit in S-Köper abgebundenem Schuss), aus dem Verlauf der Nähte, aus der Anordnung der Stickereien sowie aus materialspezifischen und motivischen Besonderheiten eindeutig hervor.[25]

Bei dem rekonstruierten Radmantel handelt es sich höchstwahrscheinlich um eine im Inventar der Schenkungen Bonifaz' VIII. an die Kathedrale von Anagni beschriebene Glockenkasel, also um einen vorn durch einen T-förmigen Besatz geschlossenen Radmantel von identischer Form und Machart wie das Pluviale.[26] Dies würde bedeuten, dass die Besätze der heutigen Kasel mit der Darstellung einer in Christus kulminierenden Königsreihe und einer in Petrus mündenden Apostelreihe, die ebenfalls Spuren

25 So tritt auf allen zweitverarbeiteten Teilen dieses Paraments eine besondere Variante des Doppeladlers auf; das Tier ist im Gegensatz zu den Doppeladlern des Pluviales gekrönt. Zur Rekonstruktion des Radmantels vgl. Elster 2017b, Kapitel 2.1 und 7.1.2.

26 *Una planeta de samito laborato de auro cum acu ad leones, pappagallos, grifos, et aquilas cum geminis capitibus et aurifrisio de samito laborato de auro ad ymagines genealogiae Salvatoris cum pernis et lapidibus pretiosis.* Inventar Schenkungen Bonifaz' VIII. Anagni, Fenicchia 1979, Nr. 9. Bei der Hinzufügung der Löwen zu den Tieren, mit denen das Parament bestickt war (Papageien, Greifen, Doppeladler) handelt es sich vermutlich um einen Irrtum des Inventarschreibers.

einer Umarbeitung aufweisen, von dem ursprünglichen Parament stammen. Die mittig über Brust und Rücken verlaufenden Besätze ordnen das profane, an weltlicher Herrschaftsikonographie orientierte figürliche Programm in einen christlichen und auf das Papsttum ausgerichteten Kontext ein (Abb. 3).

Die Datierung und Lokalisierung der Goldstickereien ist in der Forschung noch immer umstritten; zum gegenwärtigen Zeitpunkt ist ein westlicher Herstellungskontext sicher anzunehmen, wobei neben dem in der Literatur vielfach genannten Sizilien eine Verortung der Stickereien nach Zypern ernsthaft geprüft werden sollte. Denn in den päpstlichen Schatzinventaren aus den Jahren 1295 und 1311 wird das Konvolut an liturgischen Textilien, aus dem die nach Anagni geschenkte Gruppe stammt, als *opus cyprense* bezeichnet.[27] Otto von Falkes frühe Verortung der Goldstickereien nach Zypern wurde in der Forschung bald zurückgewiesen und erst jüngst wieder durch David Jacoby aufgegriffen.[28]

Die in Medaillons eingeschriebenen stilisierten Tiere, nämlich Greifen, Doppeladler und Papageienpaare, lassen eine Imitation von gewebten, rapportierenden Seidenstoffen mit einem medaillonförmigen Rahmensystem erkennen, wie es für Seidengewebe aus Byzanz, dem Vorderen Orient und Zentralasien typisch ist. Zwar stellen die stilisierten Tiere ein geläufiges Motivrepertoire der gesamten Seidenindustrie der Spätantike und des frühen Mittelalters dar, doch ist die Differenzierung zwischen byzantinischen und anderen Kulturräumen des Orients zugehörigen Geweben an dieser Stelle nicht unbedingt wesentlich, da im lateinischen Westen vielfach auch Seiden aus dem Mittleren und Fernen Osten als ›byzantinisch‹ wahrgenommen wurden, vermutlich weil sie ihn über Byzanz erreichten.[29] Auffällig ist in jedem Fall der Medienwechsel des Zitats: Denn die Textilien imitieren die im Westen bekannten und aufgrund ihrer Kostbarkeit und Seltenheit hoch geschätzten byzantinischen Seiden im Medium der Stickerei.[30] Dabei bildeten die ausladenden, figürlich gefüllten Kreismuster eine ›ikonographische Chiffre‹, die für

27 Vgl. Anm. 22.

28 Falke 1913, Bd. 2, S. 21–22; Jacoby 2014, S. 108–109. Die bislang in der Forschung alternativ vorgeschlagenen Zuschreibungen nach Byzanz und Sizilien sind beide problematisch, da sie ausschließlich auf stilkritischen Überlegungen basieren und sich weitgehend nicht auf Schriftquellen und technische Analysen stützen. Sie werden ausführlich diskutiert in Elster 2017a (im Druck) und Elster 2017b, Kapitel 3.2.3.

29 Vgl. Muthesius 1995, S. 136, 139–140, 142.

30 Der Medienwechsel hatte einerseits technische Gründe, denn im Westen wurde erst seit dem 12./13. Jahrhundert Seide gewonnen und die Technik der Seidenweberei entwickelt. Vorher fehlten komplexe Webstühle und damit die technologischen Voraussetzungen zur Herstellung feinteiliger Muster in regelmäßiger Wiederholung. Davon abgesehen erlaubte es die Stickerei aber auch, die den Kreismedaillons eingeschriebenen figürlichen Darstellungen beliebig zu drehen und damit bei Gewändern ihre Lesbarkeit zu erhöhen.

den Wert und die Kostbarkeit byzantinischer Seiden stand und als solche auch gelesen und verstanden wurde.[31]

Im byzantinischen Reich spielten kostbare Seidengewebe eine wichtige Rolle innerhalb des Zeremoniells am kaiserlichen Hof in Konstantinopel und wurden als ein auf den Kaiser und seinen Hofstaat bezogenes Machtsymbol gedeutet. Sie wurden in den direkt am Hof ansässigen kaiserlichen Werkstätten produziert; Handelsbeschränkungen und Exportverbote stellten die exklusive Verfügbarkeit des Luxusartikels für den Kaiser sicher.[32] Schriftquellen aus der mittelbyzantinischen Zeit überliefern stilisierte Tiermotive auf der Hoftracht der kaiserlichen Familie und der höfischen Beamten; ab dem 12. Jahrhundert tauchen sie auf den Gewändern, der Fußbekleidung und verschiedenen Accessoires des Kaisers selbst auf.[33] In der sogenannten *Ekphrasis* des Turniers Manuels I. (1143–1180) wird das äußere Erscheinungsbild des Kaisers ausführlich beschrieben, einschließlich seiner Gewandung. Der Text schildert u. a. einen gelben Mantel, der mit aus Gold und Perlen gestickten Greifen dekoriert gewesen sei. Die roten Schuhe des Kaisers seien mit weißen, in Perlstickerei gefertigten Adlern verziert gewesen. Sowohl der Adler als auch der Greif werden als Symbole der Tugenden des Kaisers gedeutet und auf seine Erhabenheit bezogen, die weißen Perlen werden darüber hinaus als Zeichen seiner Unbeflecktheit interpretiert. Als Bedeutungsträger fungieren neben den Motiven auch die Farben der Gewänder und die Materialien der Stickereien:

> »Der Peplos [Mantel] des Kaisers war hellgelb, mit Gold gestickt. [...] Und es war der Peplos kaiserlich und wertvoll (?), kaiserlich, weil er sich durch Glanz auszeichnete, wertvoll, weil der kaiserliche Peplos Reichtum bedeutet. An den Schultern flattern in einem roten Kreis Greifenvögel aus Gold und mit vielen Perlen versehen; so wurde es durch den Kreis, durch die Art der Vögel und die Farbe für jedermann angedeutet, daß der Kaiser hoch und erhaben ist und wie vom Himmel her gewaltig donnernd Wunderbares vollbringt. [...] Die Schuhe sind rot und wirklich kaiserlich. Weiße Adler sind mit Perlen auf den Schuhen abgebildet, damit durch das Weiß der Perlen und den Höhenflug der Vögel die ganze Erhabenheit des Kaisers dargestellt wird. Die Perlen bedeuten, daß der Kaiser unbefleckt ist, und die Adler, daß er in der Höhe schwebt.«[34]

31 Vgl. Stauffer 2013, S. 12–16.

32 Vgl. Bauer 2010, S. 22–23; Muthesius 1995, S. 231–232; La Barre Starensier 1982, S. 181–279, 456–464, 480–495.

33 In der Zeremonienschrift *De Ceremoniis Aulae Bizantinae* Kaiser Konstantins VII. Porphyrogenetos (913–959) werden Seidengewänder des Kaisers und der kaiserlichen *familia* beschrieben, die u. a. mit Adlern, Greifen und Ochsen geschmückt waren. Vgl. Constantinus Porphyrogenetos, De Ceremoniis II, 15, Reiske 1829, Bd. 1, S. 577f. Dazu Muthesius 1995, S. 214, Anm. 27; Muthesius 2004, S. 228.

34 Rom, Biblioteca Vaticana, Vat. Gr. 1409, fol. 277–277v, ediert in Schreiner 1996, S. 235–241, hier S. 240.

Auch Bildquellen überliefern aus Seidengeweben mit stilisierten Tieren wie Greifen und Doppeladlern gefertigte Gewänder des Kaisers und hoher Ränge des byzantinischen Beamtenapparats, z.B. ein Bildnis des Kaisers Alexios V. Dukas Murtzuphlos (reg. 1204) aus der ersten Hälfte des 14. Jahrhunderts (Abb. 5).[35]

Dass am päpstlichen Hof des späten 13. Jahrhunderts byzantinische Stoffe mit Tiermedaillons bekannt waren, verraten zahlreiche Einträge im päpstlichen Schatzverzeichnis von 1295. Dort wird u.a. eine Dalmatika beschrieben, deren Trägerstoff aus einem mit Doppeladlern gemusterten Gewebe byzantinischer Herkunft gefertigt war, das explizit als kaiserlicher Stoff bezeichnet wird: *Item, dalmaticam rubeam de panno imperiali de Romania ad aquilas magnas cum duobus capitibus sine ornamentis;* [...].[36] Denkbar ist, dass dieses Gewebe als diplomatisches Geschenk des byzantinischen Kaiserhauses in den päpstlichen Schatz gelangt und in Rom zu einer Dalmatika weiterverarbeitet worden war. Den päpstlichen Inventarschreibern war jedenfalls nicht nur die byzantinische Provenienz des Stoffes bekannt, sondern auch sein Rang als ein spezifisch für den Kaiser bzw. seinen Hofstaat bestimmtes Gewebe.[37]

Aber die auf Byzanz bezogenen Rezeptions- und Adaptionsprozesse, die in den nach Anagni geschenkten Paramenten in *opus cyprense* fassbar sind, gehen womöglich sogar über die Bildmotive hinaus und umfassen auch das Gewand an sich als materielles Objekt und in seiner symbolischen Zeichenhaftigkeit als Herrschaftsinsignie. Es stellt sich nämlich die Frage, ob es sich bei dem roten Pluviale in seiner päpstlichen Erstverwendung um ein päpstliches *mantum* gehandelt haben könnte. Im Hinblick auf seine Form und Farbigkeit war das *mantum* im 12. und 13. Jahrhundert vermutlich mit einem roten Pluviale identisch, worauf auch die Terminologie der Quellen dieser Zeit hinweist, denn *mantum*, *cappa (rubea)*, *chlamys (rubea)* und *pluviale (rubeum)* werden in der Regel synonym benutzt.[38] Das rote *mantum* war neben Pallium, Tiara und dem weißen Zelter spätestens seit dem 11. Jahrhundert Teil der päpstlichen Herrschaftsinsignien. Die *immantatio*, also Bekleidung des Papstes mit dem *mantum* unmittelbar nach seiner

35 Weitere Beispiele bei Woodfin 2012, S. 150–163, Stauffer 2013, S. 10–11.

36 Inventar päpstlicher Schatz 1295, Molinier 1885, S. 30, Nr. 959.

37 Möglicherweise war der Stoff mit einer Inschrift versehen, die ihn als Erzeugnis der kaiserlichen Werkstätten in Konstantinopel auswies, wie es z.B. bei der um 1000 entstandenen Elefantenseide im Karlsschrein in Aachen der Fall ist. Vgl. Wilckens 1991, S. 52–54. Zu diplomatischen Textilgeschenken der byzantinischen Kaiser an die Päpste vgl. Schreiner 2004, S. 271–280, Nr. 6a, 7, 9, 43.

38 Vgl. Braun 1907, S. 351–352. Um die Bedeutungskomponenten genauer herauszuarbeiten, müssten die genannten Begriffe einer philologischen Kontextanalyse unterzogen werden. Es ist denkbar, dass der Terminus *mantum* im Unterschied zu *pluviale* und *cappa* nicht einen spezifischen Gewandtyp bezeichnet, sondern auf spezifische Handlungen der päpstlichen Liturgie bezogen ist, vor allem das Ritual der *immantatio*. Ich danke Sible de Blaauw sehr herzlich für diesen Hinweis. Gegen diese Vermutung spricht jedoch die Austauschbarkeit der Begriffe *mantum* und *pluviale* bei den Beschreibungen der *immantatio* in den päpstlichen Ordines und Zeremonienbüchern des 11. bis 13. Jahrhunderts. Vgl. dazu Anm. 39.

Abb. 5: Niketas Choniates, *Historia*, Kaiser Alexios V. in Seidengewändern, Konstantinopel, 1. Hälfte 14. Jahrhundert. Wien, Österreichische Nationalbibliothek, Cod. Hist.Gr. 53, fol. 291v.

Wahl, brachte die Investitur des Electus in das Papstamt zum Ausdruck und symbolisierte die Übergabe der päpstlichen Regierungsgewalt.[39]

Das *mantum* gehörte zu den Privilegien, welche die Konstantinische Schenkung dem Papsttum zugesichert hatte.[40] Das im 15. Jahrhundert als Fälschung entlarvte *Constitutum Constantini*, das die Konstitution der weltlichen Macht des Papsttums um die Mitte des 8. Jahrhunderts (Pippinische Schenkung) dokumentiert und die Grundlage der *imitatio imperii*-Bestrebungen des Reformpapsttums bildete, übertrug dem Papsttum nämlich nicht nur Rom, den kaiserlichen Lateranpalast und die Herrschaftsgewalt über das weströmische Reich, sondern auch die Insignien und den Herrscherornat Kaiser Konstantins des Großen (306–337). Zu diesem gehörten neben dem Diadem, das Papst Silvester I. (314–335) aus Demut ablehnte, und dem *phrygium* (Tiara) auch die Herrschaftsgewänder (*omnia imperialia indumenta*), nämlich der Loros, die purpurfarbene Chlamys und die scharlachrote Tunika.[41] Das *mantum* stellte also eines der materiellen Zeichen für die programmatische Aneignung der Herrschaftsinsignien des römischen Kaisertums durch das Papsttum dar.[42] Im Zusammenspiel mit den anderen Insignien machte es den Papst zu einem Abbild des antiken römischen Herrschers. Dabei wurde jedoch das zeitgenössische Kaisertum in Byzanz als Referenzpunkt genutzt, verkörperte es doch für die Päpste ein Kontinuum und gleichsam ein lebendes Modell des römischen Kaisertums.

Die herausgearbeiteten, auf Byzanz bezogenen Bedeutungskomponenten des päpstlichen Pluviales von Anagni beziehen sich aber natürlich ausschließlich auf eine mögliche päpstliche Erstverwendung des Gewandes. Für die Empfänger der Schenkung, das Domkapitel in Anagni, dürften sie dagegen keine Rolle gespielt haben. In den Inventaren der Kathedrale von Anagni wurde das Parament zwar bis weit in die Neuzeit hinein als Geschenk Papst Bonifaz' VIII. erinnert, aber stets als rotes Pluviale bezeichnet.[43]

39 Vgl. de Blaauw 2002, S. 365; Herklotz 1985, S. 8–10; Eichmann 1951, S. 33–35. Die *immantatio* des neuen Papstes wird erstmals in der Vita Gregors VII. für das Jahr 1076 erwähnt, dort aber als herkömmlich bezeichnet (*indutus rubea clamide sicut moris est*, Liber pontificalis, Duchesne 1955, Bd. 2, S. 361). Die Zeremonie wird auch im *Liber Censuum* des Cencius Savelli vom Ende des 12. Jahrhunderts beschrieben, wo der Mantel des einzusetzenden Papstes als *pluviale rubeum* bezeichnet wird: [...] *prior diaconorum ipsum de pluviali rubeo ammantat, et eidem electo nomen imponit* [...].« Liber Censuum, Fabre/Duchesne 1905, Bd. 1, S. 311. Laut dem päpstlichen Ordo von 1273 zog der die Papstwahl leitende Kardinalarchidiakon dem Electus zunächst seine gewöhnliche *cappa* aus, legte ihm dann Rochett, Albe und Stola an, und bekleidete ihn zuletzt mit dem *mantum*, wobei er die Worte sprach: *Investio te de papatu romano, ut praesis urbi et orbi.* Le Cérémonial Papal, Dykmans 1977, Bd. 1, S. 159.

40 Eichmann 1951, S. 34; Miller 2014b, S. 64–67.

41 Constitutum Constantini 14, Fried 2007, S. 135.

42 Vgl. Herklotz 1985, S. 9–10.

43 Vgl. Inventar Schenkungen Bonifaz' VIII. Anagni, Fenicchia 1979, Nr. 38; Anagni, Archivio Capitolare, Serie 4: Finanze e Patrimonio (1566–1962), 1. Inventari (1576–1688); dazu Elster 2017b, Kapitel 5.3.1.

Abb. 6: Pluviale mit christologischen Szenen, Märtyrerpäpsten, Bekennerpäpsten und vier Päpsten des 13. Jahrhunderts, Metall- und Seidenstickerei auf Leinengrund, England (?), zwischen 1265 und 1288. Ascoli Piceno, Pinacoteca Civica.

Der Referenzcharakter auf den päpstlichen Schenker blieb also erhalten, während die mögliche Funktion als päpstliche Herrschaftsinsignie nicht erinnert wurde.

Ein weiteres Beispiel für ein aus dem päpstlichen Schatz stammendes Textilgeschenk ist das aus einer Schenkung Papst Nikolaus' IV (1288–1292) an die Kathedrale von Ascoli Piceno stammende und heute in der dortigen Pinacoteca Civica aufbewahrte Pluviale in *opus anglicanum*[44], das zwischen 1265 und 1288 zu datieren ist und entweder für Papst Clemens IV. (1265–1268) oder für Gregor X. (1271–1276) bestimmt gewesen sein dürfte (Abb. 6).[45] Papst Nikolaus IV. schenkte das Gewand 1288 der Kathedrale seiner Heimatstadt Ascoli Piceno.[46] Die Schenkung des Pluviales durch den damals erst seit etwa fünf Monaten im Amt befindlichen Papst scheint wesentlich auf das Werben um politische Loyalität der päpstlichen Heimatstadt ausgerichtet gewesen zu sein. Diese wurde nämlich 1288, zur Zeit seines Amtsantritts, durch politische Unruhen erschüt-

44 Zum *opus anglicanum* vgl. Elster 2017a (im Druck); Elster 2014, S. 179, Anm. 15; Ausst.-Kat. London 2016.

45 Für die Datierung bildet die Wahl Clemens' IV., des letzten der vier im unteren Register dargestellten Päpste, am 5. Februar 1265 einen *terminus post quem*, während der Schenkungsakt nach Ascoli Piceno kurze Zeit vor dem 28. Juli 1288 den *terminus ante quem* darstellt. Vgl. Ausst.-Kat. London 2016, S. 144–146, Kat.-Nr. 22; Bonito Fanelli 1990; Gagliardi/Piccinini-Fabi 1990; Christie 1938, S. 89–94, Kat.-Nr. 50.

46 Ein am 28. Juli 1288 in Rieti ausgestelltes päpstliches Schreiben überliefert die Schenkung und ihre Umstände. Demnach war das Pluviale kürzlich (*nuper*) im Auftrag des Papstes durch einen Boten, den Franziskaner Lamberto da Ripatransone, nach Ascoli Piceno überbracht worden. Paris, Bibliothèque Nationale, Ms. Lat. 4047, fol. 20v–21r; ediert in: Les Registres de Nicolas IV., Langlois 1905, Bd. 2, S. 959, Nr. 7101.

tert, die mit kirchenfeindlichen Aktionen einhergingen. Um die Stadt stärker an das römische Papsttum zu binden, setzte sich Nikolaus IV. kurz nach seiner Wahl selbst als *podestà* von Ascoli Piceno ein und schickte verschiedene Verbündete als Friedensvermittler, u. a. den Franziskaner Lamberto da Ripatransone.[47] Letzterer überbrachte wenige Monate später als Bote das textile Geschenk Nikolaus' IV.

Dass es sich bei diesem Pluviale um ein explizit päpstliches Kleidungsstück handelte, das entweder durch ein Mitglied der Kurie in England in Auftrag gegeben worden oder als diplomatisches Geschenk des englischen Königshauses[48] nach Rom gelangt sein dürfte[49], geht vor allem aus dem ungewöhnlichen, das römische Papsttum verherrlichenden Bildprogramm des Objekts hervor. Die senkrechte Mittelachse zeigt die *Vera Icon*, die Kreuzigung und eine thronende Madonna mit Kind. Diese christologisch ausgerichtete Mitte wird von einer genealogisch anmutenden Folge heiliger Päpste flankiert. Während im ersten Register beginnend mit Petrus, der zur Rechten des Heiligen Antlitzes platziert ist, die Märtyrertode heiliger Päpste des frühen Christentums zu sehen sind, werden darunter von Kardinälen flankierte heilige Bekennerpäpste im Lehrgestus dargestellt.[50] Im dritten Register erscheinen schließlich vier Vertreter des Papsttums des 13. Jahrhunderts, nämlich (von links nach rechts) Alexander IV. (1254–1261), Urban IV. (1261–1264), Clemens IV. (1265–1268) und Innozenz IV. (1243–1254). Die zeitgenössischen Päpste werden wie die Bekennerpäpste als Lehrende zwischen zwei Kardinälen gezeigt und mit Hilfe des derart vereinheitlichten Kompositionsschemas programmatisch als deren Nachfolger präsentiert (Abb. 7). Die reihende Darstellung der Päpste, die mit ihren Kardinälen im Dialog stehen, betont die Einbindung der letzteren in die Leitung der Kirche, zugleich aber auch die päpstliche, auf Christus und seinen Stellvertreter Petrus gründende Autorität, der sie sich unterstellen. Die apostolische Sukzession

47 Vgl. Ascoli Pontificia, Franchi 1999, Bd. 2, S. 176–201, Nr. 156–181; Grelli 2000, S. 272 f.; Franchi 1990, S. 163–170, 268.

48 Mehrere Pluviale in *opus anglicanum* sind als diplomatische Geschenke des englischen Königshauses an Päpste des 13. und 14. Jahrhunderts bezeugt. Schriftlich überliefert sind z. B. Schenkungen von Pluvialen durch Eduard I. (1272–1307) an Nikolaus IV. und Bonifaz VIII. Vgl. oben, Anm. 20.

49 Auftragskontext und Herstellungsort des Pluviales sind in der Forschung umstritten. Die Forschungsgeschichte des Pluviales stellt ein interessantes Beispiel für nationale Befangenheiten in der Kunstgeschichtsschreibung des 19. und 20. Jahrhunderts dar, die unterschwellig bis heute fortwirken. Englische, französische und italienische Kunsthistoriker stritten sich um die Lokalisierung des Pluviales nach England, Frankreich oder Rom: Für Frankreich plädierten Bertaux 1897 und Braun 1907, S. 339. Für England sprachen sich Morris 1904/05, Lee 1932/33, Lethaby 1929 und Ladner 1984, S. 131–134, aus. Der römische Kunsthistoriker Carlo Cecchelli schließlich brachte Rom ins Spiel und argumentierte, das Pluviale sei dort durch am päpstlichen Hof beschäftigte englische Sticker angefertigt worden: Cecchelli 1952, S. 338. Zur Forschungsgeschichte vgl. Ertl 2010, S. 104–106.

50 Die Päpste werden durch Inschriften namentlich bezeichnet. Märtyrerpäpste: Johannes I., Marcellus I, Petrus, Clemens I, Stephan I., Fabianus. Bekennerpäpste (Confessores): Leo I., Hilarius, Silvester I., Gregor I., Lucius I., Anastasius I.

Abb. 7: Detail des Pluviales in Ascoli Piceno: Papst Clemens IV. (1265–1268).

der Päpste wird auf dem Pluviale in einer Art narrativen Genealogie entfaltet, die auf den Papst ausgerichtet ist, für den das liturgische Gewand bestimmt war. Im Fall von Clemens IV. wäre der Adressat des Pluviales in die Papstreihe aufgenommen worden, denn er ist der letzte der im untersten Register dargestellten Päpste aus dem 13. Jahrhundert. Es ist allerdings fraglich, ob eine so prominente Darstellung eines amtierenden Papstes unter Clemens IV. bereits denkbar ist.[51] Daher ist zu vermuten, dass das Pluviale für einen der Nachfolger Clemens' IV. bestimmt war, wahrscheinlich Gregor X. Er als

51 Dass päpstliche Paramente auch mit Bildnissen amtierender Pontifices dekoriert sein konnten, ist erst für das Pontifikat Bonifaz' VIII. sicher zu belegen. Aus einem Eintrag in einem Inventar des Schatzes von Alt-St. Peter aus dem Jahr 1361 geht hervor, dass ein aus einer Schenkung Bonifaz' VIII. stammendes Pluviale

intendierter Träger des Pluviales bildet, gleichsam ›in Fleisch und Blut‹, den Abschluss der darauf repräsentierten Papstreihe. Daher bedurfte es seiner Aufnahme in die Sequenz der Papstbildnisse nicht.

Diese wird zugleich in einen christologisch-petrinischen, auf Rom bezogenen Kontext gestellt. Denn das an zentraler Stelle gezeigte Antlitz Christi referiert auf die in Alt-St. Peter aufbewahrte Reliquie der *Vera Icon* und verweist damit auf Rom als rechtmäßigen Sitz des Papsttums. Die reihende Darstellung von ausgewählten Vertretern des Heiligen Stuhls erinnert zudem an die in Rundmedaillons eingeschriebenen Papstreihen in römischen Kirchen seit der Spätantike, z. B. in S. Paolo fuori le mura.[52] Im Gegensatz zu den statischen Bildnissen dieser Papstreihen wird beim Pluviale jedoch ein erzählerischer Darstellungsmodus gewählt, der auf die Heiligkeit der dargestellten Päpste und ihre Zuordnung zu spezifischen Heiligenständen, d. h. Märtyrern und *Confessores*, abzielt. Ein übergreifendes Element, das alle dargestellten Päpste miteinander verbindet und das zugleich ein selbstreferentielles Moment in das Bildprogramm des liturgischen Mantels einführt, stellt ihre Kleidung dar: Alle Päpste werden im pontifikalen Ornat und mit der Tiara bekrönt gezeigt, sogar die frühen Märtyrerpäpste einschließlich des kopfüber am Kreuz hängenden Petrus. Die Gewänder der Päpste und die der sie flankierenden Kardinäle sind zudem mit heraldisch anmutenden, in Goldstickerei ausgeführten Motiven wie Leoparden, Löwen, Lilien, Adlern und Schlössern verziert und dadurch im Hinblick auf ihren materiellen Wert und ihre Kostbarkeit als dem realen Pluviale ebenbürtig ausgewiesen.[53] Als verbindendes Element zwischen dem päpstlichen Träger des Pluviales und seinen darauf gezeigten heiligen Vorgängern steht die Gewandung für den Fortbestand des Amtes, trotz des kontinuierlichen Wechsels seiner jeweiligen Inhaber.

Im Zuge der Schenkung wurde der liturgische Mantel mit diesem explizit auf die römische Institution des Papsttums und einen päpstlichen Träger ausgerichteten Bildprogramm nach außen gegeben und im Hinblick auf seine räumliche Umgebung und liturgische Verwendung neu kontextualisiert. Was bedeutete dies für seine Funktion sowie Wahrnehmung und Deutung durch das Empfängerkollektiv? Interessant ist in

---

in *opus anglicanum* mit einem Bildnis des Pontifex geschmückt war. Inventare Schatz St. Peter, Müntz/Frothingham 1883, S. 19.

52 Die Reihe der paarweise angeordneten Papstmedaillons oberhalb der Arkaden und unterhalb der Mosaikfelder wurde unter Papst Leo dem Großen (440–461) begonnen. Im 13. Jahrhundert wurde der Zyklus unter Nikolaus III. (1277–1280) restauriert und erweitert. Alle Päpste werden als Halbporträts in streng frontaler Haltung gezeigt. Vgl. Romano 2012, S. 340–343.

53 Zu der Möglichkeit, dass es sich um spezifische heraldische Anspielungen mit Bezug auf England, Frankreich, das Heilige Römische Reich und Kastilien handelt, vgl. Kyser 1990. In jedem Fall rezipieren die Motive mit stilisierten Tieren bestickte päpstliche und bischöfliche Gewänder, ähnlich denjenigen oben besprochenen aus den Schenkungen Papst Bonifaz' VIII. an die Kathedrale von Anagni.

diesem Kontext ein das Textilgeschenk betreffende Begleitschreiben Nikolaus' IV., das auf den 28. Juli 1288 datiert und Anweisungen zum Umgang mit dem päpstlichen Parament enthält:

> » [...] damit ihr jenes [Pluviale] an feierlichen und festlichen Tagen verwendet, je nachdem wie es eurem Urteilsvermögen schicklich erscheinen wird. Damit es aber nicht gelingt, dass ein Dieb die genannte Kirche um den Gebrauch desselben Pluviales betrügt, verfügen wir deutlich durch die Autorität der Anwesenden, dass das genannte Pluviale aus keinem evtl. Bedürfnis derselben Kirche heraus verkauft oder verpfändet werden darf oder auf irgendeine andere Weise veräußert werden darf. [...]«[54]

Zum einen wird den Empfängern der Schenkung, dem Domkapitel von Ascoli Piceno, vorgeschrieben, dass es das Pluviale an den kirchlichen Hochfesten benutzen solle. Es wird also zur Einbindung des päpstlichen Textilgeschenks in die eigene Liturgie verpflichtet. Zum anderen spricht der Papst ein Verkaufs- und Verpfändungsverbot aus und legt damit die Unveräußerlichkeit des geschenkten Paraments fest. Das Domkapitel musste somit für eine unbefristete Aufbewahrung und Erhaltung des textilen Geschenks Sorge tragen.[55]

Die aktive Erinnerung des päpstlichen Schenkers durch das Empfängerkollektiv bildete folglich ein zentrales Anliegen dieser Textilschenkung. Solche mit den Schenkvorgängen einhergehenden Verpflichtungen der Empfänger gegenüber den päpstlichen Schenkern schufen politische Abhängigkeits- und Loyalitätsverhältnisse; sie wirkten, wie es bereits Marcel Mauss in seiner Gabentheorie darlegte, beziehungsstiftend.[56] Sein Verweischarakter auf seine Provenienz aus dem päpstlichen Schatz und auf den Schenker machte das päpstliche Textilgeschenk abgesehen von seiner primären Funktion als

54 [...] *ut illo, prout vestra viderit decere discretio, diebus utamini sollempnibus et festivis. Ut autem ipsius pluvialis usu predictam non contingat ecclesiam imposterum defraudari, auctoritate presentium districtius inhibemus ne pluviale prefatum pro quavis ipsius necessitate vendatur ecclesie vel obligetur pignori aut quomodolibet distrahatur.* Les Registres de Nicolas IV., Langlois 1905, Bd. 2, S. 959, Nr. 7101 (wie oben, Anm. 46).

55 Auch für andere päpstliche Geschenke von Textilien und liturgischen Geräten des späten 13. Jahrhunderts sind Veräußerungsverbote schriftlich überliefert. Vgl. dazu Elster 2017b, Kapitel 4.3.2. Die Grundlage für diese Verbote bildete eine Festlegung des III. Laterankonzils von 1179, der zufolge es Klerikern verboten war, Geschenke stellvertretend für eine geistliche Institution anzunehmen und diese anschließend von dort zu entfernen bzw. zu veräußern. Vgl. Concilium Lateranense III 1179, Canon 15, in: Decrees of the Ecumenical Councils, Tanner 1990, Bd. 1, S. 219.

56 Laut Marcel Mauss stellt die Reziprozität das entscheidende Charakteristikum des Gabentausches dar, der sich aus den drei verpflichtenden Elementen Geben, Nehmen und Erwidern zusammensetzt und dauerhafte soziale Beziehungen stiftet. Der Empfänger ist also zur Erwiderung des Geschenks verpflichtet, wobei das Reziprozitätsprinzip nicht meint, dass der Gabentausch einen materiellen Ausgleich zwischen Geber und Empfänger einfordert. In asymmetrischen Tauschbeziehungen können Gaben auch immateriell ausgeglichen werden. Vgl. Mauss 1968 [1923–1924].

Bekleidungsstück innerhalb der christlichen Liturgie der Empfängerkirche zu einem ›Erinnerungsträger‹.[57] Die erinnerungsstiftende Funktion der päpstlichen Textilgaben wird auch durch die Adaption der Artefakte an die Erfordernisse zeitgenössischer Verwendungskontexte deutlich. Gebrauchsspuren sowie auf Umarbeitungen und konservatorische Maßnahmen zurückgehende Veränderungen der Paramente bezeugen sowohl ihre langwährende Verwendung in der Liturgie der Empfängerinstitutionen zu ausgewählten Anlässen als auch ihre sorgfältige Erhaltung und Musealisierung.[58]

Zusammenfassend kann festgehalten werden, dass päpstliche Textilschenkungen des späten 13. Jahrhunderts als vielgestaltige Akte symbolischer Kommunikation mit beziehungsstiftender Funktion zu deuten sind. Die textilen Gaben zeichneten sich im Hinblick auf ihre Materialität und Ikonographie durch Heterogenität aus. Ihre Bildprogramme reichten von aus der weltlichen Herrschaftsikonographie stammenden stilisierten Tieren bis zu figürlichen Darstellungen und Bilderzählungen aus der christlichen Ikonographie. Was ihre päpstliche Erstverwendung angeht, sind für einen Teil der verschenkten liturgischen Gewänder auf Byzanz bezogene Rezeptions- und Adaptionsprozesse charakteristisch, die den weltlichen Machtanspruch des Papsttums in der Nachfolge des römischen Kaisertums zum Ausdruck brachten. Typisch für die päpstlichen Textilgaben ist darüber hinaus ihre Ambiguität als Gebrauchsgegenstände und Erinnerungsträger. Einerseits waren die Textilgeschenke auf die praktische Verwend- und Nutzbarkeit durch die Empfänger abgestimmt. Andererseits wurden sie im Zuge der Schenkungen zu auf den päpstlichen Schenker verweisenden Erinnerungsobjekten. Indem die Päpste mit Hilfe der Schenkungen von Textilien und anderen Objekten einen Teil der materiellen Kultur des päpstlichen Hofes an strategisch wichtige Orte Roms und des Kirchenstaates verlagerten, erweiterten sie ihre Repräsentation über die Räume hinaus, an denen sie persönlich präsent waren. Die Verpflichtung zur Erhaltung der geschenkten Textilien und zu ihrer liturgischen Nutzung bei ausgewählten Anlässen stellte die Erinnerung der päpstlichen Schenker durch die beschenkten Kollektive sicher und zielte auf ihre politische Loyalität mit der römischen Kirche.

57 Hier wird von einem weitgefassten Erinnerungsbegriff ausgegangen, der Erinnerung als einen kreativen, schaffenden Akt versteht, der zu einer fortwährenden (Re-) Konstruktion der Vergangenheit entsprechend der sich wandelnden Bezugsrahmen der Gegenwart führt. Vgl. Assmann 1992; Fried 2004. Zum Begriff des ›Erinnerungsträgers‹ vgl. Späth 2007; Albrecht 2003, S. 14–15.

58 Vgl. Elster 2017b, Kapitel 5.

Bibliographie

Archivalien

Anagni, Archivio Capitolare, Serie 4: Finanze e Patrimonio (1566–1962), 1. Inventari (1576–1688).

Lateran, Archivio Capitolare, AAA 5.

Quellen

Ascoli Pontificia, Franchi 1999, Bd. 2 Ascoli Pontificia, Bd. 2: dal 1244 al 1300. (Testi e Documenti 4), hg. von Laura Ciotti und Antonino Franchi, Ascoli Piceno 1999.

Constantinus Porphyrogenetos, De Ceremoniis, Reiske 1829, Bd. 1 Constantini Porphyrogeniti imperatoris, De Cerimoniis Aulae Byzantinae, 2 Bde., hg. von I. I. Reiske, Bonn 1829–1830.

Constitutum Constantini, Fried 2007 Constitutum Constantini, hg. von Johannes Fried, Donation of Constantine and Constitutum Constantini. The Misinterpretation of a Fiction and its Original Meaning, Berlin/New York 2007.

Decrees of the Ecumenical Councils, Tanner 1990, Bd. 1 Decrees of the Ecumenical Councils, Bd. 1: Nicaea I to Lateran V, hg. von Norman P. Tanner, London 1990.

Descriptio Lateranensis Ecclesiae, Valentini/Zucchetti 1946, Bd. 3 Descriptio Lateranensis Ecclesiae, in: Codice Topografico della Città di Roma, Bd. 3 (Fonti per la storia d'Italia 90), hg. von Roberto Valentini und Giuseppe Zucchetti, Rom 1946, S. 326–373.

Gesta Innocentii III, in: PL 214 (1890), Kap. CXLV, Sp. 203–211, Kap. CXLIX, Sp. 226–228.

Inventar päpstlicher Schatz 1295, Molinier 1882–1888 Inventaire du trésor du Saint Siège sous Boniface VIII (1295), hg. von Émile Molinier, in: Bibliothèque de l'École des Chartres 43 (1882), S. 19–310, 626–646, 45 (1884), S. 31–57, 46 (1885), S. 16–44, 47 (1886), S. 646–667, 49 (1888), S. 226–237.

Inventar päpstlicher Schatz 1311, Regesti Clementis Papae V 1892 Inventarium thesauri ecclesiae Romanae apud Perusium asservati iussu Clementis Papae V factum anno MCCCXI, in: Regesti Clementis Papae V ex vaticanis archetypis sanctissimi domini nostri Leonis XIII Pontificis Maximi iussu et munificentia nunc primum editi cura et studio Monachorum Ordinis S. Benedicti, Appendices: Tomus I, Rom 1892, S. 369–513.

Inventar Schenkungen Bonifaz' VIII. Anagni, Fenicchia 1979 L'inventario dei paramenti e degli oggetti di sacra suppellettile donati da Bonifacio VIII alla cattedrale di Anagni, hg. von Vincenzo Fenicchia, in: Palaeographica Diplomatica et Archivistica. Studi in onore di Giulio Battelli (Storia e Letteratura. Raccolta di Studi e Testi, 140), Bd. 2, Rom 1979, S. 513–525.

Inventare Schatz St. Peter, Müntz/Frothingham 1883 Eugène Müntz und Arthur L. Frothingham: Il tesoro della basilica di S. Pietro in Vaticano dal XIII al XV secolo con una scelta d'inventari inediti, in: Archivio della R. Società Romana di Storia Patria 6, 1883, S. 1–137.

Le Cérémonial Papal, Dykmans 1977, Bd. 1 Le Cérémonial Papal de la fin du Moyen Âge à la Renaissance, Bd. 1: Le Cérémonial Papal du XIIIe siècle, hg. von Marc Dykmans (Bibliothèque de l'Institut historique belge de Rome 24), Brüssel/ Rom 1977.

Les Registres des Nicolas IV, Langlois 1905, Bd. 2 Les Registres de Nicolas IV. Recueil des Bulles de ce pape, hg. von Ernest Langlois (Bibliothèque des Écoles Françaises d'Athènes et de Rome, 2e Série 5), Paris 1905, Bd. 2.

Liber Censuum, Fabre/Duchesne 1905, Bd. 1 Le Liber Censuum de l'Église Romaine, 3 Bde., hg. von Paul Fabre und Louis Duchesne, Paris 1905–1932.

Liber Pontificalis, Duchesne 1955, Bd. 1 und Bd. 2 Le Liber Pontificalis: texte, introduction et commentaire par l'Abbé L. Duchesne, 3 Bde., hg. von Louis Duchesne, Paris 1955–1957 [Erstveröffentlichung 1886–1892].

Sekundärliteratur

Ausst.-Kat. London 2016 English Medieval Embroidery. Opus Anglicanum, hg. von Clare Browne, Glyn Davies und M. A. Michael, London 2016.

Ausst.-Kat. Rom 2000 Bonifacio VIII e il suo tempo. Anno 1300 il primo giubileo, hg. von Marina Righetti Tosti-Croce, Mailand 2000.

Albrecht 2003 Stephan Albrecht: Die Inszenierung der Vergangenheit im Mittelalter. Die Klöster von Glastonbury und Saint-Denis (Kunstwissenschaftliche Studien 104), München/Berlin 2003.

Andaloro 1990 Maria Andaloro: Il Tesoro della basilica di S. Giovanni in Laterano, in: San Giovanni in Laterano, hg. von Carlo Pietrangeli, Florenz 1990, S. 271–297.

Andaloro 2003 Maria Andaloro: Immagine e immagini nel Liber Pontificalis da Adriano I a Pasquale I, in: Atti del colloquio internazionale »Il Liber Pontificalis e la storia materiale«, Roma, 21.–22.2.2002 (Medelingen van het Nederlands Instituut te Rome 60–61), hg. von Herman Geertman, Assen 2003, S. 45–103.

Assmann 1992 Jan Assmann: Das kulturelle Gedächtnis. Schrift, Erinnerung und politische Identität in frühen Hochkulturen, München 1992.

Bauer 2004 Franz Alto Bauer: Das Bild der Stadt Rom im Frühmittelalter. Papststiftungen im Spiegel des Liber Pontificalis von Gregor dem Dritten bis zu Leo dem Dritten, Wiesbaden 2004.

Bauer 2009 Franz Alto Bauer: Gabe und Person. Geschenke als Träger personaler Aura in der Spätantike (Eichstätter Universitätsreden 116), Eichstätt 2009.

Bauer 2010 Franz Alto Bauer: Byzantinische Geschenkdiplomatie, in: Byzanz – Das Römerreich im Mittelalter. Teil 3: Peripherie und Nachbarschaft (Monographien des Römisch-Germanischen Zentralmuseums 84,3), hg. von Falko Daim und Jörg Drauschke, Mainz 2010, S. 1–55.

De Blaauw 2002 Sible De Blaauw: Contrasts in Processional Liturgy. A Typology of Outdoor Processions in Twelfth-Century Rome, in: Art, Cérémonial et Liturgie au Moyen Âge. Actes du colloque de 3e Cycle Romand de Lettres Lausanne-Fribourg, 24.–25.3., 14.–15.4., 12.–13.5. 2000, hg. von Nicolas Bock et al., Rom 2002, S. 357–394.

Bertaux 1897 Emile Bertaux: Ascoli Piceno et l'orfèvre Pietro Vanini, in: Mélanges d'Archéologie et d'Histoire 17, 1897, S. 77–112.

Bolton 1999 Brenda M. Bolton: Qui fidelis est in minimo: The Importance of Innocent III's Gift List, in: Pope Innocent III and his World, hg. von John C. Moore, Aldershot 1999, S. 113–140.

Bonito Fanelli 1990 Il piviale duecentesco di Ascoli Piceno. Storia e restauro, hg. von Rosalia Bonito Fanelli, Ascoli Piceno 1990.

Braun 1907 Joseph Braun: Die liturgische Gewandung im Occident und Orient nach Ursprung und Entwicklung, Verwendung und Symbolik, Freiburg i. Br. 1907.

Brel-Bordaz 1982 Odile Brel-Bordaz: Broderies d'ornéments liturgiques XIII–XIV siècles, Paris 1982.

Cecchelli 1952, Bd. 1 Carlo Cecchelli: La vita a Roma nel medioevo, Bd. 1, Rom 1952.

Christie 1938 Archibald Grace I. Christie: English Medieval Embroidery – a brief survey of English embroidery dating from the beginning of the tenth century until the end of the fourteenth: Together with a descriptive catalogue of the surviving examples: Illustrated with one hundred and sixty plates and numerous drawings in the text, Oxford 1938.

Eichmann 1951 Eduard Eichmann: Weihe und Krönung des Papstes im Mittelalter, München 1951.

Elster 2014 Christiane Elster: Liturgical Textiles as Papal Donations in Late Medieval Italy, in: Dressing the Part: Textiles as Propaganda in the Middle Ages, hg. von Kate Dimitrova und Margaret Goehring, Turnhout 2014, S. 65–79.

Elster 2017a (im Druck) Christiane Elster: Inventories and Textiles of the Papal Treasury around the Year 1300 – Concepts of Papal Representation in Written and Material Media, in: Inventories of Textiles. Textiles in Inventories (Late Medieval and Early Modern Period), hg. von Thomas Ertl und Barbara Karl, Wien 2016 (im Druck).

Elster 2017b Christiane Elster: Die textilen Geschenke Papst Bonifaz' VIII. (1294–1303) an die Kathedrale von Anagni – päpstliche Paramente des späten Mittelalters als Medien der Repräsentation, Gaben und Erinnerungsträger, Petersberg 2017 (in Vorbereitung).

Ertl 2010 Thomas Ertl: Die Gier der Päpste nach englischen Stickereien. Zu Bedeutung und Verbreitung von Opus Anglicanum im späten Mittelalter, in: Reiche Bilder. Aspekte zur Produktion und Funktion von Stickereien im Spätmittelalter. Beiträge der internationalen Fachtagung des Deutschen Textilmuseums Krefeld und des Zentrums zur Erforschung antiker und mittelalterlicher Textilien an der Fachhochschule Köln (20.–21. November 2008), hg. von Uta-Christiane Bergemann und Annemarie Stauffer, Regensburg 2010, S. 97–114.

Von Falke 1913, Bd. 2 Otto von Falke: Kunstgeschichte der Seidenweberei, Bd. 2, Berlin 1913.

Franchi 1990 Antonino Franchi: Nicolaus Papa IV: 1288–1292 (Girolamo d'Ascoli), Ascoli Piceno 1990.

Fried 2004 Johannes Fried: Der Schleier der Erinnerung: Grundzüge einer historischen Memorik, München 2004.

Gagliardi/Piccinini-Fabi 1990 Giannino Gagliardi und Marilena Piccinini-Fabi: Il Piviale di Ascoli, Ascoli Piceno 1990.

Gardner 2000 Julian Gardner: Legates, Cardinals and kings: England and Italy in the thirteenth-century, in: L'Europa e l'arte italiana. Per i cento anni dalla fondazione del Kunsthistorisches Institut in Florenz, hg. von Max Seidel, Venedig 2000, S. 74–93.

Gordon 2001 Stewart Gordon: A World of Investiture, in: Robes and Honor. The Medieval World of Investiture, hg. von Stewart Gordon, New York 2001, S. 1–19.

Grelli 2000 Maria Elma Grelli: Niccolò IV (Girolamo d'Ascoli), in: I papi marchigiani. Classi dirigenti, committenza artistica, mecenatismo urbano da Giovanni XVIII a Pio IX, hg. von Fabio Mariano und Stefano Papetti, Ancona 2000, S. 268–274.

Herklotz 1985 Ingo Herklotz: Der Campus Lateranensis im Mittelalter, in: Römisches Jahrbuch für Kunstgeschichte 22, 1985, S. 1–44.

Jacoby 2014 David Jacoby: Cypriot Gold Thread in Late Medieval Silk Weaving and Embroidery, in: Deeds Done Beyond the Sea. Essays on William of Tyre, Cyprus and the Military Orders presented to Peter Edbury, hg. von Susan B. Edgington und Helen J. Nicholson, Farnham 2014, S. 101–114.

Keupp 2014 Jan Keupp: Des Kaisers alte Kleider. Zum Kontext herrscherlicher Textilgeschenke im Hochmittelalter, in: Textile Kostbarkeiten staufischer Herrscher. Werkstätten – Bilder – Funktionen. Tagungsband zum internationalen Kolloquium im Rahmen der Ausstellung »Die Staufer und Italien« am 20. und 21. Januar 2011 in den Reiss-Engelhorn-Museen Mannheim (Studien zur internationalen Architektur- und Kunstgeschichte 99), hg. von Irmgard Siede und Annemarie Stauffer, Petersberg 2014, S. 67–76.

Kyser 1990 Susan Kyser: Una Lettura del Piviale, in: Il piviale duecentesco di Ascoli Piceno. Storia e restauro, hg. von Rosalia Bonito Fanelli, Ascoli Piceno 1990, S. 137–151.

La Barre Starensier 1982 Adele La Barre Starensier: An Art Historical Study of the Byzantine Silk Industry, 1982 (Dissertation Columbia University, Typoskript).

Ladner 1984 Gerhart B. Ladner: Die Papstbildnisse des Altertums und des Mittelalters, Bd. 3 (Monumenti di antichità cristiana 2 serie 4), Vatikanstadt 1984.

Latour 2007 [2005] Bruno Latour: Eine neue Soziologie für eine neue Gesellschaft. Einführung in die Akteur-Netzwerk-Theorie, Frankfurt a.M. 2007 [engl. Originalausgabe: Oxford 2005].

Lee 1932/1933 Rensselaer W. Lee: An English gothic embroidery in the Vatican, in: Atti della Pontificia Accademia Romana di Archeologia. Memorie 3, 1932/1933, S. 1–34.

Lethaby 1929 William R. Lethaby: English Primitives: The Ascoli Cope and London Artists, in: The Burlington Magazine 54, 1929, S. 304–308.

Martiniani-Reber 1999 Marielle Martiniani-Reber: Tentures et Textiles des églises romaines au haut Moyen Âge d'après le Liber Pontificalis, in: Mélanges de l'École Française de Rome, Moyen Age 111, 1999, S. 289–305.

Mauss 1968 [1923–1924] Marcel Mauss: Die Gabe: Form und Funktion des Austauschs in archaischen Gesellschaften, übersetzt von Eva Moldenhauer,

Frankfurt a. M. 1968 [Original: Essai sur le don. Forme et raison de l'échange dans les sociétés archaïques, in: L'Année Sociologique, seconde série, 1923–1924].

Miller 2014a Maureen C. Miller: Clothing the Clergy. Virtue and Power in Medieval Europe, c. 800–1200, Ithaca/London 2014.

Miller 2014b Maureen C. Miller: Vestire la Chiesa. Gli abiti del clero nella Roma medievale (La corte dei papi 26), Rom 2014.

Morris 1904–1905 May Morris: The Ascoli Cope, in: The Burlington Magazine 6, 1904–1905, S. 440–448.

Mortari 1963 Luisa Mortari: Il Tesoro della Cattedrale di Anagni, Rom 1963.

Muthesius 1995 Anna Muthesius: Studies in Byzantine and Islamic Silk Weaving, London 1995.

Muthesius 2004 Anna Muthesius: Studies in Silk in Byzantium, London 2004.

Romano 2012 La pittura medievale a Roma 312–1431. Corpus, Bd. 5: Il Duecento e la Cultura Gotica, 1198–1287 ca., hg. von Serena Romano, Rom 2012.

Saxer 1996/1997 Victor Saxer: Le informazioni del Liber Pontificalis sugli interventi dei papi nella decorazione tessile delle chiese romane: L'esempio di S. Maria Maggiore (772–844), in: Atti della Pontificia Accademia Romana di Archeologia, Rendiconti 69, 1996/1997, S. 219–232.

Schramm 1957 Percy Ernst Schramm: Herrschaftszeichen: gestiftet, verschenkt, verkauft, verpfändet. Belege aus dem Mittelalter, in: Nachrichten der Akademie der Wissenschaften in Göttingen. Philologisch-historische Klasse 1957, Göttingen 1957, S. 162–226.

Schreiner 1996 Peter Schreiner: Ritterspiele in Byzanz, in: Jahrbuch der Österreichischen Byzantinistik 46, 1996, S. 227–241.

Schreiner 2004 Peter Schreiner: Diplomatische Geschenke zwischen Byzanz und dem Westen ca. 800–1200: Eine Analyse der Texte mit Quellenanhang, in: Dumbarton Oaks Papers 58, 2004, S. 251–282.

Späth 2007 Markus Späth: Verflechtung von Erinnerung. Bildproduktion und Geschichtsschreibung im Kloster San Clemente in Casauria während des 12. Jahrhunderts (Orbis mediaevalis. Vorstellungswelten des Mittelalters 8), Berlin 2007.

Stauffer 2013 Annemarie Stauffer: Seide aus Byzanz im Westen, in: Seide im früh- und hochmittelalterlichen Frauenstift. Besitz – Bedeutung – Umnutzung (Essener Forschungen zum Frauenstift 11), hg. von Thomas Schilp und Annemarie Stauffer, Essen 2013, S. 9–28.

Volbach 1942 Wolfgang-Fritz Volbach: Tessuti. Catalogo del Museo Sacro della Biblioteca Apostolica Vaticana III, 1, Vatikanstadt 1942.

Von Wilckens 1991 Leonie von Wilckens: Die textilen Künste. Von der Spätantike bis um 1500, München 1991.

Woodfin 2012 Warren T. Woodfin: The Embodied Icon. Liturgical Vestments and Sacramental Power in Byzantium, Oxford 2012.

Abbildungsnachweis

von Christina Wawrzinek und Stephanie Herrmann

Titelabbildung:
Arnolfo di Cambio, Papst Bonifaz VIII. Foto: © Musei Vaticani, Governatorato dello Stato della Città del Vaticano, tutti i diritti riservati. Divieto di copia e di ulteriore riproduzione, se non su esplicita autorizzazione scritta dalla Direzione dei Musei.

Vladimir Ivanovici: Building prestige. Processions, visual codes, and episcopal power in fifth-century Rome (S. 11–28)
Abb. 1: Foto D-DAI-ROM-31.728. Der Autor dankt den Musei Vaticani für die freundliche Genehmigung.
Abb. 2: © akg-images / Nimatallah
Abb. 3: Repro: V. Ivanovici
Abb. 4: Foto D-DAI-ROM-61.2591
Abb. 5: Foto V. Ivanovici
Abb. 6: Der Autor dankt S. de Blaauw für die freundliche Genehmigung.

Antonella Ballardini: Von Johannes VII. zu den Renaissancepäpsten. Die Öffnung der Heiligen Pforte in Alt-St. Peter (S. 29–54)
Abb. 1: © [2017] per concessione della Biblioteca Apostolica Vaticana, ogni diritto riservato
Abb. 2: Repro: Bibliotheca Hertziana - Max-Planck-Institut für Kunstgeschichte, Rom
Abb. 3: © [2017] per concessione della Biblioteca Apostolica Vaticana, ogni diritto riservato
Abb. 4: Bibliotheca Hertziana – Max-Planck-Institut für Kunstgeschichte, Rom
Abb. 5: Die Autorin dankt der Fabbrica di S. Pietro für die freundliche Genehmigung.
Abb. 6: Die Autorin dankt M. Carpiceci und G. Dibenedetto für die freundliche Genehmigung.
Abb. 7: Die Autorin dankt E. Viscontini für die freundliche Genehmigung.
Abb. 8: © bpk / Bayerische Staatsgemäldesammlungen
Abb. 9–10: Albertina, Wien
Abb. 11: Paris, Cabinet de Médailles de la Bibliothèque Nationale

Manuela Gianandrea: Geschichtsschreibung und Erinnerung. Die Rolle von Papst Silvester in der Selbstdarstellung des römischen Papsttums (6.–12. Jahrhundert) (S. 55–76)
Abb. 1: Nach Wilpert/Tabanelli
Abb. 2: Foto G. Alfano © SSBAR. Die Autorin dankt der Soprintedenza Speciale per i Beni Archeologici di Roma für die freundliche Genehmigung.
Abb. 3: Foto: Bibliotheca Hertziana – Max-Planck-Institut für Kunstgeschichte, Rom (Roberto Sigismondi)
Abb. 4: Bibliotheca Hertziana – Max-Planck-Institut für Kunstgeschichte, Rom, Foto Sigismondi, Roberto
Abb. 5: Universitätsbibliothek Heidelberg, Ciampini, De sacris aedificiis a Constantino Magno constructis, 1693, Tafel II
Abb. 6: Foto Autorin

Galliano Ciliberti: Musik und Liturgie bei päpstlichen Zeremonien im Mittelalter: Gesten, Symbole, Strukturen (S. 77–92)
Abb. 1–3: Gallica.BnF.fr / Paris, Bibliothèque Nationale de France, ms lat. 903, f. 116v
Abb. 4, 6: Gallica.BnF.fr / Paris, Bibliothèque Nationale de France, MS Latin 903, f. 117r.
Abb. 5: Gallica.BnF.fr / Paris, Bibliothèque Nationale de France, MS Latin 903, f. 26v.

Erik Thunø: The Power and Display of Writing: From Damasus to the Early Medieval Popes (S. 95–114)
Abb. 1: D-DAI-ROM-F90.1, Foto: F. Schlechter
Abb. 2: D-DAI-ROM-90.60, Foto: F. Schlechter
Abb. 3: Bibliotheca Hertziana – Max-Planck-Institut für Kunstgeschichte, Rom (Arnaldo Vescovo)
Abb. 4: © akg-images / Andrea Jemolo
Abb. 5: Zeichnung von James Huemoller nach Guyon, Damase e l'illustration des martyrs
Abb. 6–7: Foto E. Thunø
Abb. 8: © akg-images / Andrea Jemolo

Norbert Zimmermann: Inhalte und Intentionen bildlicher Kunst in Sakralräumen zwischen Damasus und Sixtus III. in Rom (S. 115–142)

Abb. 1: Der Autor dankt L. Spera für die freundliche Genehmigung.

Abb. 2: Nach Weiland 1994, Fig. 4. Mit freundlicher Genehmigung von A. Weiland.

Abb. 3: Der Autor dankt M. Limoncelli für die Anfertigung.

Abb. 4: nach: Cimitero di Domitilla, Album-Ricordo, Tav. IX, preparata da G. B. De Rossi per il IVo tomo della sua Roma Sotterranea, o. J. Foto Verf.

Abb. 5: nach J. Wilpert, W. N. Schumacher, Die römischen Mosaiken der kirchlichen Bauten vom IV.–XIII. Jahrhundert, Freiburg 1976, Taf. 48.

Abb. 6: nach Freyberger/Ertel 2016, Farbtaf. 8c. Der Autor dankt S. Freyberger für die freundliche Genehmigung.

Alessandro Taddei: Papst Theodor (642–649) und die Künste: ein ›pragmatisches‹ Verhältnis (S. 143–160)

Abb. 1: nach Carlo Ceschi, S. Stefano Rotondo, Atti della Pontificia Accademia Romana di Archeologia. Serie III. Memorie, 15, 1982, S. 10

Abb. 2: nach Carlo Ceschi, S. Stefano Rotondo, Atti della Pontificia Accademia Romana di Archeologia. Serie III. Memorie, 15, 1982, Taf. 1

Abb. 3: Der Autor dankt dem Collegio Germanico-Ungarico für die freundliche Genehmigung.

Abb. 4: Der Autor dankt C. Palombi für die freundliche Genehmigung.

Abb. 5: Der Autor dankt L. Spera für die freundliche Genehmigung.

Abb. 6–7: Der Autor dankt M. Luchterhand für die freundliche Genehmigung.

Abb. 8:Der Autor dankt dem Collegio Germanico-Ungarico für die freundliche Genehmigung.

Lucrezia Spera: Das Papsttum und Rom im 8. Jahrhundert. Neudeutung der institutionellen ›Wende‹ anhand der archäologischen Dokumentation (S. 161–188)

Abb. 1, 2a-2b: Die Autorin dankt F. Carboni für die freundliche Genehmigung.

Abb.2 c, 3, 6: Foto L. Spera

Abb. 4: Die Autorin dankt L. Saguì/M. Cante für die freundliche Genehmigung.

Abb. 5: Die Autorin dankt E. Steinby für die freundliche Genehmigung.

Giulia Bordi: Die Päpste in S. Maria Antiqua. Zwischen Rom und Konstantinopel (S. 189–212)

Abb. 1, 3–6: Foto G. Alfano © SSBAR. Die Autorin dankt der Soprintedenza Speciale per i Beni Archeologici di Roma für die freundliche Genehmigung.

Abb. 2: Foto Verf. Die Autorin dank V. Valentini für die freundliche Genehmigung.

Abb.7: nach Wilpert 1914, IV, Pl. 167,1

Abb. 8: Die Autorin dankt M. Carpiceci und G. Dibenedetto für die freundliche Genehmigung.

Dieter Blume: Die Aula Gotica von Santi Quattro Coronati – Kosmos, Antike und Tugenden im Selbstverständnis der Kurie (S. 213–234)

Abb. 1–5, 7–10: Polo Museale del Lazio - Archivio Fotografico

Abb. 6: Foto Codices Electronici AG, www.e-codices.ch

Donatella Nuzzo: Bildung und Umbildung kirchlicher Strukturen in Italien zwischen Spätantike und Frühmittelalter (S. 251–270)

Abb. 1: © [2017] per concessione della Biblioteca Apostolica Vaticana, ogni diritto riservato

Abb. 2: D-DAI-ROM-58.1684

Christiane Elster: Päpstliche Textilgeschenke des späten 13. Jahrhunderts – Objekte, Akteure, Funktionen (S. 287–310)

Abb. 1: Foto Musei Vaticani, per concessione dei Musei Vaticani

Abb. 2–4: Bibliotheca Hertziana – Max-Planck-Institut für Kunstgeschichte (Alessandro Iazeolla)

Abb. 5: Wien, Österreichische Nationalbibliothek, Cod. Hist.Gr. 53, fol. 291v.

Abb. 6–7: Ascoli Piceno, Pinacoteca Civica: Stefano Papetti

Sollte es vorgekommen sein, dass Rechtinhaber nicht genannt sind oder nicht ausfindig gemacht werden konnten, bitten wir um entsprechende Nachweise die beteiligten Urheber betreffend, um diese in künftigen Auflagen zu berücksichtigen oder/und im Rahmen der üblichen Vereinbarung für den Bereich wissenschaftlicher Publikationen abgelten zu können.

Namenregister

von Mona Kirsch